THE LEGAL SYSTEMS OF AFRICA SERIES

GENERAL EDITOR
KENNETH R. REDDEN
Professor of Law, University of Virginia, U.S.A.
Former Fulbright Professor of Law, Haile Sellassie I University, Ethiopia

CONGO-KINSHASA
By John Crabb

ETHIOPIA
By Kenneth R. Redden

FRENCH-SPEAKING AFRICA
Volume I (Africa South of the Sahara); Volume II (North Africa)
By Jeswald W. Salacuse

GHANA
By T. A. Mensah

KENYA
By Ojwang K'Ombudo

LESOTHO
By Vernon V. Palmer and Sebastian M. Poulter

LIBERIA
By Michael Kitay and Robert Culp

MALAWI
By Vern G. Davidson and Colin A. Baker

NIGERIA
By M. L. Marasinghe and Shirley Zabel

SOMALI REPUBLIC
By Haji N. A. Noor Muhammad

SUDAN
By Zaki Mustafa

ZAMBIA
By J. J. R. Collingwood, J. L. Barrington-Jones, L. K. Young and B. P. Cullinan

Additional volumes on other countries are in preparation and will be made available in the immediate future.

MOROCCO
TUNISIA
IFNI
ALGERIA
LIBYA
U.A.R. (EGYPT)
SPANISH SAHARA
MAURITANIA
MALI
NIGER
SENEGAL
GAMBIA
PORT GUINEA
GUINEA
UPPER VOLTA
CHAD
SUDAN
SIERRA LEONE
GHANA
TOGO
NIGERIA
Fr. SOMALILAND
LIBERIA
IVORY COAST
DAHOMEY
CAMEROON
CENT. AFRICAN REP.
ETHIOPIA
SOMALI REPUBLIC
EQUATORIAL GUINEA
CONGO
UGANDA
KENYA
GABON
DEMOCRATIC REPUBLIC OF CONGO (KINSHASA)
RWANDA
BURUNDI
TANZANIA
ANGOLA
MALAWI
ZAMBIA
SOUTH WEST AFRICA
RHODESIA
MOZAMBIQUE
MALAGASY REPUBLIC
BOTSWANA
SWAZILAND
LESOTHO
SOUTH AFRICA

THE LEGAL SYSTEM of LESOTHO

By

VERNON V. PALMER

SEBASTIAN M. POULTER

THE MICHIE COMPANY
Law Publishers
CHARLOTTESVILLE, VIRGINIA
1972

Library of Congress Catalog Card No. 71-185225

To Our Parents

PREFACE

This book is intended to fill a need obvious to all those who have to deal with the legal system of Lesotho, and in particular to those who teach and study law and government there. When we started lecturing in the Department of Law at the University of Botswana, Lesotho and Swaziland in 1967, we were immediately struck by the lack of any general works dealing with the legal systems of the countries to which the University owes allegiance. It was necessary for both lecturers and students to rely heavily upon books stating the legal position in say, England, South Africa, or Nigeria, adapting what was written, with difficulty, to local circumstances. But very often the alien legal rules were quite simply inapplicable.

Thus, to take a few examples, whereas the reception or introduction of English law into West and East Africa had been the subject of much study over the previous decade, there had been no detailed examination of the introduction of Roman-Dutch law into Southern Africa (save in relation to South Africa itself). Again, while much substantive customary law was to be found in books like Duncan's *Sotho Laws and Customs* and Schapera's *Handbook of Tswana Law and Custom,* no book had yet tackled the question of when the customary law was applicable in the three countries. Finally, although the constitutions of the three countries followed in the main the Westminster model, they presented certain unique features upon which the constitutional texts of other countries could not be expected to touch.

With this need in view we have tried to write a book that would be of use to a wide variety of readers, including practitioners, judicial and administrative officers, students, and foreign readers. Our purpose was to introduce the legal system of Lesotho: its dual private law, its written constitution, and its court structure. For reasons of space we have not dealt at length with many substantive areas of the Roman-Dutch law such as the criminal law, contract, mercantile law, marriage, succession, and the like. Where common law or statutory rules apply, the law of Lesotho is often similar (though not identical) to South African law and there are numerous South African works that can be read with profit. So far as the substantive customary law is concerned, sufficient research has not yet been done to permit a really detailed picture to be drawn, and Duncan's book remains a useful introduction.

The features we selected to stress are intended to comprise a kind of profile of the legal system. In our view they are the features that are most striking and noteworthy and that set the law of Lesotho apart not only from that of South Africa but from that of Botswana and Swaziland as well. Indeed if this book possesses any unifying theme it would be that Lesotho's law is in many respects different, even unique, and cannot be taught or learnt as if it were the law of some other country.

The reader must be warned, however, that the legal statements contained in this book are subject to a cutoff date with an importance beyond that normally associated with a legal text. In January, 1970, long after our work seemed to be complete and was in the hands of the publisher, a *coup d'etat* occurred in Lesotho that substantially threatened the relevance of much of what we had written. The Prime Minister, Chief Jonathan, after declaring a state of emergency and seizing power following an apparent defeat by the opposition party at the general election on January

27, 1970, instituted rule by decree and shortly afterwards the King, Moshoeshoe II, went into temporary exile in Holland. Parliament did not reconvene and since the *coup* legislative power has been vested exclusively in "The Council of Ministers" which is the new title adopted by Chief Jonathan's former cabinet. The general change is that the new regime has suspended operation of the 1966 Constitution, which had received such detailed treatment in Part Two and in portions of Part Three of this book. But even though the government suspended the Constitution, it has not yet provided the country with another and thus none was available at the time this book was ready for press.

The choices left to us by this turn of events were limited and unpleasant. We could have awaited the eventual day when a new constitution might be drafted, but this might have meant waiting for years. In the interim the publication of other valuable legal material unrelated to constitutional law would be delayed, perhaps for an indefinite period, because there would always be the possibility that another revolution might destroy even a successor constitution.

Instead it seemed better, though hardly satisfying, to leave the manuscript in its original form and to place a cutoff at January 1, 1970. In making this decision we rejected the alternative approach of shifting verb tense and sentence structure so that the account would read as a historical development of the constitutional position in Lesotho. It is nothing new for authors of African texts to elect to adopt the strategy we have. As Professor Harvey has stated, "Anyone writing about Africa today must be content to write history. The pace of change is so rapid that currency may not survive the period required for publication. In these circumstances the only expedient is to choose an arbitrary cutoff date." *(Law and Social*

Change in Ghana, Princeton 1966, p. *x*). In addition we would offer the following justification for the approach we have adopted. On the one hand, Part Two of this book was intended as more than a description of the constitution of one country. Rather our discussion of the Constitution has been woven into a more general framework of constitutional theory dealing with such questions as the power of judicial review, the justiciability of constitutional conventions, and the legal effect of fundamental human rights' provisions. What merit such a general enquiry might possess does not depend upon a change of governments.

And on the other hand, if *law* is indeed more than a synonym for *power,* the Constitution survives, however unheeded, as a legal inspiration. It is an imaginative document which contains both technical innovations and substantive reform.

The present work is divided into three parts.

Part One is devoted to the sources of law, namely the common law, the customary law, and legislation. It starts with a discussion of the reception of the Cape Colonial law and the extent of its operation in Lesotho. This involves an investigation of how far courts in Lesotho are bound to follow South African decisions. There follows a treatment of the customary law including questions of its ascertainment and proof, its applicability in the various courts in particular cases, and its future place in the general legal system.

Part Two traces the constitutional development of Basutoland from colonial days to its emergence in 1966 as the independent state of Lesotho. It describes and analyzes the main features of the 1966 Constitution, concentrating particularly on the Fundamental Human Rights provisions.

Part Three, entitled "The Courts and the Legal Profession," examines the structure and jurisdiction of the courts as well as the appointment, qualifications, and tenure of the judiciary and the magistracy. Short sections at the end deal with admission to the legal profession, legal education, and law reporting.

A recent decree of the Council of Ministers entitled the Court of Appeal and High Court Order, 1970 has altered the law regulating these two courts and has also abolished future appeals from Lesotho to the Privy Council. This decree is referred to in various footnotes at the appropriate places in the text.

We should like to take this opportunity of expressing the enormous debt of gratitude which we owe to Mr. J. E. Beardsley of Los Angeles, formerly Head of the Department of Law at the University of Botswana, Lesotho and Swaziland. His constant encouragement, perceptive judgment, and general enthusiasm for the publication of this book have been a powerful inspiration to both of us. He has read Parts One and Two, suggesting valuable criticism and saving us from numerous errors. We should also like to express our thanks to Dr. A. Milner, Fellow of Trinity College, Oxford, who kindly read the draft of Part One and also provided much helpful comment and criticism. We need hardly add that while they merit thanks for improving our work, they can be in no way responsible for its shortcomings.

Our thanks are also due to Mrs. V. Wiltshire who over many months successfully deciphered our often illegible and labyrinthine drafts. Heroically, she typed the bulk of the manuscript. Finally, we must acknowledge the generous financial assistance provided by the University of Botswana, Lesotho and Swaziland which enabled us to cover the costs of the typing.

The general format and style of the book is the responsibility of the publisher. For style they have followed *A Uniform System of Citation,* 11th ed., published by The Harvard Law Review Association.

V. V. PALMER
Tulane University
New Orleans, Louisiana
S. M. POULTER
U.B.L.S.
Roma, Lesotho

TABLE OF ABBREVIATIONS

1. Law Reports

A.C. .... Appeal Cases (United Kingdom)

A.D. .... Appellate Division Reports (South Africa)

A.I.R. .... All Indian Law Reporter (India)

A.L.R. .... African Law Reports (Commercial Series) (Africa)

All E.R. .... All England Reports (United Kingdom)

All N.L.R. .... Nigerian Law Reports (1961 and later) (Nigeria)

App. Cas. .... Appeal Cases Law Reports (United Kingdom)

B.A.C. .... Buchanan's Appeal Cases (South Africa)

Bech. L.R. .... Bechuanaland Law Reports (Botswana)

C.A. .... Court of Appeal (Lesotho)

C.L.R. .... Commonwealth Law Reports (Australia)

C.P.D. .... Cape Provincial Division Reports (South Africa)

C.W.N. .... Calcutta Weekly Notes (India)

Ch.D. .... Chancery Division Law Reports (United Kingdom)

Co. Rep. .... Coke's King's Bench Reports (United Kingdom)

Cowp. .... Cowper's King's Bench Reports (United Kingdom)

Cranch .... Cranch's Supreme Court Reports (United States)

D.Ct. .... Divisional Court (Gold Coast/Ghana)

E.A.C.A. .... East Africa Court of Appeal (East Africa)

E.&B. .... Ellis & Blackburn's Queen's Bench Reports (United Kingdom)

F.S.C. .... Selected Judgments of the Federal Supreme Court of Nigeria (Nigeria)

G.L.R. .... Ghana Law Reports (Ghana)

H.C.T.L.R. .... High Commission Territories Law Reports (Lesotho, Botswana, and Swaziland)

H.C.T.L.R.(C.A.) .... High Commission Territories Law Reports (Court of Appeal Cases) (Lesotho, Botswana, and Swaziland)

I.L.R. .... Indian Law Reports (India)

I.R. .... Irish Reports (Ireland)

J.C. .... Judicial Commissioner's Cases (Unreported) (Lesotho)

K.B. .... King's Bench Law Reports (United Kingdom)

L.J. .... Law Journal (United Kingdom)

M.P.C.C. .... Moore's Privy Council Cases (United Kingdom)

M.P.C.C.(N.S.) .... Moore's Privy Council Cases (New Series) (United Kingdom)

N.A.C. .... Reports of the Native Appeal Courts (South Africa)

N.L.R. .... New Law Reports (Ceylon)

N.P.D. .... Natal Provincial Division Reports (South Africa)

N.R.N.L.R. .... Northern Region of Nigeria Law Reports (Nigeria)

Nig. L.R. .... Nigerian Law Reports (before 1961) (Nigeria)

O.P.D. .... Orange Free State Provincial Division Reports (South Africa)

O.R. .... Ontario Reports (Canada)

P.C. .... Privy Council (United Kingdom)

P.L.D. .... Pakistan Legal Decisions (Pakistan)

Q.B. .... Queen's Bench Law Reports (United Kingdom)
R.L.R. .... Rhodesian Law Reports (Rhodesia)
R & N .... Rhodesian and Nyasaland Law Reports (Rhodesia)
Ren. .... Renner's Reports (Gold Coast)
S.A. .... South African Law Reports (South Africa):
C. Cape Provincial Division
E. Eastern Districts Local Division or Eastern Cape Division
N. Natal Provincial Division
O. Orange Free State Provincial Division
S.W.A. South Wales Africa Division
T. Transvaal Provincial Division
W. Witwatersrand Local Division
S.C. .... Cape Supreme Court Reports (South Africa)
S.C.A. .... Supreme Court Appeals (India)
S.C.R. .... Supreme Court Reports (India)
S.R. .... Southern Rhodesian High Court Reports (Rhodesia)
S.R.N. .... Southern Rhodesian Native Appeal Court Reports (Rhodesia)
Sar. F.L.R. .... Sarbah's Fanti Law Reports (West Africa)
T.H. .... Reports of the Witwatersrand High Court (Transvaal) (South Africa)
T.L.R. .... Times Law Reports (United Kingdom)
T.L.R.(R) .... Tanganyika Law Reports (Revised) (Tanzania)
T.P.D. .... Transvaal Provincial Division Reports (South Africa)
T.S. .... Transvaal Supreme Court Reports (South Africa)

U.L.R. .... Uganda Law Reports (East Africa)
U.S. .... United States Supreme Court Reports (United States)
W.A.C.A. .... West African Court of Appeal (West Africa)
W.A.L.R. .... West African Law Reports (West Africa)
W.L.D. .... Witwatersrand Local Division Reports (Transvaal) (South Africa)
W.L.R. .... Weekly Law Reports (United Kingdom)
W.R.N.L.R. .... Western Region of Nigeria Law Reports (Nigeria)
Wheat .... Wheaton's Reports (United States)

2. Legal Periodicals

Camb. L.J. .... Cambridge Law Journal
Colum. L. Rev. .... Columbia Law Review
Harv. L. Rev. .... Harvard Law Review
J.A.L. .... Journal of African Law
J.C.L.I.L. .... Journal of Comparative Legislation and International Law
L.Q.R. .... Law Quarterly Review
Mod. L.R. .... Modern Law Review
R.L.R. .... Rhodesian Law Review
R.N.L.J. .... Rhodesian & Nyasaland Law Journal
S.A.L.J. .... South African Law Journal
Wis. L.R. .... Wisconsin Law Review
Yale L. J. .... Yale Law Journal

3. Miscellaneous Abbreviations

AALS .... American Association of Law Schools
C.U.P. .... Cambridge University Press
Cmd. .... Command Papers
G.N. .... Government Notice

H.C.N. .... High Commissioner's Notice
H.M.S.O. .... Her Majesty's Stationery Office
O.U.P. .... Oxford University Press
S.I. .... Statutory Instrument
Stat. R.&O. .... Statutory Rules and Orders (United Kingdom)
U.N.C.P. .... University of North Carolina Press
W.H.O. .... World Health Organization

Table of Contents

Part Two. The Constitution

by V. V. Palmer

Part Three. The Courts and the Legal Profession

by S. M. Poulter

INTRODUCTION

INTRODUCTION

The independent kingdom of Lesotho came into being on 4th October 1966. Prior to that time it was known as the British colony of Basutoland. A member of the British Commonwealth and of the United Nations, Lesotho is situated in the southeastern part of Africa some six hundred miles south of the Tropic of Capricorn.

A. Geography

Lesotho is completely surrounded by the Republic of South Africa and in the graphic words of Austin Coates,

> shares with the Republic of San Marino the distinction of being one of the only two countries in the world to be entirely enveloped by another country, to have no access to the exterior except through that country, and thus by that country's grace and favour.[1]

The borders of Lesotho adjoin those of Natal in the east, of the Cape Province to the south, and of the Orange Free State in the west and north. The total area of the country is 11,716 square miles, which makes it virtually the same size as Belgium and slightly larger than the state of Maryland. Lesotho has been variously described as the "Switzerland of Africa," the "roof of Southern Africa," and the "sponge of Southern Africa." All these appellations

---

1. A. Coates, Basutoland 1 (H.M.S.O. 1966).

serve to point to its distinctive geographical features. Lesotho is a mountainous country, having the highest peak in southern Africa, Thabana Ntlenyana (11,425 feet). In winter the mountains are often covered with snow. Moreover, that part of the Drakensberg range which lies within Lesotho, the Maloti, contains most of the major sources of South Africa's most important river, the Orange.

The country can conveniently be divided into five regions:[2]

(i) the border lowlands, a small triangular area in the extreme west with lower rainfall and poorer soil than the lowlands proper and part of which lies below 5,000 feet;

(ii) the lowlands (5,000—6,000 feet), which run inland from the western border and contain most of the main centers, including the capital, Maseru (population 18,797). This area, while making up only about twelve percent of the total land surface, possesses by far the greatest concentration of population since it is easier to cultivate than most of the areas further east. However the fertility of the soil is low and yields are poor;

(iii) the Orange River Valley, which runs between the southern mountains and penetrates into the heart of the country, and which closely resembles the lowlands in altitude and rainfall;

(iv) the mountain valleys or foothills, which are situated between 6,000 and 8,000 feet. This region includes some of the most fertile land in the country and is fairly densely populated; and

(v) the mountains, which comprise 58 percent

---

2. *See* SMIT, LESOTHO: A GEOGRAPHICAL STUDY 3-4 (Pretoria 1967); Smits, *The Distribution of the Population in Lesotho and Some Implications for Economic Development*, 1968 LESOTHO NOTES AND RECORDS, 21-23.

of the total surface area and make up the whole of the eastern half of the country. This region, which is the least densely populated, runs from 8,000 feet to over 11,000 feet. It is essentially grazing land, although attempts have been made at cultivation despite the very steep slopes.

The country as a whole therefore rises steadily from just below 5,000 feet in the west to over 11,000 feet in the east. The vast majority of the population lives in the lower lying cultivated areas, with hardly any permanent settlements in the high mountains. The average temperature decreases and the average rainfall increases as one moves eastward. The average annual rainfall is about 29 inches in the lowlands, but the deciding factor from the agricultural viewpoint is whether the rain comes in steady, soaking showers at intervals suitable to the growth of the staple crops or whether it comes in short and heavy storms and runs to waste. In recent years many crops have failed because of poor timing of the rains.

In the lowlands, temperatures rise to a maximum of 90° F or more in summer and do not usually fall below 20° F in winter. However in the mountains, temperatures below zero are common. Frost may occur in all parts of the country at any time of year, but out of season it is much less frequent and less severe in the lowlands than in the mountains.

B. Terminology

The African inhabitants of Lesotho are known as *Basotho,* which is the plural form of *Mosotho.* The term *Sotho* is now generally used to indicate the peoples of the central high grasslands of southern Africa. These people constitute a well-defined ethnographical group characterised by a considerable degree of cultural and linguistic homogeneity.[3] The Basotho are often described as Southern Sotho because of their location within the wider Sotho grouping. Their language is *Sesotho* (or Southern Sotho). The word Sesotho is also used by the Basotho to describe anything characteristic of their culture and this usage is adopted in this book, *e.g.*, Sesotho law and custom means the customary law of the Basotho.

During much of the colonial period, the use made of the prefixes added to "Sotho" was often inconsistent. Moreover "Sotho" was usually spelt "Suto," a relic of an earlier orthography. This accounts for the employment of expressions like "Basuto law" (for Sesotho law), "Basutos" (for Basotho) and "Basutoland" itself (for Lesotho). The position is further complicated by the fact that "Sotho" is pronounced more or less as if it rhymed with "Pluto," *i.e.*, "suto."

The modern forms will be used throughout this book save where direct quotations use the older forms.

C. History [4]

The first people to live in Lesotho about whom

---

3. SHEDDICK, THE SOUTHERN SOTHO 9 (London I.A.I. 1953).

4. The following works on the history of the country may be found of interest: TYLDEN, THE RISE OF THE BASUTO (Juta 1950) (a military history covering the years 1824-1946); ELLENBERGER AND MACGREGOR, HISTORY OF THE BASUTO, ANCIENT AND MODERN (London 1912) (extremely rich in information about early customs and traditions); CASALIS, THE BASUTOS (Struik reprint 1965) (a valuable account by a gifted missionary); LAGDEN, THE BASUTOS Vols. I and II (London 1909) (a thorough description by a former Resident Commissioner); HAILEY, NATIVE ADMINISTRATION IN THE BRITISH AFRICAN TERRITORIES Part V (H.M.S.O. 1953) (a detailed, thorough, and impartial survey); HAILEY, SOUTH AFRICA AND THE HIGH COMMISSION TERRITORIES (O.U.P. 1963) (this work covers in detail the efforts to incorporate Lesotho into South Africa).

we have any considerable knowledge were the Bushmen. As an organised people they disappeared from the country around 1870, but their remarkable cave paintings endure to this day and the "click" sounds in the Sesotho language are of Bushman origin.

The first major settlements of people occurred during the 18th Century when Bantu tribesmen, probably of Nguni origin, entered Lesotho from a northeasterly direction. Later, Sotho-speaking tribes joined them in settling the country. About the year 1820, however, their relatively peaceful life was violently shattered by the Zulu despot Chaka in Natal, whose powerful regiments (*impis*) drove the remnants of defeated Zulu tribes into exile in Lesotho. The incessant strife they caused was known as the *Lifaqane* or "Wars of Calamity." Constant warfare and great famine characterised this time of troubles and the lack of food reached such proportions that cannibalism became commonplace.

In the midst of these violent times an obscure young chieftain began to acquire the dominant power and respect that eventually would nationalise the many diverse clans and tribal groups and would make him their Paramount Chief. This was Moshoeshoe I, one of the outstanding personalities of his time, a man who combined in rare degree the arts of diplomacy and war. The former attribute may have been due in part to Mohlomi, a chief renowned for his wisdom and foresight, who accepted Moshoeshoe as his protegé. No doubt Moshoeshoe's competence in war, however, derived from his early experience as a master cattle raider. Indeed it was this expertise that led to his acquisition of the name Moshoeshoe, which is an onomatopoeia expressing the élan with which he swept off a herd of cattle in his youth.

His victory in 1831 over the dreaded Motselekatse,

a lieutenant of Chaka, illustrates Moshoeshoe's style. After breaking the Zulu's assault on his famous mountain stronghold, Thaba Bosiu, by hurling down an avalanche of stones, Moshoeshoe sent presents to the retreating enemy with this message: "Moshesh [5] salutes you. Supposing that hunger has brought you into this country, he sends you these cattle, that you may eat them on your way home." [6] In this manner, allying the weak and fragmented clans under his leadership, but using fully the natural fighting advantages afforded by the impregnable Thaba Bosiu (Mountain of Night), he succeeded in repelling the Zulu invaders from the territory.

Soon afterwards, however, the arrival of the Boers presented a grave threat to the country. Dutch settlers had arrived at the Cape of Good Hope in 1652. After the abolition of slavery in the Cape in 1833, Dutch families began trekking north beyond its borders in quest of new lands and cheap labor. By 1836 they were at the threshold of Lesotho. The main dispute with the white pioneers concerned rights to land. Moshoeshoe was prepared to permit them temporary occupation, but the settlers regarded their token presents to Moshoeshoe as payment for land title or else they asserted that the land, being previously empty, was theirs by virtue of occupation.

Concerned with the problem of negotiating with the foreigners, Moshoeshoe had already invited, in 1833, three members of the Paris Evangelical Missionary Society to act as his advisers and intermediaries. Moshoeshoe was apprehensive of the increasing encroachments, tensions, and disputes that developed between the Boers and the Basotho. He felt that the

5. An earlier spelling of Moshoeshoe.

6. This account of the battle is taken from CASALIS, *supra* note 4, at 23.

only solution for his country would be British protection. But despite his constant pleas to the Crown between 1842 and 1868, British protection did not come until the Basotho stood at the brink of national disaster.

After an initial request for protection in 1842, Moshoeshoe became the ally of the Cape Government in 1843 by virtue of the Napier Treaty, and in 1848 the British Government declared its sovereignty over Lesotho and other territories north of the Orange River, including that occupied by the Boers.

In 1852 occurred "the Affair at the Berea" which provided Moshoeshoe with another opportunity to employ one of his diplomatic master-strokes, this time against the British who were endeavouring to maintain order in the area. The Basotho had been raiding for cattle within Boer territory, and the British commander, Lieutenant-General Cathcart was determined to teach them a lesson. He demanded that Moshoeshoe hand over 10,000 head of cattle and 1,000 horses within three days—an impossible ultimatum. He declared that if this were not done his men would come and collect them. In the ensuing battle the British forces suffered heavier casualties than the Basotho and were forced to retreat. At this opportune moment Moshoeshoe sent Cathcart a letter in the following terms:

> Your Excellency—This day you have fought against my people, and taken much cattle. As the object for which you have come is to have compensation for Boers, I beg you will be satisfied with what you have taken. I entreat peace from you, you have shown your power, you have chastised, let it be enough I pray you; and let me be no longer considered an enemy of the Queen. I will try all I can to keep my people in order in the future.

This communication, described by Theal as the "most politic document ever penned in South Africa," had the desired effect and an armistice was arranged at the time when Moshoeshoe's forces were completely exhausted.[7]

In 1854 British sovereignty was withdrawn and the Orange Free State acquired its independence. With British authority now departed, Moshoeshoe and his people were left to face the Boers alone.

In 1858 the Free State commenced an attack on the Basotho, but they were badly outnumbered and defeated at Thaba Bosiu, and therefore sued for peace. In the second Free State War (1865-1868), however, the Boers had reduced the Basotho to desperate straits. But just when most of the country was lost and starvation prevalent, Moshoeshoe's earlier appeals to the British reaped their reward. Acting on the advice of Sir Philip Wodehouse, the High Commissioner in the Cape, the Crown declared by Proclamation of 12th March 1868 that Lesotho was British territory.[8] Throughout the ensuing 98 years of colonial rule the country was known officially as Basutoland. Moshoeshoe died in 1870 and was succeeded as Paramount Chief by his son, Letsie I.

In 1871, without prior consultation of the Basotho, Basutoland was annexed to the Cape Colony.[9] The country was divided for administrative purposes into four districts. Resident Magistrates with civil and criminal jurisdiction were appointed. The Basotho were not represented in the Cape Parliament, although they requested this. The relationship with the Cape soon foundered, however, on the decision in 1880 to disarm the Basotho. Their implacable opposition to

---

7. This account is taken from TYLDEN, *supra* note 4, at 53-65.

8. For the constitutional effect of this see pp. 254-255.

9. Act 12 of 1871.

surrendering their guns resulted in the Gun War (1880—1881) in which certain chiefs went into rebellion against the Cape authorities. Peace was finally arranged, but the Basotho remained armed and the Cape Government, disillusioned by the heavy expense of this unsuccessful police action, requested the Imperial Government to take charge of the territory. Accordingly, Basutoland was disannexed from the Cape in 1883 [10] and the British Government, after determining the desires of the Basotho, took control in 1884.[11] This marked the beginning of an administration uninterrupted until the grant of independence in 1966.

The disadvantage of British protection, however, was the element of false security. Born of reluctance, it might be revoked if the right opportunity arose. Indeed the central fear of succeeding years was whether Britain might not hand Basutoland over to South Africa. Events soon after the turn of the century confirmed that this fear was well founded.

Following its victory in the Anglo-Boer war (in which Basutoland observed neutrality), Britain granted independence to the Union of South Africa in 1909. Prior to that, the transfer of the High Commission Territories of Basutoland, the Bechuanaland Protectorate, and Swaziland to the proposed union was discussed without seeking the advice of their peoples. Fearful of losing their independence, the Basotho sent a deputation of chiefs to England to seek an assurance that incorporation would not occur. In their prayer to King Edward VII they expressed "grave anxiety that our national existence will cease, our old native laws and customs be cast aside, and our whole

10. Act 34 of 1883.
11. Proclamation 2B of 1884.

constitution . . . will be shattered."[12] However the main assurance they received was that when transfer did take place, the land would be preserved for their use. A provision in the South African Constitution of 1909 later formalised the proposed transfer while acknowledging this limitation.[13] Fortunately for the Basotho, however, the ideological differences between the Afrikaners and the Cape liberals stood in the way. By tradition the Afrikaners opposed any African enfranchisement whereas the Capetonians desired to extend to the territories the common-law principle of equality for all before the law. In all subsequent discussions the impasse on African civil rights remained the underlying issue.

Over the next 50 years the question of incorporation received intermittent attention by the governments of Britain and South Africa. The distractions of two world wars made negotiations difficult. Though the matter was revived in 1935 it was again readily shelved until after the war. Following the accession of the Nationalist Party to power in 1948, South Africa began to insist that the transfer be carried out. In light of the doctrine of apartheid, however, it became evident to the British that this would have amounted to a breach of trust on their part. Basutoland was becoming noted for its relative absence of racialism. By 1965 the contrast with encircling South Africa was very great, for the Constitution of Basutoland rejected racial discrimination in access to public accommodation, public education, and civil rights.[14] Furthermore nationalist elements in Lesotho were beginning to demand independence. By 1959 Britain had

---

12. Quoted from LAGDEN, *supra* note 4, at 621.
13. South Africa Act, 1909, Schedule § 14.
14. For details, *see infra* pp. 408-440.

agreed to this in principle and the first constitutional steps were under way.[15]

D. Population

(1) ETHNIC STRUCTURE

The many clans and other tribal groups that were moulded together by Moshoeshoe I to form the Basotho Nation during the last century were predominantly Sotho in origin and, within that category, predominantly Koena. Since then most of the non-Koena Sotho have come to conform to the Koena pattern of life to a considerable degree. The non-Sotho people are Nguni in origin, but while these show cultural diversity they are numerically small.[16] The position is summarised by Smits who states: [17]

> Originally, the various groups constituting the Basotho Nation of today each showed specific ethnic characteristics, *e.g.*, the Batlokoa and Baphuthi. In the past certain areas experienced a history slightly different from that of the rest of the country, *e.g.*, the Quthing District. Nevertheless it can be said that, on the whole, regional differences among the population of Lesotho can no longer be explained primarily through differences in historical, political or social characteristics. As a result of the forging of Lesotho's heterogeneous population groups into one Basotho Nation under the great Moshoeshoe I, Lesotho is now already for more than a century one relatively homogeneous area, with its people sharing basically the same historical and political events, undergoing fundamentally the same social and cultural influences and transformations.

(2) SIZE AND COMPOSITION

The total population today is just over one mil-

---

15. *See infra* pp. 224-225.
16. *Supra* note 3, at 13-14.
17. *Supra* note 2, at 23.

lion. The most recent census in 1966 gave the *de facto* population as 852,361, *i.e.*, this was the number of persons present in the country during the enumeration period. In addition there were calculated to be 117,273 persons absent who had been away for less than five years. This gave a *de jure* total of 969,634 and it was later estimated that the one million mark was reached in 1967. According to the 1966 census figures, 53.8 percent of the population is under twenty years of age.

Of the *de facto* population in 1966, 850,013 were Basotho, 1,582 were Europeans, and 766 were Asiatics. One of the striking features of these figures is the tiny number of Europeans in comparison with their presence in many other African countries. This is explained by the fact that non-Basotho have never been permitted to own land in that country and thus never became genuine colonial settlers. The small number of Europeans is made up in the main of government officials, traders, missionaries, and teachers.

The attitude of the Basotho to foreigners entering the country was made unmistakably clear by Moshoeshoe in his Law of Trade in 1859:

> I, Moshesh, write for any trader, whoever he may be, already in my land, and for any who may come to trade with the Basutos; my word is this:
> Trade to me and my Tribe is a good thing; I wish to promote it.
> Any trader who wishes to establish a shop, must first obtain permission from me. Should he build a house, I grant him no right to sell it. Further, I do not grant him liberty to plough the fields, but only to plant a small vegetable garden. The trader who fancies that the place he is sojourning in belongs to him, must dismiss the thought; if not, he is to quit; for there is no place belonging to the whites in my land, and I have granted no white man a place, either by word, or by writing . . . .[18]

18. Quoted in LAGDEN, *supra* note 4, at 304.

There can be no doubt that this policy, which was endorsed by the British when they were the colonial power, has obviated many of the political and economic difficulties that have been encountered elsewhere.

(3) DISTRIBUTION

The 1960 agricultural census shows that about 50 percent of the population lives in the lowlands, the border lowlands, and the Orange River Valley which together form only about 26 percent of the total surface area. The other 50 percent inhabit the foothills and the mountains. Thus a population density of over 200 persons per square mile is to be found in the lowlands, whereas in the mountains the average is 39 per square mile. The average overall density for the whole of Lesotho is around 73 persons per square mile, but the more meaningful figure is the density per square mile of land capable of being cultivated; this is around 630.[19]

(4) EMPLOYMENT

The vast majority of the country's labour force, probably somewhere in the region of 85 percent, is engaged in subsistence farming. However, because there is an acute shortage of land suitable for cultivation and because there has been a great increase of population, the Basotho have for many years been forced to sell their labour in mines and industries and on farms in South Africa. The jobs they take are unskilled and the wages are low, but through lack of employment opportunities in Lesotho they have been presented with little choice.

It is generally thought that these migrant workers constitute at any given time around 43 percent of

---

19. *See* SMIT, *supra* note 2, at 17-19.

the adult male population of Lesotho.[20] While the money earned, including remittance payments and deferred pay, contribute substantially to the wealth of the population of Lesotho, the overall social and economic consequences are a cause for considerable concern. Family life is disrupted and many villages are deprived of their menfolk. Cultivation of the fields has to be carried on by women and children whose shallow ploughing has deleterious effects on the productivity of the land. Moreover the fact that the option of migrant labour is open to the Basotho prevents them from ever becoming serious and efficient cultivators and stock farmers. As production from the land decreases it becomes more necessary to seek employment abroad and thus a vicious circle is created.[21]

It appears that migrant labour is drawn in the main from the lowland areas where the pressure on land is greatest, while in the mountains the function of relieving population pressure due to the scarcity of arable land is performed by pastoralism at cattle posts.[22] However the number of men absent at cattle posts is very small.

The Bureau of Statistics concluded from the 1966 census that the rates of underemployment and unemployment respectively were around 39 percent and 14 percent for the *de facto* African population aged 15 to 64 years.[23]

(5) EDUCATION

Lesotho has long claimed one of the highest literacy rates in Africa. The primary school enrolment has

---

20. *See* SPENCE, LESOTHO: THE POLITICS OF DEPENDENCE 64 (O.U.P. 1968).

21. *See* SMIT, *supra* note 2, at 33.

22. Smits, *supra* note 2, at 26-27.

23. 1966 POPULATION CENSUS REPORT Part II at 143.

indeed been high owing to the emphasis placed by the missionaries upon elementary education.[24] However the situation beneath the surface is far from satisfactory. Thus while 72 percent of the female population attends school at some stage, only about 50 percent of the male population does so.[25] This is because many boys of school age are entrusted by their families with the herding of livestock. Moreover, neither secondary education nor vocational or technical training has up to now been adequately developed, with the result that Lesotho is desperately short of skilled manpower.

There are 1,077 primary schools, 26 secondary and high schools, seven teachers' training colleges, and five technical and vocational schools. Ninety-eight percent of these schools are run by missionaries although most are now largely government aided. The wastage (dropout) rate in the schools is extremely high, with only about twelve percent of primary school enrolments reaching the final year. Of these few, only about a quarter proceed to secondary school and barely an eighth of these complete the course. Thus while in 1967 there were about 44,000 children in the first year of primary school, only 166 were in their final year at secondary school.[26]

From an economic viewpoint the results in this sphere have been disappointing. The relatively high rate of investment in education has altogether failed to stimulate more productive farming, to lead to a

24. The 1966 Census report (p. 141) defines literacy in terms of successful completion of the first two years at primary school, after which a child should be able to read and write Sesotho. On this basis it estimates a literacy rate of 47.5% for the *de facto* population. This is much lower than the rather extravagant figures given in some earlier assessments.

25. *Supra* note 23, at 142.

26. ANNUAL STATISTICAL BULLETIN 49-52 (1967).

dynamic change in traditional social patterns, or generally to contribute significantly to the modernization of Lesotho.[27] In 1966 the country possessed only 180 Basotho graduates and the vast majority of the people still cannot look beyond subsistence farming and periodic migrations to unskilled work in South Africa.

The need for education to match the manpower requirements of the country was reflected in the appointment of two commissions in 1969. The Pickard Commission was given the task of reporting on the development of vocational and technical education, while the Alexander Commission was asked to assist the University of Botswana, Lesotho and Swaziland to prepare a development plan for the period 1970-1985 designed to meet the high level manpower requirements of the three countries.

The University came into being in 1964, having taken over the grounds and buildings previously used by the Roman Catholic College of Pius XII which prepared students for degrees of the University of South Africa. The University (commonly known as U.B.L.S.) serves Botswana, Lesotho, and Swaziland, and although at present its principal location is at Roma, 21 miles from Maseru, preparations are being made to establish substantial centres in the other two countries. In 1969-70 there were 386 full-time students, including 155 from Lesotho, studying in the fields of science, the humanities, social and economic studies, and education. The University awards its own degrees, diplomas, and certificates. The entry of students is usually after they have passed the Cambridge Overseas School Certificate examination (equivalent to O-level) and bachelors' degrees generally take four years.

---

27. LEISTNER, LESOTHO: ECONOMIC STRUCTURE AND GROWTH 5 (Pretoria 1966).

(6) HEALTH

Despite Lesotho's healthy climate and the absence of tropical diseases the general health of the people is not good. In 1960 a World Health Organisation report[28] stated that over 75 percent of all Basotho were undernourished to a significant degree and that endemic goitre, pellagra, and kwashiorkor were widespread. Tuberculosis is also a serious problem.

There are seventeen hospitals in the country (with a total of 1,616 hospital beds), 42 health centres, and 31 dispensaries. The total number of doctors is 34, *i.e.*, one for every 25,000 persons.[29] A flying doctor service operates from Maseru to treat patients who are in the remote mountain areas.

Various voluntary agencies such as the Catholic Relief Services, the Save the Children Fund, Oxfam, World Food Aid Programme, and the Freedom from Hunger Campaign give assistance with food for hospitals and feeding programmes for schools. Also on a number of occasions each year a team of South African doctors visits Queen Elizabeth II Hospital in Maseru to perform operations and give consultations on a voluntary basis.

(7) RELIGIOUS AFFILIATIONS

The various churches have played a leading part in the life of the country for well over 100 years, especially in the spheres of education, health, politics, and literature. The first missionaries, who were from the Paris Evangelical Missionary Society, arrived in 1833. One of these was Eugène Casalis who later be-

---

28. J. A. Munoz and M. Anderson, Report and Recommendations on a Nutrition Survey conducted in Basutoland (W.H.O. Regional Office for Africa South of the Sahara, 1956-60, mimeographed).

29. ANNUAL STATISTICAL BULLETIN 43-45 (1967).

came Moshoeshoe I's political adviser. The first Roman Catholic priests arrived in 1862. Although it came to Lesotho later, the Catholic Church is today extremely influential. The 1966 census figures show that of the *de facto* African population, 38.7 percent is Roman Catholic, 24.3 percent adheres to the Lesotho Evangelical Church (an autonomous church which resulted from the endeavors of the Paris Evangelical Missionary Society), 10.4 percent is Anglican, other Christian denominations account for 8.4 percent and 10.4 percent is non-Christian.

E. Economy

Lesotho's economic position does not rest upon very sure foundations. The country had a trade deficit of 19.6 million rand in 1967 [30] and very substantial aid is still required from the United Kingdom to balance the budget.[31] Known natural resources are limited to diamonds and water, both of which are expensive to exploit because of their location in the remote mountain areas. Livestock farming and crop cultivation at the subsistence level are the mainstay of the people, and industry is still at its infant stage. The infrastructure is very far from adequate for economic takeoff. The average annual *per capita* income was estimated in 1966-67 to be 57.7 rand [32] which is one of the lowest in Africa.

Lesotho's currency is the South African rand (R) which at current rates of exchange is equivalent to $1.40 or 11/8d sterling.

---

30. ANNUAL STATISTICAL BULLETIN 22-23 (1967).

31. The grant-in-aid for 1966-67 was R5.5 million and total British aid for 1968-69 amounted to £4.018 million.

32. ANNUAL STATISTICAL BULLETIN 36 (1967).

(1) AGRICULTURE

According to the 1966 census figures, around 87 percent of the population is dependent upon agriculture. In 1966-67 agriculture accounted for over 70 percent of the gross domestic product. At present 11.6 percent of the total land surface is under cultivation and of this only 62 percent can be considered truly arable because of the acute slopes that characterise the remainder.[33]

Crops are grown to meet immediate subsistence needs and traditional attitudes and techniques continue to prevail over the introduction of modern methods. Leistner has summarised the obstacles in the way of reform as follows:

> What basically impedes the development of a dynamic agricultural economy is the interaction between an archaic form of land tenure, a social system biased against rapid change, mounting population pressure, and the physical features of the land. From the interaction of these four factors has evolved a pattern of eroding soils, declining output per unit of land, malnutrition, and labour migration, with all the attendant social and moral evils.[34]

Soil erosion is the most striking and at the same time the most disheartening feature of the Lesotho countryside. Strenuous efforts are now being made to reclaim land lost in this way, as well as to encourage better agricultural practices by agricultural extension services, a "progressive farmers" scheme, and the enactment of legislation. The Land Husbandry Act 1969[35] provides for the Minister of Agriculture to make regulations for improving the use of land and

---

33. SMIT, *supra* note 2, at 25-26.

34. *Supra* note 27, at 6-7.

35. Act No. 22 of 1969 discussed *infra* pp. 182-183.

water resources, contravention of which would render a farmer liable to a fine.

The land tenure system,[36] under which an individual may only obtain the right to use the land and not its ownership, is hardly conducive to substantial investment in the land. Nor does it encourage the growing of cash crops. The Basotho have generally planted only the traditional crops, *e.g.*, maize, sorghum (kaffircorn), summer wheat, beans, and pumpkins. These are all one-season crops. After they have been harvested the rest of the community is entitled to turn its stock to feed on the stubble. The planting of certain cash crops, *e.g.*, winter wheat, would conflict with these communal grazing rights.[37]

The population increase has led to the fragmentation of holdings so that the average size for a family holding had decreased by 1960 to five acres. Moreover it is general practice for a family's fields to be scattered. This makes scientific farming virtually impossible.[38]

Poor farming methods include failures to use fertilizers or to put animal manure on the fields, to let land lie fallow and to rotate crops, the lack of essential implements, and ploughing across contour lines which results in soil erosion.

Thus, Lesotho's crop production is not sufficient to feed her population and substantial imports of cereals are required. Although maize is grown on about half the cultivated land in the country it was still necessary in 1967 to import further quantities at a cost of R893,000.

---

36. The land tenure system and its future are discussed in detail *infra* pp. 172-189.

37. *See* Henry *The Economy of Lesotho* in LESOTHO, BOTSWANA AND SWAZILAND (Stevens ed. London 1967).

38. LEISTNER, *supra* note 27, at 8.

The physical nature of Lesotho makes it more suitable for stock farming than for cultivation, and pastoralism supplements the growing of crops. Cattle are of great social significance, especially because they represent bridewealth *(bohali)*. This tends to lead people to concentrate on the quantity rather than the quality of their cattle, and as a result the country is badly overstocked.[39] Nevertheless earnings from the export of hides and skins are relatively high.

Sheep and goats are kept in large numbers and wool and mohair represent a very substantial proportion of the country's exports. However here again poor farming practices have been prevalent, *e.g.*, lack of grazing control and allowing valuable angora goat rams and merino rams to crossbreed with inferior stock, thus reducing the quality of the wool clip.

(2) INDUSTRY

Industrial development has been very slow and until recently it was limited to two printing works run by the churches, four furniture-making establishments, a few small mills, and a tiny handful of other minor enterprises.[40] In 1966 only 1,880 people were employed in this sector of the economy.

Since independence, and more especially within the last year or so, limited but steady progress has been made in establishing a wider range of small industries. These are in the main run by foreigners and they include a candle factory, a tyre retreading plant, a brewery, a paint factory, four handicraft centres, carpet weavers, a stone crushing plant, a maize mill, and a factory to manufacture steel products for the construction industry.[41]

---

39. SMIT, *supra* note 2, at 35.

40. LEISTNER, *supra* note 27, at 22.

41. ANNUAL ECONOMIC REVIEW FOR BOTSWANA, LESOTHO, AND SWAZILAND 14-15 (Standard Bank Group 1969).

The Lesotho National Development Corporation was set up in 1967 [42] to promote and initiate the development of mining, commerce and manufacturing and processing industries. It has participated in a number of the ventures referred to above, as well as acted as a valuable stimulant.

In 1969 two acts of parliament were passed that were designed to encourage private investment in industry. The Pioneer Industries Encouragement Act [43] grants tax incentives to manufacturers and related industries in the form of either a six-year tax holiday or substantial tax deductions on items such as the cost of new machinery and equipment, factory buildings, and housing for employees. To qualify for the incentives the industry must be registered in Lesotho, establish a new factory or plant or expand its existing one, and satisfy the Pioneer Industries Board that it will contribute to the economic development of Lesotho. The Act offers similar incentives to hotels, casinos, and building developers.

The Industrial Licensing Act [44] authorises the granting of an exclusive right to a manufacturer to produce a specified product for up to five years at a time.

(3) MINING

Lesotho's mineral resources have for a long time been the subject of controversy owing to inadequate geological surveys and the half-hearted interest shown by the colonial administration.[45] Moreover the assessments of large-scale mining concerns have not always been the same. The Basotho have always held that the

---

42. By Act No. 20 of 1967.
43. Act No. 19 of 1969.
44. Act No. 27 of 1969.
45. Henry, *supra* note 37, at 101-103.

country possessed substantial resources, but it can readily be appreciated that in view of the dire economic position in other respects this could have been mere wishful thinking.

During the past thirty years there have been eight different surveys. The reports of these surveys show that there are diamondiferous pipes in the Maloti Mountains.[46] Consequently the government has recently concluded two prospecting and mining agreements with international companies. The first was with the Rio Tinto Zinc Corporation in respect of an area at Letšeng-la-Terae; the Bethlehem Steel Corporation of America has agreed to join in these operations, and the Lesotho Development Corporation will also be participating. The second was with Lonrho Ltd. in relation to a diamond pipe at Mothae which is about seven miles from Letšeng-la-Terae. The companies are expected to make substantial investments in these projects. Part of their investment will be in the construction of access roads since the mining zones are in very remote areas of the mountains.[47]

The individual Basotho diggers who used to conduct very primitive mining operations at Letšeng-la-Terae have been moved to other areas to make way for the Rio Tinto Zinc Corporation.

The value of diamonds exported rose sharply from R136,932 in 1961-62 to R1,017,623 in 1967.[48] There was a decline in 1968 largely due to the changeover at Letšeng-la-Terae, but 1969 showed a recovery and exports were again valued at over R1 million.

In 1967 a diamond weighing 601 carats, and said to be the seventh largest ever found, was discovered

---

46. DEPARTMENT OF MINES ANNUAL REPORT 1-2 (1968).
47. *Id.* at 4-5.
48. *Id.* at 11.

by an individual Mosotho digger at Letšeng-la-Terae. It was exported at a price of over R200,000.

(4) TAXATION

As in most underdeveloped countries, direct forms of taxation in Lesotho constitute a much smaller proportion of total revenue than indirect forms. Thus in 1966-67 direct taxes contributed only 35 percent of the total tax receipts while indirect taxes made up the balance of 65 percent.[49]

The three direct personal taxes are basic tax, graded tax, and income tax. Basic tax has replaced the earlier hut and poll taxes and is levied upon every adult male resident in the country. There is a standard rate of R3-50 but if the taxpayer has more than one wife he has to pay an extra R2-50 in respect of each additional wife up to a maximum of R5-00,[50] which would bring his total maximum tax to R8-50. In 1966-67 this tax brought in a total of R772,700.[51]

Income tax is levied broadly speaking on the British pattern,[52] but the tax is only payable by those who have a taxable income of over R600. The rate of assessment rises from six percent of a person's taxable income at the lowest point, through around 13 percent on an income of R6,000, to around 30 percent on R20,000 in respect of the income of a married couple. In 1966-67 this tax brought in R428,100.

Graded tax has two purposes. The first is to impose an additional tax to basic tax on those who earn between R250 and R600. The tax rises from R4 on an

---

49. ANNUAL STATISTICAL BULLETIN 39 (1967).

50. Basic and Graded Tax (Consolidation) Act, No. 24 of 1968, § 4.

51. ANNUAL STATISTICAL BULLETIN 39 (1967).

52. See the Income Tax (Consolidation) Proclamation, No. 30 of 1959.

income of R300 to R8 on an income of R600. The second purpose is to levy a graduated tax, in addition to the other two taxes, on those who have incomes of over R600. The amounts are relatively small, rising proportionately to a maximum of R100 on an income of over R2,000. Consequently, the tax only contributed R11,000 to the country's revenue in 1966-67.

Company tax is levied at the rate of 30 per cent in respect of taxable income up to R8,000 and 37½ percent thereafter.[53] Mining companies pay a 50 percent profits tax from which they are able to deduct the sales tax of 15 percent, which is also imposed.[54]

Revenue from indirect taxes has come mainly from Lesotho's share of the customs levy under the Customs Agreement with South Africa. Under the agreement there is a free flow of goods to and fro across the border, with a few exceptions which include diamonds and alcoholic liquor. Lesotho's percentage in terms of the original 1910 agreement was 0.88575 percent of the total tariffs levied on imports into South Africa. This figure was reached on the basis of the trade figures for 1906-08 and has long been recognised to be in need of revision. The extent of Lesotho's dependence upon these payments is shown by the fact that they constituted half the country's total territorial revenue up to 1964. In 1964 the proportion was revised to 0.47903 for a trial period.[55] Even this reduced share amounted to R1,335,200 in 1966-67, or one-third of the total territorial revenue.

The 1910 agreement was renegotiated in 1969 with South Africa, Botswana, and Swaziland, which should result in Lesotho's receiving a substantially

---

53. Income Tax (Rates) Act, No. 25 of 1969, § 2.

54. DEPARTMENT OF MINES ANNUAL REPORT 4 (1968).

55. HALPERN, SOUTH AFRICA'S HOSTAGES 232 (Penguin 1965).

greater amount than at any time previously.[56] This should have the effect of lessening the country's reliance upon the United Kingdom's aid to balance the budget.

Other indirect taxes are the export levies on mohair, wool, and diamonds, motor vehicle and trading licenses, and duties on alcoholic liquor.

(5) COMMUNICATIONS

The topography of Lesotho has considerably hampered the creation of an efficient communications' network. All the main centres except two are found along the western part of the country and these are connected by a main road running 228 miles from north to south. Seventy-six miles of this road have been tarred recently as a result of a loan from the International Development Association, and it is hoped that further sections may be tarred later. There is a road called the Mountain Road which runs eastwards from the capital city of Maseru into the mountains for about 90 miles. Apart from this, there are only tracks connecting the lowlands with the higher parts of the country.

Lesotho has no railway system of its own, but it is linked with the South African system by one mile of rail running between Maseru and the border. From there the line continues to Marseilles which is on the Bloemfontein-Natal main line.

Light aircraft are used quite extensively to give access to the remoter mountain areas and there are 33 airstrips scattered throughout the country, five of which are served by scheduled flights by Lesotho Airways. There is no road linking one of the main centres in the east, Qacha's Nek, with the western parts

56. The agreement is annexed to G.N. 193 of 1969.

of Lesotho and unless plane travel is used it is necessary to drive in a very wide circle outside Lesotho to get there.

Scheduled air services between Maseru and Johannesburg operate twice a week in each direction. One flight is performed by Lesotho Airways and the other by South African Airways.

(6) DEVELOPMENT PLANS

The provisional development plan drawn up soon after independence appears to have been abandoned and the Prime Minister has instructed the government to prepare a new five year National Development Plan during 1970, designed to accelerate the rate of economic and social progress.

Because it is a member of the Rand currency union, Lesotho has no central bank of its own, and most of its functions are carried out by the South African Reserve Bank. However the government plans to establish a Development Bank that would become a depository for local savings which could then be utilised for providing credit in the fields of small industries, agriculture, and housing.

Perhaps the most promising development project for the future is the Oxbow scheme under which the massive water resources of Lesotho would be put to productive use.[57] The scheme envisages the construction of a series of dams and tunnels for storing and diverting waters from the Malibamatšo River (a tributary of the Orange) and for regulating their flow. Water for industrial purposes would then be sold to the Republic of South Africa, where there is a shortage. At a later stage hydroelectric power could be provided both for the Republic and for Lesotho. This scheme

57. *See* Henry, *supra* note 37, at 103-106; SMIT, *supra* note 2, at 38-41.

has been the subject of much discussion for many years. Its implementation is dependent upon South African agreement to purchase the water and upon obtaining financing for the operations, which would cost many millions of rands because of the remoteness of the area where the dams would be situated. The signs are at last encouraging since South Africa has agreed in principle to purchase water and hydroelectric power from Lesotho and the U.N. Development Programme has been called in to undertake feasibility studies at a cost of R1.2 million.[58]

(7) OUTLOOK

Lesotho's prospects of being economically viable in the near future and at the same time carrying through the social and economic changes demanded by its people are undeniably slender. The obstacles to economic development often appear to be overwhelming —the topography of the country renders much of the land unfit for cultivation and makes it costly to exploit the limited natural resources that are known to exist; there is a scarcity of trained manpower; many of the people are conservative by nature; and Lesotho is geographically vulnerable, being encircled on all sides by South Africa. All these factors suggest that the struggle for economic independence will be far more difficult than that which achieved political independence.

However, the years since 1966 show that the government is determined to make progress. Steps have been taken to improve agricultural techniques and increase production from the land, to encourage and promote industries and mining, to attract private foreign investment and mobilise local savings, to make

58. ANNUAL ECONOMIC REVIEW FOR BOTSWANA, LESOTHO, AND SWAZILAND 16 (1969).

communications better, and to pursue the Oxbow scheme. This scheme, if implemented, would not only provide revenue from the sale of water and power, but would offer much-needed employment for Basotho within their own country. It would also improve irrigation and supply hydroelectric power for Lesotho's own projected industrial development.

Finally, consideration is being given to promoting tourism in Lesotho, and this should meet with a good measure of success. The first luxury hotel and casino costing R1 million will soon be in operation on the banks of the Caledon River at Maseru. The country has magnificent mountain scenery including some of the highest waterfalls in Africa. There are some very fine Bushman cave paintings and dinosaur footprints that are said to be over 180 million years old. In addition, it is good riding and fishing country.

F. Government [59]

The early government of the Basotho rested upon the aristocratic powers of the chiefs. Each of the federated clans was ruled by a hierarchy of its own chiefs and subchiefs. Over and above these tribal chiefs was the Paramount Chief of the nation who held central authority. In calling Moshoeshoe the "supreme master" of the country, however, Casalis probably exaggerated the extent of that authority.[60] Cer-

---

59. The traditional and colonial government structures of Lesotho receive some treatment in the historical works cited *supra* note 4. In particular, however, the reader is referred to the cited works of HAILEY and LAGDEN. In addition, *see* ASHTON, THE BASUTO (2d ed. 1967); STEVENS, LESOTHO, BOTSWANA, AND SWAZILAND (London 1967); and the penetrating analysis of JONES in BASUTOLAND MEDICINE MURDER, CMD. No. 8209 (H.M.S.O. 1951).

60. Quoted from GERMOND, CHRONICLES OF BASUTOLAND 517 (Morija 1967).

tainly he commanded the armies in battle, sat as highest court of appeal, and promulgated general laws. Furthermore, he possessed the prerogative known as the power to place. By "placing" his sons and other relatives over the chiefs of an allied tribe he could further extend his power.[61]

In the tradition of the Basotho chieftainship, however, their powers were not despotic. A measure of truth lies in the brocard *Morena ke morena ka batho:* "A chief is a chief by the people." Though the chieftainship is hereditary, it rests partly on popular approval. Moshoeshoe always emphasised that on important matters he required the advice and consent of the great chiefs under him. This may have been partly due to the basis of his military alliance, but by custom every chief had kinsmen and councillors with whom he was required to consult.[62]

One reason for popular control was that Basotho chiefs were not deemed to have religious or magical powers. Further, though Casalis noted the people's almost "superstitious respect" for chiefs,[63] this has diminished greatly in modern times. Another reason is the custom of calling together *pitsos* (public meetings) to discuss important matters. Early observers of Basotho life, witnessing the freedom of criticism directed at chiefs by commoners on such occasions, stressed the democratic nature of the *pitso*.[64] The first National *pitso* was called in 1874 and it was intended that they be held annually. Unfortunately this practice was abandoned in the colonial era.

---

61. *See* Jones, *Chiefly Succession in Basutoland* SUCCESSION TO HIGH OFFICE 57 *et seq.* (Goody ed. Cambridge 1966).

62. ASHTON, *supra* note 59, at 216-217.

63. CASALIS, *supra* note 4, at 214.

64. *See, e.g.,* LORD BRYCE, TRAVELS IN SOUTH AFRICA 339 (1899).

(1) COLONIAL GOVERNMENT

It was a cardinal principle of British policy toward Basutoland that the authority of the chiefs and the way of life of the Basotho should be interfered with as little as possible. The advantages of this course were that it was inexpensive, ostensibly altruistic,[65] and in accord with the original wish of the Basotho, who desired protection but rejected control. To detractors on the other hand, its defect was that it led to inevitable stagnation.

In any event the indigenous structure of government by the chiefs was retained and a small force of British administrators, headed by a Resident Commissioner in Maseru and a High Commissioner in South Africa,[66] was established as a kind of parallel government. Two limitations always checked their actions. The Administration was instructed first to accomplish no more than the "protection of life and property" and secondly to observe the principle that expenditure should never exceed revenue. On these premises few economic or political developments in the country took place. From the constitutional standpoint, however, two developments may be noted. First, the Paramount Chief Lerotholi (r. 1893-1905), succeeded in subduing dissident elements, thus securing for the Paramount Chieftainship an unquestioned overall superiority. Secondly, in place of the disused national *pitsos,* a National Council (later called the Basutoland Council) was established in 1903 as a means of broadening the decision-making process.

---

65. HOBSON, for example, argued that Britain's *laissez faire* attitude in Basutoland illustrated how an imperial policy could in fact be moral—IMPERIALISM 245-246 (3d ed. 1938). *But see* ROBINSON, THE DILEMMAS OF TRUSTEESHIP 68-70 (1965).

66. For the implications of this *see* pp. 228-230.

Comprised originally of the leading chiefs, the Council was the forerunner of the present Legislature. One of its first undertakings was the drafting of the Laws of Lerotholi, an unofficial written restatement of the leading principles of Sesotho customary law.[67]

Important reforms were introduced in 1938.[68] Spurred by the 1934 enquiry of Sir Alan Pim who severely criticised the prior policy of noninterference, the Crown introduced the well-known system of "indirect rule." It was an attempt to rouse Basutoland after 50 years of stagnant slumber. Even allowing for a world depression, Basutoland's economy and social services in 1934 were in a deplorable condition. Politically, the chieftainship was abusing its powers. It had lost much respect and was out of touch with the people. The *pitso* lay in desuetude and a substantial number of chiefs flouted the Laws of Lerotholi. Furthermore the extravagant use of "placings" was an unquestionable evil. The switch to indirect rule sought to eliminate such problems by bringing the chieftainship securely under the control of the colonial government.

Under indirect rule the chiefs were recognised not by virtue of customary law but by notice in the Government Gazette. Their numbers were substantially reduced. A statutory obligation was imposed on them to maintain law and order. Furthermore the valuable prerogative of each chief to hold a court was eliminated, thereby depriving many of an important source of income. Whereas in 1939 there were 1,300 recognised courts, this was reduced by 1949 to 106.[69] When

---

67. Discussed *infra*, pp. 106-107.

68. The most extensive discussion of the 1938 reforms is to be found in HAILEY, NATIVE ADMINISTRATION IN THE BRITISH AFRICAN TERRITORIES Part V, 70-111.

69. The implications and history of this change in the court structure is discussed *infra* pp. 489-493.

a National Treasury was established in 1946, the administrative services of the chieftainship became salaried and their sources of income in turn came under control. A House of Chiefs was established in 1959 mainly for the purpose of requiring the senior chiefs to police and administer the chieftainship.[70]

Several changes of importance took place soon afterwards in the Basutoland Council. The colonial government had conferred increased power. The Council could now demand to be consulted before laws affecting the administration of the country were enacted. Furthermore the Council broadened its membership by admitting elected representatives from the District Councils, which had been created in 1945. By 1950, 36 out of a total of 100 members were elected in this manner.[71] Finally in 1948, the Council prevailed upon the acting Paramount Chief to accept an advisory board or Privy Council from its ranks. The advisers consisted of three members selected from a list of eighteen members nominated by the Council.

(2) INDEPENDENCE AND AFTER

From 1955 onwards the Council began to press for measures leading to Independence [72] and this was finally granted in 1966 under a Westminster form of government featuring a Parliament (National Assembly and Senate),[73] Cabinet system,[74] and Constitutional Monarch.[75]

---

70. For further discussion, *see infra*, pp. 221-222. For the latest attempt to reform the chiefs, *see* The Chieftainship Act, No. 22, of 1968.

71. For the future development of the Basutoland Council under the Constitutions of 1959 and 1965, *see infra*, pp. 214-237, respectively.

72. Discussed in detail *infra*, pp. 212-213.

73. Discussed *infra*, pp. 244-251.

74. Discussed *infra*, pp. 252-254.

75. Discussed *infra*, pp. 239-244.

In the first elections in 1965 the present ruling party, the Basotho National Party (B.N.P.), obtained 41.6 percent of the vote and 31 of the 60 seats in the National Assembly. The main opposition party, the Basutoland Congress Party (B.C.P.), captured 39.7 percent of the votes and 25 seats in the National Assembly. The B.N.P. appears to be a pro-Catholic, conservative party which is strongly anti-Communist and favorable to *rapprochement* with South Africa. Its leader, the present Prime Minister, is Chief Leabua Jonathan. The B.C.P. on the other hand, led by Ntsu Mokhehle, has been described as a radical, pan-Africanist mass party and has often appeared to be hostile towards South Africa. Indeed on paper there is a great ideological gap between the two main parties.[76]

The centre position is occupied by the royalist Marematlou Freedom Party (M.F.P.) which allied itself in the first parliament with the B.C.P.

There are three explosive issues in Basotho politics on which feelings run very deep between the parties: (1) relations with South Africa, (2) plans for economic growth, and (3) the position of the King. A possible fourth issue, the question of land tenure reform, is also important but it is to a certain extent controlled by constitutional provisions.[77]

To B.N.P. thinking the first two issues, in the Lesotho context, are in reality much the same. Economic growth depends upon good relations with South Africa. In the 1965 elections the electorate apparently

---

76. For analyses of party attitudes and policies, *see* WEISFELDER, DEFINING NATIONAL PURPOSE (Ohio University Center for International Studies, Papers in International Studies: Africa Series No. 3, 1969) and Macartney, *African Westminster? The Parliament of Lesotho* XXIII PARLIAMENTARY AFFAIRS 121-140 (No. 2, 1970).

77. Discussed *infra*, pp. 254-268.

split radically here, the slight plurality opting for a foreign policy with the Republic friendly enough to guarantee the mainstays of the economy, which include (a) the vital customs union agreement, (b) the security of Basotho employed in South Africa, (c) foreign aid, and (d) communications and transit facilities for goods and personnel. The last is indispensable if the country is to attract educators, tourists, technicians, and foreign investors. On the other hand if the B.C.P. came to power, it is foreseeable that South Africa might restrict the economy along some or even all of these lines; this could put the country to an extreme survival test. However, at least 40 percent of the electorate apparently felt that in principle non-cooperation (as opposed to direct confrontation) with South Africa was worth the risk.[78]

The King was dissatisfied with the prospect of a position as a constitutional monarch and opposed Independence under the 1966 Constitution.[79] Following disturbances in December 1966 he was placed under palace arrest on order of the Prime Minister. Under pressure he eventually signed a written undertaking to observe strictly his limited role under the Constitution.[80] The leaders of the B.C.P. and the M.F.P. were imprisoned in connection with the same incident.

The unanswered issues for the future are how the political neutrality of the King can be restored and

78. Future relations with South Africa are discussed by SPENCE, *supra* note 20, at 79-80.

79. The King wanted powers equivalent to those which the Resident Commissioner held at Independence.

80. The text of the instrument is fully set out in Weisfelder, *Power Struggle in Lesotho* 12 AFRICA REPORT 5 at 12 (No. 1 1967). The legality of the instrument is subject to much doubt. Aside from the question of duress, there is no reason to think that the King's entrenched rights are subject to change by mere private agreement.

how constitutional limitations on his power can gain general acceptance. The current strategy of the government is to place an embargo upon the vote-getting use of the King's name by the politicians [81] and to consider any indecorous political breach of Westminster conventions by the King as tantamount to abdication. Neither the King nor the Prime Minister, however, seems satisfied with the present arrangement.

81. § 85. Electoral Act No. 23 of 1968.

PART I
THE LAWS

CHAPTER 1

INTRODUCTION

The advent of independence in October 1966 did not effect any momentous change in the basic content of the laws of the country. The newly independent state of Lesotho took over the existing laws that had previously been in force in Basutoland, though they were in future to be construed with any modifications, adaptations, qualifications, and exceptions required to bring them into conformity with the Independence legislation, namely the Constitution and the Order in Council to which it was scheduled.[1]

The basic legal structure which was in force dur-

---

1. The Independence Order in Council (§ 1. No. 1172 of 1966) provides as follows:

> The existing laws shall, as from the appointed day, be construed with such modifications, adaptations, qualifications, and exceptions as may be necessary to bring them into conformity with the Lesotho Independence Act 1966 and this Order. (§ 4(1).)
>
> For the purposes of this section the expression "existing law" means any proclamation, law, rule, regulation, order, or other instrument made or having effect as if it had been made in pursuance of (or continuing in operation under) the existing Order or the existing Court of Appeal Orders, [S. I. Nos. 1369 of 1954, 1187 of 1964, and 133 of 1965] and having effect as part of the law of Basutoland immediately before the appointed day or any act of the Parliament of the United Kingdom or Order of Her Majesty in Council so having effect and includes the customary law of Basutoland and any other unwritten rule of law so having effect. (§ 4(5).)

The "existing Order" referred to was the Basutoland Order, 1965, which revoked *inter alia* the Basutoland (Constitution) Order, 1959, but preserved the validity of existing laws with the necessary modifications, etc. The Basutoland (Constitution) Order, 1959, had previously revoked the Order in Council dated 2nd February 1884 while preserving the validity of existing laws with necessary modifications, etc. In this manner continuity was preserved throughout the successive constitutional changes.

ing colonial days and has been carried through into independence originates from the General Law Proclamation of 29th May 1884.[2] This was a proclamation of the High Commissioner in whom legislative power had been vested following the disannexation of Basutoland from the Cape Colony in February 1884.[3]

This proclamation provided for the operation of Cape Colonial laws and the customary law in Basutoland in the following manner:

> In all suits, actions, or proceedings, civil or criminal, the law to be administered shall as nearly as the circumstances of the country will permit, be the same as the law for the time being in force in the Colony of the Cape of Good Hope: Provided, however, that in any suit, action, or proceeding in any Court, to which all the parties are natives, and in all suits, actions, or proceedings whatsoever, before any Native Chief exercising jurisdiction as aforesaid, native law may be administered: And provided further, that the laws set out in the Schedule hereto and Acts passed after the 29th day of September 1884, by the Parliament of the Colony of the Cape of Good Hope, shall not apply to the said territory. (§ 2.)

Only the first part of this section remains intact today, the two provisos having been amended in 1960 by the Law Revision Proclamation.[4]

The purpose of the amendments was to take account of the fact that the customary law was no longer

2. Proc. No. 2B of 1884.

3. Part II of the Disannexation of Basutoland from the Colony of the Cape of Good Hope Order in Council of 2nd February, 1884 (proclaimed by Cape Proclamation No. 75A of 1884) provided *inter alia* that all laws in force in Basutoland at that time should continue in operation until repealed or altered by proclamation of the High Commissioner.

4. Proc. No. 12 of 1960, § 7(2).

administered by chiefs but by courts, and to delimit and specify the Cape legislation still in force.

The provisos therefore now read as follows:

> Provided, however, that in any suits, actions, or proceedings in any Court to which all of the parties are Africans, and in all suits, actions, or proceedings whatsoever before any Basuto Court, African law may be administered; and provided further that no law enacted by the legislative authority of the Colony of the Cape of Good Hope, or any legislative authority succeeding thereto in the Cape of Good Hope, shall have effect in Basutoland unless it is included in the First Schedule or the Third Schedule to the Law Revision Proclamation or has been specially applied therein by the Legislature of Basutoland.

Recognition is thus accorded by the Proclamation to three sources of law: namely, Cape Colonial common law, African customary law, and certain Cape statutes. In addition there is the post-1884 legislation passed by the legislative authority in the country from time to time. These sources will now be considered in turn.

CHAPTER 2

THE COMMON LAW

A. The Reception of Cape Colonial Law
B. The Content of the Law Retained

A. The Reception of Cape Colonial Law

The General Law Proclamation directs that the law to be administered shall, as nearly as the circumstances of the country will permit, be the same as the law for the time being in force in the Colony of the Cape of Good Hope. The process by which the general law of one country is introduced into another is known as "reception." Thus a territory colonised by Britain may be said to have "received" the amount of foreign law which it was allotted by the Imperial Government. In the case of Basutoland this was accomplished by means of the High Commissioner's Proclamation of 1884.

It is, however, clear from the first proviso to the Proclamation that there was no intention to supplant the indigenous or customary law, and this system still regulates the lives of the vast majority of people living in Lesotho today. Preservation of this law was, of course, in line with the conventional practice of English constitutional law to maintain so far as possible the existing law in force in territories acquired by settlement, conquest, cession, or the extension of possession,[5] and so far as Basotho [6] are concerned their customary law still stands on an equal footing with the common law.

---

5. Campbell v. Hall, [1774] 1 Cowp. 204, 209.

6. The spellings "Basotho," "Sesotho," and "Mosotho" conform with current usage and will be used throughout save where a quotation is given that uses the older "Basuto," etc.

The General Law Proclamation deviated from the current English practice in two respects.[7]

First, it was normal at the turn of the century to export the English common law together with the doctrines of equity and English statutes of general application. There were, however, precedents for this departure since Roman-Dutch law had been continued in force in Ceylon in 1799 and in Demerara and Essequebo in 1803.

Secondly, it was usual to stipulate what we may for the sake of convenience describe as a "cutoff date." Thus by the Law of England (Application) Ordinance of the Gambia[8] the Supreme Court there was empowered to administer "the common law, the doctrines of equity, and the statutes of general application in force in England on the 1st November, 1888." In Sierra Leone the date was 1st January 1880,[9] and in the former Gold Coast it was 24th July 1874.[10]

The Proclamation of 1884 was therefore exceptional in that it neither imported English law into Basutoland, nor did it fix a date so that the importer would know which year's model it had acquired. Instead of the English common law, provision was made for the reception of the law of the Cape Colony and this we may loosely refer to as Roman-Dutch law. It should be borne in mind that the word "reception" is being used here in a wider sense than is usual, for

---

7. For full discussions of the reception of English law in Africa, *see* ALLOTT, ESSAYS IN AFRICAN LAW chs. 1-2 (Butterworths 1960), and A.E.W. PARK, THE SOURCES OF NIGERIAN LAW ch. 3 (Sweet & Maxwell 1963).

8. Ch. 104, § 2 of the LAWS OF THE GAMBIA (1966).

9. § 37 of the Courts Ordinance—ch. 7 of the LAWS OF SIERRA LEONE (1959).

10. § 83 of the Courts Ordinance—ch. 4 of the LAWS OF THE GOLD COAST (1951 Revision), which has since been repealed by the Courts Act, 1960.

when the 1884 Proclamation provided for the application of Cape law this was not the first time such law was introduced into Basutoland. While the territory was annexed to the Cape [11] from 1871 to 1884 the law of the Cape was being applied.[12] Thus it is more accurate to speak of the "retention" of Cape law in 1884, and this too may be regarded as an application of the settled English rule allowing ceded territories to keep their existing laws. The reasons for permitting Basutoland to retain Cape law were clearly its geographical contiguity to the Cape Colony and the corresponding advantage of administering the same system in both colonies.

This same system of law was later to be introduced into the Bechuanaland Protectorate [13] and the colony of Southern Rhodesia.[14]

B. The Content of the Law Retained

In order to discover the content of the common law retained by Basutoland under the 1884 Proclamation it is first necessary to consider by what reference date the law of the Cape Colony is to be ascertained. It is a general principle that a statute speaks from the date of its enactment unless special provision is made for it to come into force at a different date. If this rule were to be applied, then 29th May 1884 would be the crucial date and the law as at that date would be the common law of Lesotho today.

---

11. By Cape Act 12 of 1871.

12. *See* § 8 of Cape Proclamation No. 74 of 1871, and §§ 12 and 24 of Cape Proclamation No. 41 of 1877.

13. By § 19 of the High Commissioner's Proclamation of 10th June 1891, which was subsequently repealed and replaced by § 2 of Proc. No. 36 of 1909.

14. By the High Commissioner's Proclamation of 10th June 1891, § 19.

On the other hand it may be that the law applicable is that administered at the present time in the Cape Province of the Republic of South Africa, which is the geographical successor to the Colony of the Cape of Good Hope.

A third alternative is that the law is that which was in force in the Colony of the Cape of Good Hope in 1909 before the Colony became merged in the Union by the enactment of the South Africa Act.

The theory that judges merely declare what has always been the common law would suggest that it does not make any difference which date is taken since the law is always the same.[15] Thus a decision of the Cape Supreme Court before 29th May 1884 would be just as applicable to Lesotho as a decision handed down by the Cape Provincial Division today. However it is submitted that the idea that judges merely reveal the common law is now generally discredited. Moreover the South African courts have in fact converted Roman-Dutch law into South African law, not by a process of interpretation but by making and moulding a new common law. This question is examined in more detail below.[16]

Fourthly, it must be considered whether the law of Lesotho can be described as Cape Colonial, Roman-Dutch, or South African law, not by reference to decisions given at particular periods of time but as a broad system of the common law spanning a number of jurisdictions.

(1) "THE LAW FOR THE TIME BEING IN FORCE IN THE COLONY OF THE CAPE OF GOOD HOPE"

If we accept the view that judges make law, what

---

15. This argument is dealt with by ALLOTT, *supra* note 7, at 31, and PARK, *supra* note 7, at 22.

16. *See infra*, pp. 55-58.

is the effect of the words in the General Law Proclamation "the law *for the time being*[17] in force in the Colony of the Cape of Good Hope"?

It appears that the phrase "for the time being" may have different meanings according to its context. It may, for instance mean the present time or denote a single period of time. On the other hand it may have the sense of time indefinite and refer to an indefinite state of facts that will arise in the future and that may, and probably will, vary from time to time.[18]

The context in which the phrase is used in the General Law Proclamation in fact affords scant assistance. The surrounding words do not, in themselves, show clearly whether the intention was to import the Cape Colonial Law of 29th May 1884 or the living system of law administered in the Cape from time to time.

Support for the first interpretation comes from various quarters. There are two reported judicial utterances on the question in Lesotho, the first being that of Schreiner J. A. delivering the judgment of the Court of Appeal in *Khatala v. Khatala*[19] in 1964. He referred to ". . . section 12 [*sic*] of Proclamation No. 26 [*sic*] of 1884, which applies the then existing law of the Cape of Good Hope to Basutoland . . . ."

This was followed in 1966 by a statement from Benson C. J. in *Motsamai Pholo v. The Principal Chief of Mokhotlong*[20] in which he said:

---

17. Our italics.

18. *See, e.g.*, STROUD'S JUDICIAL DICTIONARY 2058-59 (2d ed.).

19. [1963-66] H.C.T.L.R. 97, 99.

20. [1963-66] H.C.T.L.R. 188, 189. This statement is, with respect, inaccurate in its reference to a "common law of South Africa" before 1884. There was, of course, no such thing. The courts of the Cape Colony, the Orange Free State, Natal, and the Transvaal (and later the South African Republic) went

> A Declaratory Order is sought and also an Interdict as an alternative; the law regarding Declarations of Rights in Basutoland is governed by the common law of South Africa as it was prior to the 29th May 1884.

A note in similar vein is to be found in Allott's *Judicial and Legal Systems in Africa*[21] as follows:

> The effect of the Order in Council, 1884, and the High Commissioner's Proclamation is that the Roman-Dutch law in force in 1884 in the Colony of the Cape of Good Hope and such statutes, not discontinued by proclamation, are in force in Basutoland.

None of these three statements, however, contains any reason or explanation for the interpretation given and it is submitted that the alternative construction is to be preferred.

Professor Allott in his *Essays in African Law*[22] also contends that the same expression, used in a similar context, gives validity to the living system of law. Taking the hallowed reception clause from the Gold Coast Courts Ordinance,

> . . . the common law, the doctrines of equity, and the statutes of general application which were in force in England on the 24th day of July, 1874, shall be in force . . .

he concludes that the cutoff date applies to all three branches of the law and not only to the statutes by necessary intendment. Arguing *per contra* he goes on to state,

> Had the intention of the legislature been different,

their own ways in many particulars. One of the purposes of creating an Appellate Division in 1909 was to bring some uniformity into the interpretation of the law.

21. ALLOTT, JUDICIAL AND LEGAL SYSTEMS IN AFRICA 183 (Butterworths 1962).

22. *Supra* note 7, at 20 and 30-31; *also see supra* note 1.

> the relevant words might have followed those of section 17 of the Courts Ordinance which provided that the Gold Coast Supreme Court was to exercise matrimonial jurisdiction "in conformity with the law and practice for the time being in force in England." [23]

Apart from its use in connection with the incorporation of foreign law, the phrase "for the time being" is found in section 32(2) of the Lesotho Independence Constitution in a context which clearly suggests the living law. The section states:

> The King shall do all things that belong to his office in accordance with the provisions of this Constitution and of all other laws for the time being in force.

It could hardly be contended that it was the legislature's intention that the King should act in conformity with laws in force on the date of independence regardless of their amendment or repeal, and should not be required to act in conformity with post-independence legislation.

In the English case of *Governments Stock and Other Securities Investment Company v. Manila Railway Company* [24] Lord Macnaghten said in respect of a debenture:

> A floating security is an equitable charge on the assets for the time being of a going concern. It attaches to the subject charged in the varying condition in which it happens to be from time to time.

This statement, it is submitted, reflects the true meaning of the expression in Lesotho's General Law Proclamation, namely that it relates to the situation as it may exist from time to time and thus stands in op-

---

23. *See* ALLOTT, *supra* note 7, at 31. *See also* PARK, *supra* note 7, at 17, who emphatically adopts the same viewpoint.

24. [1897] A.C. 81, 86.

position to the idea of a settled body of law at a fixed date.[25] To take the analogy of a debenture further, the law of the Cape Colony is comparable to a floating charge as contrasted with a fixed charge. Thus it is the living common law as it changes year by year that was incorporated into Lesotho by the proclamation of 1884, subject to the modifications discussed below. However, although the charge was originally a floating one it may be argued that it crystallised in 1909, upon the demise of the Cape Colony. Has the effect of the South Africa Act[26] been to provide a cutoff date for the law of the Cape so far as Lesotho is concerned? It seems unlikely that the future unification of the provinces of South Africa was present to the mind of the High Commissioner when the 1884 proclamation was drafted and we are left to interpret the words used as they stand.[27]

---

25. This appears to be the view of Sir Kenneth Roberts-Wray; *see* his COMMONWEALTH AND COLONIAL LAW 564 (Stevens 1966).

26. [1909] 9 Edward VII, c. 9.

27. Whatever the interpretation to be placed on the wording of the 1884 proclamation as it was originally enacted, it must now be construed together with the amendments made in 1960. The proviso introduced in that year by the Law Revision Proclamation, in dealing with statutes of the Cape, refers to "law enacted by the legislative authority of the Colony of the Cape of Good Hope, or any legislative authority succeeding thereto in the Cape of Good Hope" and declares that no such law shall have effect in Basutoland unless specified in the Law Revision Proclamation itself or specially applied by the Legislature of Basutoland.

Since this amendment leaves untouched the reference earlier to "the law for the time being in force in the Colony of the Cape of Good Hope," could the implication be that a cutoff date at 1909 was being introduced for the common law, since no reference here is made to a successor to the Cape Colony, whereas it is in regard to statutes?

While this interpretation is just conceivable, it is submitted

The present Cape Province is the geographical successor to the old Cape Colony. From the point of view of the administration of the law, the judicial system has been altered, but not, it is submitted, fundamentally. Before 1910 there were three superior courts in the Cape Colony. These were the Supreme Court, itself, operating under the Charter of Justice of 1832, as amended, and its two local divisions, namely the Eastern Districts Court (E.D.C.) founded in 1864, and the High Court of Griqualand (H.C.G.) founded in 1880. Their counterparts today are the Cape Provincial Division, the Eastern Cape Division, and the Griqualand West Local Division.

It should be noted that all these three courts continue to exercise jurisdiction, even though their names may have been changed and areas slightly altered,[28] within the bounds of what was formerly the Colony

---

that the explanation of the inclusion of the words "or any legislative authority succeeding thereto in the Cape of Good Hope" is that some acts of the Union Parliament had been specially applied by the Basutoland Legislature and it was desired to retain some of these in force as well as certain Cape Colonial statutes. *See infra* pp. 200-206. It must be borne in mind that the purpose of the Law Revision in 1960 was basically to collate the statutes in force and not to iron out difficulties in relation to the common law. It would be wrong therefore to attribute any definite intention in relation to the meaning of the words "the law for the time being in force in the Colony of the Cape of Good Hope" to a legislator dealing with the specific problem of how best to specify what extraneous statutes were in force in Basutoland.

In addition, the fact that the proviso about statutes refers to enactments after 1884 at all suggests that the words "for the time being" in the main body of the Proclamation connoted a living system of law extending beyond 1909.

28. *See generally*, HERBSTEIN AND VAN WINSEN, THE CIVIL PRACTICE OF THE SUPERIOR COURTS IN SOUTH AFRICA 2-12 (2d ed.), where the development of the courts is traced down to the present day.

of the Cape of Good Hope. They are clearly the lineal successors of their predecessors and inherit their decisions.[29] This position was not affected by the declaration of a republic in 1961.[30]

The largest change in the judicial system made by the South Africa Act[31] was the creation of an Appellate Division, which is an appeal court common to all the courts of the former colonies. This means that the Appellate Division has power to make law for the whole Union regardless of the province from which the appeal emanates. However, while this change introduced a new element into the legal system at the Cape there remained the right of further appeal to the Privy Council, which existed before Union. Such appeals were only abolished in 1950.[32]

In the light, therefore, of the fact that the judicial structure in the Cape has altered so little since 1884, and because the Cape Province is the same geographical entity as the former Cape Colony, it is submitted that the common law to be administered in Lesotho is basically the common law in force in the Cape Province of the Republic of South Africa today, and not that applied in 1909.

(2) WHAT IS CAPE COLONIAL COMMON LAW?

Having decided that Lesotho's common law is basically the same as the common law of the Cape as it is today, and not that administered there in 1884 or 1909, the next question relates to the nature of that law.

There is little doubt that in the old days it was

29. S. A. Farmers Representatives v. Bonthuys [1930] C.P.D. 132, 135.

30. By Act 32 of 1961.

31. By § 96.

32. By the Privy Council Appeals Act (No. 16 of 1950).

Roman-Dutch law, the system that applied in the province of Holland during the Dutch Republic from 1581 to 1795 and which was transplanted to the Cape during the course of the Republic's commercial expansionism.[33] This system was composed of the Roman law of Justinian as interpreted by the Glossators[34] and Commentators,[35] together with medieval Dutch law, which had its origin to a great extent in Germanic customs. In Holland in the 16th Century Roman law was a subsidiary common law. However it soon came

---

33. Jan van Riebeeck, an officer of the Dutch East India Company, occupied the Cape in 1652. The common law of Holland was taken to the Cape, rather than the law of any other province, because of the predominant influence of Holland in the affairs of the Dutch East India Company. *See generally* on the history of Roman-Dutch Law, HAHLO AND KAHN, THE SOUTH AFRICAN LEGAL SYSTEM AND ITS BACKGROUND Pt. II (Juta 1968), and WESSELS, HISTORY OF THE ROMAN-DUTCH LAW (African Book Co. Ltd. 1908).

34. The school of the Glossators flourished from late in the 11th Century to the middle of the 13th Century. Its centre was the law school at Bologna and two of its leading figures were Irnerius (1055-1130?) and Accursius (1182-1260?). The method of the Glossators was exegetical, *i.e.*, it was concerned with the interpretation of the *corpus juris* of Justinian and concentrated mainly on achieving consistency among all passages. The school gets its name from the glosses which its members added in the margins of the Roman texts. These ranged from commentaries to case discussions and from questions to general maxims.

35. The Commentators (also known as the Post-Glossators) concentrated on correlating Roman law to the law of their own times, especially Germanic customary law. They were thus attempting to build a unity out of two divergent systems, one written and the other largely unwritten—which is the problem facing African law today. The Commentators wrote commentaries on the Roman texts and usually followed the opinions of the majority of the Roman jurists on any particular issue. They were followed by the Humanistic School which took a broader view of the Roman texts, demanding that they give way if they were not in accordance with justice and reason.

to play a greater role than it was theretofore allotted. First, it was applied more easily than the customary law, since the latter had to be proved. Secondly, it had infiltrated its rules into numerous statutes.[36] Both of these features illustrate the advantages a written system holds over one that is unwritten. There is an interesting parallel in the dualism of African customary law and the common law today.

The Roman-Dutch law transported by the colonists from the Netherlands to the Cape Colony came from a number of different sources.[37] There was legislation in the form of *placaaten;*[38] there were collections of decisions in the courts, often kept privately by the judges since there was no system of law reporting. There were collections of the opinions of advocates,[39] legal dictionaries, encyclopedias and the works of the institutional writers whose treatises form such an important part of modern South African law. Among the most notable writers were Grotius, Groenewegen, Vinnius, Van Leeuwen, Huber, Voet, Bynkershoek, Van der Keesel, and Van der Linden.[40] Voet is cited more extensively in the South African courts today than any of the others. Although Huber wrote on the law of Friesland he has always been treated as an authority for the law of Holland also.

The Roman-Dutch law which was in force in Holland during the 17th and 18th Centuries was very

---

36. HAHLO AND KAHN, *supra* note 33, at 503-04 and 516.

37. *Id.* at 543-62.

38. These were enacted by the States General of the United Netherlands, the States of Holland, and other subordinate legislative authorities.

39. The most famous being the HOLLANDSCHE CONSULTATIEN.

40. For a discussion of the works of these writers and their relative significance, see HAHLO AND KAHN, *supra* note 33, at 548-62.

little different from that of the other provinces of the Netherlands or indeed of the other countries in western Europe. Thus in his treatise on the *Partiarian Lease* [41] Mr. Justice van den Heever was able to write:

> Were we bound to follow Dutch writers and them alone, there would be no point in consulting French, Italian, German, Spanish, and Belgian authorities; these are constantly quoted in our courts and rightly, for Roman-Dutch law is really a misnomer; that system was for centuries the common law of Western Europe.

In Holland in 1809 Roman-Dutch law was abolished, and replaced in 1811 by the Napoleonic Code. Roman-Dutch law continued, however, to live on in Southern Africa, and also in Ceylon and what was later known as British Guiana.[42]

The question, not a substantial one but merely one of nomenclature, is whether it is still sensible to continue to refer to the Cape law as Roman-Dutch. Over the years English law has had an enormous impact upon the law of the Cape. Some English rules and ideas have been introduced in almost every field, sometimes *in toto,* sometimes only partially, both by statute and by the judges.[43] In constitutional and administrative law both the law of the prerogative [44] and the rules relating to the validity of subordinate legislation

---

41. THE PARTIARIAN AGRICULTURAL LEASE IN SOUTH AFRICAN LAW 7 (Juta 1943).

42. It was replaced in 1916 in British Guiana (now Guyana) by English law—*see* the Civil Law of British Guiana Ordinance of 1916.

43. *See generally,* SCHREINER, THE CONTRIBUTION OF ENGLISH LAW TO SOUTH AFRICAN LAW AND THE RULE OF LAW IN SOUTH AFRICA Ch. 4. (Hamlyn Lectures, Stevens 1967), and HAHLO AND KAHN, *supra* note 33, at 576-78.

44. *See, e.g.,* Sachs v. Donges N.O., [1950] 2 S.A. 265 (A.D.) and Fellner v. Minister of the Interior, [1954] 4 S.A. 523 (A.D.) (the passport cases).

are English. The doctrine of *stare decisis*[45] was introduced from England, albeit in a more flexible form, and now forms a basic element in South African law.[46] In the sphere of adjective law, the English rules of civil and criminal procedure as well as those of evidence have likewise been imported. Similarly, there are English features in the law of obligations.[47] The mercantile law of South Africa is in many areas almost a total replica of the English original,[48] as is the law relating to copyright, trademarks, and patents. Even in the law of persons the English influence has been felt, *e.g.*, in the concept of constructive desertion in divorce, the reduction of the age of majority, and the adoption of the underhand will. There has also been a limited borrowing in the law of trusts.

In view of all this the expression "Roman-Dutch law" only tells half the story today. The other half is made up of the injection of English rules and the body of South African decisions on a system already made up of three component elements.[49] South Africa is thus neither a truly civil law jurisdiction nor is it a member of the common-law system. Rather it may be said to possess a mixed system. That the only proper description of the present day Cape law is South

---

45. *Infra* pp. 72-95.

46. SCHREINER, *supra* note 43, at 12.

47. *E.g.*, in contract, the rules of offer and acceptance, misrepresentation, undue influence, rectification for mistake, covenants in restraint of trade, the penalties and liquidated damages classification (until the enactment of the Conventional Penalties Act No. 15 of 1962), and the doctrine of time being of the essence of the contract; in delict, rules of vicarious liability, the maxim *res ipsa loquitur*, omissions by highway authorities and, until recently, defamation and nuisance.

48. *E.g.*, in agency, negotiable instruments, marine and life insurance, company law, and bills of lading.

49. *I.e.*, Roman law, Dutch law, and English law.

African law has been recognised in a number of judgments, and despite the rash of Afrikaner nationalism which occasionally breaks out and desires to revert to pure Roman-Dutch law [50] (whatever that may be), it is submitted that these decisions reflect the true position.

Thus in the South West Africa case, *R. v. Goseb* [51] Claassen J. P. recently remarked:

> I consider that the term "Roman-Dutch" law is a confusing term, for in fact, the common law of the Union [now Republic] or for that matter the Cape of Good Hope is not Roman-Dutch law. It is South African common law. It is true that Roman-Dutch law forms the basis of our law and as such has supplied the more fundamental and elementary principles of our law. The law has been continuously developed and improved by the courts as well as by legislation. Other systems of law have had a marked influence, particularly English law. . . . In view of all these influences it seems to me that it is more correct to speak of South African common law rather than of Roman-Dutch law.

This is also apparent from the earlier observation of Kotze J. A. in the Appellate Division decision in *R. v. Mlooi*: [52]

> The point has, of course, to be decided by our law and not by the rules of Roman-Dutch jurisprudence, which are only applied as subsidiary common law where our law and practice are silent on the subject.

It is to be observed not only that the common law

---

50. *See, e.g.*, Trust Bank van Afrika Bpk v. Eksteen, [1964] 3 S.A. 402 (A.D.), especially the judgment of Steyn C. J. This blinkered attitude is also reflected in the habit, now alas becoming all too frequent, of having most cases in the South African Law Reports only published in the Afrikaans language.

51. [1956] 2 S.A. 696 (S.W.A.), 698.

52. [1925] A.D. 131, 149.

has changed very substantially from its reception at the Cape in the 17th Century, but also that it is continuing to change. We shall have more to say on this subject later,[53] in view of the fact that Lesotho is, up to a point, tied to the living law of South Africa.

For our present purpose however, it is sufficient to reiterate that the common law of Lesotho is, with substantial qualifications, South African common law and this expression or simply "the common law" will be used to designate that system throughout the succeeding pages.[54]

It is clear that when the common law is altered by statutory enactment in the Republic of South Africa this has no effect at all on the position in Lesotho. This is apparent from a series of cases concerned with the question whether *furtum usus* is a crime or not. In the Cape case of *R. v. Fortuin*[55] which was decided before 1884 it was held that the theft of the use of an ox was not a crime. This decision was followed and applied in South Africa for 65 years until the Orange Free State Provincial Division in *R. v. Mtaung*[56] reached the opposite conclusion in 1948. It would appear that since the law retained by Lesotho was the law of the Cape the position would have remained unaltered by the decision in *R. v. Mtaung*. However in the case of *R. v. Goseb*[57] the High Court of South West Africa held that it was not bound by the Cape

53. *Infra* pp. 70-72.

54. This term is considered preferable by SCHREINER, *supra* note 43, at 7 and by HAHLO AND KAHN, THE UNION OF SOUTH AFRICA—THE DEVELOPMENT OF ITS LAWS AND CONSTITUTION (Stevens 1960). *See also*, Proculus 68 S.A.L.J. 306 (1951); Mulligan 69 S.A.L.J. 25 (1952); Proculus Redivivus 82 S.A.L.J. 17 (1965).

55. [1883] 1 B.A.C. 290.

56. [1948] 4 S.A. 120 (O).

57. *Supra* note 51.

decisions and decided to follow *R. v. Mtaung*. Since under its reception proclamation South West Africa acquired the law of the Cape,[58] this was a somewhat startling departure which the courts in Lesotho probably would not have embarked upon. Immediately after *R. v. Goseb* the Appellate Division pronounced on the subject in the case of *R. v. Sibiya,*[59] holding the law to be that laid down in *R. v. Fortuin,* and thus overruling *R. v. Mtaung*. This provoked legislative action in the Union of South Africa in the form of the General Law Amendment Act, 1956,[60] which made it an offence to appropriate unlawfully the use of another's property. There are no reported decisions on *furtum usus* by the courts of Basutoland during the period 1948 to 1955, but in 1962 the point was considered by the High Court in the case of *R. v. Lenyehelo Motlatsi.*[61] The accused had taken the complainant's horse without permission and used it for two days, but with the continuous intention of returning it to the owner. The court held that since Lesotho had no legislation comparable to the General Law Amendment Act of 1956, the decision in *R. v. Sibiya* must be regarded as correctly stating the law on the subject. Thus an intent permanently to deprive the owner

---

58. The reception of Roman-Dutch law into South West Africa was accomplished by Proc. 21 of 1919 (S.W.A.) which provided: "The Roman-Dutch law as existing and applied in the Province of the Cape of Good Hope at the date of the coming into effect of this Proclamation shall from and after the said date, be the common law of the Protectorate . . . ." The Proclamation came into effect on 1st January 1920. Since there was a "cutoff date" it is all the more surprising that the court felt free to follow the decision in the Free State in view of the long line of Cape cases supporting R. v. Fortuin.

59. [1955] 4 S.A. 247 (A.D.).

60. Act 50 of 1956, § 1.

61. [1961-62] H.C.T.L.R. 105.

is still an essential element in the crime of theft in Lesotho.[62]

(3) "AS NEARLY AS THE CIRCUMSTANCES OF THE COUNTRY WILL PERMIT"

The second clause in the General Law Proclamation which calls for comment states that the Cape Colonial common law is only to apply "as nearly as the circumstances of the country will permit."

It was a common feature of the reception of a foreign law, be it English or Roman-Dutch, into a colonial territory that provision was made for the exclusion or modification of laws that did not fit the circumstances of the receiving country. Thus these foreign laws were generally imported subject to their applicability to local circumstances. The East Africa Order in Council 1902 [63] as amended by the East Africa Order in Council 1911,[64] for example, contains this proviso:

> Provided always that the said common law, doctrines of equity, and statutes of general application shall be in force in the protectorate so far only as the circumstances of the protectorate and its inhabitants and the limits of Her Majesty's jurisdiction permit and subject to such qualifications as local circumstances render necessary.

The effect of this proviso was considered by the English Court of Appeal in 1955 in the case of *Nyali Ltd. v. Attorney-General.*[65] By an agreement under seal, the Government of Kenya Colony and Protectorate had given Nyali Ltd. permission to erect a pontoon bridge connecting the island of Mombasa with the mainland. Provision was made for the company to charge tolls to persons using the bridge, but

---

62. *See also*, Molungoa v. R., [1963-66] H.C.T.L.R. 116.
63. [1902] STAT. R. & O. (No. 661).
64. [1911] STAT. R. & O. (No. 243).
65. [1955] 1 All E.R. 646.

it was contended on behalf of the Crown that this right, known as the right of pontage, could only be granted by prerogative of the Crown and that in order to be valid it must be made by matter of record, *i.e.*, by royal charter or letters patent under the Great Seal. The validity of the company's right was thus called in question since it merely arose from an agreement under the respective seals of the two parties.

The court decided unanimously that the Crown had power to make a grant in such manner as should be appropriate having regard to local circumstances and that the necessity of making a grant in the special manner required by the English common law was thereby obviated.[66] Denning L. J. made the following salutary remarks about the effect of the proviso:

> This wise provision should I think be liberally construed. It is a recognition that the common law cannot be applied in a foreign land without considerable qualifications. Just as with an English oak, so with the English common law. You cannot transplant it to the African continent and expect it to retain the tough character which it has in England. It will flourish indeed but it needs careful tending. So with the common law. It has many principles of manifest justice and good sense which can be applied with advantage to peoples of every race and colour all the world over: but it has also many refinements, subtleties, and technicalities which are not suited to other folk. These offshoots must be cut away. In these far off lands the people must have a law which they understand and which they will respect. The common law cannot fulfill this role except with considerable qualifications. The task of making these qualifications is entrusted to the judges of these lands. It is a great task. I trust that they will not fail therein.[67]

---

66. This finding was not disturbed in the House of Lords; *see*, [1956] 2 All E.R. 689.

67. [1955] 1 All E.R. 653.

It is true that the Kenya proviso specifically permits qualification of the imported law as well as exclusion, but it is submitted that the judge's power to exclude rules encompasses also the right to modify them. Thus the end result is that judges in Lesotho have powers as wide in this respect as judges in Kenya and are in a position to adopt the line taken in the *Nyali* case.

Some instances are given below of situations in which it is thought that the proviso in the Lesotho General Law Proclamation will or might warrant an exclusion or modification of the South African common law.

First, there is the difference in approach towards African laws and customs in relation to the family, especially in respect of marriage and divorce. Since customary law is given general statutory recognition in Lesotho [68] and the validity of customary marriages is expressly preserved,[69] the attitude of nonrecognition adopted by the South African common law is not applicable in Lesotho. However, even in the administration of the common law, the Lesotho courts will have to take account of polygyny and other features of traditional family law. To decide otherwise would be to deprive a section of the population of full legal recognition of their personal law and beliefs.[70] The South African common law has never given full recognition to potentially polygynous unions [71] (though

68. By the General Law Proclamation, *supra* at pp. 42-43.

69. The validity of marriages contracted in accordance with African law or custom is expressly preserved by § 7 of the Marriage Proclamation No. 7 of 1911.

70. *Cf.*, Maleksultan v. Sherali Jeraj [1955] 22 E.A.C.A. 142, and *see*, J. N. D. Anderson [1957] J.A.L. 14-19.

71. Seedat's Executors v. The Master, [1917] A.D. 302; and see the departure from this view by the Rhodesian Federal Supreme Court in Estate Mehta v. The Master, [1958] R & N 570. *See also* S.A.N.T.A.M. v. Fondo, [1960] 2 S.A. 467 (A.D.).

various statutes have done so for limited purposes),[72] and this is reflected in the South African definition of the crime of bigamy. The standard South African textbook on Criminal Law and Procedure [73] states:

> Bigamy is committed by any person who, during the subsistence of a valid marriage to which he or she was one of the parties, purports to contract a legally recognised ceremony of marriage with another person.

This definition relates the crime to civil marriages only, since customary marriages are unrecognised at common law and are deemed illicit unions. But were the definition to be applied in Lesotho where such marriages are valid and do fall within the terms of "a legally recognised ceremony of marriage," this would make polygyny a crime. It is clear therefore that the South African common law definition must be discarded, and a new one sought.

It seems to be accepted that the basic reason for recognising a crime of bigamy at all is in order to punish an affront upon public decency by the profanation of the solemn ceremony of marriage.[74] The falsification of the marriage register and deceit (where it occurs) can both be penalised under different heads. However, even the justification of profanation of the marriage ceremony has been strongly criticised as archaic and anomalous [75] and it is submitted that the crime should be carefully circumscribed in Lesotho.

---

72. *E.g.*, § 11(1) of Act 38 of 1927 and § 31(1) of Act 76 of 1963.

73. GARDINER AND LANSDOWN, 2 SOUTH AFRICAN CRIMINAL LAW AND PROCEDURE 1181 (6th ed.).

74. FITZGERALD, CRIMINAL LAW AND PUNISHMENT 77 (O.U.P. 1962).

75. *See* Glanville Williams 61 L.Q.R. 76-78, and FITZGERALD, *Id.* at 77-78.

One writer[76] has suggested that Lesotho should follow the Rhodesian approach and make it bigamy where one of the "marriages" is by civil rites, regardless of whether the other is a civil or a customary "marriage," and notwithstanding the order in which they take place.[77]

This is thought to be unsatisfactory for two reasons. First, this approach casts its net very wide, rendering bigamous all cases of two subsisting marriages save where both are under the customary law.

Secondly, there appear hitherto to have been no charges of bigamy brought in Lesotho and one reason for this is probably uncertainty as to the existing law. It is thought that these doubts should lead us to restrict the operation of the offence until the question is clarified by legislation. As has been pointed out,

> It would be a pity if it [the offence of bigamy] were resurrected unless this were part of an attempt to provide and enforce a satisfactory comprehensive system of marriage law. Lesotho is particularly vulnerable, because of its close relationship with a country with a cynical disregard for African family life, traditional or modern. It has not the resources to deal with the social casualties caused by broken homes. The law should not exist to create social problems. . . .[78]

It appears that the percentage of polygynous marriages in Lesotho is steadily decreasing, and considerations of public policy might tend towards accelerating this development. However the Basotho have always been tolerant of different approaches to mar-

---

76. Harlow 1966 J.A.L. 168.

77. R. v. Moyo, [1946] S.R. 12; R. v. Ncube, [1960] 2 S.A. 179 (S.R.).

78. Harlow, *supra* note 76 at 172.

riage [79] and to attempt to foster the adoption of monogamy by the extension of the crime of bigamy would be out of character as well as unwise.

Therefore it is submitted that at present the crime of bigamy should be limited to a situation where there are two "marriages" by civil rites.[80] Bigamy would thus be committed by any person who, during the subsistence of a valid marriage, contracted in terms of the Marriage Proclamation, to which he or she was one of the parties, purports to contract a subsequent marriage under the proclamation with another person.

This definition has the advantage that it links up with section 18 of the Proclamation, which relates only to marriages contracted in terms of the proclamation,[81] and which runs as follows:

> No person may marry who has previously been married to any other person still living unless such previous marriage has been dissolved or annulled by the sentence of a competent Court.

Again, the South African common law inevitably does not take account of the extended family which is an integral part of traditional African society. The

---

79. *See, e.g.*, the evidence of Chiefs Jobo and Nehemiah Moshesh, and Philemon Moeletsi given to the 1872 Commission on the Laws and Customs of the Basotho—*Report and Evidence* at 49, 52-53, 54.

80. *Cf.*, the *obiter dictum* of Evans J. in Rakhoabe v. Rakhoabe (1969—unreported) that a civil marriage followed by a customary marriage would amount to bigamy.

81. Section 18 is contained in Part II of the Proclamation whereof § 7 provides—"This Part [*i.e.*, Part II] shall apply to all marriages solemnised in Basutoland after the date of this Proclamation save and except marriages contracted in accordance with African law or custom. . . ." The section then proceeds, ". . . nothing herein contained shall be taken as in any manner affecting or casting doubts upon the validity of any such last-mentioned marriages . . . ."

range of the duty of support which a person owes his dependants is correspondingly narrower and needs modification to cater for the needs of the Basotho.

In addition, account must be taken of the special position of land in Lesotho. Traditionally, and now as a matter of constitutional law, all land in Lesotho is vested in the Basotho Nation.[82] Thus, for instance, there can be no question of anyone acquiring ownership of land by purchase or acquisitive prescription. Nor can arable lands be disposed of by will.[83] Similarly, if a deed or document uses words which under the common law would connote absolute ownership by an individual they will be inapplicable. Thus in the Privy Council case of *Oyekan v. Adele* [84] (from Nigeria) it was held that the words contained in a grant, ". . . to . . ., His heirs, executors, administrators, and assigns for ever . . ." should be rejected as meaningless in their African setting.

It also seems that account may be taken of the geographical features of the country. Much of it is very mountainous and remote, features that do not exist to anywhere near the same extent in the Cape Province of the Republic of South Africa. The highest peaks in southern Africa are in the portion of the Drakensburg Mountains which form the eastern part of Lesotho, and communications are poor. In *Teboho Seboka v. R.* [85] faction fights had broken out and the appellants had been convicted of public violence. On appeal it was argued that the charge had omitted an essential averment, namely:

> . . . and by the said means to assail or set at defiance the authority of the police and others

82. § 92 of the Constitution.
83. *See* LAWS OF LEROTHOLI, Part I, § 7 (5).
84. [1957] 2 All E.R. 785, 790.
85. [1960] H.C.T.L.R. 72.

> in public authority there established to maintain law and order.

According to the standard treatise on South African Criminal Law [86] this was a necessary element of the crime. The court held that even if resistance to the authority of the police is usually involved, it is not essential to the crime and Romer J. went on to say:

> It is common knowledge that faction fights, which are a form of public violence, often take place in remote areas where there are no police habitually present and there is no public authority responsible for law and order other than perhaps the Chiefs, and if a faction fight took place in such an area I do not think it could be said that this was not public violence merely because no policemen were there to be resisted. And furthermore it might conceivably happen that the Chief himself was involved in one of these faction fights, and then I do not think it could be said that this was not public violence because he had not resisted his own authority.[87]

Finally, it is felt that, as in other African countries, account should be taken of the fact that a substantial portion of the population is illiterate, at any rate in English, the *lingua franca.* In the field of contract the South African common law imposes a strict rule to the effect that a person signing a contract is bound by the conditions therein, even though he is unable to read it.[88] However a Privy Council decision on appeal from West Africa has held that where an illiterate has signed a document any other party who relies on that document must prove that it was read over and interpreted to the illiterate and that he fully

---

86. GARDINER AND LANSDOWN, *supra* note 73, at 1012, *et seq.*

87. *Id.* at 74.

88. *See* Burger v. C.S.A.R., [1903] T.S. 571; Bhikagee v. Southern Aviation (Pty.) Ltd., [1949] 4 S.A. 105 (E.).

understood the meaning and effect of the document.[89] It is submitted that this approach is more consistent with the circumstances of Lesotho than the South African decisions.

There is of course, a great variety of other differences between the circumstances of the Cape and those of Lesotho, which may or may not be relevant in particular cases. Lesotho has a democratic form of government, whereas the Cape is part of a political system which by no stretch of the imagination even borders on a democracy. Lesotho is a constitutional monarchy while the Cape is a province within a Republic with a president as head of state. Nor do chiefs stand in the same position in the two places.

Moving from the political to the economic field, the Cape is partly industrialised and in certain areas predominantly so. Lesotho has hardly any industry and is undoubtedly an underdeveloped country, if not an undeveloped one. All these factors may be relevant where a decision turns on a question of public policy. Lesotho has chronic unemployment and there are many people "wandering abroad and having insufficient visible means of support" who might not be able to give very satisfactory accounts of themselves if questioned. However, although technically they might be deemed to be idle and disorderly persons within the orbit of the Cape Vagrancy Act which is in force in Lesotho [90] such prosecutions are very rarely brought.

Whereas South Africa is a racialist state, Lesotho has the principle of nondiscrimination entrenched in its Constitution.[91] This distinction is, of course, a

---

89. Atta Kwamin v. Kufuor, [1914] Ren. 808, [1874-1928] P.C. 28, followed in Union Trading Co. v. Tetteh, [1965] A.L.R. Comm. 100 (Ghana).

90. Act 23 of 1879. (*See* 2 LAWS OF BASUTOLAND 1044). *See infra* p. 201.

91. § 17.

fundamental one. While in South Africa it would be quite justifiable to refuse a person a room in a hotel, or a place on public transport, or access to public baths upon grounds of race, such action in Lesotho would amount to an *injuria.*

The equality of races in Lesotho will necessitate a different approach in the field of defamation. This is because the views of right-minded members of the two countries diverge and this criterion is the one adopted by the law in the determination of whether a statement is defamatory or not.[92] In South Africa it has accordingly been held that it is defamatory of a person to say that he is an advocate of miscegenation.[93] It appears that it may also be defamatory to say of a man that he is of a different race from his true race.[94] Clearly such statements could not be defamatory *per se* in Lesotho.

These differences reflect a marked dichotomy of trends, some of them so important that they are bound to have a significant impact upon the future development of the legal systems with which they are closely linked. What direction will Lesotho take? That the South African common law is steadily changing has already been shown.[95] In *Daniels v. Daniels* [96] the Appellate Division was unanimous in declaring that the common law is not static and that there is "no good reason to hold that our law of divorce stopped growing when our forbears came to South Africa; the indications are strong that it did not." [97] In a simi-

92. *See* MCKERRON, THE LAW OF DELICT 162 (6th ed.).

93. Brill v. Madeley, [1937] T.P.D. 106.

94. Pitout v. Rosenstein, [1930] O.P.D. 112; *but cf.* Maskowitz v. Pienaar, [1957] 4 S.A. 195 (A.D.), 197.

95. *Supra* pp. 56-58.

96. [1958] 1 S.A. 513 (A.D.).

97. *Id.* at 523.

lar vein are Lord Tomlin's remarks in the Privy Council appeal of *Pearl Assurance v. Union Government*: [98]

> That law is a living, virile system of law, ever seeking as every such system must, to adapt itself, consistently with its inherent basic principles to deal effectively with the increasing complexity of modern organised society.

A quarter of a century earlier Innes C. J. had depicted the role of the judges in the remoulding of the law in the following language:

> There come times in the growth of every living system of law when old practice and ancient formulae must be modified to keep in touch with the expansion of legal ideas, and to keep pace with the requirements of changing conditions. And it is for the courts to decide when the modifications, which time has proved to be desirable, are of a nature to be effected by judicial decision, and when they are so important or so radical that they should be left to the legislature. . . . And it seems to me that this is an instance where we shall be fully justified in initiating a change of procedure, which is not in conflict with any fundamental principle of the Roman-Dutch law, and which will assist in keeping that law what we desire to see it, a living and effective instrument for the administration of justice.[99]

When we look at the growth of South African law we must ask whether Lesotho is bound to develop her law on the same lines. It seems virtually certain that the answer will be in the negative. The state of Lesotho, launched as an independent nation in 1966, is at present having to sail close to her larger neighbour. Because of her weak economy she may have to tack

---

98. [1934] A.D. 560 (P.C.), 563. *See also,* Jajbhay v. Cassim, [1939] A.D. 537, 542; O'Callaghan v. Chaplin, [1927] A.D. 310, 327.

99. Blower v. Van Noorden, [1909] T.S. 890, 905.

along in this way for some little time to come. But her buoyancy is not in doubt. The aspirations of her people diverge from those in power in the Cape and they look steadfastly northwards towards their kinsmen. It is there that new nations will be moulding new laws to fit new needs and a new era. Mr. Justice Holmes in *The Common Law* [100] wrote:

> The life of the law has not been logic; it has been experience. The felt necessities of the time, the prevalent moral and political theories, intuitions of public policy, avowed or unconscious, even the prejudices which judges share with their fellow-men, have had a good deal more to do than the syllogism in determining the rules by which men should be governed.

This statement, which was originally made with reference to the English common law, is no doubt equally true as a prediction of the law of Lesotho. It was endorsed in relation to South African law by Schreiner J. A. in *Daniels v. Daniels* [101] in 1958. As Lesotho changes, so will her law. Great developments are taking place in the legal systems of independent Africa to take account of the great awakening of her peoples. It cannot be long before Lesotho is on the march to join them.[102]

(4) JUDICIAL PRECEDENT

(a) General Introduction [103]

If the common law of present day Lesotho is,

---

100. At 1 (Macmillan & Co. 1882).

101. *Supra* note 96, at 522-23.

102. This is not, of course, to advocate the overthrow of the present system of law and the adoption of, *e.g.*, English law.

103. *See generally*, (Mr. Justice) J. G. Kotzé in 34 S.A.L.J. 280 (1917); CROSS, PRECEDENT IN ENGLISH LAW (O.U.P. 1961); T. B. SMITH, THE DOCTRINES OF JUDICIAL PRECEDENT IN SCOTS LAW (Green 1952); Kahn *The Rules of Precedent applied in South African Courts* 84 S.A.L.J. 43, 175, & 308 (1967).

broadly speaking, the current South African common law as administered in the Cape Province subject to modifications necessitated by the special circumstances of Lesotho, the next question is where that South African common law is to be found.

The common law of England is made up of the decisions of the courts piled one upon another over many centuries. It is the accumulation of decisions given in particular cases. The common law of South Africa is made up not only of decided cases but also of the views expressed by the celebrated Roman-Dutch writers of the 17th and 18th Centuries, together with certain statutes that were in force in the province of Holland. Both systems make very extensive use of judicial precedent, by which we mean that courts in deciding cases refer back to previous decisions for authority and guidance. It is clearly a basic principle of the administration of justice that like cases should be decided alike, but apart from this there is a variety of reasons why judges all over the world, at any rate to some extent, tend to follow previous decisions.

In the first place many judges feel happier about their judgments if they have been able to discover that an earlier judge took the same view as they do. Secondly, to decide similar cases in the same way should make for certainty in the law and thus enable people to organise their affairs in the reasonably sure knowledge of the legal significance of their acts. In the criminal law it provides for equality of treatment for those charged with offences. Thirdly, in many legal systems judges are only appointed from among those who have had a long experience of the law. Such men tend to be conservative in their later years and may often be temperamentally disinclined to depart from established practice. Fourthly, no judge likes to be overruled on appeal and therefore he is likely to follow decisions of courts superior to his.

However, although there is this almost universal element of uniformity, different legal systems show marked divergences at various points. In particular two questions require discussion. First, to what extent are previous decisions binding upon courts in Lesotho in hearing subsequent cases? Secondly, what authorities, though not binding, are persuasive? Before dealing with these problems, however, it will be necessary to examine the approaches of the South African and the English legal systems.

The Roman-Dutch writers' views on judicial precedent followed, broadly speaking, the doctrine of Roman Law. Thus Van der Linden held that whilst judicial decisions do not have the force of law,

> . . . yet we must not lightly depart from such an opinion, pronounced after due deliberation, and certainly not unless we have convincing reason and ground, which after careful consideration induce us to arrive at an opposite conclusion, as being more agreeable to the spirit and analogy of the law.[104]

Earlier decisions should not be blindly followed in later cases, but on the other hand there must be a strong reason such as a palpable error if any departure is to be justifiable. Voet adopted Justinian's decree *non exemplis sed legibus judicandum est* [105] but held that a chain of invariably consistent decisions interpreting an enactment had the force of law.[106]

South African law, as mentioned earlier, is a

---

104. VERZAMELING V. MERKW GEWIJSDEN Inleid (Leyden, 1803). Van der Linden took a middle path in the controversy that raged in Holland on the question during the 17th and 18th Centuries—*see* T. B. SMITH, *supra* note 103, at 4.

105. CODE 7.45.13; *but see also* DIGEST 1.3.34; DIGEST 1.3.38; and CODE 8.52.1 which seem to permit past decisions some authority.

106. VOET, AD PANDECTAS 1.3.19.

mixed system with elements taken from both civil-law and common-law jurisdictions. The law in most countries with a civil-law system is codified and the function of the courts in the particular cases that come before them is to interpret the relevant sections of the code. Thus

> [t]he practice of the courts does not become a source of law until it is definitely fixed by the repetition of precedents which are in agreement on a single point.[107]

A French judge does not have to follow a previous decision in a single case, but rather he searches for the trend of recent decisions on the point under consideration. This trend is known as *la jurisprudence constante*.[108] South African law, however, has been much more deeply influenced by English law than by the civil law in this field. The English legal doctrine of *stare decisis* (keep to what has been previously decided) became incorporated into South African law as a result of the training of the earlier judges and advocates. This doctrine, which is based on a judicial hierarchy, has two special features. First, a court must follow an earlier decision of a court that is higher in the hierarchy. This is so even if there is only a single decision on the point and even if the lower court considers it wrong. This shows the strongly coercive effect of the doctrine and the fact that a court is not entitled to look for a trend in judicial decisions—a single decision in point is binding. Secondly, it used to be the position that most English courts were in addition bound to follow their own previous decisions. However the former rigidity of this second aspect of the English rule has been avoided by the South African courts

---

107. Lambert, *Case Method in Canada* 39 YALE L.J. 14.

108. LAWSON, NEGLIGENCE IN THE CIVIL LAW 234 (O.U.P. 1962).

which have always felt themselves free to refuse to follow their own earlier decisions when satisfied that they are wrong.[109] In addition, in neither system does a decision given *per incuriam* have to be followed. This expression is used to cover not only situations where statutes have been overlooked by the court,[110] but also where relevant decisions in earlier cases have not been brought to the attention of the court, and perhaps even where there has not been full argument of the point before the court.[111]

There is no doubt that the views of the old Roman-Dutch writers that decisions of the courts do not form part of the law have now been superseded. Judicial decisions in South Africa are firmly ensconced as a source of law [112] and decisions of higher courts are binding in subsequent cases on lower courts.

The various South African provincial and local divisions correspond to the High Court of Lesotho,[113] and the Appellate Division is roughly equivalent to the Lesotho Court of Appeal. The rules of precedent applied by the South African courts—which are of some relevance to the position in Lesotho—are as fol-

---

109. *See, e.g.*, Habib Motan v. Transvaal Government, [1904] T.S. 404, 413; R. v. Faithfull and Gray, [1907] T.S. 1077, 1080-81.

110. *E.g.*, Natalite Motor Spirit Co. v. Davies, [1923] A.D. 1, 11-13; and Kahn, *supra* note 103, at 176.

111. *See, e.g.*, Harris v. Minister of the Interior, [1952] 2 S.A. 428 (A.D.), 471; Penny v. Nicholas, [1950] 2 All E.R. 89, 91-92; and A-G of N. Rhodesia v. Dimakopoulos, [1961] R & N 833. In the Botswana case of Moatlhodi v. Mekgwe (Civil Appeal No. 8 of 1967) the High Court held it was not bound to follow its earlier decision in Marcos v. Wellio (Civil Appeal No. 2 of 1967) as the latter was partly founded on a concession.

112. *See, e.g.*, Daniels v. Daniels, *supra* note 96.

113. The High Court of Basutoland established by Proc. 18 of 1954 (which is a predecessor of the present High Court) was created with "all the jurisdiction, power, and authority vested in the Supreme Court of South Africa"—*see* § 2(2).

lows: A provincial or local division is generally bound to follow a decision of the Appellate Division,[114] but decisions of one provincial division are not binding on another though they are of high persuasive authority.[115] Full benches or single judges of the provincial and local divisions seem in principle bound to follow their own previous decisions and have adopted the Appellate Division's approach of departing from them only when satisfied that they are erroneous.[116]

The Appellate Division has decided that as a general rule it is bound to follow its own decisions, but that there are recognised exceptions to this rule.[117] The position is summarised by Stratford J. A. in *Bloemfontein Town Council v. Richter* [118] as follows:

> The ordinary rule is that this court is bound by its own decisions and unless a decision has been arrived at on some manifest oversight or misunderstanding, that is, there has been something in the nature of a palpable mistake, a subsequently constituted court has no right to prefer its own reasoning to that of its predecessors—such preference, if allowed, would produce endless uncertainty and confusion. The maxim *stare decisis* should therefore be more rigidly applied in this the highest Court in the land than in all others.[119]

A recent case in which the Appellate Division declined to follow one of its earlier decisions was *Harris*

---

114. Collett v. Priest, [1931] A.D. 290, 297; *Ex parte* Sadie, [1940] A.D. 26, 30.

115. MacRobert v. Pretoria Municipal Council, [1910] T.P.D. 931, 942; *Ex parte* Hansmann, [1938] W.L.D. 89, 93.

116. Kaplan v. Union Govt., [1924] T.P.D. 532, 534; *Ex parte* Hansmann *supra* note 115; Klaassen v. Benjamin, [1941] T.P.D. 80, 90; R. v. Philips Dairy (Pty.) Ltd., [1955] 4 S.A. 120 (T.), 122.

117. R. v. Nxumalo, [1939] A.D. 580, 586.

118. [1938] A.D. 195.

119. *Id.* at 232.

v. Minister of the Interior,[120] the famous coloured voters case. The court departed from its decision in *Ndlwana v. Hofmeyr N.O.*[121] given fifteen years earlier. This procedure was justified by the court on the ground that the earlier decision had been pronounced *per incuriam* on a question of vital constitutional importance without the court hearing argument for and against the main conclusion which it reached. A further powerful reason permitting the departure was the fact that the earlier decision "did not lead to the coming into existence of any right accruing to, or obligations devolving on private individuals. That decision, if correct, enabled Parliament to deprive by a bare majority in each House, sitting separately, individuals of rights which were solemnly safeguarded in the Constitution . . ." [122] Finally the court considered its earlier decision to have been wrong.

It appears that much of the rigidity attributed to the English version of the *stare decisis* rule has now disappeared with the announcement of the Lord Chancellor (Lord Gardiner) on behalf of himself and the Lords of Appeal in Ordinary on 26th July 1966 that the House of Lords will no longer be bound to follow its own decisions.[123] The pronouncement ran as follows:

> Their Lordships regard the use of precedent as an indispensable foundation upon which to decide what is the law and its application to individual cases. It provides at least some degree of certainty upon which individuals can rely in the conduct of their affairs, as well as a basis for orderly development of legal rules.

---

120. [1952] 2 S.A. 428 (A.D.).

121. [1937] A.D. 229.

122. *Supra* note 120, at 471-72, per Centlivres C.J.

123. For a comment on the announcement, *see* Kahn, 83 S.A.L.J. 503 (1966).

> Their Lordships nevertheless recognise that too rigid adherence to precedent may lead to injustice in a particular case and also unduly restrict the proper development of the law. They propose therefore to modify their present practice and, while treating former decisions of the House as normally binding, to depart from a previous decision when it appears right to do so.
> In this connection they will bear in mind the danger of disturbing retrospectively the basis on which contracts, settlements of property, and fiscal arrangements have been entered into and also the especial need for certainty as to the criminal law.
> This announcement is not intended to affect the use of precedent elsewhere than in this House.

Since the House of Lords is now free to depart from its earlier decisions whenever it feels it is right to do so, whereas the Appellate Division may only do so if satisfied its previous decision was wrong, it appears that the constricting boot of rigidity is now on the other curial foot. The House of Lords will be free to depart from a previous decision on the basis that the proper development of the law requires it while acknowledging that the decision was correct for the time in which it was given. The Appellate Division on the other hand cannot adopt this approach and must first reach the conclusion that the earlier decision was mistaken.

It is clear that the English and South African interpretations of the *stare decisis* rule are now much closer than previously was the case. It is arguable that less rigidity is needed in the context of a system administering Roman-Dutch law since there are always the old authorities (and in the last resort Roman law) to fall back upon as the ultimate reservoir of the law. The reason the English courts adopted *stare decisis* was in response to a keenly felt need for certainty in a system where there was no background of legal rules and customs for reference.[124]

Finally a word should be said about "distinguishing." It always falls to a subsequent court to decide whether or not it is bound by an earlier decision. In practice it is far more likely to follow such a decision because it agrees with it or decline to follow it because it can find grounds for distinguishing it (showing it is irrelevant) than to examine its authority as a precedent according to the hierarchy of the courts.

(b) Stare Decisis *within the Lesotho Judicial System*

From the discussion above it is clear that in the modern South African law, judicial precedent is recognised as a source of law and it is also apparent that the rules as to which decisions are binding upon what courts under what circumstances are different in South Africa from those in England where the doctrine of *stare decisis* originated.

As a leading authority on precedent has pointed out:[125]

> The rule that judicial decisions make law is theoretically distinct from the doctrine of precedent which is based on the practices by which the courts give effect to that rule. The two cannot be separated in practice because, once it is established that judicial decisions make law for the future, a decision on a point of law comes to be called a "precedent" and some doctrine concerning the weight to be attached to the different precedents becomes essential.

---

124. *See* Goodhart, 50 L.Q.R. 40 at 61-62. In Scotland the courts were able to fall back upon Roman law principles and the institutional writers and thus did not need the rigidity of the English doctrine—*see* T. B. SMITH, *supra* note 103, at 68-69.

125. CROSS, *supra* note 103, at 3.

If we take the view that the technique of weighing different precedents is a doctrine, *i.e.*, that it embodies rules of substantive law, it follows that the South African common law on the subject is broadly in force in Lesotho. This would mean that the rules applicable to the relevant part of the hierarchy of South African courts, *i.e.*, basically the Cape Provincial Division and the Appellate Division, would apply in Lesotho "as nearly as the circumstances of the country will permit" with the substitution of Lesotho's court structure for the South African one, and consequential modifications.

If, on the other hand, we adopt the approach that whilst there is a legal doctrine that judicial precedent is a source of law, the rules of precedent are a matter of practice only, then we should look for special local rules in the practice of the Lesotho courts. Unfortunately the courts of Lesotho have not pronounced on the subject, nor has the legislature laid down any rules about the form the practice should take.

The first view finds support in certain *obiter dicta* of Clayden F. J. in the Southern Rhodesian case of *Estate Mehta v. The Master* [126] in 1958. He considered the right of a court to disregard its own previous decisions to be a matter of law rather than one of practice and procedure. The learned judge's remarks have been the subject of strong criticism [127] and there is much authority for the opposite viewpoint.[128] Thus in

126. *Supra* note 71.

127. *See* Palley *Stare Decisis and the Federal Supreme Court* 1962 R.N.L.J. 126.

128. *See supra* note 44 at 529-32 per Centlivres C.J.; and the views of Glanville Williams 70 L.Q.R. 470; CROSS *supra* note 103, at 104, 247, and 250; and Lord Reid in Scruttons v. Midland Silicones Ltd., [1962] 1 All E.R. 1, 11-12 culminating in the announcement by Lord Gardiner quoted pp. 78-79.

the South African case of *Habib Motan v. Transvaal Government,*[129] Solomon J. said:

> The statement that any court is bound by its own decisions can never mean more than that it is a rule of practice of such court to follow its previous decisions . . .

Whilst this view is preferred and thus the Lesotho courts are thought to be free to alter their practice at any time in the same way as the House of Lords has done and are not bound to follow the South African practice, there remains the difficulty of ascertaining what rules they are operating under at present. It would be open to the Judicial Committee of the Privy Council as the highest court for Lesotho to lay down the practice, but this has not occurred. It is therefore proposed to examine the South African practice so as to obtain some guidance.

Applying with necessary modifications the South African version of *stare decisis* to the courts of Lesotho,[130] the position appears to be as follows:

(1) The inferior courts [131] are bound to follow a decision of the High Court, Court of Appeal, or Judicial Committe of the Privy Council.

(2) The High Court is not bound to follow its own previous decision or that of its predecessor, if satisfied it was wrong.[132] Indeed, it is its duty to reconsider the matter.[133] To permit a departure on this basis the instant court must be convinced that the previous court's decision was quite erroneous because of an obvious oversight or misunderstanding. However the High Court must follow decisions of the old and

129. [1904] T.S. 404, 420-21.

130. The court structure is dealt with in Part III.

131. Molungoa v. R., [1963-66] H.C.T.L.R. 116, 117.

132. Letlaka v. R., [1963-66] H.C.T.L.R. 1, 3.

133. *Cf.* Theron v. Behr, [1918] C.P.D. 443, 459.

courts usually prefer not to investigate too deeply the question of what precedents are binding and will tend instead either to follow an earlier decision because they agree with its reasoning or to distinguish it because they disagree with it.

If the South African version of *stare decisis* is regarded as applicable, it is thought the courts may adopt the following positions. Since decisions of one provincial division are not binding in another division, and since the Lesotho High Court is clearly of similar standing and jurisdiction to a provincial division, it will not be bound to follow decisions of the Cape Provincial Division, the Eastern Cape Division, and the Griqualand West Local Division and their various predecessors, though such decisions will of course still be of persuasive authority.

It may be asked whether since the reception statute refers specifically to Cape colonial law such decisions are not authoritative for Lesotho in the absence of an Appellate Division decision. However it seems preferable for the High Court of Lesotho to wait until the particular point is settled by the highest court for the Cape which has the power to make a final declaration of what the law there is.[136]

On the other hand, decisions of the Appellate Division will be binding—at any rate upon the Lesotho High Court and the subordinate courts. It is submitted that the subordinate courts in Lesotho should not be bound to follow decisions of the Cape Provincial Division, Eastern Cape Division, and Griqualand West Local Division and their various predecessors. In the first instance, they should look for decisions of the superior

---

136. *See*, the statement of Lord Dunedin in Robins v. National Trust Co., [1927] A.C. 515 (*infra* pp. 91-92). A similar approach to English decisions in Nigeria is adopted by PARK, *supra* note 7, at 62.

courts in Lesotho and, if there are none, follow Appellate Division decisions.[137]

The only justifications for departing from an Appellate Division decision would appear to be the following:

(1) That the decision is not applicable because the circumstances of Lesotho do not permit it. This would include departures on the basis that the South African law is a growing system which will inevitably continue to change in accordance with political and moral attitudes and public opinion, and that Lesotho's attitudes, policies, and needs do not coincide. It would also permit a reassessment of an old precedent in the light of contemporary needs.

(2) That the decision is inconsistent with the provisions of the Lesotho Constitution or any other statute in force in the country.

(3) That the decision was given *per incuriam.*

(4) That the decision was interpreting a statute not in force in Lesotho.

(5) That the decision is inconsistent with a decision of the House of Lords or the English Court of Appeal or High Court on a matter where Lesotho applies English law and not Cape Colonial law (see below).

(6) That the decision has been abrogated by disuse in Lesotho.[138]

(7) That the decision is inconsistent with a decision of the Lesotho Court of Appeal or the former Court of Appeal for Basutoland, the Bechuanaland Protectorate, and Swaziland, or with a decision of the Privy Council that is applicable to Lesotho.

---

137. A similar approach for Nigerian courts in relation to English decisions is recommended by PARK, *supra* note 7, at 63-64.

138. Abrogation by disuse is discussed *infra,* note 489.

The second approach to this whole problem is to take the view that no South African decisions are binding in Lesotho and that at the most they are merely highly persuasive authorities. According to this view the system of common law in force in Lesotho may be styled Roman-Dutch, Cape Colonial, or South African law but the courts in Lesotho are free to interpret that law as they wish without being fettered in any way by what has previously been decided in South Africa. They may, and often do in practice, look to South African decisions and follow them, but they are not compelled to do so. They may prefer instead to adopt the reasoning of a Ceylonese or a Rhodesian court or pursue a line of their own in a given sphere.

This approach of giving free rein to the courts in Lesotho is undoubtedly more consonant with the concept of independence. However, while it fits in well with nationalistic and patriotic sentiment within Lesotho, it seems unlikely that the granting of independence itself can be said to have automatically achieved this position. The direct legal effect of independence was only a transfer of legislative power which enables the Lesotho Parliament to amend the law if it so wishes. Until the law is in fact amended the Lesotho Parliament is presumed to desire the position to remain as it stands.

The pressure for Lesotho courts to be free to choose their own path (in the event of the second approach being rejected) will no doubt increase when Basotho fill the bench, when a strong and well-trained legal profession emerges, when more attention is given to the reform of the law, and when ideas from other independent African states begin to filter through to the legal profession generally.

In the meantime it would seem highly desirable for the legislature to place the question of the authority of South African decisions beyond doubt by amending legislation. The wording of the General Law Proclamation is problematical in relation to both the common law and customary law, and dates back to a distant colonial past. It should be repealed forthwith and replaced by a clear statement to the effect that South African decisions are only of persuasive authority.[139]

(d) The Authority of English Decisions in Lesotho

Two statutes, emanating from the Cape Colony, that are still in force in Lesotho incorporate the English law into the legal system. They are the Mercantile Law Amendment Act and the Evidence in Civil Proceedings Ordinance.

The Mercantile Law Amendment Act of 1879 [140] introduces certain rules of English law in the following terms: [141]

> In every suit, action, and cause having reference to questions of fire, life, and marine assurance,

---

139. An attempt has recently been made to do just this in § 7(2) of the Court of Appeal and High Court Order, No. 17 of 1970 which came into force on 8th May 1970, but unfortunately the subsection has been poorly drafted and contains an ambiguity. The relevant part of the provision is as follows:

> Notwithstanding anything to the contrary in any other law contained, no court and no person in Lesotho shall be bound by any judgment, order, ruling or opinion given by any tribunal, court, person or authority outside Lesotho after the date of commencement of this Order.

It is not clear whether all extraneous decisions cease to be binding as from 8th May 1970 or whether it is only extraneous decisions given after that date which will cease to be binding in Lesotho. Probably on the wording of the provision the latter interpretation is to be preferred, which leaves the basic problem referred to in the text unresolved.

140. Cape Act 8 of 1879.

141. *Id.* § 2.

> stoppage *in transitu*, and bills of lading which shall henceforth be brought in the High Court or in any other competent court of Basutoland, the law administered by the Supreme Court of Judicature in England for the time being, so far as the same shall not be repugnant to, or in conflict with, any Ordinance, Act of Parliament, or other statute having the force of law in Basutoland, shall be the law to be administered by the said High Court or other competent Court.

Taking the expression "for the time being" to have the same meaning as in the General Law Proclamation, and thus to connote the living law, this means that the Lesotho High Court must follow decisions of the English Court of Appeal and the House of Lords in the mercantile matters specified.†

The English High Court and Court of Appeal are part of the Supreme Court of Judicature. The House of Lords, while not part of the Supreme Court, has power to make decisions binding upon those courts since it is the final appeal court in terms of the Appellate Jurisdiction Act, 1876. It is submitted that since the High Court of Lesotho is of roughly co-ordinate jurisdiction with the English High Court it is not absolutely bound to follow the decisions of the latter.

The Evidence in Civil Proceedings Ordinance of 1830 [142] brings in certain English rules in relation to evidence and refers to evidence admissible "in any similar case depending in the Supreme Court of Judicature in England." [143] The matters on which the law is to be the same as the English law include the privilege of professional advisers, evidence of charac-

---

† For the recent amendment contained in the Court of Appeal and High Court Order, 1970, *see* note 139, *supra*.

142. Ordinance 72 of 1830. See *infra* pp. 203-204.

143. §§ 15, 18, 21, and 22, and similar language is to be found in §§ 12, 23, 25, and 26.

ter, proof of appointment to a public office, the admissibility of testimony of absent or deceased witnesses, hearsay evidence, refusal to answer certain questions, privilege on the grounds of public policy or public interest, and the impeachment and support of a witness's credibility.

The use of the word "depending" must refer to the present time and thus have the effect of introducing the law for the time being in force in the Supreme Court in England. Again, decisions of the Court of Appeal and House of Lords will be binding on the Lesotho High Court.††

The Criminal Procedure and Evidence Proclamation,[144] dating from 1938 and modelled upon a South African statute also introduces the English law of evidence at various points. Broadly speaking, they cover the same subjects as the Evidence in Civil Proceedings Ordinance.

(e) The Classification of Judicial Precedent

From the foregoing discussion it appears that decisions of the Judicial Committee of the Privy Council, the Appellate Division, the House of Lords, and the English Court of Appeal may all, on occasion, be binding on the superior courts in Lesotho.

Assuming that such decisions are relevant and applicable in a given case what is their respective standing?

First, English decisions will only be authoritative within the areas laid down in the Mercantile Law Amendment Act of 1879, the Evidence in Civil Proceedings Ordinance, and the Criminal Procedure and Evidence Proclamation. In the event of two conflicting

†† See †, supra.

144. Proc. 59 of 1938 as amended. *See* §§ 220, 221, 226, 230, 237, 249, 250, 251, and 272.

decisions, one of the English courts and the other of the Judicial Committee, it is submitted that a decision of the latter is to be preferred. There is no doubt that it can be argued forcefully that, applying the wording of the Proclamation, the English courts are the final arbiters not only of the English law in these spheres but also of the law of Lesotho.[145] However the Judicial Committee is the highest court for Lesotho and this is strong justification for its pronouncements being entitled to greater authority. While, in the absence of a Privy Council decision the Lesotho High Court will be bound by a decision of the English Court of Appeal [146] or the House of Lords, it is thought that the Lesotho Court of Appeal, if placed in a similar situation, is only bound to follow a decision of the House of Lords. Support for this contention is provided by the Privy Council in the Canadian appeal of *Robins v. National Trust Company* [147] where Lord Dunedin stated:

> . . . when an appellate court in a colony which is regulated by English law differs from an appellate court in England, it is not right to assume that the colonial court is wrong. It is otherwise if the authority in England is that of the House of

---

145. As does Kahn, 84 S.A.L.J. 329 (1967) in dealing with the South African position, which differs of course from that of Lesotho here since the Judicial Committee is no longer the highest court of appeal in South Africa; *but see* Van der Linde v. Calitz, [1967] 2 S.A. 239 (A.D.), 280. In this case the Appellate Division preferred the Privy Council decision in Robinson v. State of S. Australia (No. 2), [1931] A.C. 704 to that of the House of Lords in Duncan v. Cammell, Laird & Co. Ltd., [1942] A.C. 624.

146. For a case in which a South African court exercising original jurisdiction held itself bound to follow the English Court of Appeal in similar circumstances, *see* Yusaf v. Bailey, [1964] 4 S.A. 117 (W.).

147. [1927] A.C. 515, 519 (Ontario).

> Lords. That is the supreme tribunal to settle English law, and, that being settled, the colonial court, which is bound by English law, is bound to follow it.[148]

If this was the proper approach when Lesotho was a colony how much more it is in keeping with its independent status today.

Secondly, if the first approach to South African authorities outlined above is adopted, decisions of the Appellate Division must be followed within the areas of the law where they are applicable. In the event of a difference between the Appellate Division and the Privy Council it is again submitted that the decision of the latter should be followed. There are stronger arguments in favour of this conclusion here than in the case of decisions of the House of Lords. One reason is that before the abolition of appeals from South Africa to the Privy Council in 1950 [149] all South African courts regarded themselves as absolutely bound by decisions of the Judicial Committee on appeal from South Africa.[150] Thus the Privy Council stood towards the Appellate Division then as it stands towards the Lesotho Court of Appeal today, and as the House of Lords stands to the English Court of Appeal. While it is true that since 1950 the Appellate Division has felt free to depart from previous Privy Council decisions [151] it is thought that this does not have the effect of elevating the Appellate Division to an equal status with the Privy Council so far as Lesotho is

148. *But cf.* Trimble v. Hill, [1879] 5 App. Cas. 342 (New South Wales) and Chettiar v. Mahatmea, [1950] A.C. 481 (Ceylon).

149. By the Privy Council Appeals Act (No. 16 of 1950).

150. Estate Cato v. Estate Cato, [1915] A.D. 290, 303.

151. John Bell & Co. Ltd. v. Esselen, [1954] 1 S.A. 147 (A.D.).

concerned. It rather reflects the consummation of the purpose of abolishing appeals to the Privy Council by enabling South African courts to be the final arbiters of the law in that country in practice as well as in theory.

Moreover as pointed out above it is more correct to think of the Lesotho Court of Appeal as of equal standing with the South African Appellate Division. For these reasons it is thought that in the absence of a Privy Council decision, though the Lesotho High Court is basically bound by Appellate Division decisions, the Court of Appeal should have a free hand.[152] It is true that the Appellate Division is the final arbiter of the law in force in the Cape, but both the nationalistic concept of independence and the standing of the present Lesotho Court of Appeal militate against any doctrine that it is fettered by what the Appellate Division has previously decided.

(f) Ratio Decidendi *and* Obiter Dicta

In the preceding section the binding effect of the decisions of various courts has been considered. The word "decision" has been used in a special sense since not everything that a court decides is binding on a later court. Only the *ratio decidendi* binds, and this may be defined as the judge's pronouncement of law in relation to the material or relevant facts before him. In the South African case of *Pretoria City Council v. Levison*[153] Schreiner J. A. put it in the following terms:

> As I understand the ordinary usage in this connection, where a single judgment is in question, the reasons given in the judgment, properly inter-

---

152. *Cf.* PARK, *supra* note 7, at 62 where he holds that House of Lords' decisions bind all courts in Nigeria.

153. [1949] 3 S.A. 305 (A.D.), 317.

> preted, do constitute the *ratio decidendi,* originating or following a legal rule, provided (a) that they do not appear from the judgment itself to have been merely subsidiary reasons for following the main principle or principles, (b) that they were not merely a course of reasoning on the facts and (c) (this may cover (a)) that they were necessary for the decision, not in the sense that it could not have been reached along other lines, but in the sense that along the lines actually followed in the judgment the result would have been different but for the reasons.

Judges often make pronouncements that are not necessary for their decision, *e.g.,* on hypothetical facts, and these are called *obiter dicta* (remarks "by the way" or "on the side.") *Obiter dicta* are never binding on subsequent courts; they may be of great persuasive authority but a later court never has to follow them.

Considerable difficulty may be experienced in practice in discovering the exact *ratio decidendi* of a case and a certain amount of subtlety may be resorted to by a later judge in order to "distinguish" an earlier case on the ground that its material facts were different from those in the case under consideration.

Decisions of the courts play a dual role in the development of the law. In the first place they attempt to do individual justice in the particular cases that arise. Secondly they interpret statutes, the old Roman-Dutch authorities, and earlier decisions, and indeed adapt the last two to the changing conditions and needs of society. The Roman-Dutch common law has now been dealt with and discussed in so many cases that it is becoming increasingly unnecessary to resort to the old authorities any more, let alone Roman law. It is partly for this reason that it has been argued earlier that the proper name for the common law in force in the Cape and also in Lesotho is South African law.

(g) Persuasive Authorities

Apart from those authorities that are binding on the courts, there are lesser authorities that may have a great influence on a decision though they are not absolutely binding. These are often called "persuasive authorities." The difference between a binding authority and a persuasive authority is that the former must be followed by a lower court even if that court is convinced that it is wrong.

Persuasive authorities include, for instance, decisions given by either the Privy Council or the Appellate Division in cases where such decisions are not binding upon the Lesotho courts within the rules outlined above. *Obiter dicta* of these courts are also persuasive.

The degree of persuasiveness of a particular pronouncement by a court, *i.e.*, the amount of respect it is entitled to in subsequent cases, will vary according to the status of the court, whether or not the decision was unanimous, the standing of the judges, and whether the pronouncement was a *ratio* or merely *obiter*. It is impossible to be more specific than this, and often the court hearing the instant case will decide the issue without any careful consideration of the strength of the persuasive authorities cited.

Finally, on this subject, it remains to point to two important peculiarities of South African law. The first is the use it makes of authorities outside its own system. We have already adverted to the borrowings and adoptions of English rules.[154] Here we are not concerned with authorities that are binding on the courts but those that may be cited by counsel to induce

---

154. *Supra* pp. 56-57.

the court to follow them on the basis that they constitute good rules that have been applied in the past elsewhere.

South African law is the child of the two great legal systems of the western world—the common law and the civil law. It has therefore been able to look to both parents for guidance and as Professor Lawson has said, "South African lawyers have on the whole been pretty canny in their choice of legal rules . . . ."[155]

Cases may be found in which English and American decisions have been quoted and also those of the Privy Council on appeal from other countries. This reflects the common law influence.

The civil law background is illustrated by the references not only to the old Dutch authorities but also to other continental writers. This approach, as we have already seen, was justified by Mr. Justice van den Heever[156] on the ground that the Roman-Dutch law was for centuries a branch of the shared common law of the whole of Western Europe.

By way of illustrating the breadth of authority to be found cited, even today, we may look briefly at two cases heard by the South African Appellate Division.

In *Consolidated Diamond Mines v. Administrator S.W.A.*[157] the authorities cited to the court included *inter alia* a House of Lords decision, a Privy Council decision on appeal from Canada, three Roman-Dutch writers (Grotius, Gudelinus, and Voet), and various German writers. The Prussian Code was also referred to, as were the *Institutes* and *Digest* of Justinian.

---

155. JOURNAL OF COMPARATIVE LEGISLATION AND INTERNATIONAL LAW 101 (3d series, Vol. XXXIII, 1950).

156. *Supra* p. 56.

157. [1958] 4 S.A. 572 (A.D.).

Moreover all these authorities were used by the court in its judgment.

And in *Jajbhay v. Cassim* [158] the judgments of the Appellate Division on the question of illegality in contract referred to English and Scottish decisions, three English textbooks, Halsbury, an American textbook and the American Restatement, Pothier and Gluck, as well as three Roman-Dutch writers, and not unpredictably Justinian's works as well.

Nor is it only the institutional writers of the past who may be quoted as authority for a point of law. Modern textbook writers are often cited and followed.[159] This is in marked contrast with the position in English law. However, one should point out that the influence of writers, especially the ancient ones, is gradually waning as more and more of the law is covered by judicial decisions. These are of course more readable and accessible, and the cases in which reliance will be placed exclusively on the old authorities are likely to be less frequent as time goes on. At present, the extent to which modern courts rely on the old authorities varies with the branch of the law under consideration. They are still vigorously applied in the law of persons for instance, but no longer play a large part in contract and mercantile law.

The second characteristic is the practice of treating statements of principle in earlier cases with great respect despite a wide divergence between the sets of facts in the instant case and the earlier case. The courts lean towards the adoption of the principle in

---

158. [1939] A.D. 537. For breadth of citation, *see also* the short judgment of the Appellate Division in Gibson v. van der Walt, [1952] 1 S.A. 262 (A.D.)

159. *E.g.*, WILLE, PRINCIPLES OF SOUTH AFRICAN LAW (Juta) and LANDLORD AND TENANT IN SOUTH AFRICA (Juta); MCKERRON, THE LAW OF DELICT (Juta).

subsequent cases, whereas generally in English law the tendency of the court is to distinguish prior decisions that have laid down broad principles, declaring that the statement of principle must be limited to the particular facts of the case.

CHAPTER 3

THE CUSTOMARY LAW

A. The Place of Customary Law in the Legal System
B. The Ascertainment of Customary Law
C. When May Customary Law Be Administered?
D. The Validity of Customary Law in the Basotho Courts
E. Summary as to the Applicability of Customary Law
F. The Future of Customary Law in Lesotho

A. The Place of Customary Law in the Legal System

In the following pages the expressions "customary law," "Sesotho law," "Sesotho law and custom," "Sotho law and custom," and "African law" are used indiscriminately to describe the same system, namely the customary law recognised and applied among the Basotho people in Lesotho.[160] The General Law Proclamation [161] provides for the application of customary law in two respects. First in Basotho courts generally, and secondly in other courts where all the parties to the proceedings are Africans. Furthermore the Independence Order 1966 [162] in making provision for the continuance in force of existing laws defines "existing law" as including the customary law of the country, and the Constitution itself defines law as including "the customary law of Lesotho." [163]

It may therefore be stated categorically that so far as the African inhabitants of Lesotho are concerned, African law stands basically on an equal footing with the common law. In no sense is the customary law placed in a fundamentally inferior or subsidiary

---

160. The most correct terms are "customary law" and "Sesotho law."

161. No. 2B of 1884.

162. § 4(5).

163. § 139(1).

position as it is in some other African countries, *e.g.*, Botswana [164] and Swaziland.[165]

This is, of course, largely as it should be. On the cession of Basutoland in 1884 it was only necessary to retain the Roman-Dutch common law for the benefit of the few Europeans then resident, most of whom would have found it both difficult (through ignorance of its contents and lack of written records) and abhorrent (owing to their background) to regulate their affairs in accordance with Sesotho law. Earlier, when Basutoland was annexed to the Cape Colony [166] the subordinate legislation enacted to deal with the administration of the country [167] did give some recognition to the customary law, especially in the fields of marriage, divorce, *bohali* (payment of cattle in connection with marriage), and guardianship. Thus it was only right and proper to maintain in a prominent position the law that was being successfully applied among the vast majority of the population. This is not meant to belittle the value of the common law to the development of the country at the present time, especially in the field of mercantile law where customary rules are, on the whole, notably absent.

Whereas formerly the courts *(khotla)* applied

---

164. Proc. 36 of 1909, which governs the general law to be administered, does not mention customary law; nor does the earlier reception Order in Council of 9th May 1891 incorporate such law as part of the general law though it does give some recognition to it. *See* § 4.

165. No reference is made to customary law in the General Law and Administration Proclamation (No. 4 of 1907). *See further* Baruti v. Mdiniso, [1961-2] H.C.T.L.R. 46 (C.A.).

166. By Cape Act 12 of 1871.

167. *See* G.N. of 13th May 1870 (draft regulations) and Proc. 51 of 1871. In 1872 a Commission of the Basutoland Magistrates was appointed to enquire into the customary law. For their amendments to the Proclamation see Proc. 41 of 29th March 1877.

Sesotho law as a matter of custom, the jurisdiction of the courts is now regulated by statute. The General Law Proclamation, the Independence Order, and the Constitution are the matrices of this jurisdiction which is reinforced by enactments such as the Central and Local Courts Proclamation [168] and the Marriage Proclamation.[169]

Four particular problems arise in connection with the application of the customary law in Lesotho.

First, how is such law to be ascertained?

Secondly, when may customary law be administered? This involves an examination of the way in which courts may exercise their discretion.

Thirdly, what are the criteria for the validity of customary law in the Basotho courts? These are the courts that only have jurisdiction to administer customary law and are staffed exclusively by Basotho.

Fourthly, what sort of future is there for customary law in Lesotho?

B. The Ascertainment of Customary Law

Since customary law forms part of the general law of Lesotho in cases where all the parties are Africans and since many magistrates as well as the entire judiciary are European and thus to a very great extent unfamiliar with customary law, how is such law to be accurately discovered and applied?

(1) Ascertainment in the non-Basotho Courts

The problem of ascertainment is not nearly so acute in the Basotho courts and therefore we shall start by considering the position in the non-Basotho courts. The way in which customary law is to be dis-

168. Proc. 62 of 1938 as amended.
169. Proc. 7 of 1911.

covered and the legal justification for the method adopted to achieve this are problems that have bedevilled judges and academic writers alike throughout the African continent.[170] Although presumably a practical compromise is reached in the daily quota of decided cases, a satisfactory theoretical basis for what in fact goes on has yet to be worked out. It is clear that in the courts' endeavours to discover law that is basically unwritten they do in fact make extensive use of assessors, and we deal with this form of ascertainment first.

(a) Assessors

The High Court Act 1967 provides: [171]

> The High Court may call to its assistance at any civil or criminal trial or appeal not more than four Assessors, whose duty it shall be to give, either in open court or otherwise, such assistance and advice as the Judge may require, but the decision shall be vested exclusively in the Judge.

The Subordinate Courts Proclamation provides: [172]

> In any action the court may summon to its assistance one or more persons to sit and act as assessors in an advisory capacity.

A Judicial Commissioner's Court has the same power to summon assessors as do the subordinate courts.[173]

Assessors are widely used in these three courts and they make a significant contribution in two respects. In the first place they advise the court on mat-

---

170. For discussions of the problem, *see* ALLOTT, *supra* note 7, Ch. 4; PARK, *supra* note 7, Ch. 6.

171. §§ 8 and 9.

172. § 19.

173. Judicial Commissioners Proclamation, § 2(2).

ters of Sesotho law and custom. Since the courts are still largely staffed by non-Basotho, this operates as a guarantee to the Basotho people that their customs and practices will be taken into consideration in reaching a decision. As the Privy Council stated in the Swaziland case of *Mahlikilili Dhlamini v. R.:* [174]

> It must further be remembered that the provision for giving the judge, at his request, the assistance of a native assessor cannot be regarded solely from the point of view of aid given to the judge. It operates and no doubt is intended to operate, as a safeguard to natives accused of crime, and a guarantee to the native population that their own customs and habits of life are not misunderstood.

In relation to the advice given on customary law, it may be asked whether the assessors are taking part in the hearing as expert witnesses. Although the High Court Proclamation no longer requires assessors to be chosen from among "Chiefs, Sub-Chiefs, Headmen, or other Africans suitably qualified to aid the court," [175] they are nevertheless picked from those well versed in the customary law.

The practice of using assessors [176] originated in British India and in the Indian case of *King Emperor v. Tirumal Reddi* [177] the judge explained their functions as follows:

> [A]ssessors are analogous to expert witnesses and in principle the opinion of an assessor is substantially on the same footing as the opinion evidence

---

174. [1943] 1 All E.R. 463, 466.

175. High Court Proclamation 1954, § 8 repealed by Proc. 1 of 1963, § 2.

176. *See generally,* on the use of assessors, ALLOTT, *supra* note 7, at 76-81; Sir John Gray 1958 J.A.L. 5 and J.H. Jearey 1961 J.A.L. 82.

177. [1901] I.L.R. 24 Madras 523.

> of expert witnesses . . . . Thus it will be seen that provision was made by the legislature for Europeans administering justice in a foreign land and therefore deficient in their knowledge of the customs and habits of the parties and witnesses appearing before them and also deficient in judging of their demeanour in the witness box, having the benefit of the opinion of two or more respectable natives of the land as assessors possessing such knowledge and judgment . . . the opinion of an assessor given upon the whole case tried before a Court of Session or any portion of such case is, in principle, on the same footing as the opinion evidence of a person specially skilled in foreign law, science, or art.

This advisory capacity of assessors is most apparent in civil cases, but it may also play an important part in criminal cases, especially when an assessor is able to point to a Sesotho law or custom as a justification for, or an explanation of, what appears to be a serious offence.[178]

It appears that it is still an open question whether the views of an assessor on a matter of custom constitute evidence that can be admitted to prove the existing state of the law. If they are, there should naturally be an opportunity for these opinions to be challenged by either party. On the other hand these views may be treated as findings of fact similar to those of a jury and thus unimpeachable save on exceptional grounds. In East Africa it has been held that the opinion of assessors, unsupported by the evidence of witnesses, is not of itself admissible as a conclusive statement of customary law.[179] It is interesting to note that the consensus at the Conference on the Future of Law in

---

178. *See* Sir John Gray, *supra* note 176, at 6-7.

179. Ndembera v. R., [1947] 14 E.A.C.A. 85; *but cf.* Benyamini Pande v. R., [1951] 18 E.A.C.A. 263.

Africa in 1960 was that assessors were not a suitable way of discovering customary law.[180]

The second function of assessors is to assess and weigh the evidence and in this they may have an easier task than the judge (especially where an interpreter is used) since through a deeper understanding of modes of behaviour and speech they can form a clearer picture as to the credibility of a party or a witness. In criminal trials an omission by the judge to direct the assessors to any aspect of the defence may be fatal, as may a misdirection.[181] As Lord Denning said in the Fijian appeal to the Privy Council in *Bharat s/o Dorsamy v. R.:* [182]

> He [the trial judge] has in truth by his misdirection disabled the assessors from giving him the aid which they should have given, and thus, in turn, disabled himself from taking their opinion into account as he should have done. This is a fatal flaw.

In this respect assessors stand in a similar position to a jury, but the analogy breaks down because a judge is bound by the verdict of a jury while he is free to reject the opinions of assessors.[183] It is no longer necessary for assessors to give their opinions in open court nowadays.[184]

(b) Written Evidence of Customary Law

Reliable written evidence of Sesotho customary law is limited to the following sources. First, there is the evidence that was given before a Special Commis-

---

180. THE FUTURE OF LAW IN AFRICA 14 (record of the proceedings of the London Conference of 1960, Butterworths).

181. *But cf.*, DANIELS, *supra* note 134, at 202 and the West African decisions cited there.

182. [1959] 3 All E.R. 292, 294.

183. § 9 of the High Court Act, 1967.

184. *Id.*

sion on the Laws and Customs of the Basotho, appointed by the Governor of the Cape on 19th August 1872.[185] Evidence was given by *inter alia* the chiefs Letsie, George Moshesh, Sofonia Moshesh, Jobo, and Tsita Mofoka. It dealt among other things with marriage, *bohali,* divorce, circumcision, homicide, incest, seduction, arson, damage to property, theft, assault, rape, land tenure, and succession. This early document is of immense value, not only as reflecting the customary law of the period but also as a demonstration of the interest shown in the local law by the Cape authorities.

Secondly, there are the Laws of Lerotholi which contain in their first part an incomplete Declaration of Sesotho Law and Custom, originally drawn up by the Basutoland Council and confirmed by Paramount Chief Lerotholi in 1903, and subsequently amended on a number of occasions, the most recent edition being dated 1959. They do not have the force of a statute, however, since at none of the relevant times did the Basutoland Council (or National Council) or the Paramount Chief have legislative authority. However these were the authorities traditionally entitled to make and declare the law and thus the "Laws" have been accepted as binding by the Basotho people despite the fact that they do not all date from time immemorial.

The nature of the laws was discussed by the Judicial Commissioner in the case of *Monare v. Koela*[186] in 1959. As a frequent interpreter of their provisions his remarks carry special weight. He stated:

> Coming to the Laws of Lerotholi, Part I is a Declaration of Basotho Custom and it is of course

185. REPORT AND EVIDENCE OF COMMISSION ON NATIVE LAWS AND CUSTOMS OF THE BASUTOS (1873; reprinted by Morija Printing Works, Lesotho).

186. J.C. 89/1959.

> far from exhaustive and complete and it has not been drafted by legal draftsmen and leaves much to be desired in its lack of precision which gives rise to a great deal of unnecessary litigation and difficulties of interpretation and enforcement. This Declaration was amended in recent years when it was sought to make lands inheritable . . . and this section has repeatedly been ruled invalid for Custom cannot be changed by altering a Declaration of Custom[187]. . . . Parts II and III are on quite a different footing and embody Paramount Chief's orders issued and promulgated under proper statutory authority.[188] But even Part II combined with Part I is far from representing a comprehensive set of customs. . . . Further the laws and customs of the Basuto have never been codified. While this has the defect of lack of precision which is reflected in case after case heard in this Court, it has the inestimable advantage of not crystallising outmoded laws and customs which are being abandoned in favour of customs evolving as more suitable to modern conditions.

Thirdly, a former Judicial Commissioner, Patrick Duncan, has written a slim volume entitled *Sotho Laws and Customs*.[189] This brings together the Evidence given to the 1872 Commission, the Laws of Lerotholi, and many decisions from the Judicial Commissioner's Court as well as a few from the High Court and the Basotho courts.

Fourthly, there are a few monographs that cover certain aspects of the customary law. The outstanding work is undoubtedly Sheddick's *Land Tenure in Basutoland*,[190] but there are also Ashton's *The Ba-*

---

187. *E.g.*, in Lesitsi v. Mafa, J.C. 84/1953; *see also* Sekoboto v. Possa, J.C. 74/1964 where it was held that LL. § 6 of Part I could not alter the custom that a husband is liable for his wife's delicts.

188. *See also* ASHTON, THE BASUTO (2nd ed. O.U.P. 1967).

189. DUNCAN, SOTHO LAWS AND CUSTOMS (O.U.P. 1960).

190. SHEDDICK, LAND TENURE IN BASUTOLAND (H.M.S.O. 1954).

suto,[191] Ellenberger and Macgregor's *History of the Basuto,*[192] Sekese's *Mekhoa le Maele a Basotho,*[193] and Casalis' *The Basutos.*[194] Sheddick has also written on the Southern Sotho in the series of ethnographic surveys in Africa.[195]

Fifthly, there are the decisions of the Courts. Comparatively few cases have reached the High Court or Court of Appeal, but some of those that have are reported in the High Commission Territories Law Reports from 1926 to 1966, though by no means all the significant ones. A very large number of appeals do however reach the Judicial Commissioner's Court, but these decisions are not published. Some of the more important judgments during the years 1952-1968 in the fields of marriage, divorce, succession, delict, and contract have recently been collected by the Law Department at the University of Botswana, Lesotho and Swaziland. No attempt has so far been made to collect together or publish the judgments of the Basotho courts.

Sixthly, there has recently been completed a survey under the auspices of the Restatement of African Law project at the School of Oriental and African Studies in London, namely a Restatement of the Sesotho Law of Marriage by a panel under the chairmanship of Advocate A. M. Ramolefe.

(c) The Proof of Customary Law

What is the correct procedure to be followed in

---

191. *Supra* note 188.

192. ELLENBERGER AND MACGREGOR, HISTORY OF THE BASUTO (Caxton 1912).

193. SEKESE, MEKHOA LE MAELE A BASOTHO (Morija 1908, reprinted in 1968).

194. CASALIS, THE BASUTOS (London 1861, in translation from the French).

195. ETHNOGRAPHIC SURVEY OF AFRICA (Forde ed. London I.A.I., 1953).

trying to prove a point of customary law? How should a court set about the task of discovering the customary law? Is the analogy of the proof of local custom at common law relevant?

The rules of the common law of England [196] and South Africa coincide on the method by which a local custom may be proved and thus become a source of law. In the leading South African case of *van Breda v. Jacobs* [197] the requirements of an enforceable custom were listed as follows:

(a) The custom must be ancient or long established;

(b) The custom must have been uniformly observed;

(c) The custom must be reasonable;

(d) The custom must be certain.

These matters must be proved as facts before the court. One objection to employing this technique to customary law however, is that these rules are applied to permit a custom to derogate from the general law of the land, whereas in Lesotho the customary law forms a part of this general law, applicable to the Basotho people generally.[198] As Professor Allott says:

> Nevertheless, as far as the Africans who are members of that tribe are concerned, their customary law is not an occasional variant from the general law applicable to them; it is their general law *prima facie* applicable in civil and criminal matters. The tests for its application and the method by which its rules are ascertained, should not be

196. See HALSBURY, 10 LAWS OF ENGLAND, paras. 6-22 (Hailsham ed.).

197. [1921] A.D. 330.

198. However these rules may be applicable where a court in Lesotho has no jurisdiction to apply customary law as law. This is the position in the subordinate courts in cases where not all the parties to the proceedings are Africans; *see infra*. pp. 153-154.

blindly borrowed from the English law relating to local custom.[199]

Conventionally, common law courts establish legal and factual points by utilising one of two approaches. On the one hand, the common law that they administer and the statutes they apply they discover for themselves, and they are free to use their own knowledge of such laws even if these are not expressly referred to during the hearing. Thus we say that the courts take judicial notice of these laws.[200]

Foreign laws, on the other hand, must be proved as matters of fact by witnesses, and commonly expert evidence is given of them.

Ordinary facts span both these approaches. Some facts must be proved by evidence, whereas judicial notice is taken of others and these need not be proved. The latter are regarded as patently true or "notorious" and cover such diverse matters as, *e.g.*, the number of days in a year, the existence of a state of war, and the fact that among the purposes for which a university exists is the advancement of learning.[201]

Where does customary law fit into these approaches? In 1916 in the case of *Angu v. Attah* [202] the Privy Council stated:

> As is the case with all customary law it has to be proved in the first instance by calling witnesses acquainted with the native customs until the particular customs have, by frequent proof in the courts, become so notorious that the courts will take judicial notice of them.

Although these remarks were made *obiter* they are of course entitled to great respect, emanating as

---

199. *Supra* note 7, at 74-75.

200. *See* CROSS, EVIDENCE 133 (2d ed.); HOFFMAN, SOUTH AFRICAN LAW OF EVIDENCE 130-32 (Butterworths 1963).

201. Re Oxford Poor Rate case, [1857] 8 E. & B. 184.

202. [1874-1928] P.C. 43, 44 (1916).

they do from Lesotho's highest court, especially as the *dictum* has been reiterated by the Board itself,[203] and because it has been followed frequently elsewhere in Africa.[204]

Thus in the first instance witnesses must be called to prove the existence of a point of customary law. The experience and qualifications of the witness will affect the weight to be attached to his evidence in the same way as those of a doctor, engineer, or other expert would be relevant in considering *his* evidence.

There is support for this approach to the proof of customary law in the Lesotho case of *Joel Motsoene v. Sir Edward Harding*.[205] The decision turned on the customary law relating to the remarriage of widows, and counsel for the plaintiff had argued that a custom could only be proved by specific instances of its existence and had cited authorities relating to the common law method of proving customs and usages of trade. Huggard C. J., however, dismissed this contention in the following manner:

> In my opinion such authorities have no application to the present case. It is true that in the phrase "Basuto law and custom" the word "custom" is used, but in fact what we are dealing with here is a "law." And that law being an unwritten law,

---

203. Amissah v. Krabah, [1936] 2 W.A.C.A. 30 and Golightly v. Ashrifi (P.C. appeal No. 31 of 1958 from Ghana, reported 1961 J.A.L. 52).

204. *See* from Uganda, Kigizi v. Lukiko of Buganda, [1943] 6 U.L.R. 113, 117. Similar rules have been propounded by the Nigerian courts: *see* Buraimo v. Gbamboye, [1940] 15 Nig. L.R. 139 and Giwa v. Erinmilokun, [1961] 1 All N.L.R. 294. *See also* the Nigerian Evidence Act (Cap. 62), § 14 which has adopted the principles of the rule in Angu v. Attah. Authorities from Sierra Leone, Malawi, and Zambia are also cited in ALLOTT, *supra* note 7, at 77.

205. [1954] H.C.T.L.R. 1 (reporting a decision given in 1940).

> the best evidence one can obtain regarding it is the evidence of those who by virtue of their experience may be expected to be familiar with it.[206]

Expert testimony need not be given orally but may be presented in the form of a textbook or other documentary record written by someone with special knowledge of the subject. The author need not be a lawyer, but his work must be held in high repute for it to be entitled to the court's consideration. Since the field of customary law is largely the domain of anthropologists and sociologists, it is natural for recourse to be had to their works, *e.g.*, the copious references made in Botswana to Professor Schapera's studies of Tswana Law and Custom.[207] In the same way a mountaineer or explorer might give expert evidence as to the physical geography of the Andes or the Drakensberg in a boundary dispute case, even though he were not himself a geographer. The reason is that his researches and experience might give him a greater knowledge of the subject than an armchair geographer.

Very little use seems to be made in practice of precedent. By and large, decisions of one Basotho court are not circulated to another, there is no system of publishing reports of such decisions, nor are decisions of the Judicial Commissioners' courts circulated sys-

---

206. *Id.* 13-14.

207. SCHAPERA, TSWANA LAW AND CUSTOM was cited with approval in, *e.g.*, Bagwasi & Louno v. R., [1926-53] H.C.T.L.R. 38, 40 and Wetshootsile v. R., [1959] H.C.T.L.R. 110, 111; and his TRIBAL LEGISLATION AMONG THE TSWANA OF THE BECHUANALAND PROTECTORATE in Samotsoko v. Palane, [1958] H.C.T.L.R. 75, 76 and 78. However, there may be a danger in citing an anthropologist's classifications, *e.g.*, of crimes and torts, or customs and laws, rather than the content of customary law. *See, e.g.*, the use of LEWIS, THE PEOPLES OF THE HORN OF AFRICA in the Somali Republic case of H.A. Abdulla Saad v. Arap Samaneh, Boho Samaneh (1962) reported in 1964 J.A.L. 139.

tematically or published in an accessible form. One should also bear in mind the essential difference between the common law and customary law. The former is self-sufficient; it depends on itself and can only be altered by itself or by statute. Customary law on the other hand depends on the usage of the people and can change from time to time. A decision on a matter of customary law given ten years ago cannot be blindly followed today as it may no longer represent the law. However for there to be constructive and uniform growth and development rather than haphazard fluctuation in the law it would seem desirable for some system of precedent and publication of reports to be introduced. This would make more sense of the system of appeals from local to central courts and from central courts to that of the Judicial Commissioner.

An illustration of the need to recognize changes in the customary law is afforded by the decision of the Basutoland High Court in *Bereng Griffith v. 'Mantsebo Seeiso Griffith*,[208] often referred to as the *Regency Case*. This was a dispute in 1943 about the appointment [209] of the defendant as Regent and Acting Paramount Chief during the minority of her stepson, the heir to the Paramount Chieftainship. The plaintiff claimed that he should have been appointed instead and sought to prove that, being a woman, the defendant was by Sesotho law and custom incompetent to succeed to a Chieftainship or to hold office as Regent and Acting Paramount Chief. He also sought to show for the same reasons that she was incompetent to be the guardian of her stepson or to administer the estate of her late husband and that, on the contrary, she was herself under guardianship. Thirdly, he argued that

208. [1926-53] H.C.T.L.R. 50.

209. The appointment was recognized by the High Commissioner—*see Id.* at 53.

under customary law on the death of his brother, the late Paramount Chief, he obtained the right to assume his place as husband of his brother's widows, or if they should object to cohabitation, as guardian of them and their children, and controller and administrator of their respective houses and their property.

In the course of a long and carefully reasoned judgment Lansdown J. disposed of the plaintiff's first two contentions concerning the incompetence of the defendant as a woman under customary law. His findings about the changes that had come about are instructive in showing how very significant alterations in a matter of great social importance were occurring at the time. He found that under the traditional system, which was polygamous and involved each wife having a separate establishment or "house," there was little room for the exercise of authority by a wife or widow. During her husband's lifetime she was under his guardianship and after his death she was merely entitled to be maintained out of the estate which passed to the eldest son. However a new custom had grown up, under which when the husband died, if his eldest son were still a minor the widow could become the controller and administrator of the affairs of her own "house," subject only to the influence and advice of the male head of the family. Moreover in cases where the husband was a chief, his widow was often appointed as regent until such time as the eldest son attained majority and succeeded to his father's office.[210] The court therefore concluded that, at any rate among the chieftain class, there had been a development in the status of women and they were entitled to hold administrative office, to act as guardians of their children, and to control and administer property.[211]

Lansdown J. then turned to the plaintiff's third

210. *Id.* at 54-55.
211. *Id.* at 57.

contention that under the custom of *kenela* he was entitled to step into his deceased brother's place vis-a-vis the defendant and become her husband, at any rate to the extent of controlling her "house" and becoming guardian of her and her child. He found that whereas the practise of *kenela* was general in the early history of the Basotho and had then much to commend it, it had fallen into decay and was no longer a universally practised custom at the time of the hearing.[212]

This case therefore clearly points to the fact that since the customary law is in a state of change, decisions of the courts can only be of limited value as precedents. A court may certainly commence by looking at earlier decisions on the matter but must always be on the lookout for changes in the law brought about by a metamorphosis in the operation of the custom among the Basotho people, in the same way in which it must take notice of an alteration in the law effected by statutory enactments.

We are now in a position to summarise the position under the first branch of the rule laid down by the Privy Council in *Angu v. Attah* that until the particular customs have, by frequent proof in the courts, become so notorious that the courts will take judicial notice of them they must be proved as facts by the evidence of witnesses.

It is submitted that customary law should not be equated with local custom or foreign law in this connection. It is neither local nor foreign within Lesotho.[213] To adopt such a viewpoint is to perpetuate

212. *Id.* at 67.

213. For South African decisions on judicial notice and the dissimilarity between customary law and foreign law, *see Ex parte* Minister of Native Affairs: *In re* Yako v. Beyi, [1948] 1 S.A. 388 (A.D.), 394; R. v. Dumezweni, [1961] 2 S.A. 751 (A.D.), 757; Ngcobo v. Ngcobo, [1929] A.D. 233, 236-37; Mosii v. Motseoakhumo, [1954] 3 S.A. 919 (A.D.), 930-31.

the ethnocentricity which has been such a disastrous feature of the approach of Europeans to African systems of government and land tenure. Customary law must be looked at as an institution *sui generis* and it should be examined in its own terms and against its own sociological background, rather than through the eyes of the analytical jurisprudence of the Western world.

Its three chief characteristics are that it is very much law in the sense that it is enforceable as such through the courts; that being dependent upon the practises of those who are subject to it, it is liable to change in accordance with usage and is therefore not constant; and that it is difficult of access for those who do not regulate their lives by it since it is still largely unwritten. It is essential to bear these matters in mind in considering its application.

It has often been suggested that customary law be written down and this controversial question is considered below.[214] But in the meanwhile, until this task is undertaken in a comprehensive manner, the burden of ensuring that customary law moves into line with the new aspirations of the Basotho people will fall squarely upon the courts. And, more significantly, this burden may increasingly come to rest upon the shoulders of the superior courts and must be satisfactorily discharged if they are to retain the respect of the general public.

Bearing in mind the three characteristics of customary law outlined above, we must determine what type of proof of a customary rule can legitimately be required. Its first characteristic is that it is law, and therefore it must be established that it is regarded as legally binding among its subjects just like any other law, and not just a rule of morals or etiquette.

---

214. *Infra* pp. 193-197.

Secondly, since customary law is law partly because it is practised in Basotho society and actually lived out by those subject to it there is a clear need for it to be well established. By this we mean that it should be sufficiently current in that it is being put into operation as law and that people are managing their affairs and regulating their behaviour on this basis. Expectations of society must be taken into account. The extent of its recognition need not be universal but it must be substantial.[215] This may prove a thorny problem in practise but it has to be faced, and the courts should take sympathetic account of modern trends and variations. Though such changes and modifications must be given effect for the proper development of customary law, a custom which is only just beginning to grow up is too young to have the force of law, and on the other hand a custom that is rapidly falling into desuetude likewise does not warrant enforcement. Many customs may disappear as a result of increasing contact with urban development and a money economy together with their emphasis upon individualism rather than the extended family. The practise of *kenela* was dying out at the time of the hearing of the *Regency Case* (above). Lansdown J. declared:

> No system or course of practice can indeed be said to amount to a reasonable and well-established custom with force of law which having once flourished is now decadent and to a considerable degree, in disuse.[216]

215. The need for recognition by the community was expressed by Lord Atkin in the Judicial Committee appeal in Eleko v. Government of Nigeria, [1931] A.C. 662, 673 in the following terms, "It is the assent of the native community that gives a custom its validity, and therefore barbarous or mild it must be shown to be recognised by the native community whose conduct it is supposed to regulate."

216. *Supra* note 208, at 69. In Lembemba v. Nswima, a

It will be noticed that Lansdown J. refers to a criterion of reasonableness.[217] The third feature of customary law is the fact that it is unwritten. This explains its penchant for generality and reflects the fact, previously noted, that it acquires its force largely from consistent usage rather than from interpretation. Without writing there cannot be much interpretation and this accounts for the relative paucity of customary law jurisprudence. These matters are relevant in considering what criterion of reasonableness it is justifiable to expect for the validity of a customary rule. The justification for the requirement of reasonableness in the proof of local custom at common law is that the common law is considered innately reasonable by the judges and that if there is to be any derogation from it this too should be reasonable. The common law is looking outwards at something alien. It argues by analogy with its own rules to see if there is sufficient "reasonable" content in the custom to warrant its limited application despite the fact that its own rules are not always reasonable themselves. Neither the concept of the inclusion of an extraneous rule nor the jurisprudential approach is applicable to proof of customary law. It would be quite improper for a European judge to impose his own views, based on his own background, to hold that a rule of customary law is unreasonable. Many Sesotho customs when examined from such an ethnocentric viewpoint do not appear reasonable. The judiciary will therefore have to

---

case from the N. Rhodesian High Court, reported in (1958) J.A.L. 127 the court similarly refused to enforce a Bemba custom that a son-in-law should render free service to his father-in-law in a form of marriage by service, because it was found to be dying out in the urban areas where the parties lived.

217. This is regarded as a requisite by VOET 1.3.28 so far as proof of custom in Roman-Dutch law is concerned.

approach the question from the point of view of the people who practise the custom themselves and see whether the rule is reasonable in its sociological context. It seems that the requirement of reasonableness may, in reality, be a formal one without very specific content, as appears to be the position in English law. Thus Sir Carleton Allen writes:

> [T]he chief purport of these rules or tests is to determine whether the general and particular customs of our law are, *as a matter of established fact*, proved to be recognised social practise. Beyond this English courts seldom go, if ever; and it is, I submit, a mistake to represent modern judges as exercising any extensive critical faculty with regard to established usages . . . *if a custom is proved in an English court by satisfactory evidence to exist and to be observed, the function of the court is merely to declare the custom operative law*. . . . Further it has always been laid down that the court has power to declare a custom, though proved in fact, unreasonable in its origin and no longer to be observed. As I shall attempt to show, this latter rule belongs to theory rather than to practise and has little effect upon the operation of custom in English law. (Emphasis added.)[218]

---

218. LAW IN THE MAKING 126, 127, 129, 130 (6th ed. O.U.P.). For another view, *see* SALMOND, JURISPRUDENCE (11th ed. 1957):

> The authority of usage is not absolute, but conditional on a certain measure of conformity with justice and public utility. It is not meant by this that the courts are at liberty to disregard a custom whenever they are not satisfied as to its absolute rectitude and wisdom, or whenever they think that a better rule could be formulated in the exercise of their own judgment. This would be to deprive custom of all authority, either absolute or conditional. The true rule is, or should be, that a custom, in order to be deprived of legal efficacy, must be so obviously and seriously repugnant to right and reason, that to enforce it as law would do more mischief than that which would result from the overturning of the expectations and arrangements based on its presumed continuance and legal validity. (At 242.)

Sir Carleton concluded from his examination of English cases that the few occasions on which a custom was held unreasonable fell into two basic categories. Firstly where the custom was oppressive or prejudicial to a class of persons, and secondly where its range had been improperly extended to persons who were strangers to the local area of operation.[219] In any event the onus is on the party disputing the custom to prove that it is unreasonable.[220] Since customary law and the common law stand on an equal footing for Africans in Lesotho it is hard to see why one should have to be proved to be reasonable and the other not.

It is submitted that there is no necessity for the custom to be long established or to have existed from time immemorial,[221] since this would have the effect of refusing to recognise the progressive development of customary law. Nor need there be complete uniformity of practice, since this again would jeopardise the present adaptation of the law and during a process of modification there would be no rule at all. Both these points are clear from Lansdown J.'s judgment in the *Regency Case* (above).

With regard to the actual process of proof it is instructive to examine the way in which the court in *Bereng Griffith v. 'Mantsebo Seeiso Griffith* approached the question of the competence of women in Basotho society.

First, it tried to discover the extent to which there were women presidents of the 1,300 native courts that

219. *Id.* LAW IN THE MAKING Appendix I at 599-617.

220. *Id.* at 136.

221. It has recently been held that a custom does not have to have existed from time immemorial to be valid in South African Law—Catering Equipment Centre v. Friesland Hotel, [1967] 4 S.A. 336 (O).

were in operation in 1938, and found there were many who exercised not only their judicial functions but also administrative functions as chiefs, sub-chiefs or headmen, both in their own capacities and as regents for their minor sons. Ten of these women gave evidence before the court. The court found that the women collected taxes, allotted lands, and issued cattle permits.

Secondly, the court examined court records to discover whether or not a woman had *locus standi in judicio*. It found 22 cases between 1929 and 1941 in which women had sued and been sued in their own names.

Thirdly, the court rejected the idea that it should seek guidance from Seymour's *Native Law and Custom*,[222] on the grounds that it specifically related to the Transkei. It was pointed out that for approximately a century the Basotho had been separated from the rest of the Bantu-speaking peoples and their customs had therefore inevitably been subject to divergent developments.[223] This approach was, with respect, clearly correct though it has not always been observed elsewhere.[224]

Fourthly, the court considered Laws of Lerotholi calling them the Lerotholi Code but rightly declared:

> No legislative authority or official recognition has been extended to this Code; nevertheless it is helpful, though not conclusive, on any question as to the existence or extent of any customary practise among the Basuto people. . . . Now the Lerotholi Code is in no sense written law. Its

---

222. SEYMOUR, NATIVE LAW AND CUSTOM (Jutas 1960).

223. *Supra* note 208, at 59.

224. Thus SARBAH, FANTI CUSTOMARY LAWS has often been cited in West Africa as an authority in non-Fante cases, *e.g.*, the Ashanti cases of Ntrama v. Attia, [1956] 1 W.A.L.R. 94 and Kojo v. Anane, [1956] 1 W.A.L.R. 131.

provisions, though reduced to print, do not emanate from any lawgiver.[225]

Fifthly, the court adopted some of the evidence given in 1872 before the Special Commission on the Laws and Customs of the Basothos by Chief George Moshesh, son of the first Paramount Chief.

Sixthly, the court examined the census figures for 1911 and 1936 in order to discover whether or not polygamy was dying out and thus indirectly whether the practice of *kenela* still operated. It found the census figures would not permit of the continuance of a general system of polygamy.

Seventhly, the court closely examined the ten women chiefs, sub-chiefs, and headmen as to whether they had ever been *kenelaed.* Considerable evidence was also given by other witnesses on the prevalence of the practise. The court also distinguished an unreported case in which, it was contended, the custom of *kenela* was directly affirmed.

Finally, the court accepted the evidence as to *kenela* of the Government Secretary who had had 33 years of varied service in the country.

The second branch of the rule in *Angu v. Attah* states that after frequent proof in the courts, a customary rule may have become so notorious that the courts will take judicial notice of it. The rule was applied by the Privy Council itself in *Aryeh v. Ankrah* [226] in a matter relating to intestate succession among the Ga people of Ghana, and Mr. de Silva in giving the judgment of the Board stated:

> Their Lordships will now examine the decisions cited to them in order to ascertain whether any principles relevant to the determination of the question before them have been proved and recog-

225. *Supra* note 208, at 58, 59.

226. P.C. appeal No. 1 of 1952 reported in 1958 J.A.L. 26.

> nised so frequently that judicial notice can be taken of them.

Having considered various cases the Board held there was no

> . . . series of decisions from which any relevant principles have crystallised in the manner indicated in the case of *Kobina Angu v. Cudjoe Attah*. . . .[227]

It seems clear that the Committee was looking for a series or line of decisions in order to bring the second branch of the rule into play. An isolated decision would not appear to have been enough, though recently the Nigerian Federal Supreme Court held that judicial notice could be taken of a rule propounded in a single case.[228]

Even where rules of customary law are judicially noticed, subsequent courts must be careful to ensure that the rule has not been abolished or modified by an intervening change of practice, otherwise the law will quickly fall out of line with custom and cease to be entitled to respect.[229] It is clear that counsel must be permitted to advocate the reappraisal of a rule of customary law that has been judicially noticed,[230] and it should not be beyond judicial technique to continue the dynamic process of adaptation and development to meet modern needs, which has been such a strong characteristic of the common law.

It should be borne in mind that non-Basotho courts

---

227. *Id.* at 30 and 31. On judicial notice and its application in West African cases, *see further* PARK, *supra* note 7, at 92 *et seq.*

228. *See* Cole v. Akinyele, [1960] 5 F.S.C. 84 relying on Alake v. Pratt, [1955] 15 W.A.C.A. 20.

229. *See* Amodu Tijani v. Southern Nigeria (Secretary), [1921] 2 A.C. 399, criticised by ALLOTT, *supra* note 7, at 290 and PARK, *supra* note 7, at 95.

230. In support see PARK, *supra* note 7, at 95; *contra* ALLOTT, *supra* note 7, at 290.

are faced with the difficulty of ascertainment not only in cases at first instance, but also in hearing appeals from Basotho courts.

As we shall see below, Basotho courts take judicial notice of the customary law, and evidence of a customary rule is not required. Appellate courts have greater hesitation over upsetting a lower court's finding of fact than they do about reversing its finding of law. We have already emphasised that customary law is indeed law and therefore a non-Basotho court hearing an appeal from a Basotho court ought not to be overcautious about rejecting a finding on a matter of Sesotho law and custom.[231] If the appellate court is reluctant to interfere with such findings it can hardly be said to be performing any useful function at all and it may well allow a wrong finding of customary law to establish itself as a precedent almost unnoticed.[232] Provided the evidence of expert and other witnesses and the reasons of assessors are on the record, the appellate court is in just as strong a position as the court of first instance for reaching the correct decision. The same applies where a court is exercising its powers of review. The Privy Council statement in the Indian appeal of *Devi v. Roy* [233] that

> [T]he Board will always be reluctant to depart from the practice [of not interfering with concurrent findings of fact of the local courts] in cases which involve questions of manners, customs,

---

231. *See* Allott 1968 J.A.L. 3 at 31.

232. In the Nyasaland (now Malawi) case of Chitema v. Lupanda, [1962] R & N 290, the High Court held that where the court of first instance takes judicial notice of customary law the appellate court should do likewise. It is submitted that this approach may lead to the appellate court putting a rubber stamp to findings of law in the court of first instance where the former is staffed by non-African judges, and that such a practice should be restricted in its operation.

233. [1946] A.C. 508.

> or sentiments peculiar to the country or locality from which the case comes whose significance is specially within the knowledge of the courts of that country . . . ,

is understandable for the Privy Council, but it should not be used by appellate courts within Lesotho to evade their wider responsibilities.

It remains finally to consider whether the rule in *Angu v. Attah* is still the best approach to the problem facing the non-Basotho courts.[234] The rule was laid down in 1916 against the background of the English law of local custom and at a time when views of African customary law were very different from those of today.

At the outset it is worth remembering two factors. First, that the rule was designed for courts staffed by non-Africans who were likely to be ignorant of customary law. That position is no different in Lesotho at the present time.

Secondly, the place of customary law in Lesotho's legal system has remained largely unaltered between 1916 and today.

The argument that could be levelled against the rule is that since customary law is part of the general law of the land, the judges should have to make the effort to discover it for themselves if they do not know it. To do this, of course, they could use all the documentary evidence available. But the onus would be upon them to find it and not upon the parties to establish it by expert evidence.

The difficulty lies in the fact that to date so little

---

234. The rule was recently declared by Crabbe J. A. (dissenting) in Kimani v. Gikanga, [1965] E.A.C.A. 735 to be fast becoming out of date and therefore inapplicable in Kenya. However Kenya has a provision in its Evidence Act 1963 which specifically provides that the courts are to take judicial notice of the customary law. (See § 60.)

has been written about Sesotho law and custom that the judges would find it an extremely exacting task, if not an impossible one.

The immediate aim will naturally be to have Basotho judges on the bench and these will of course have a greater knowledge of customary law than their predecessors. They may not know every rule but they will be in a better position to inform themselves of the law than the expatriate judiciary. Thus perhaps we may look forward to a time in the not too distant future when the rule in *Angu v. Attah* will be superseded by a policy of taking judicial notice of the customary law in the same way as the courts presently take judicial notice of the common law and statutes.

(2) ASCERTAINMENT IN THE BASOTHO COURTS

In the previous discussion we have been dealing only with the non-Basotho courts in their endeavours to discover the customary law. Basotho courts, on the other hand, clearly take judicial notice of the customary law. But can we assume that there is no problem for the judiciary of Basotho courts since they are Basotho and thus familiar with the customary law? It has been suggested that:

> [A]s the customary law becomes more and more modified to suit modern conditions, and as the personnel of the African courts becomes increasingly non-traditional, the old assumptions will serve no longer.[235]

Although Lesotho is a small country and is now composed of a single people with uniform customs[236] there is a danger that the Basotho courts may not keep up to date, especially when one considers the remote-

---

235. ALLOTT, *supra* note 7, at 96.

236. In Ndlungwane v. Setokwe J.C., 135/1961 the Judicial Commissioner's Court rejected the contention that the Laws of Lerotholi did not govern all African inhabitants of Lesotho.

ness of some of them and the fact that there is not much pooling of information of decisions given by other courts and the Judicial Commissioner's Court. It is also often a mistake to assume that all Basotho know their customary law in detail, especially the younger generation from among whom, no doubt, future court presidents will be chosen. Moreover legal practitioners are not permitted to appear in civil causes before the Basotho courts,[237] and thus the courts are without the benefit of their argument and research.

Nevertheless it has been held by the West African Court of Appeal that the rule in *Angu v. Attah* does not apply to the proceedings of African courts on the basis that such courts should be familiar with the customary law.[238]

C. When May Customary Law Be Administered?

(1) INTERNAL CONFLICT OF LAWS

It has already been seen that the General Law Proclamation provides that customary law may be administered in the Basotho courts, and in any other court where all the parties are Africans. Since the word "may" is used this clearly gives the court a discretion, enabling it to choose between the customary law and the common law. Upon what principles is this discretion to be exercised? The expression "internal conflict of laws" [239] has been coined to describe this problem of the choice of law. It demonstrates that this field has certain similarities with private

237. Proc. 62 of 1938 as amended, § 20.

238. *See* Ababio 11 v. Nsemfo, [1947] 12 W.A.C.A. 127, on appeal from the Gold Coast (as it then was). *Contra semble* the Nigerian decision in Fijabi v. Odumola, [1955-56] W.R.N.L.R. 133.

239. The phrase was originally coined by ALLOTT, *supra* note 7, at 154, note 3.

international law, which deals with conflicts between the legal systems of different countries ("external conflict of laws") while pointing the contrast that the conflicting laws we are considering here spring from the same legal system.

In many parts of Africa there are detailed statutory rules that lay down when the common law is to be applied and when customary law is the proper law to decide the case.[240] Lesotho lacks such specific directions in the general administration of the law and the General Law Proclamation leaves everything to the discretion of the court. However, specific directions *are* to be found in relation to the jurisdiction of the Basotho courts[241] and also in respect of particular areas of the law, for instance marriage[242] and inheritance.[243]

At the outset it may be said that the choice of court the parties make may determine the law to be applied. This is not to say that there is any racial classification of courts, for this distinction was abolished in 1965.[244] Any person may bring an action before any court in Lesotho. However, since Basotho courts are basically only empowered to administer customary law and not the common law, the effect of commencing proceedings in such a court is to elect to have the matter determined by the customary law.

(2) APPLICATION OF CUSTOMARY LAW IN THE BASOTHO COURTS

So far as Basotho courts are concerned, the pro-

---

240. For Nigeria, *see* PARK, *supra* note 7, at 149-151, Appendix III.

241. Central and Local Courts Proclamation, § 9.

242. Marriage Proclamation (No. 7 of 1911), § 7.

243. Administration of Estates Proclamation (No. 19 of 1935), § 3(b).

244. By the Native Courts Proclamation and Rules (Amendment) Regulations 1965, § 3.

vision in the General Law Proclamation that they "may" administer African law has been converted by the Central and Local Courts Proclamation into a "must." This is an example of the construction of the word "may" in a statute as having mandatory connotations where a duty is imposed by another statute.[245] The Central and Local Courts Proclamation provides in section 9 that such courts "shall administer—(a) the native law and custom prevailing in the Territory . . . ." Thus no discretion is vested in the Basotho courts. If they are to administer any law at all it must be African law or a law that falls within certain other restricted categories specifically mentioned in the Proclamation,[246] but not including the common law. If the court decides that African law does not apply to the case its proper course is to decline jurisdiction and transfer the case to a subordinate court.[247] Examples of situations in which the court would clearly not apply African law would be most matters of mercantile law (*e.g.*, cases relating to insurance companies and bills of exchange) and passing off actions in the law of delict.

It may be as well, at the outset, to clarify the question of whether a Basotho court is free to apply customary law to a non-African. The question is a complicated one and it is proposed to approach the matter historically.

The original wording of the 1884 General Law Proclamation [248] included the following proviso:

> Provided, however, that in any suit, action, or proceeding in any Court, to which all the parties

245. *See* MAXWELL ON THE INTERPRETATION OF STATUTES 231 *et seq.* (11th ed. Sweet and Maxwell).

246. *See infra* pp. 493-494.

247. Such transfer is provided for by rule 31 of the Basuto Courts (Practise and Procedure) Rules (G.N. No. 21 of 1961).

248. Proc. 2B of 1884, § 2.

> are natives, and in all suits, actions, or proceedings whatsoever before any Native Chief *exercising jurisdiction as aforesaid,* native law may be administered. (Emphasis added.)

It is clear that whether the case was before a court or a chief, customary law could only be administered where all the parties were Africans.

In 1938 courts styled "Native Courts" were established [249] to replace the system of Chief's Courts. The Native Courts Proclamation of that year limited the jurisdiction of these courts to cases in which all the parties were "natives." [250]

Despite the revision in the laws that took place in 1949 the wording of the General Law Proclamation remained the same. In the wording of the 1960 revision, however, the proviso had been amended to read as follows:

> Provided, however, that in all suits, actions, or proceedings in any Court, to which all the parties are Africans, and in all suits, actions, or proceedings whatsoever before any Basuto Court African law may be administered.[251]

By that time the word "African" was regarded as a necessary replacement for "native" and the Basuto Courts Proclamation 1958 [252] (although it never came into force) had started the practice of using "Basuto courts" as a substitute for "Native courts" or "courts of Native Chiefs." [253]

However the alteration of the wording of the proviso did more than merely substitute these expressions for the old ones since it omitted the crucial words "exercising jurisdiction as aforesaid" which

---

249. By Proc. 62 of 1938.
250. *Id.* §§ 6 and 7.
251. LAWS OF BASUTOLAND Vol. I, at 340.
252. Proc. 23 of 1958.
253. *Id.* § 1(2).

referred to the requirement that all the parties be African before customary law could be administered.

This was, perhaps, an unintentional alteration, but it was followed in 1965 by the Native Courts Proclamation and Rules (Amendment) Regulations [254] which directly abolished the racial restriction on the jurisdiction of the Basotho courts. However the effect of these regulations made by the Resident Commissioner [255] cannot be to override the provisions of the General Law Proclamation and therefore we must return to this to ascertain the true position.

An ambiguity appears from the use in the proviso of the words "any court" and later "any Basuto court." The proviso declares that in all suits, actions, and proceedings in a Basotho court, African law may be administered (without any specification as to the race of the parties), whereas in proceedings before "any court," which *prima facie* includes a Basotho court, African law may only be administered when all the parties are Africans.

It is submitted that the ambiguity can be resolved by interpreting the words "any court" to mean "any court other than a Basuto court." [256] To interpret them as including Basotho courts is to render superfluous the phrase "and in all suits, actions, or proceedings whatsoever in any Basuto court."

In the Rhodesian case of *Loewerstein v. Commissioner of Taxes* [257] Murray C. J., giving the judgment of the Federal Supreme Court declared:

---

254. LAWS OF BASUTOLAND 511 (1965). *See* § 3.

255. Pursuant to § 13 of the Basutoland Order 1965 in the interim before Independence.

256. In Thipanyane v. R., [1926-53] H.C.T.L.R. 203, it was held that the word "court" in the Criminal Procedure and Evidence Proclamation did not include a Basotho court.

257. [1956] 4 S.A. 766, 770-1. *See also* CRAIES ON STATUTES 89 *et seq.* and 98, 99 (5TH ed.).

> It is, I imagine, indisputable that one of the cardinal rules of statutory construction is that, despite the fact that frequency of tautology or surplusage even in an Act of Parliament is by no means an uncommon phenomenon, the Legislature must normally be taken to have intended that effect should be given to every word of the language employed by it.

And Viscount Simon made a similar statement in *Hill v. William Hill (Park Lane) Ltd.*:

> When the Legislature enacts a particular phrase in a statute the presumption is that it is saying something that has not been said immediately before. The rule that a meaning should if possible be given to every word in the statute implies that, unless there is good reason to the contrary, the words add something which would not be there if the words were left out.[258]

These views were recently endorsed by the Lesotho High Court in *Molapo v. Seeiso* [259] and their application to the present problem leads to the inescapable conclusion that the jurisdiction of the Basotho courts was not intended to be based upon the races of the parties to proceedings. In addition the use of the strong words "in *all* suits, actions, or proceedings *whatsoever* in any Basuto court" supports this interpretation.

In most cases, obviously, a non-African would not be subject to customary law. However there may be numerous situations in which he could find it being applied to him even if only to a limited extent, *e.g.*, if he married a Mosotho or if he adopted a Basotho way of life, or in matters relating to the allocation of land, grazing rights, assisting at burials, and charging for ferry boat crossings.[260] His subjection to custom-

---

258. [1949] 2 All E.R. 452, 461.

259. [1963-66] H.C.T.L.R. 150, 159.

260. LAWS OF LEROTHOLI Part I, § 7; Part III, § 13; Part II, §§ 30 and 37.

ary law might be general or special and would probably be based upon the "mode of life" test discussed below.[261]

(3) APPLICATION OF CUSTOMARY LAW IN OTHER COURTS

Whereas a Basotho court can basically only administer African law and thus if it finds this inapplicable has to wash its hands of the case, the other courts have a much wider discretion since they may choose whether they administer African law or the common law. This discretion must be exercised in a judicial manner. The discretion granted to such courts by the General Law Proclamation is limited to cases where all the parties are Africans and we must first consider who an African is. The answer is given in the General Interpretation Proclamation [262]

> . . . "African" means and includes any aboriginal African belonging to any tribe of Africa, and all persons of mixed race living as members of any African community, tribe, kraal, village, or location in the Territory.

This is a wide definition covering peoples throughout the continent, but it imposes a "mode of life" test [263] on persons of mixed blood. However, the question arises whether the limitation to cases between Africans contained in the General Law Proclamation has survived independence. The Independence Order

---

261. For examples of a non-African being held to be subject to customary law, *see In re* Bethell, [1888] 38 Ch.D. 220; [1886-90] All E.R. 614 (marriage of Englishman to girl of the Barolong tribe held valid under Tswana law); Adjei & Dua v. Ripley, [1956] 1 W.A.L.R. 62 (European father must maintain his child under Gold Coast customary law).

262. Proc. 12 of 1942, § 2(17) as amended by Proc. 13 of 1954.

263. *See infra* p. 135 *et seq.*

1966 [264] saves existing laws but they are thenceforth to be construed with such modifications, adaptations, qualifications, and exceptions as may be necessary to bring them into conformity with that Order, to which is scheduled the Constitution. The Constitution in section 110(1) confers upon the High Court "unlimited original jurisdiction to hear and determine any civil or criminal proceedings under any law. . . ." and "law" is defined [265] to include the customary law. Since the High Court's jurisdiction to hear cases under customary law is specified to be unlimited it may be contended that the limitation to cases in which all the parties are Africans has been abolished. The limitation was in any event anomalous after the removal of the restriction as to the parties' race in cases before the Basotho courts in 1960, since the High Court must have had appellate jurisdiction to apply customary law on appeal from these courts in cases where the parties were of different races.

However it may be argued equally strongly that the words "under any law" in section 110(1) refer back to the General Law Proclamation itself with its limitation to cases between Africans.

There remains the difficult question of the subordinate courts. Here the racial restriction of the General Law Proclamation appears to have been left untouched by the Independence Order and therefore their original jurisdiction in applying customary law is limited to cases where all the parties are Africans save where in applying the common law, that law itself is prepared to recognise the validity of a custom as a matter of fact.[266]

It is submitted that not only the necessity for a

---

264. § 4.
265. § 139.
266. *See infra* pp. 153-154.

unified legal system but also the ambiguities and uncertainties of current laws call for immediate amending legislation.

(a) The "Mode of Life" or Environmental Test

One of the tests frequently propounded for deciding whether or not customary law should be applied to the parties in a particular case, is the "mode of life" test. The court focusses its attention on the way in which a person lives and tries to reach a conclusion that fits the law to the man. He may in this way gain either total (general) exemption from customary law or partial (special) exemption. In Mozambique and Angola, an African may be declared "assimilado" and in the Congo "immatriculé" and acquire total exemption in this manner, but this process of official declaration is impossible in Lesotho.

The "locus classicus" on the subject in South Africa is the Appellate Division decision in *Ex parte Minister of Native Affairs: In re Yako v. Beyi*.[267] The judgment, in which the other four members of the court concurred, was delivered by Schreiner J. A., presently a distinguished member of the Lesotho Court of Appeal. It is thus entitled to the greatest respect.

In South Africa, the Native Commissioner's Courts have a discretion whether or not to apply "native law" (*i.e.*, customary law) under the Native Administration Act of 1927,[268] and in *Yako v. Beyi* the relevant court had decided to apply customary law in a seduction case and held that under such law the woman seduced could not sue the man responsible, because the right of action resided in her guardian and not herself.

Schreiner J. A. first dealt with the exercise of dis-

---

267. [1948] 1 S.A. 388 (A.D.).

268. Act No. 38 of 1927, § 11(1). For early decisions under this section, *see* LEWIN, STUDIES IN AFRICAN NATIVE LAW Ch. 5 (Hortors 1947), and 58 S.A.L.J. 365 (1941).

cretion in clear-cut cases, pointing out that some cases so obviously called for the application of customary law that the commissioner would not be exercising his discretion judicially if he chose any other law. On the other hand an action arising out of a party's membership or directorship of a limited liability company patently could not be decided by rules of customary law.[269]

The learned judge then dismissed the suggestion that customary law is in any sense the primary law for cases between Africans, and therefore that resort could only be had to the common law where customary law could provide no answer. The discretion of the court should be untrammelled by any assumption as to the primacy of one system over another. This is in line with the position in Lesotho where neither system is the primary one. With regard to the procedure the commissioner should adopt, Schreiner J. A. stated:

> I think that he should only finally decide which system of law he is going to apply after considering all the evidence and argument as part of his eventual decision on the case; but it would probably be convenient in many cases for him to indicate at an earlier stage, and possibly even at the commencement of the trial, what law he would provisionally regard as applicable.[270]

It is submitted, with great respect, that this is the correct approach. Clearly much time and expense will be saved if the court indicates as early as possible the system it considers appropriate, since if the common law were chosen there would be no need to call expert witnesses to prove customary rules. However, the decision on this preliminary point is of the greatest importance, as it may determine the final result of the

---

269. *Supra* note 267, at 395.
270. *Id.* at 397.

case or at any rate the extent of the remedy granted (if any). The court would no doubt find its task much simplified if the parties in their pleadings stated the system they relied upon. The Appellate Division, however, held this was not necessary and that it was for the commissioner to decide what relief was available after he had selected the correct system of law. Nevertheless a speedy choice by a subordinate court in Lesotho would, if it decided in favour of customary law, enable it to transfer the case to a Basotho court on the basis that it could more conveniently be dealt with there.[271] This would save costs and dispense with the necessity for calling evidence to prove the customary rules.

Turning to the factors to be considered in making the choice of law, the Appellate Division held that the determination must be ". . . which system of law it would be fairest to apply in deciding the case between the parties."

The court considered that it would not necessarily be improper to apply the common law in a particular case on the ground that the parties were "educated, civilised, urbanised, or detribalised." In some actions, *e.g.*, for *injuria,* it was often only possible to do justice by taking into account the whole personality of the person injured, including his or her social and economic standards. Moreover the prevalent public opinion in the group to which he or she belonged was certainly a factor to be borne in mind in the assessment of damages.[272]

This environmental or "mode of life" test has the great virtue of attempting to tailor the type of law to the plaintiff's needs and to take account of his or her

271. Under the provisions of the Subordinate Courts Proclamation as amended, § 16(2).

272. *Supra* note 267, at 398-99.

reasonable expectations in ordering his or her affairs the way they are. However, it suffers from a grave defect if it only considers the plaintiff's position. What of the mode of life and reasonable expectations of the defendant and other persons who may be affected by the decision? Are these not legitimate factors which the court ought to take into account? Moreover it may be asked whether the plaintiff ought to be permitted to deprive another of a cause of action by unilaterally so organising his affairs that he falls under one system rather than the other. On occasion, of course, the mode of life of all relevant persons may be the same and no problem will arise.[273] But often this is not the case. The defendant may have lived under a different system.

A seduction action such as *Yako v. Beyi* affords a good illustration of the way in which a person not a party to the action may be affected. At common law the proper person to bring a seduction claim is the woman seduced, whereas in customary law, as in English law it is her parent or guardian. It may be thought unlikely that the court would make the seducer liable under both systems of law and thus the choice of law will determine which of the two can succeed, and either the woman or her parent or guardian will be deprived of a remedy she or he would have had if the other system had been chosen. Thus let us assume that an educated schoolmistress living in an urban area is seduced and under the environmental test the common law is chosen with the result that she rather than her father succeeds in her claim for damages. Her father may have acted out his entire life according to Sesotho law and custom and may have lived in the expectation of getting full *bohali* for his daughter when she marries. Suddenly he finds that the *bohali* is reduced by

273. A good example is afforded by Lembemba v. Nswima, a case from Northern Rhodesia (reported in 1958 J.A.L. 127).

the seduction and yet he is entitled to no compensation for this loss from the seducer. In this way he is effectually deprived of a right of action by his daughter's unilateral departure from a customary mode of life. Yet there appears to be nothing to prevent the daughter's snapping her traditional social links in this way and with these consequences if the mode of life test is adopted.

The next question relates to the way in which a person's mode of life is established; in other words, What are the peculiar features of a customary mode of life and a "modern" mode of life, respectively? The leading case in Lesotho is *Mokorosi v. Mokorosi*[274] which involved the application of section 3(b) of the Administration of Estates Proclamation,[275] which, after declaring that the estates of Africans are generally to continue to be governed by the customary law, provides for an exception in the case of Africans who ". . . have abandoned tribal custom and adopted a European mode of life, and who, if married, have married under European law."

The court, in considering whether the deceased came within the exception, pointed to the following features as being characteristic of the customary way of life of the Basotho: first, the supervision and control exercised by chiefs and headmen especially over land allocations and grazing rights; secondly, the marriage system with its payment of *bohali* and the recognition of separate "houses" in cases of polygamy; thirdly, the rights of succession which depend upon the position of the children in the different "houses" and whereby the property goes to the eldest son who has obligations to others in his "house"; fourthly, the state of perpetual tutelage of a woman under the male

---

274. Civil Trial No. 4 of 1955 (unreported).
275. Proc. 19 of 1935.

head of her family (though there had been a limited degree of emancipation under the influence of Christianity);[276] fifthly, the pastoral and agricultural life based upon the land, as opposed to life in towns based upon employment in commerce or industry.

In the particular case, the deceased was found to have abandoned the customary mode of life and adopted a European one because of a variety of considerations. First, the deceased had not followed the customary marriage system. He was himself married in a Protestant Church and his children were similarly married according to Christian rites. In no case was *bohali* paid or received. He ate and slept with his family in a European way. Secondly, he worked in a shop and later carried on various businesses of his own, including a café and a butchery. He wore European clothes and he owned a motor truck. He lived in a reserve and had no grazing or ploughing rights. He loaned out his cattle to others. Thirdly, he had belonged to a Protestant Church and none of his sons or daughters had been to initiation school. Fourthly, he was in the habit of consulting a firm of attorneys and they assisted him in relation to his business affairs and in drafting his will.

The court explained that even though by living in the reserve the deceased owed allegiance to the Paramount Chief, it still was not an indication that he followed a customary mode of life since every Mosotho owed this allegiance. Nor was payment of basic tax through a headman such an indication because the tax was levied upon all adult male Africans, and the chiefs and headmen were the authorised collectors of this tax.

In the recent case of *Hoohlo v. Hoohlo*,[277] which

276. *See* the Regency Case, *supra* note 208.

277. Civil Application No. 38 of 1968 (unreported).

also involved the application of the proviso in the Administration of Estates Proclamation, the High Court referred to two additional factors that did not arise in *Mokorosi v. Mokorosi* which tended to show the adoption of a European mode of life. First the making of a will in which the dispositions did not reflect the customary rules of inheritance, and secondly the fact that the deceased had taken out three life insurance policies.

One of the most difficult questions in this area of the choice of law is to assess the legal consequences of a partial abandonment or adoption of a mode of life. For example, what is the effect of contracting a marriage in terms of the Marriage Proclamation [278] in lieu of a customary law marriage? It would seem that this will at the most affect the status of a man and his family. Thus the common law or statute will govern questions of the status of the spouses,[279] divorce,[280] nullity, judicial separation,[281] restitution of conjugal rights, adultery,[282] bigamy,[283] and the legitimacy of

---

278. Proc. 7 of 1911.

279. *See* Nko v. Nko (Civil Trial No. 3 of 1968—unreported).

280. *Id., also see* Nthunya v. Nthunya (Civil Trial No. 34 of 1968—unreported).

281. *See* Rakhoabe v. Rakhoabe (1969—unreported).

282. It has been held both in South Africa and in Southern Rhodesia that the law to be applied should be that under which the marriage was contracted. *See* Mdodana v. Nokulele [1911] 2 N A.C. 138; Mtshengu v. Mawengu [1954] N.A.C. 172 (S); Thomas v. Josiah [1959] S.R.N. 655. *See also* the Ghanaian case of Ackah v. Arinta [1893] Sar. F.L.R. 79 cited in ALLOTT, *supra* note 7, at 221. However it was held in the Ugandan case of Ibrahim s/o Alimasi v. John s/o Adraa (Civil Revision No. 3 of 1963) (reported in 1964 J.A.L. 46) that a man married under the Marriage Ordinance could sue under customary law someone who had committed adultery with his wife.

283. *I.e.*, a man cannot contract another civil marriage during the subsistence of the first. *See supra* p. 66.

the children [284] as they are intimately bound up with the marriage and its resulting rights. On the other hand the spouses could still fall under customary law in other matters, *e.g.*, those relating to the marital property regime,[285] succession,[286] *bohali* contracts,[287]

---

284. But marrying under the Proclamation will not have the effect of legitimating children born previously out of wedlock according to the decision in Mosoang v. Mosoang, J.C. 234/1966/32/1967 where customary law was held applicable. The Judicial Commissioner's judgment contained the following statement:

> The marriage was both customary and civil. The fact of a civil marriage does not make a person join the customs of a different people except in regard to dissolution of that marriage and the mutual obligations of the husband and wife are different in a civil marriage, but I do not believe it follows that a child born illegitimately 8 years before the natural parents marry is automatically legitimated according to Sesotho custom.

With respect, it is submitted that the court's reasoning is confused and that no attempt was made to determine which system of law should govern the legitimation question. *See also* Bamgbose v. Daniel, [1954] 3 All E.R. 263.

285. *See* Khatala v. Khatala, [1963-66] H.C.T.L.R. 97 (C.A.); *but cf.* Rakhoabe v. Rakhoabe, (C.A.) Civil Appeal No. 5 of 1969 (unreported).

286. *See* Khatala v. Khatala *Id.* The contracting of a civil marriage will not preclude a spouse from making a will under customary law—*see* Shang v. Coleman (*infra* note 292). Sesotho customary law has long recognised testamentary dispositions—*see* Laws of Lerotholi § 14(1) of Part I and DUNCAN, *supra* note 189, at 18. *See also* Mokorosi v. Mokorosi, [1954] H.C.T.L.R. 24.

287. Support for this view is found in § 8 of the Central and Local Courts Proclamation which provides that these courts shall have no jurisdiction to hear "cases in connection with marriage other than a marriage contracted under or in accordance with native law and custom, except where and insofar as the case concerns the payment or return or disposal of dowry." The section clearly contemplates the courts' hearing *bohali* cases connected with civil marriages and since the courts only have jurisdiction to apply the customary law, the inevitable

most delicts,[288] and commercial contracts.

This important point was recognised as far back as 1924 in the West African case of *Smith v. Smith* [289] where Van der Meulen J. declared:

> It would be quite incorrect to say that all the persons who embrace the Christian faith, or who are married in accordance with its tenets, have in other respects obtained the stage of culture and development as to make it just or reasonable to suppose that their whole lives should be regulated in accordance with English laws and standards. Any such general proposition would in my opinion be no less unjust in its operation and effects than the converse proposition . . . that because a man is a native the devolution of his property must be regulated in accordance with native law and custom, irrespective of his education and general position in life. The fact that a man has contracted a marriage in accordance with the rites of the Christian Church may be very strong evidence of his desire and intention to have his life generally regulated by English laws and customs, but it is by no means conclusive evidence.

The recent Lesotho case of *Khatala v. Khatala* [290]

---

conclusion is that one system of law may be applied to the marriage and other to the *bohali.*

Further support for this view is afforded by the case of Mokhesuoe v. Moiloa, J.C. 10/1967/100/1967 where the wife was found to be pregnant on her arrival at her husband's home. The husband told his father not to pay the *bohali.* The court held that as the parties had married by civil rights, any question of divorce was a matter for the High Court; the Basotho courts however would have power to deal with the repayment of *bohali* if a divorce were granted, but in the meanwhile the *bohali* must be paid.

The dichotomy of marriage and *bohali* may also be considered in terms of a composite decision—*see infra* pp. 150-153.

288. Thus a husband will still be liable for his wife's delicts—*see* Sekoboto v. Possa, J.C. 74/1964.

289. [1924] 5 N.L.R. 105.

290. *Supra* note 285.

on intestate succession bears this out. The deceased married his first wife both under customary law and under the provisions of the Marriage Proclamation, and by her he had one son, the appellant. After his first wife's death the deceased had married the respondent, similarly both under the provisions of the Marriage Proclamation and under customary law. The dispute concerned the inheritance of certain of his property on his death. The respondent based her claim on the fact that she was married to the deceased in community of property, while the appellant claimed to be the deceased's heir. The deceased and the respondent had continued to live according to Sesotho law and custom during their marriage. The court accordingly held that upon the deceased's death, the disputed property devolved upon his heir (the appellant) according to customary law, and did not pass to his widow (the respondent) under the common law. The respondent's contention that she was entitled to half the deceased's property because the marriage was in community of property was rejected. The Court of Appeal held:

> In the absence of express provision to that effect, there is no good reason for holding that all marriages under the provisions of the Marriage Proclamation carry the consequences of a marriage governed by Roman-Dutch Law. It is unnecessary to express a view on whether all marriages by Basutos in Basutoland have identical proprietary consequences; it is enough to say that where, as here, Basutos living "according to the Basuto custom" marry according to Basuto rites as well as according to Christian rites, their proprietary relations during their joint lives and their intestate succession rights after the death of one of them are governed by Basuto law.[291]

It is clear that merely marrying under the Marriage Proclamation does not have conclusive propri-

---

291. *Id.* at 100.

etary consequences, and it is submitted that the decision would not have been different if this had been the only form of marriage entered into by the spouses.

A similar conclusion was reached by the Court of Appeal of Ghana in the case of *Shang v. Coleman*[292] in 1959. Spouses were married under the Ghanaian Marriage Ordinance[293] but continued to live according to customary law. The court held that a person subject to the customary law who marries under the Ordinance does not cease to be subject to customary law merely by reason of his marriage. The customary law would still be applied to him except in matters specifically excluded by the statute and those which were necessary consequences of marrying under the Ordinance.

The matters in which the customary law would not apply were considered by the court to be bigamy, divorce, and the legitimacy of the children. However customary law would still apply to the husband if, *e.g.*, he committed adultery with the wife of another person married under customary law. The court also held *obiter* that the right to make a will was unaffected by the form of marriage entered into and that therefore a person subject to customary law, though married under the Marriage Ordinance could make a valid customary nuncupative will *(Samansew)*.[294]

To take another example, if the parties to a commercial contract were civil servants working in Maseru there would be a very strong presumption that the common law would govern the contract.[295] But this

---

292. Civil appeal No. 41/59 reported in 1960 J.A.L. 160. The decision was affirmed on appeal to the Privy Council; *see* Coleman v. Shang, [1961] 2 All E.R. 406 (P.C.) although the Board did not deal with the particular features of the judgment of the Court of Appeal mentioned here.

293. Ch. 127 (1951 revision of the Laws).

294. Thus overruling *Re* Otoo, [1927] D. Ct. 1926-1929, 84.

295. Thus in Bakare v. Coker, [1934] 12 Nig. L.R. 31 where

would not prevent their marrying under customary law and regulating matters of status and succession according to African law. We can, in these examples, either say that the parties had partially changed their mode of life and thus effected a partial exemption from the application of customary law, or that the choice of law depended on the nature of the issue which fell to be adjudicated.

(b) The "Remedy" Test

A second test put forward as a guide to the choice of law a court should make asks which system provides a remedy. On this basis if only one of the systems grants the plaintiff his claim, this system should be applied. It will be readily appreciated that this test inevitably gives a great advantage to the plaintiff, and may be unsatisfactory for this reason. It suffers in this respect from the same defect as the mode of life test above.

However as the court pointed out in *Yako v. Beyi,* there is no objection to a plaintiff trying to persuade the court to adopt the system which affords a remedy, for he is after all only asking that the court's discretion be exercised in favour of selecting what he regards as the correct legal system to govern the case.[296]

However, Schreiner J. A. recognised the competing claims of a defendant to a fair exercise of the

---

one Nigerian had given the other a signed and stamped promissory note the court held they had evinced an unmistakable intention that the transaction should be governed by the common law. The presumption that the common law was to apply would be almost irrebuttable if the parties expressly stated that it was to govern their contract. The commercial relationship of the parties and the urban environment were considered very important factors in the choice of law in Lembemba v. Nswima (Northern Rhodesia, 1958) *supra* note 273.

296. *See supra* note 267, at 397-98.

court's discretion, and he went on to develop this important point as follows:

> It is, however, right I think, to point out that it would not necessarily and in all cases lead to a juster result to apply the system of law which alone gives the plaintiff a remedy or which gives him or her the more adequate remedy. Generally, no doubt, if a remedy exists under one of the two systems but not under the other, this would be a reason for applying the former, since the existence of a remedy especially under a more advanced system of law itself provides some ground for believing that its general application would be in the interests of justice. But in some cases it may seem preferable to give effect to a defence that the defendant has under the one system and not under the other.[297]

This passage exposes both the advantage and the disadvantage of applying this test. The selection of the system providing the remedy would thus appear to be entirely arbitrary and unjustified, and place the defendant in an intolerable position.

So far we have been considering this test where both systems of law have rules applicable to the point at issue. The test may not be so unfair where one system has never considered the matter. Thus it is arguable that customary law should be applied in matters of chieftainship, while the common law should be chosen for cases concerned with limited liability companies and negotiable instruments. An election on this basis may alternatively be considered as part of the environmental test, since a person who becomes involved in matters of companies or negotiable instruments must impliedly expect to have his affairs with respect to these matters regulated by the common law,

---

297. *Id.* at 399-400; *see also* Umvovu v. Umvovu, [1953] 3 S.A. 195 (A.D.), at 201.

and conversely he could not possibly anticipate that chieftainship affairs could be similarly governed. It is, in a sense, a situation of partial subjection to one system or the other, as outlined above. Another way of looking at it is to say that the choice depends upon the nature of the transaction (see *infra*). However it is a mistake to assume that all mercantile transactions should be governed by the common law since customary law certainly recognises certain contracts of sale, barter, loan, and agency as well as the specialised *bohali* contract.

In the field of delict the rules of the common law and the customary law are often found to be similar, and the problem of choice is not so acute. However an example of a case where the common law was applied on the basis of being the system that afforded a remedy is the decision in *Nyovane v. Murungwana* [298] from Southern Rhodesia. The appellant had assaulted the respondent at a beer party and had broken his jaw. The court found that whereas both systems recognised liability for personal injury in much the same way, customary law provided no standard or method for calculating the damages to be awarded. The court therefore applied the common law both to the question of liability and to the measure of damages. It is submitted that but for the actual wording of the relevant statute [299] the court might easily have given a "composite decision" (see *infra*) and applied customary law to the question of liability and the common law to the damages aspect.

---

298. [1956-7] 4 S.R.N. 1.

299. The Native Law and Courts Act (ch. 73), now replaced by the African Law and Courts Act (ch. 104) states in § 3 that if African law and custom is "inapplicable to the cause or matter before the court" then the common law must be applied. This may mean that one system or the other must be applied to cover the whole case.

(c) The Test of the Nature of the Transaction

This method of deciding the choice of law question has been adverted to earlier, but it appears peculiarly applicable to the problem of prescription of actions.[300] The customary law rule is that there is no bar, for a debt never dies. The common law rule is that the limitation period varies from one to thirty years depending upon the cause of action. On top of this the Cape Prescription Act [301] is still in force in Lesotho and this imposes shorter periods of limitation, again depending on the particular type of action instituted. The customary rule has always been applied to suits for the payment of *bohali* and in *Majake v. Litjamela* [302] the Judicial Commissioner's Court stated:

> It is admitted that in dowry claims no prescription applies according to custom but the burden of proof increases with the passing of time.

Earlier in *Ntjeke v. Ranthiba* [303] the same court declared:

> [T]his court knows of no legislative or customary authority for such procedural bar to claiming debt. "Debt does not rot" is still applicable and prescription is still foreign to Sesuto custom.

It is submitted that these are correct decisions and should be applied in the superior courts too when a choice of law is to be made in relation to a *bohali* debt.

In some actions at customary law, *e.g.*, for damages for abduction [304] it has been held that the customary rule is contrary to justice and this approach is considered below.[305]

---

300. The distinction is not appreciated by Duncan, *supra* note 189, at 114-15.

301. Act 6 of 1861.

302. J.C. 4/1963.

303. J.C. 61/1959.

304. Pulenyane v. Matela, J.C. 242/1959.

305. *See infra* p. 162.

However, actions that arise out of commercial transactions clearly governed by the common law should, it is submitted, attract the common law rule of prescription. In practice many of them will be governed by the periods of limitation laid down in the Prescription Act.

(4) THE ROLE OF PRECEDENT IN CHOICE OF LAW

This very difficult question of choice of law may become easier when a body of case law has grown up on the way in which the judicial discretion should be exercised.[306] However, it is likely to be a long time before precedents will solve this problem.

(5) COMPOSITE DECISIONS

Finally we should consider to what extent, if at all, it is possible for a court to decide to apply a mixture of customary and common law in the same case. The old view was that the systems were entirely separate and should be kept well apart.[307] However, great developments have been taking place since then and there are decisions from various parts of Africa that reflect the desire of the courts to integrate the dual systems they operate. A spark has thus been lit which may assist in the eventual fusion of the laws. In the Nigerian case of *Balogun v. Balogun* [308] a wealthy businessman left money by his will to trustees upon trust (an English legal concept) to hold it and pay it out in accordance with certain native laws and customs. The West African Court of Appeal construed the will in such a way that English law was applied to give effect to the operation of the trust but customary law

---

306. This point was adverted to in Yako v. Beyi, *supra* note 267, at 400-01.

307. *See, e.g., Re* Williams, [1941] W.A.C.A. 156; Labinjoh v. Abake, [1924] 5 N.L.R. 33.

308. [1935] 2 W.A.C.A. 290.

was applied in its beneficial distribution. To have applied English law to the latter question would have had a different effect, out of keeping with the circumstances of the case.

In another Nigerian decision *Bamgbose v. Daniel,*[309] the Privy Council interpreted the English Statute of Distribution[310] which governed Nigerian intestate succession in that case, so as to include as legitimate those children of the deceased who were legitimate by native law and custom, in spite of the fact that they were issue of polygamous unions. Thus the English statute was restricted to governing the order of distribution, whereas customary law was permitted to determine which children were legitimate within the meaning of the statute.

In a South African case[311] concerned with divorce on the grounds of malicious desertion under the common law, the court held that failure by the husband to pay *lobolo* justified the wife in deserting him. (*Lobolo* is the Zulu and Xhosa equivalent of the Sesotho *bohali.*) While the payment of *lobolo* is essential to a customary union, it is optional under common law; but the court felt able to mix the two systems to reach a fair result.

It would, on this sort of basis, seem possible for a court to decide a question of the custody of a child under the common law by applying the principle that the paramount consideration is the welfare of the child, and yet interpret the meaning of welfare in the context of customary law. In *Yako v. Beyi*[312] the Appellate Division mentioned the usefulness of composite

---

309. [1954] 3 All E. R. 263. For a discussion of the decision and of the law of legitimacy in Nigeria *see* Nwogugu (1964) J.A.L. 91.

310. Statute of Distribution 1670 (22 & 23 Car. 2, c. 10).

311. Mbani v. Mbani, [1939] N.A.C. (C. & O.) 91.

312. *See supra* note 267, at 400.

decisions in connection with the possibility of allowing both the woman and her guardian to recover in full in a seduction case, each under the legal system that favoured his or her case.

The recognition that rules from both systems can be fused in a single decision is implicit in the recent judgment of the Lesotho Court of Appeal in *Khatala v. Khatala*,[313] mentioned above. This was a dispute (which went to five appeals) between the deceased's son by his first wife, and his second wife, as to who was entitled to inherit his Post Office savings account of £300. The problem was finally resolved in favour of the son by the application of customary law in the form of the relevant section of the *Laws of Lerotholi*.[314] However whereas customary law was applied to determine the succession question, it was implicit in the court's judgment that the legal mechanism for dealing with the money was governed by the common law. Thus the court ordered the second wife to deliver the Post Office savings bank book to the son and to take all necessary steps to complete his title thereto. Thus the cession of a debt with its attendant formality of the delivery of the document evidencing the debt was being decreed.[315]

Another example of a composite decision is the dissenting opinion of Schreiner J. A. in the case of *Fraenkel N.O. v. Sechele*.[316] He considered that Chief Kgari Sechele's will was valid and that its dispositions should take effect according to the law of the Bechuanaland Protectorate (as it then was), but that the appointment of an executor was invalid and therefore the will should be administered by senior members of the deceased's family, according to customary law.

---

313. *Supra* note 285; *see supra* pp. 143-144.
314. Part. I, § 11.
315. *See* Smith v. Farrelly's Trustee, [1904] T.S. 949, 956.
316. [1964-65] Bech. L.R. 5 (C.A.).

It should be noted that although there is a productive intermingling of the dual systems in the above examples of composite decisions, this is usually only permissible where the issues can be kept distinct. The courts, in using their discretion, do not however possess *carte blanche* to create new legal principles comprised of the better qualities of each of the present systems.

Nevertheless it would inevitably be beneficial for the law to be unified as soon as this is practically possible, and this topic is discussed below.

(6) THE APPLICATION OF CUSTOMARY LAW UNDER COMMON LAW RULES

From the discussion earlier [317] of the application of customary law in the non-Basotho courts, it emerged that the subordinate courts only had jurisdiction under the General Law Proclamation and under any other statute to apply customary law in cases in which all the parties were Africans. Where this is not the position, they are limited to applying the common law and statutes. However, to the extent to which the common law *itself* recognises custom as a source of law they will be able to apply customary law in such cases. The requirements at common law for the validity of a local custom were laid down in *van Breda v. Jacobs*.[318] The custom must be ancient or long established; it must have been uniformly observed; it must be reasonable; and it must be certain.

Support for the application of customary law in this indirect manner is to be found in the judgment of Schreiner J. A. in *Yako v. Beyi*,[319] where he stated that if native commissioners' courts were not given

317. *Supra* p. 134.

318. [1921] A.D. 330, and *see* VOET 1.3.27-31.

319. *Supra* note 267, at 394.

specific power to decide cases in accordance with customary law:

> [T]he law they would have to apply would be the general law of the land. Native customs would then be provable and would have effect according to the principles generally applicable to customs (*see van Breda v. Jacobs . . .*).

This method of proving a point of customary law as fact is, as has been pointed out earlier, very different from establishing it as a matter of law.

D. The Validity of Customary Law in the Basotho Courts

It will be recalled that the Central and Local Courts are to administer *inter alia*

> . . . the native law and custom prevailing in the territory, so far as it is not repugnant to justice or morality or inconsistent with the provisions of any law in force in the Territory.[320]

This proviso gives two reasons why a customary rule may not be applied, but to a large extent rules that might in the past have been caught in the meshes of the first now find themselves constricted by the net of the second, since customs that are considered "repugnant" have normally been abolished by legislation and are therefore now inconsistent. Thus the practice of witchcraft and divination has been outlawed by the Medicine Men and Herbalists Proclamation.[321] Moreover the custom whereby a girl could be forced

---

320. Central and Local Courts Proclamation, § 9.

321. Proc. 44 of 1938 as amended. In 1855 Moshesh had promulgated a law against witchcraft, making it the offense of murder to kill upon the word of a wizard and thus rendering the practices of "smelling out" and "eating up" subject to the death penalty; *see* HAILEY, NATIVE ADMINISTRATION IN THE BRITISH AFRICAN TERRITORIES Pt. V., 46 (H.M.S.O. 1953).

to marry against her wishes[322] has also been rendered unlawful.[323] Thus in the future it is likely that only customs of which the legislature was unaware will be rejected for repugnancy. In reality, moreover, some rules are rejected by the courts on the ground that it would be inequitable to apply the custom to a particular person.[324]

We will now examine the interpretation to be given to the expressions used. The word "prevailing" has been held by a Nigerian court interpreting a similar clause to mean "dominant."[325] This is clearly correct and the customary law that predominates in Lesotho is, of course, Sesotho law and custom.

The other expressions need more lengthy treatment.

(1) "SO FAR AS IT IS NOT REPUGNANT TO JUSTICE OR MORALITY"

This expression or a similar one, "repugnant to natural justice, equity, and good conscience," is to be found in statutes[326] throughout the continent, and courts have been called upon to consider them in a variety of cases. One of the earliest interpretations, which will serve as a starting point, is that of Wilson J. in the Tanganyika case of *Gwao bin Kilimo v.*

---

322. George Moshesh in giving evidence to the 1872 Commission said, "It does sometimes happen that parents compel their daughters to marry men against their wishes by beating them, etc., but this happens very seldom." REPORT AND EVIDENCE 40.

323. The Marriage Proclamation provides in § 2, "It shall not be lawful for any person to compel any woman to enter into a contract of marriage or to marry against her wish."

324. *See, e.g.*, Cole v. Cole, [1898] 1 N.L.R. 15, and Koykoy Jatta v. Menua Camara reported 1964 J.A.L. 35.

325. R. v. Ilorin Native Court ex parte Aremu, [1953] 20 N.L.R. 144.

326. *See, e.g.*, the High Court Laws of Nigeria appendixed in PARK, *supra* note 7, at 149-151.

Kisunda bin Ifuti.[327] He had to decide whether an attachment of the cattle of the judgment debtor's father, rather than an execution upon the property of the debtor himself was to be upheld, a practice apparently permitted under customary law. He stated:

> But on the other question—as to whether the application of the "law" in question to the present case would be "repugnant to justice and morality" —I hold more positive views, though I am far from unmindful of the difficulty of construing the meaning of that phrase. Morality and justice are abstract conceptions and every community probably has an absolute standard of its own by which to decide what is justice and what is morality. But unfortunately, the standards of different communities are by no means the same. To what standard, then, does the Order in Council[328] refer—the African standard of justice and morality or the British standard? I have no doubt whatever that the only standard of justice and morality which a British court in Africa can apply is its own British standard. Otherwise we should find ourselves in certain circumstances having to condone such things for example, as the institution of slavery. . . .
>
> Is it just according to our ideas to take away a man's property in order to compensate a party who has suffered injury at the hands of the man's son, the son being of full age and fully responsible in law for his own actions? I hold most strongly the opinion that it is not just.

The passage has a certain colonial ring about it which may sound arrogant to modern ears and it may betray a failure to understand the rules of the family property regime in question and their significance within the particular society. However, it brings out clearly the historical fact that the common law (whether English or Roman-Dutch) is the imposed

327. [1938] 1 T.L.R. (R.) 403.

328. Tanganyika Order in Council, 1920, Art. 24.

system, tolerating customary law only on its own terms wherever the repugnancy clause is used. The colonial viewpoint was the one adopted,[329] and therefore to retain the clause after independence is to perpetuate a complete anachronism. It is difficult to imagine many customary rules regarded as immoral by those who live by them. However, while the clause is retained it calls for examination. In origin it reflects the desire of the Imperial power to retain certain fundamental ideas about justice. Some principles are considered so important by the common law that the term "natural justice" [330] has been coined to make the point that these are felt to arise from the *jus naturale*, a law common to all people everywhere. This is probably the correct meaning to be given to the word "justice" in the repugnancy clause, but it is a misapprehension to think of natural justice in terms of a universal concept.

The two cardinal principles of "natural justice" are firstly, that no man should be a judge in his own cause and, secondly, that no party ought to be condemned unheard. Accused persons must be given an

---

329. "Morality and justice must of course mean British and not African conceptions of these. Were that not so British justice would be looking in two different directions at once. . . . I have sometimes been asked . . . 'How do you justify the application of English principles of justice to so many different peoples, whose outlook and mentality vary so much from our own, especially when English ideas pass their understanding?' . . . We believe that these ideas are the best that can regulate our administration of justice, and an Englishman because he is an Englishman and not someone quite different, cannot adopt other persons' conception of justice"—Sir Sidney Abrahams' *The Colonial Legal Service and the Administration of Justice in the Colonial Dependencies* (1948) 30 J.C.L.I.L. 1, at 8 and 11.

330. For discussion of natural justice see WADE, ADMINISTRATIVE LAW Ch. V (O.U.P. 1961); ROSE-INNES, JUDICIAL REVIEW OF ADMINISTRATIVE TRIBUNALS IN S. AFRICA 144 *et seq.* (Juta 1963).

opportunity to present their arguments [331] and for this right to be effective they must know the cases against them and have a reasonable time to prepare a rebuttal.[332]

These two principles relate largely to the administration of the law, and violations of them are outlawed (if ever this was the practise) by the making of the Basuto Courts (Practise and Procedure) Rules.[333] These rules have to a great extent swept away traditional procedure and replaced it with much the same patterns as are used in the subordinate courts.

Turning to questions of morality, what rules of customary law are likely to be found repugnant by the Lesotho courts? The matter was discussed by the High Court in *Malofotsane v. Mpho.*[334] This was a dispute as to the devolution of the deceased's estate and the appellant based her claim upon the fact that she was a child of the first house through a practise permitted by Sesotho law. The deceased had arranged a marriage between the appellant's mother and the still-born child of his first wife, and then appointed his nephew to raise up seed to provide an heir for the first house.

The court, relying on a prohibition contained in the *Laws of Lerotholi,*[335] found that this practice did not in fact accord with Sesotho law, but Elyan C. J. went on to say that he and his assessors regarded such a marriage entered into with a still-born child as

---

331. In Guri v. Hadejia Native Authority, [1959] 4 F.S.C. 44 (Nigeria), a rule of Maliki law that prevented persons accused of highway robbery from defending themselves was declared invalid.

332. For West African cases *see* DANIELS, *supra* note 134, at 274-79.

333. G.N. No. 21 of 1961.

334. [1959] H.C.T.L.R. 107.

335. Part II, § 34(3).

repugnant to morality. The appellant had contended that even if such repugnancy existed at the time of the hearing, it did not necessarily follow that it existed at the time of the marriage. Elyan C. J. dealt with this point by stating:

> The determination of what is repugnant to morality — (rules it may be said very briefly, which though not positive law, regulate the conduct, of groups of human beings and relating—*inter alia*—to moral behaviour) necessarily varies from time to time, with the principles which for the time being inform public opinion. To invite this court to take the view that the test of such repugnancy should relate back to the time of the marriage in question is to invite the court to enforce a claim founded upon a transaction which the Court and the Assessors view as being repugnant to morality judged by present day standards, whatever may have been the view in the past. In my opinion, as to this, it suffices if the marriage in question is repugnant to morality as judged by present day standards in Basutoland for such marriages to be in conflict as aforesaid. And that it is so repugnant is the view of the Court and the Assessors.[336]

West African courts have often found rules based on slavery repugnant to morality,[337] but these can have no application for Lesotho, where slavery has never been recognised. And in recent cases in the Lesotho and Gambian courts, forcible circumcision of a girl under customary law has been held repugnant. In the Gambian case [338] the customary law of one tribe was being imposed on a child of another tribe, and the court was not prepared to enforce it. In the Lesotho case [339] it was being imposed as a reprisal for peeping

336. *Supra* note 334, at 109.

337. *See Re* Effiong Okon Ata, [1930] 10 N.L.R. 65, and Kodich v. Affram, [1930] 1 W.A.C.A. 12. *See also* DANIELS, *supra* note 134, at 272-73.

338. Koykoy Jatta v. Menua Camara, *supra* at note 324.

339. Mothobi Maele v. R., [1963-66] H.C.T.L.R. 218.

at a circumcision school. Again the court was not prepared to countenance it.

Also the courts have often spoken out against practises relating to the guardianship of children which they found offensive.[340] The principle that the welfare of the child is the paramount consideration has tended to become the court's guiding light.

In the Southern Rhodesian case of *Tabitha Chiduku v. Chidano* [341] it was stated by Tredgold C. J. that the repugnancy clause should only operate to invalidate "such customs as inherently impress us with some abhorrence or are obviously immoral in their incidence." It is not enough that they merely would not meet with the approval of many members of non-African societies. Thus the Privy Council in the Nigerian appeal of *Dawodu v. Danmole* [342] has recently warned:

> [T]he principles of natural justice, equity, and good conscience applicable in a country where polygamy is generally accepted should not be readily equated with those applicable to a community governed by a rule of monogamy.

Similarly in a recent English decision [343] recognising the validity of a polygamous marriage between Nigerian Muslims contracted in Nigeria, the court found there was nothing repugnant about a girl of thirteen marrying a man of 35 under that law, however the average Englishman might view it in terms of his own society.

---

340. *See, e.g.*, in South Africa Nowamba v. Nomabetshe, [1906] N.A.C. 36, (an agreement to supply *lobolo* on the condition that the issue of the marriage should belong to the supplier of *lobolo*).

341. [1922] S.R. 55.

342. [1962] 1 W.L.R. 1053, 1060.

343. Mohamed v. Knott, [1968] 2 All E.R. 563.

It appears that no set formula can be, or even ought to be, worked out for deciding when a court should reject customary law on grounds of repugnancy. Morality, as Elyan C. J. pointed out above, changes. Increasingly, too, the judiciary will be composed of Africans who will be able to approach customs with a greater insight than is possible for non-African judges. However, one should perhaps plead that until such changes in staffing come about, customs that might look repugnant at first sight should be examined extremely closely before they are rejected, and preferably through the eyes of right-minded members of the society and not subjectively.[344] In this matter, of course, assessors can play a vital role in explaining the background and function of the custom. Two decisions of the Judicial Commissioner's Court in Lesotho call for particular mention on this score.

In *Nako v. Nako*[345] it was contended by the respondent that she was entitled to the appellant's earnings since she was the head of his family and he was still unmarried. According to Sesotho law, a man is a minor until he marries. However the court found the respondent's claim repugnant since the appellant was a man of 30 years of age.

And in *Khabele v. Khabele*[346] the court held that the rule that a *seantlo* wife should take precedence over one married to her husband before she was, could not be enforced on grounds of repugnancy. A *seantlo* wife is one who takes the place of her deceased sister as a man's wife, often because there is no issue of the first house.

In issue in these two cases were customs deeply

---

344. *See* DANIELS, *supra* note 134, at 284-85.
345. J.C. 141/1949.
346. J.C. 319/1948.

ingrained in Basotho society, both in the field of family law. One of the reasons why the head of a family is entitled to property acquired by a minor son is that the head of the family is bound to pay *bohali* for that son's first wife. Upon marriage, and only then, does he attain majority. The practice is an entirely rational one and there is no immorality attached to it.[347]

The second custom—that of *seantlo*—again has a rational basis in the context of Basotho society. One of the purposes of paying *bohali* on marriage is to obtain for the husband's family the reproductive powers of his wife. If she dies early, a younger sister relation may be substituted, sometimes for half the original number of cattle. Since the new wife is stepping into the shoes of her deceased sister and taking over the upbringing of any children already born, it is natural she should take the precedence her relative had among the wives. It is a well-known custom and subsequent wives marry on these terms.[348]

It is submitted that these decisions constitute an erroneous application of the repugnancy clause. In addition, the same court has on two occasions [349] expressed the view that the customary rule "Molato ha o bole" (a debt never rots or dies) is repugnant to justice. It is hard to see why this should be the case, and in any event the Judicial Commissioner's Court has in other cases applied the customary rule.[350]

---

347. *See further* Chaule v. Makae, J.C. 166/1963 and p. 202 *infra*.

348. For criticism of the decision in Khabele's case *see* DUNCAN, *supra* note 189, at 33.

349. Pulenyane v. Matela, J.C. 242/1954; Seakhi v. Seakhi, J.C. 509/1953, *and see infra* p. 202.

350. Ntjeke v. Ranthiba, J.C. 61/1959; Mojake v. Litjamela, J.C. 4/1963—discussed *supra* p. 149.

On those rare occasions when a court is confronted with a customary rule that it finds repugnant, the court can only reject it outright and refuse to recognise and enforce rights under it. There is no power to modify the custom so that its repugnant features are struck out. As Lord Atkin said in the Nigerian appeal of *Eleko v. Government of Nigeria*: [351]

> The Court cannot itself transform a barbarous custom into a milder one. If it still stands in its barbarous character it must be rejected as repugnant to "natural justice, equity, and good conscience."

However this is not to say that distinct parts of a customary rule may not be severed one from the other, rejecting the repugnant part and enforcing the acceptable part. On the analogy of the severance of illegal provisions in a contract,[352] there would have to be separate and divisible portions that could stand alone. To revert to the custom of *kenela*, which, as we have already seen,[353] is dying out in Lesotho, it might have been possible in the past to reject as repugnant any rule that the widow must cohabit with her late husband's junior brother, while enforcing the rule that she and her children should come under his guardianship and that he should become controller and administrator of their property.[354]

It remains under this heading to point out the slightly anomalous position that is created by the in-

---

351. [1931] A.C. 662, 673.

352. *See, e.g.*, Empire Theatres Co. Ltd. v. Lamor, [1910] W.L.D. 289; Goodinson v. Goodinson, [1954] 2 Q.B. 118; [1954] 2 All E.R. 255; Bennett v. Bennett, [1952] 1 All E.R. 413.

353. *Supra* p. 117.

354. The question of whether *kenela* should be recognised in S. Africa was discussed in Mcunukelwa v. Mcunukelwa, 5 N.A.C. 168.

sertion of the repugnancy clause in the Central and Local Courts Proclamation. These courts are the ones directed to administer customary law so far as it is not repugnant. However they themselves have no criteria by which to judge such repugnancy. Their familiarity with the law is limited exclusively to customary law. The subordinate courts, the Judicial Commissioner's Court and the High Court, in the exercise of their original jurisdiction, may administer customary law without any restriction on the question of repugnancy. They do, however, have a discretion in the matter and it is arguable that it may justifiably be used to reject a repugnant rule. It is, we suppose, in the exercise of their appellate or review jurisdiction that the true impact of the repugnancy provision may be felt. For they are able to reject a repugnant rule on the basis that the central court was exceeding its jurisdiction in applying it. Presumably such rejection, if communicated to the Basotho courts would generally have the effect of prohibiting them from applying the repugnant rule in the future.

(2) "OR INCONSISTENT WITH THE PROVISIONS OF ANY LAW IN FORCE IN THE TERRITORY"

This clause presents difficulties of interpretation which have not received any consideration by the courts of Lesotho, and there is scant reported judicial construction of similar clauses to be found in comparable legislation in other parts of Africa.[355]

The first problem relates to the meaning of the word "law." This cannot include customary law although that is part of the general law in force in

---

355. The problem is discussed by ALLOTT, *supra* note 7, at 195-97; and KEAY AND RICHARDSON, THE NATIVE AND CUSTOMARY COURTS OF NIGERIA 238-245 (Sweet & Maxwell 1966).

Lesotho, since such law cannot be inconsistent with itself. But does it include the common law or relate only to statutes? If it covers the former, grave difficulties arise. Does this mean to say that whenever a customary rule is not in accord with the common law that the former is excluded? If this were the case, the majority of customary law would be inapplicable in the Basotho courts. This, however, clearly could not have been the intention of the legislature, nor is it borne out by the day-to-day activities of such courts.

The second problem relates to the exact meaning to be attributed to the word "inconsistent." Perhaps it may be argued that the word "inconsistent" does not extend to situations where the customary law is "different from," but is limited to cases where it is "absolutely incompatible" with common law. However, this is probably to strain the language used too far and is not a satisfactory argument.

It is submitted that the answer to the first problem is that "law" does in fact only refer to statutory enactments, to which customary law must inevitably yield. Support for this contention is gained from the General Interpretation Proclamation[356] which until recently defined "law" to mean and include "a Proclamation, Law, Act, Ordinance, or Order in Council, and any regulation, rule, by-law, or order made under the authority of a Proclamation, Law, Act, or Ordinance or Order in Council." Thus only written law, whether it be in the form of ordinary or delegated legislation, used to be encompassed by the word "law" in this context.

Recently the definition of the word "law" in the General Interpretation Proclamation has been amended to include "the customary law of Lesotho and

356. Proc. 12 of 1942, § 2 (15).

any other unwritten rule of law." [357] However it is hard to see that the legislature intended to alter the provisions of the Central and Local Courts Proclamation in this oblique manner, and in any event were this new definition to apply, we should be left with a direction to the courts to apply Sesotho law and custom so far as it is not inconsistent with the customary law of Lesotho, which is meaningless. Fortunately the General Interpretation Proclamation's definitions do not apply if there is something in the subject or context inconsistent with such construction,[358] and it is submitted that for this reason the new definition of law is not applicable in the present situation.

This solution obviates the need to attribute a dubious meaning to the word "inconsistent." It is submitted that the proper function of this word is to describe a situation in which the legislature has enacted a rule that is contradictory to customary law regardless of whether the statute specifically revokes the customary law or not. It must be assumed that the legislature knew of the existence of the rules of customary law and legislated with these in mind. That it was indeed apprised of the local situation is apparent from a number of proclamations that contain specific reference to customary law and leave it unaffected.

The Adoption of Children Proclamation [359] which lays down rules for the adoption of children that conflict with those of customary law states roundly:

> [N]othing in this Proclamation contained shall be construed as preventing or affecting the adoption

357. Adaptation of Existing Laws (No. 9) Regulations 1967, (G.N. No. 102 of 1967).

358. *Id.* at § 2.

359. Proc. 62 of 1952 (Vol. II of the Laws at 1076).

> of an African child by an African or Africans in accordance with Basuto law and custom.

Similarly the Administration of Estates Proclamation[360] does not apply to:

> The estates of Africans, which shall continue to be administered in accordance with the prevailing African law and custom of the Territory: Provided that such law and custom shall not apply to the estates of Africans who have been shown to the satisfaction of the Master to have abandoned tribal custom and adopted a European mode of life, and who, if married, have married under European law.

The Marriage Proclamation of 1911[361] in Part II declares:

> This Part shall apply to all marriages solemnized in Basutoland after the date of this Proclamation save and except marriages contracted in accordance with African law or custom. . . .

However Part I, which contains no such restriction, states that it shall not be lawful for any person to compel any woman to enter into a contract of marriage or to marry against her wish. It may be presumed, therefore, that this part was intended to apply throughout the population and to modify any rule of customary law to the contrary, even though this was not specifically stated.

We may therefore assume that territorial legislation that is inconsistent with customary law will render the latter unenforceable in the Basotho courts even though the abolition of the particular customary rules is not spelt out in so many words. Different considerations may, however, apply to Cape Colonial

---

360. Proc. 19 of 1935 (Vol. II of the Laws at 1453).
361. Proc. 7 of 1911 (Vol. III of the Laws at 1760).

legislation enacted before 1884 and incorporated into the law of Lesotho. This matter is discussed below.[362]

When an offence is created by statute which refers to "any person," this must encompass Africans living according to Sesotho law and custom even though the offence conflicts with customary law or is quite unknown to that law. Thus under the Arms and Ammunition Proclamation 1934 [363] it was made an offence to introduce into the country or purchase or sell within the country guns, pistols, and cartridges without permission of the Resident Commissioner or a District Officer.

On the other hand, a statute creating an offence unknown to customary law may specifically exclude its operation to Africans. Thus the provisions of the Game Preservation Proclamation,[364] which made it an offence to hunt game during the open season without a license, was specifically not extended to Africans.

A good example of inconsistency with statute law is provided by the law of prescription. The traditional law was embodied in the maxim "Molato ha o bole" (a debt never rots or dies). Thus a claim never became barred, provided it could be established. However in *Seakhi v. Seakhi* [365] it was held that the customary rule was inconsistent with the Prescription Act [366] in force in the country and therefore could not be applied. Thus the customary rule can no longer be enforced in the Basotho courts in circumstances where the Prescription Act lays down a period of limitation.[367] However, the Act only deals with certain

362. *See infra* pp. 200-206.

363. Proc. 33 of 1934 (Vol. II of the Laws at 1009).

364. Proc. 33 of 1931 (Vol. IV of the Laws at 2295).

365. J.C. 209/1953.

366. Cape Act 6 of 1861.

367. In Seakhi v. Seakhi, the action was for money had and received, which prescribes after eight years under the Act.

types of action and, apart from these, common law or customary rules are applicable.[368]

E. Summary as to the Applicability of Customary Law

We are now in a position to summarise those situations in which customary law may not be applied in Lesotho, bearing in mind that these are the exceptions to the general rule—that the customary law stands on an equal footing with the common law and with legislation as the general law of the land.

First, a court cannot administer a customary rule unless it can be proved that it exists as law with obligatory force and also that it is well established. Secondly, even if these essentials have been proved or are susceptible of such proof, a court may decide not to exercise its discretion in favour of applying customary law for any of the following reasons:

(1) Because of the nature of the action, *i.e.*, because customary law possesses no rules to deal with the action or claim, *e.g.*, in matters of limited liability companies or bills of exchange.

(2) Because of the position of the parties, *e.g.*, they have completely abandoned Sesotho law and custom or they never lived according to Sesotho law and custom. This latter category would, of course, cover most non-Basotho. This is based on the mode of life test.

(3) Because the parties have expressly or impliedly agreed that the matter should not be governed by customary law, *e.g.*, a contract contains a clause declaring the proper law to be the common law, or the parties are married under the Marriage Proclamation and the case concerns a matter of their status, or that of their children.

(4) Because the court considers that part of

---

368. *See supra* p. 149.

the case should be governed by the common law (a composite decision).

(5) Perhaps because Sesotho law does not give a remedy whereas the common law does, and the court thinks it would achieve a fair result to apply the common law.

(6) Perhaps because Sesotho law does not provide a defence to the claim and the common law does, and the court thinks it would achieve a fair result to apply the common law.

(7) Because the action is before a Basotho court or was commenced before such a court and the customary rule is repugnant to justice or morality, or inconsistent with statute law in force in Lesotho, or does not "prevail" in Lesotho, *i.e.*, is not a Sesotho custom.

(8) Because the action is before a non-Basotho court and did not originate in a Basotho court and one or more of the parties are not Africans.

F. The Future of Customary Law in Lesotho

(1) CUSTOMARY LAW OR COMMON LAW?

A long debate is in process throughout the length and breadth of the African continent as to the future role of customary law,[369] and it is appropriate to make a few remarks on this subject in relation to Lesotho.

Law exists to a large degree to serve the needs of society. The needs of Lesotho are best served not only by maintaining laws that at present satisfactorily

---

369. *See generally,* THE FUTURE OF CUSTOMARY LAW IN AFRICA, (a collection of papers read at a symposium held in Amsterdam in 1955, published by Afrika-Instituut, Leidon, 1956); THE FUTURE OF LAW IN AFRICA (report of the London Conference held in 1959 and 1960, edited by A.N. Allott, Butterworths, 1960).

regulate personal relationships, but also by taking account of the development that is desired in the future. As the Declaration of Delhi of the International Congress of Jurists insists:

> The Rule of Law is a dynamic concept . . . which should be employed not only to safeguard and advance the civil and political rights of the individual in a free society, but also to establish social, economic, educational, and cultural conditions under which his legitimate aspirations and dignity may be realised.[370]

The implementation of the second requirement may involve not only the modernisation of the law but also the creation of uniformity in various fields.

It is proposed to examine the various divisions of the law with a view to charting possible future adjustments and alterations.

(a) Family Law and Succession

This is a sphere *par exellence* of customary law. There seems no logical reason why such personal laws should not continue to regulate the affairs of those who wish it for a considerable time to come. There are no absolute values involved here, for even developed systems of law show marked divergencies in, *e.g.*, the essential requirements of a valid marriage, grounds of divorce, legitimacy of the children, and succession on death. Probably the only ground upon which the public interest might require changes in this field would be if the rules of succession to rights in land were impeding economic development. As will be seen, however, fragmentation of land holdings occurs despite rather than because of the application of Sesotho law.

---

370. INTERNATIONAL COMMISSION OF JURISTS, THE RULE OF LAW IN A FREE SOCIETY: A REPORT OF THE INTERNATIONAL CONGRESS OF JURISTS 3 (1959).

There will, no doubt, be an increasing number of Africans who desire to regulate their family relations and succession under the common law or statute, and there is nothing to prevent their exercising this option. The extended family is, of course, a traditional institution of which many Africans are justly proud. The preservation of the solidarity of the family is likely to come under increasing pressure as individuals become wage earners and move to an urban environment. They will be less likely to wish to maintain their traditional responsibilities, nor will they in all cases be content to see their property devolve according to customary law upon death. These influences are going to strike at the very heart of the system. The greater freedom of women is also going to affect the family structure. Thus in the long run we may find an adaptation of the customary law so that it concentrates its attention increasingly on the individual and thus moves closely into line with the common law and the relevant statutes.

(b) The Law Relating to Land

This is, of course, intimately linked with family law and succession. However it also has a direct bearing on the future economic progress of Lesotho and therefore wider considerations must be borne in mind than the personal desires of individuals.[371]

The cardinal principle of the customary law relating to land is now enshrined in section 92 of the Constitution, which declares that all land in Lesotho is vested in the Basotho Nation. The Constitution also carries through the traditional concept of a hierarchy of political authorities with power to allocate land to individuals.

---

371. Constitutional aspects of land law are discussed in Part II, *infra* at pp. 254-268.

Sheddick, who was a pioneer in this field, has explained the land tenure system in terms of "rights of administration" and "rights of usufruct."[372] Rights of administration are held in the first instance by the King and are exercised through the Principal Chiefs, Ward Chiefs, Chiefs, and Headmen.[373] They involve the right to allocate or distribute land to a subordinate authority and eventually to an individual subject, the right of reversion when the land falls vacant whether as a result of death or deprivation, and the duty to supervise the activities of those lower in the hierarchy including the hearing of appeals against the wrongful exercise of subordinate powers. The position is well stated in the judgment of the Judicial Commissioner in a case heard in 1953 as follows:

> The land in Basutoland first belonged to the Paramount Chief, the Paramount Chief Moshoeshoe who founded this nation. . . . The Paramount Chief appointed chiefs, sub-chiefs, and headmen as his eyes and ears in the Territory. Their duty it was to supervise their respective areas and to allocate the land for residential sites, gardens, tree plantations, burial sites, etc., and arable purposes. . . . If a man wishes to get a land he goes to his chief under whom he is resident, or to his headman. A man either goes direct or through his father or some other responsible person and asks for land. The chief issues a land if he agrees with the request, and allocates the applicant a virgin land (*thite*) or a land which has been used but which has been returned to the Chieftainship for re-allocation. Land reverts to the Chieftainship if the owner removes from the area or on the death of a husband or wife whoever dies last.[374]

Gluckman has elaborated Sheddick's terminology

372. LAND TENURE IN BASUTOLAND 4 (H.M.S.O. 1954).

373. *Id.* Ch. 9.

374. Lesitsi v. Mafa J.C. 84/1953.

and refers to "estates" of administration to emphasise the hierarchy of political status.[375] Thus there are primary, secondary, tertiary estates of administration, etc., right down to the village headman. Gluckman has also criticised Sheddick's employment of the expression "rights of usufruct" to describe the various individual rights of user over the land, and prefers to use the term "estates of production."[376]

It is the rights of individual holders and cultivators of land that are germane to the question of the reform of the law of land tenure, whatever name is given to them, and these rights are therefore examined below. This involves a comparison with the rights of absolute owners at common law, since the adoption of a system of freehold tenure is often put forward as a necessary first step in the improvement of agriculture in Africa. Thus one finds the East Africa Royal Commission on African Land Tenure advocating "a land policy which would have as its cardinal features the pregressive [*sic*] encouragement of individualisation of title in African lands. . . ."[377]

As Professor Seidman has pointed out:[378]

> If private capitalist farming for the market is the objective, the first requirement would seem to be permanence of tenure.

Despite widespread misconceptions[379] many systems of land tenure in Africa do grant the occupant more or less permanent rights in the land, and thus to propose

---

375. THE IDEAS IN BAROTSE JURISPRUDENCE 89 *et seq.* (Yale U.P. 1965).

376. *Id.*

377. LA. ANYANE, GHANA AGRICULTURE—ECONOMIC DEVELOPMENT FROM EARLY TIMES TO THE MIDDLE OF THE TWENTIETH CENTURY 191 (O.U.P. 1963).

378. 1966 WIS. L. REV. 999 at 1046.

379. *See* Bentsi-Enchill 1965 J.A.L. 114 *et seq.*

freehold tenure on this ground alone is illogical. However the position is not nearly so clear-cut in Lesotho where there is a chronic shortage of land,[380] and the limitations placed upon security of tenure by the *Laws of Lerotholi* must now be examined.

Section 7 of Part I of the Laws provides three grounds for depriving a person of his land.

First, under section 7(2), the headman is abjured to make frequent inspections of all lands allocated by him for the cultivation of crops and is empowered to take away land from people who in his opinion have more lands than are necessary for their own and their families' subsistence, and grant such land so taken away to his subjects who have no land or insufficient lands.

Secondly, under section 7(3), it is at the discretion of a chief or headman to take away land or lands which he has allocated to any of his subjects, who through continued absence or insufficient reason fail for two successive years to cultivate them properly or cause them to be cultivated. Both these grounds would seem to be consequences of the shortage of land in Lesotho.

Thirdly, a person may be deprived of his lands in the public interest.[381]

Another important factor, if land is to be put to maximum use and large capital investment to be made in it, is freedom of alienation, both during the occupier's lifetime in case he has to leave, and after his death. However among the Basotho, as the saying goes, "[arable] lands are not an inheritance" and cannot be disposed of by will, nor do they pass on intestacy

---

380. *See* SHEDDICK, *supra* note 190, Ch. 12, and Crawford 1967 S.A.L.J. 437.

381. LL. § 7(8).

to the relatives of the deceased. Instead they revert to the chief or headman for re-allocation.[382] However in the process of re-allocation, priority must be given to the requirements of any adult sons residing in the same village. Although this is the strict legal position, in practice lands are commonly handed on from father to son and the mechanism of re-allocation bypassed. When a man with a relatively large piece of land fears that he may be deprived as a result of an inspection, he divides the land among his sons and staves off a diminution of the family estate. This procedure is adopted largely as a result of the abuses by chiefs and headmen of their positions in re-allocating lands to their favourites as soon as they revert.[383] The inevitable consequence is the progressive fragmentation of holdings into smaller and smaller units.

However land allocated for residential purposes, for the growing of vegetables or tobacco, or for the purpose of planting fruit or other trees is inheritable both in practice and in theory and passes to the heir or the dependants of the deceased for their use so long as he or they continue to live there.[384]

Land is not freely alienable in the sense understood where the concept of freehold title exists. The right of occupation of land may be gratuitously and revocably granted to another, but land cannot be sold save by the allodial owner, the Basotho Nation. It follows that land cannot be mortgaged either.[385]

Finally, an occupier's right to use his land in Lesotho is not exclusive; others may enjoy various rights over the land, for instance to graze cattle there

---

382. LL. § 7(5).

383. *See* Lesitsi v. Mafa, *supra* note 374.

384. LL. § 7(7).

385. Sales and Mortgages are now prohibited by the Deeds Registry Act, No. 12 of 1967, §§ 15(1) and 27(1).

during the winter, without the necessity for the occupier's agreement.[386] Land holdings, moreover, lack precision for there is no system of land registration and boundary disputes are commonplace.

Advocates for the reform of traditional African systems of land tenure often point to them as major obstructions in the way of economic development and the attraction of foreign investment.

> [T]raditional systems, unaltered, simply will not sustain economic progress, and they are being and will be replaced by new crops and new methods.[387]

And again—

> If enterprise is to be given an opportunity to express itself there must be a break with traditional institutions which govern land.[388]

For increased returns there must be investment in the land, not only initially but annually. Moreover the size of a production unit must be such that it can sustain investment in, and the use of, modern agricultural machinery and equipment.

The most significant investigation of land law reform occurred in 1963 when four members of a land tenure research team [389] sponsored by the University of Chicago and financed by the Ford Foundation prepared some *Recommendations and Reflections on Some Problems of Land Tenure in Basutoland.* The subsequent history of the report has been described by one of the members of the team:

> A full report was made in June, 1963, making

---

386. SHEDDICK, *supra* note 372, at 165.

387. HUNTER, THE NEW SOCIETIES OF TROPICAL AFRICA 98 (O.U.P. 1962).

388. YUDELMAN, AFRICANS ON THE LAND 255 (Harvard 1964).

389. They were K. Bentsi-Enchill, D. V. Cowen, A. Dunham, and L. Fallers.

> specific recommendations for improvements in the system. But . . . a melancholy fate overcame the report; it has become a secret sequestered document. Despite strong recommendations by various persons, including Dr. Elkan in a recent Manpower Survey, the Chicago Report has never been published. After some tactful negotiation, the report was shown to the all-party Constitutional Reform Committee whose work, in 1963, led to the country's present constitution; and some of the recommendations in the Chicago document have in fact been incorporated in the Constitution, ... Nevertheless, it remains the case that accurate information concerning the land system tends to become a jealously guarded mystery, and that specific proposals for reform languish.[389a]

The Report starts by emphasising the importance of agriculture in the general scheme of development. It stresses that land policy must be directed towards the removal of those conditions that prevent the available land from being effectively utilised.[390]

Attention is drawn to the fact that for over a century the Basotho people have had to adapt themselves to a modern money economy and adjust their traditional dependence on subsistence farming accordingly.[391]

The customary law has also had to adapt itself to the growing land shortage, the large body of migrant labour working in the Republic of South Africa for various periods of time and then returning to their lands, the introduction of new cash crops, and the increasing emphasis on the raising of sheep and goats for the production of wool and mohair.

389a. Cowen, 1967 SOUTH AFRICAN JOURNAL OF ECONOMICS 58.

390. Report of K. Bentsi-Enchill *et al.* (unpublished) at 2-3.

391. *Id.* at 3. *See also* SHEDDICK, *supra* note 372, at 183 *et seq.*

The recommendations in the Report do not call for a new land law (*e.g.*, the adoption of freehold tenure), but rather suggest a comprehensive reorganisation of the administration of the system to remove uncertainty and anomalies.[392] Thus there are various recommendations concerned with streamlining the procedure for the allocation and deprivation of land, and others designed to ensure that equitable apportionments of the limited supply are made and that justice is seen to be done to each and every applicant and occupant.[393] Most of these were adopted in the 1965 Constitution—for instance, the introduction of advisory boards to consult with headmen, the necessity for authorities to give reasons for their decisions, and of a system of appeals—and these were all carried through into the Independence Constitution.[394]

To encourage development in urban areas, the Report calls for a town council to take over the functions of allocating land in the townships.[395] Allocation prob-

---

392. *See supra*, note 390, at 6.

393. Recommendations 3 (no one to participate in the allocation of land where he has a personal interest); 4 (allocating authority must work with a committee of local residents, must give names of applicants in writing, and must give reasons for not allocating to any landless person); 5 (appeals); 9 (no one to be deprived of land except on grounds expressly provided by law—appeals to the court only where land is taken *mala fide*, or irregularly, or for no stated reason, or for an unauthorised reason; other appeals, *i.e*, on the merits, to go to higher administrative authority); 10 (depriving authority to work with committee of local residents and to state reasons for deprivation in writing; necessity for inspections *in loco* where ground is improper use or occupancy of more arable land than is necessary; proposed Land Utilisation Board to prescribe standard inspection procedures to avoid suspicion of discrimination); and 11 (appeals)—*Supra* note 390, at 11-16 and 27-33.

394. *See* §§ 95, 96, 97, 99, and 101. *See also* §§ 9 and 10 of the Land Procedure Act, No. 24 of 1967.

395. *Supra* note 390, at 22-24 (Recommendation 7).

lems here are primarily ones of town planning and urban development and are unsuitable for continued handling by the chief or headman. This recommendation has not been implemented, and land in urban areas is still allocated by the Principal Chief or Ward Chief, although he must act in consultation with the local government authority concerned.[396]

Clarity of title would seem to be indispensable for fast economic and agricultural development, but there is no recommendation that a system of land registration should be adopted throughout the country. This would involve a cadastral survey which was considered too expensive at the time. However it was suggested that a survey could be commenced in the townships at once, and that in any event a simple system of record keeping be introduced immediately throughout the country in a uniform manner. A certificate should be granted upon each allocation of land to specify the boundaries of the area allotted, the conditions of occupancy or use imposed by the issuing authority, and the identity of the allocating authority.[397] However there could be no really satisfactory delineation of boundaries in such a certificate until a proper survey of the area had been made.

A significant proposal for the improvement of agricultural techniques is that a National Land Utilisation Board, subject to the government's control, should be set up with *inter alia* the following functions:

(i) To plan and develop a programme of land conservation and use in order to correct maladjustments in land use, control soil erosion and afforestation, and conserve water resources and watersheds;

(ii) To prepare and comment on plans for future

396. § 98(1) and (2) of the Constitution.

397. *Supra* note 390, at 25-26 (Recommendation 8).

industrial and other natural resource development; and

(iii) To educate and advise headmen and other persons empowered to allocate land or deprive people of land on proper standards or criteria to be used.[398]

The Constitution went some way towards the implementation of this proposal by the creation of a National Planning Board which had [399] wide functions including the following:

(i) The preparation of plans for the economic development of Lesotho, including in particular the development, conservation, and use of land and other natural resources;

(ii) Advising the government and other public authorities in relation to the economic development of Lesotho including the matters particularly specified in (i); and

(iii) Advising the Government in relation to its policy in respect of land holding.[400]

It will be noted however that the third function recommended has been omitted, despite its great importance.

The Report's recommendations on the permissible grounds for depriving a person of land are also clearly designed to encourage maximum good use of the available resources.[401] It is proposed that the ground of misuse or nonuse under § 7(3) of the *Laws of Lerotholi* be amended to empower a chief or other author-

---

398. *Id.* at 9 (Recommendation 2).

399. The National Planning Board was abolished by the Lesotho Constitution (First Amendment) Act, 1969. The Board had been given both executive and advisory powers and in relation to the former there was a conflict of responsibilities with the government. A National Planning Consultative Council is now to be set up with advisory powers only.

400. § 90 of the Constitution.

401. *Supra* note 390, at 36-40 (Recommendations 13 and 14).

ity to deprive of land a person who does not use it or does not cause it to be used for two successive years. The existing law requires the chief to assess whether or not an allottee's failure to cultivate was due to "insufficient reasons," but, as the Report states, it is hard to see what *bona fide* sufficient reason there could be since the allottee does not have to actually cultivate the land himself but merely cause it to be cultivated. The recommendation would also extend this ground of deprivation to the use of residential sites, gardens, huts, and buildings, whereas under existing law it only relates to arable land.

Secondly, the Report proposes that the chief or other authority be empowered to deprive of arable land a person who fails to use it in accordance with good agricultural methods, as laid down by the proposed Land Utilisation Board, for two successive years after notice has been given to him of his deficiencies. At present the law merely refers to land not being "properly" cultivated.

To balance this threat of forfeiture there is also a proposal that incentives in the form of economic benefits and other public assistance should be provided for those who comply with the prescribed methods.[402]

However a fine may operate as an effective sanction and deterrent, and this method was the one selected in the new Land Husbandry Act, 1969.[403] The Act empowers the Minister of Agriculture to make regulations to ensure that land is employed in the most beneficial uses, to promote soil conservation, proper management of water resources, and proper irrigation and to promote good and prevent bad agricultural practices. These regulations may make their contra-

---

402. *Id.* at 37.

403. No. 22 of 1969.

vention an offence punishable on a first conviction by a fine not exceeding R50 or, in default of payment, imprisonment for a period not exceeding three months. For subsequent convictions the maximum fine may be R150 or, in default of payment, imprisonment for up to nine months.

It is thought that a process of encouragements and assistance by the provision of credits, education, and extension services is likely to be both fairer and more beneficial in the long run than the threat of forfeiture, since comparatively few farmers use their land badly on purpose.

The Report also recommends three changes in section 7(2) of the *Laws of Lerotholi* which provides for deprivation of land where the occupant is found, on inspection, to have more land than is necessary. First, that a maximum acreage be laid down by Parliament of arable land that may be held by any person. This is because of the acute shortage of land in the country and because it appears that the present variations in acreage are excessively large,[404] and impossible to justify except on largely irrational and historical grounds.

Secondly, that land should be taken from any person who has more land than necessary to produce sufficient agricultural earnings to meet reasonable family living expenses. This criterion is to replace that of bare subsistence under the existing law. This should encourage the Basotho farmers to raise their standard of living by the adoption of improved methods without fear of being penalized.[405]

Thirdly, that in both these cases the chief or other authority be required to deprive a person of excess

---

404. The Report (*supra* note 390, at 39) refers to holdings said to be 200 acres in extent.

405. *Id.* at 39-40.

lands and not merely empowered to do so. None of these proposals has been implemented to date.

So far as transmission of rights in land upon death is concerned, the Report makes no specific recommendations about allocation, but calls for a general clarification of the existing law, particularly with reference to trading sites and the procedure concerning expatriates.[406]

Two further useful suggestions put forward concern group projects. It is proposed that a procedure be instituted whereby on a petition of a specified small percentage (*e.g.*, 20 percent) of the holders of arable land in an area the National Land Utilisation Board may delineate boundaries and propose a plan of consolidation so that

(i) after an election in which a large percentage (*e.g.*, 80 percent) of holders of land within the area approve the plan; then

(ii) the land holdings of all persons within the area may be reallocated in such a way that the former allottees are allotted consolidated holdings in accordance with the approved consolidation plans; or

(iii) the lands within the area may be allocated to one or more co-operative societies, the members of which are former allottees.[407]

The law should provide that the allocating authorities must reallocate in accordance with the approved plan. This recommendation takes into account the economic desirability of consolidating separate holdings and even of forming cooperatives for the purpose of taking full advantage of mechanized farming.[408] However, although the disadvantages of

---

406. *Id.* at 41-44 (Recommendation 15).

407. *Id.* at 45-46 (Recommendation 16).

408. Successful consolidation has already taken place in development projects at Thaba Phatsoa and ha Josiah.

small holdings were in the minds of the makers of the Report they did not tackle the problem of the fragmentation of lands by the prevailing practice of allocating to an individual some good land and some poor land, often far apart.[409]

The second proposal in this field is that a procedure be established for farmers in a given area to decide by vote that an area be designated an "enclosed area" and then be fenced off.[410] This would be useful, for instance, to farmers who have planted a crop that has a growing season requiring a modification of customary communal grazing practice. This would mean that no one other than those specified could graze their animals in the enclosed area. Neither of these two recommendations has however yet been adopted.

The penultimate recommendation in the Report deals with the important topic of security for loans.[411] The enactment of a complete mortgage or security law that would expressly deal with the rights of lenders, borrowers, and of third parties dealing with the security is advocated. A Deeds Registry Act has since been passed,[412] specifying the types of mortgage available, but this leaves the rights obtained under them to be regulated under the common law as in the past.

The Report recommends that security interests be permitted over crops, livestock, and the products of livestock, as well as over residential and industrial buildings, but not over the land on which they are situated, nor over arable land.[413]

---

409. The solution to this problem advocated later by Bentsi-Enchill is exchange and consolidation, voluntary or with varying degrees of inducement and compulsion—*see* 1965 J.A.L. 114 at 136-7.

410. *Supra* note 390, at 47 (Recommendation 17).

411. *Id.* at 48-50 (Recommendation 18).

412. Act 12 of 1967.

413. *Supra* note 390, at 49-50.

It is, perhaps, in this sphere that the Report may be criticised for not going far enough. It may well be that only by making the land itself capable of being mortgaged can the speed of agricultural development be accelerated and the desired investment in industrialisation be attained. In the absence of a proper survey, this can only be a matter of surmise, but it is possible that the added security that land gives might influence the attraction of a prospective developer. As soon as this is done and land thus takes on a commercial value, the gates are opened for free alienation and something approaching individual tenure of a common law type. Whether or not this is desirable is a matter of much debate, but at the outset it should be made clear that the introduction of such a system certainly does not mean dispensing with the traditional rule that all land is vested in the Basotho Nation.[414] Thus in English law the fee simple held by the individual owner is found perfectly compatible with the allodial ownership of the sovereign. In some American states the allodial ownership is vested in the state. As Bentsi-Enchill, a member of the Chicago team, has pointed out elsewhere:

> In this way the fee simple estate of the Anglo-American common law is a superb example of a near-maximum type of proprietary occupancy, *i.e.*, of the group member's interest in his allotment of land concerning which the ultimate or allodial title is regarded as being vested in the group—the state—of which he is a member.[415]

In considering the question of whether land should be made saleable, he goes on:

> Perhaps it should, at least among members of the community, and subject to some controls regard-

---

414. *Id.* The Report (Recommendation 1) strongly favoured the retention of this rule.

415. 1965 J.A.L. 114 at 124.

> ing excessive accumulations in a few hands, or in the hands of non-members of the community.
> But it is far from clear that haste in the general direction of making land freely alienable is necessary. Leasehold arrangements can be tried. An important value in not encouraging a person who has control of land over which he has a farming right to lose it is that whilst he retains the land he has the triple option of continuing as a subsistence farmer or becoming a cash-crop producer or being a wage earner; loss of his land reduces him to wage-earning or starvation. Why not then help him to become a cash crop farmer? This at least has the merit of achieving the goal of many a land tenure reform elsewhere, and may well be the most effective means of countering the strong drift of migratory labour to the cities of Southern Africa where apparently insecure conditions generally await them.[416]

This passage draws attention to one of the greatest reservations anyone has about making land alienable by individuals, namely that it will soon lead to the creation of a landless class who will then be exploited by the landowners. The available land will be concentrated in the hands of those with money, whether they be prosperous farmers on neighbouring lands or city dwellers speculating on a rise in prices. The Swinnerton Plan, adopted in Kenya in 1954, appeared to view this prospect with equanimity and declared that this was a normal step in the evolution of a country.[417] However in Lesotho where there is at present virtually no alternative means of earning a living this might be to condemn the landless to a choice between the Scylla of exploitation by landowners in their own country and the Charybdis of similar treatment in the South African mines and industries.

---

416. *Id.* at 138-9.

417. A plan to intensify the development of African agriculture in Kenya (1954) at 10.

The second corollary of making land freely saleable is that this will take away from the chiefs and headmen their most important remaining function. In effect it will lead to the demise of the chieftainship which is a break with tradition so large as to warrant very careful deliberation. It would be bound to lead to numerous social problems and could foster a feeling of rootlessness and uncertainty in the country at large, more especially in the remoter mountain areas.

One answer to these problems might be to set aside certain areas of Lesotho, probably the towns, where land could be subject to absolute ownership, leaving the rest to be held in the traditional manner. From a commercial point of view this system appears to be operating satisfactorily in Swaziland. This will encourage foreign investors to set up businesses in Lesotho and promote industrialisation. For it cannot be doubted that the traditional land tenure system is in practise a disincentive to the prospective investor if only because it is unfamiliar and has implications of uncertainty of operation and insecurity of tenure.

If the concept of freehold tenure, or *dominium plenum,* as it is known in Roman-Dutch law, were to be introduced at all there would, of course, have to be stringent regulations about the proper utilisation of the land by the owner because of the acute shortage of land. As Professor Dumont has explained, Roman systems of law grant the owner the *jus utendi et abutendi.*[418] The right to "abuse" such a valuable asset as land cannot be permitted under any circumstances in Lesotho today and safeguards would need to be introduced by legislation.

An alternative to free alienation of land—a sort of halfway stage—might be to permit the purchase of

418. FALSE START IN AFRICA 128 (Andre Deutsch 1966 trans. Ott).

improvements to the land. This would encourage good use of the land whilst attaching no commercial value to the land itself.[419]

If the change to any form of freehold tenure is thought undesirable, the answer may lie in increased emphasis upon cooperatives and state-farms.[420] These can develop easily from the traditional system of tenure, and a beginning could be made in accordance with the Chicago Report's recommendations in this respect.

There is no doubt that the problem of the land tenure system is not only a pressing one but extremely difficult. The members of the Chicago team were well aware, as we ourselves are, of the need to look not only at the economic aspects of any possible reforms, but also at the social and political implications these may have.[421]

(c) The Law of Contract, Commercial Law, and the Law Relating to Property Other Than Land

The fact that Duncan in his book [421a] makes no mention at all of these subjects as forming part of Sesotho law suggests that this is not an area where customary law has any well-developed body of rules. This is borne out by the paucity of appeals that reach the Judicial Commissioner's Court in this field.

However, clearly simple contracts are recognised and enforced under customary law and these reflect the traditionally agricultural mode of life of the Basotho and the fact that most of their wealth is in the form of cattle. Agreements are commonly made to place stock with another, to plough another's lands, to herd another's cattle, and of course to pay *bohali* upon marriage. Moreover transactions of loan, lease,

---

419. *See* Crawford 1967 S.A.L.J. 445.

420. *See* Seidman 1966 WIS. L. REV. 999 at 1049-51.

421. *Supra* note 390, at 1.

421a. *Supra* note 189.

partnership, and bailment are recognised in addition to sale, agency, exchange, and pledge.

So far as general principles are concerned the customary law is close to the common law in the remedies it affords [422] and in its refusal to enforce illegal or immoral agreements.[423] However, we have already seen that the maxim "A debt never dies" used to apply, but has had to yield to the Prescription Act. It is sometimes said that the requirement of delivery in sale and exchange under the common law is unknown to customary law. Ownership apparently passes under the contract. This presents a conflict of laws.

Matters of company law, insurance, negotiable instruments, copyright, and trade marks are unknown to customary law while partnership, employment, and guarantee have only sketchy rules.

It is submitted that this would be an appropriate sphere to replace the few Sesotho laws and customs that exist by the common law and legislation. This would help to bring people to terms with the inevitable repercussions of the economic development of Lesotho. The undesirable niceties and technicalities of the common law can of course always be avoided by providing that the common law shall only apply so far as the circumstances of the country permit, if this is not already the position in respect of the particular topic.

---

422. *See, e.g.*, Malope v. Khoase, J.C. 18/1958 (cancellation of contract for sale of plough for seller's failure to deliver; restitution of purchase price ordered); Matsepe v. Moeti, J.C. 58/1965 (damages).

423. Makhetha v. Molungoa, J.C. 43/1952 (agreement for sale of liquor by unlicensed person held unenforceable); Chere v. Nyenye, J.C. 41/1966 (agreement by diviner to point out person responsible for the cutting of a fence; held he could not recover the agreed fee of two bags of mealies, as the agreement was an offense under the Medicine Men and Herbalists Proc. No. 44 of 1948).

(d) The Criminal Law

Duncan states that criminal liability in Lesotho law is the same as in South African law.[424] South African criminal law is based upon the common law and is thus largely unwritten, whereas most countries in Africa have by now adopted Criminal Codes. Botswana enacted a code substantially similar to the East African codes in 1964, having prior to that date used the South African common law.

The penalties are not however the same under the common law as under customary law and there are probably a number of minor variations in the substantive law. It is difficult to resist the conclusion that there should be a single standard of justice in criminal cases applicable to all persons in Lesotho. Probably the best solution would be the enactment of a code presently being used in another part of Africa with adaptations to meet local circumstances. The advantage of pursuing this course would be that use could be made of the body of case law developing throughout the continent on the various sections of these codes, rather than relying solely on South African interpretations of the common law there. The administration of justice in the Republic is based on certain assumptions quite out of keeping with the position in Lesotho. Such a change would also provide a stimulus to the training and employment of more local magistrates rather than borrowing such personnel from the Republic.

(e) The Law of Delict[425]

The customary law of delict is a system of nominate actions that may be classified under four headings.

---

424. *Supra note* 189, at 103.

425. *See generally*, V. V. PALMER, THE ROMAN-DUTCH AND SESOTHO LAW OF DELICT (Sijthoff 1970).

Wrongs may be to the person (assault, homicide), to property (theft, trespass, damage), to family rights (seduction, abduction, adultery), and to reputation (insult, defamation). These actions are not linked together by underlying general principles, and thus the remedies stand, much as English writs, once did, as a set of exhaustive remedies.

If the view is taken that customary law changes almost imperceptibly, one would think that the gestation period for any new categorical form of relief would require many generations. However, considering the accelerated rate of economic expansion and social adjustment now called for by almost every African government, it is doubtful whether custom's leisurely pace would be adequate to meet changing conditions.

The record so far is promising for the future, for sometimes a new remedy can be imported from the common law or from some other customary law system, such as was done in regard to the action for defamation which now overlays the ancient but limited action for insult. Furthermore, customary law has shown itself capable of shifting rather rapidly in the face of such modern developments as the automobile and the tractor, thus entertaining remedies for injuries that the social and economic order had never previously considered.

One discernible trend in the development of the customary law of delict is its tendency to move toward rather than away from the common law, especially in cases where there is no customary law rule applicable to the question before the court.

The great value of the common law at the moment is that it stands by with a wealth of principle, detailed rules, and ready-made solutions to problems that are new to the Basotho courts. One day it may come to pass that the law of delict in Lesotho will represent an individual synthesis of these two systems, composed of the best and most relevant elements of each.

(f) Evidence and Procedure

As is pointed out in Part III, pp. 495-501, the procedure to be adopted in the Basotho Courts has ceased to be regulated exclusively by traditional rules, and the movement towards more modern practices is generally to be welcomed. However the virtues of the customary procedures were that they aimed at reconciliation and whilst this is, of course, still possible in extra-judicial arbitral proceedings some consideration should perhaps be given to whether it should not play a larger part in the law administered in the courts.

In England, public and legal opinion is at last recognising the important role that can be played by conciliatory bodies in settling industrial disputes and by marriage guidance officers in resolving matrimonial problems, and it would be a waste if the conciliation procedure which is at the heart of African justice were to be relegated to a position of insignificance.

(2) THE RECORDING OF CUSTOMARY LAW

As we have seen, one of the particularly difficult problems in connection with the continued application of customary law is its ascertainment. Many people have advocated the codification of such law to facilitate its administration, and there is now a growing consensus that, at any rate, customary law should be written down. If Lesotho is to retain certain branches of Sesotho law and custom, what sort of record should be made? It is instructive to commence by looking at the conclusion of the Conference on the Future of Law in Africa in 1960:

> It is desirable that there should be for each territory a record or digest of the native law and custom in relation to family relations, marriage,

> divorce, succession, and land tenure. A useful precedent is the *Digest of Customary Law in the Punjab* by Sir William Rattigan and his successors. This record should be prepared in consultation with the "elders" of each community, so as to ensure that it reflects their common opinion. It should be under the direction of a central advisory authority who should be able to collate the native law and custom of different areas with a view to co-ordinating them, where possible to ensure that the number of local variations was restricted to the minimum. The central advisory authority might well include a sociologist, an administrative officer, and a lawyer.
>
> The record should not as a rule be given statutory form, lest it might become too rigid. It should be available for guidance only so as to ensure flexibility. It should be receivable in the courts as a public document admissible without formal proof, and carry the same sort of weight as a received textbook. It should be revised as frequently as necessary so as to ensure that it keeps pace with changing conditions.[426]

There can be no doubt that this is the right type of approach.

One useful function which the recording of customary law should have is to make the law more certain for those who regulate their lives by it, as well as for the judges whose task it is to administer it. It may incidentally also tidy up the law, ironing out local deviations and perhaps even improving portions of it. The sections of customary law to be recorded are surely the right ones and a suitable blend of qualifications are recommended for those who should undertake the task. But most important of all, the documents that result should not have the force of law.[427] In Natal, a Code of Native Law was enacted as law in

---

426. Report, *supra* note 369, at 16-17.

427. *See, e.g.*, the Regency Case, *supra* note 208, at 58.

1891, and this has mummified the customary law and prevented its development since that date.[428] It was even thought to have become out of date as early as 1901.

One of the best types of digest is a handbook on the lines of Professor Schapera's *Handbook of Tswana Law and Custom*,[429] which was designed not as a legal code but as a guide for those administering the law. It was realised that a code might tend to perpetuate both undesirable customs and those that were dying out.

Professor Schapera has put another argument against having a code, as follows:

> Moreover, unless the code was very simple indeed and confined to bare statements of basic principles, it would almost certainly be largely incomprehensible to most of the people, including many of the tribal judges themselves. The Tswana in general are not sufficiently advanced in education to appreciate the subtleties of legal draughtsmanship; hence, unless and until legal practitioners are allowed to appear before tribal authorities, legislation where the outcome of a case might for example depend upon precise interpretations of wording should preferably be avoided.[430]

One might add that even with legal practitioners such decisions are hardly likely to appeal to the people themselves.

The dangers of codification appear to be greater at the present time than almost any other. African societies have been awakened by the coming of independence, and customs are undergoing a cathartic

---

428. For a discussion of codification and the Natal Code, *see* Kerr 1958 J.A.L. 82, 89 *et seq.*

429. (O.U.P. 1938).

430. SCHAPERA, *The Development of Customary Law in the Bechuanaland Protectorate* in THE FUTURE OF CUSTOMARY LAW IN AFRICA 111 (1956), *supra* note 369.

change. Reassessment and a new evaluation are taking place. Thus even a handbook will need constant revision.

This capacity for easy change is one advantage that customary law in an uncodified form has over a code. Legislation, as Fritz Kern [431] puts it,

> . . . in fact, often proves to be clumsier and less helpful than customary law. The latter quietly passes over obsolete laws, which sink into oblivion, and die peacefully, but the law itself remains young, always in the belief that it is old. Yet it is not old; rather it is a perpetual grafting of new onto the old law, a fresh stream of contemporary law springing out of the creative wells of the subconscious, for the most part not canalized by the fixed limits of recorded law and charter. Statute law on the other hand, cannot be freed from the letter of legal texts, until a new text has replaced an old one, even though life itself has long since condemned the old text to death; in the meantime the dead text retains power over life.

It was suggested at the London Conference that a contribution to the recording of customary law would be made by the School of Oriental and African Studies. Their Restatement of African Law Project is now in full swing [432] and a restatement of the Lesotho law of marriage has already been prepared though not published.

The recording of customary law in the form of a handbook or restatement, not having the force of law, leaves the development of the law firmly in the hands of the courts.[433] The courts will have the opportunity

---

431. KINGSHIP AND LAW IN THE MIDDLE AGES 179 (trans. from German by S.B. Chrimes 1939).

432. The first volume was published recently on Kenya Family Law.

433. It may be prudent to provide by statute that the restatement or textbook should be prima facie proof of a customary rule and thus place the burden of proof upon the party who dissents from the recorded rule.

of playing a dynamic role and they will be applying similar techniques to those that led in the past to the growth of the common law into the great system it is today. It seems, however, that we can only look forward to this prospect when a number of conditions are satisfied. First, there must be a unification of the judicial structure. This will involve merging the subordinate courts with the Basotho courts and giving them a new and comprehensive jurisdiction. That is to say, the new courts must be empowered to apply the whole gamut of the law in force in Lesotho—customary law, common law, and statutes—without any restriction based on the race of the parties or the matter in dispute. Only in this way will the courts acquire the habit of dynamic interpretation. Secondly, for such multipurpose courts to prove feasible there must be an improvement in the training of the lower strata of the judiciary. Only when there are legally qualified judges with legal practitioners appearing before them can we begin to envisage the progress that is desirable. Alternatively, if there are to be lay judges there must be well-qualified clerks to assist them on matters of law and procedure.

Thirdly, a proper system of law reporting is absolutely indispensable to the orderly development of customary law. It is understandable that in the past no proper reports have been compiled of judgments given in cases before Basotho courts. But the failure to make available in an accessible form the judgments of the Judicial Commissioner's Courts is inexcusable. It is essential for such a court, hearing a great quantity of appeals from Basotho courts, to circulate its judgments so as to provide the lower courts with the necessary guidance.

CHAPTER 4

STATUTE LAW

A. The Sources of Statute Law
B. The Enactment of Legislation

A. The Sources of Statute Law

It will be recalled that the Law Revision Proclamation,[434] amending the General Law Proclamation of 1884,[435] provided for the retention of only a few specified Cape statutes.

Legislation, which is now the most important source of new law in the country, has found its way onto the Lesotho statute book since 1884 through a variety of channels. At present we may point to the following types of legislative enactment that are in force:

(1) United Kingdom Legislation

Such legislation was exported to Basutoland during the colonial days. It took the form either of an Order in Council (*e.g.*, the 1966 Independence Order[436] giving Lesotho her present constitution, and the Appeals to Privy Council Order),[437] or of Proclamations of the High Commissioner (*e.g.*, the Criminal Procedure and Evidence Proclamation),[438] or more rarely of Proclamations of the Resident Commissioner. In addition there were two types of subsidiary legislation made by High Commissioners' Notices and Government Notices.

---

434. Proc. 12 of 1960—*see supra* pp. 42-43.
435. *Supra* p. 42.
436. *Supra* p. 41.
437. § 1, 1954, No. 1370.
438. Proc. 59 of 1938.

(2) LOCAL LEGISLATION

Local legislation dates back to the pre-Colonial Era when Moshoeshoe was an independent ruler. Prior to the annexation of Basutoland to the Cape Colony in 1871, Moshoeshoe had promulgated three laws for the various peoples whom he was in the process of cementing together to form the Basotho nation.[439] The first was the Liquor Law of 1854 which prohibited the sale of spirits.[440] This was followed in 1855 by a law dealing with witchcraft and in 1859 by the Law of Trade which, while welcoming traders from outside, stated that they could not acquire any permanent rights in the land.

The enactment of these laws set a precedent for the subsequent promulgation by Paramount Chief Lerotholi of Part I of the *Laws of Lerotholi*. This is a declaration of the customary law, but cannot be regarded as true legislation [441] since its enactment took place during the Colonial Era when only the Imperial government or its local representatives had power to legislate for the country.[442]

In 1959 the Legislative Council was created by Order in Council.[443] This gave the Basutoland National Council power to legislate on various matters with the consent of the Paramount Chief and the assent of the Queen.[444] Such enactments between 1960 and 1965

---

439. *See* HAILEY, *supra* note 321, at 46. These laws are no longer in force today.

440. For the text of the three laws, *see* II THEAL, BASUTOLAND RECORDS at 133, 152-53, 536-37 (Struik 1964).

441. *See supra* pp. 106-107.

442. The High Commissioner's Proclamations cannot really be regarded as local legislation since the High Commissioner was a British civil servant and anyway he was stationed in Pretoria.

443. The Basutoland (Constitution) Order in Council, 1959.

444. *Id.* § 45.

are styled "Laws." Since Independence, legislation has been enacted by the Lesotho Parliament, and these statutes are now designated as "Acts."[445] The process by which legislation is enacted today is discussed briefly below.

(3) CAPE COLONIAL STATUTES

In addition there are some pre-1884 statutes of the Colony of the Cape of Good Hope that are still in force. The only Cape statutes in force in 1960, apart from those specially applied by the Basutoland legislature,[446] were those contained in the First and Third Schedules to the Law Revision Proclamation.[447] Of these, the five relating to companies[448] have been repealed by the Companies Act of 1967, but four old Cape statutes relating to the execution of wills are still in force,[449] as are the 1873 and 1874 Law of Inheritance Acts.[450] Other significant examples are the

---

445. *Id.* § 56(9) re-enacted in § 63(7) of the 1966 Constitution.

446. An example of a Cape Colonial statute being specifically applied in Basutoland is Cape Act 14 of 1885, which became the Diamond Proclamation No. 1B of 1887 of Basutoland. It has only recently been repealed. The Law Revision Proclamation also kept in force in Basutoland laws enacted by any legislative authority succeeding the Cape Colony legislative authority (*i.e.*, the Union Parliament) that have been specially applied to Basutoland by its legislature. An example of this type of statute is Union Act 10 of 1911, which was applied as the Post Office Proclamation No. 27 of 1916 and is still in force today.

447. Proc. 12 of 1960.

448. Loans on shares (Ordinance 13, 1846); Joint Stock Companies (Act 23 of 1861); Joint Stock Companies Winding-Up (Act 12 of 1868); Companies' Trustees (Act 3 of 1873); and Banking Companies (Act 11 of 1879).

449. Wills (Execution) (Ordinance 15, 1845 as amended by Act 10 of 1879); Wills (Execution) (Act 22, 1876); Wills (Execution) (Act 3, 1878).

450. LAWS OF BASUTOLAND Vol. II 1507 (1960).

Prescription Amendment Act,[451] the Age of Majority Ordinance,[452] the Friendly Societies Act,[453] the Vagrancy Act,[454] the Mercantile Law Amendment Act,[455] and parts of the Evidence in Civil Proceedings Ordinance.[456]

From the wording of the General Law Proclamation it is clear that Cape Colonial legislation, like the common law, is only to be administered subject to the condition that the circumstances of the country permit its operation.

We have already referred to the unsuitability of the Cape Vagrancy Act of 1879.[457] People "found wandering abroad and having no visible lawful means, or sufficient lawful means, of support" who cannot give a satisfactory account of themselves may be held to be "idle and disorderly persons" under the Act.[458] Similarly it is made an offence to harbour such people.[459] Again every person found without lawful excuse wandering over any farm, or in or loitering near any dwelling house, shop, garden, or kraal is deemed and taken to be an idle and disorderly person and guilty of an offence.[460]

It is thought that such offences cannot be considered applicable as they stand because the circumstances of the country do not permit it. The activities specified as punishable are common features of everyday life.

---

451. Act 6 of 1861, see *supra* pp. 149, 168-169.

452. Ordinance 62, 1829.

453. Act 7 of 1882.

454. Act 23 of 1879.

455. Act 8 of 1879. See *supra* pp. 88-89.

456. Ordinance 72, 1830, as amended by Act 4 of 1861 and Act 21 of 1877. See *supra* pp. 89-90.

457. *Supra* p. 69.

458. *Id.* § 2.

459. *Id.* § 3.

460. *Id.* § 4.

The Prescription Act,[461] which is directly contrary to the customary law, has however been held [462] to override the traditional rule that a debt never dies, and thus it appears that it is deemed applicable to the circumstances of Lesotho.

The Age of Majority Ordinance, dating back to 1829,[463] provides:

> From and after the passing of this Ordinance, all persons when they shall attain or who have already attained the full age of twenty-one years shall be deemed to have attained the legal age of majority.

The traditional rule of Sesotho law is that only the father of a family is a major. His wives, his daughters, and his unmarried sons are all minors, and he is liable for their delicts under section 6 of Part I of the *Laws of Lerotholi* which provides:

> [T]he head of a family may be held liable for a wrongful act or debt of his minor children (*i.e.*, unmarried children living in his house and under his control).

In *Chaule v. Makae* [464] the father of a 28-year-old man was sued for compensation for a seduction by his son. His contention that his son was a major and thus liable for his own delicts was rejected by the Judicial Commissioner's Court. The court held that the 1829 Ordinance had not abrogated customary law on the point and the son was still a minor. The same conclusion was reached in a later case of assault.[465]

In *Nako v. Nako* [466] an unmarried man of 30 was held to be a major on the basis that any other rule was

---

461. Act 6 of 1861.

462. Seakhi v. Seakhi, J.C. 209/1953. See *supra* pp. 168-169.

463. Ordinance 62, 1829.

464. J.C. 166/1963.

465. Mopeli v. Rathebe, J.C. 238/1964.

466. J.C. 141/1949. See *supra* p. 161.

repugnant to justice and morality, but that decision has been criticised and must be rejected. It is clear that the custom is still operative despite the old Cape statute.

The Age of Majority Ordinance caters for marriage accelerating majority by declaring:

> Nothing herein contained shall extend or be construed to prevent any person under the age of twenty-one years from attaining his majority at an earlier period by operation of law.[467]

This coincides with the Sesotho custom that a man becomes a major upon his marriage even if he is under the age of 21.[468]

The Evidence in Civil Proceedings Ordinance [469] provides that:

> [I]t shall not, in any case, be competent to examine any person as a witness who does not understand the nature and recognise the religious obligation of an oath.[470]

Provision is however made for a solemn affirmation and declaration in lieu of an oath.[471] Nevertheless neither practice is of any significance to a non-Christian Mosotho and traditionally the people did not swear to tell the truth because it was not etiquette and because they knew it would not greatly impress the court which relied on its own ability to ascertain the truth by vigorous examination.[472]

The new Basuto courts (Practice and Procedure) Rules [473] state that the Basotho courts should admonish

---

467. § 5.
468. See DUNCAN, *supra* note 189, at 3.
469. Ordinance 72, 1830 as amended.
470. *Id.* § 6.
471. *Id.* § 31.
472. See ASHTON, *supra* note 191, at 242.
473. G.N. No. 21 of 1961, § 17(1) and (2).

all witnesses to speak the truth but the practice of administering oaths is not to be used.

The Ordinance also provides [474] that hearsay evidence shall be inadmissible in the same circumstances as it would in the Supreme Court of Judicature in England. This too is not in accordance with the customary law [475] and it is specifically laid down in the Basuto courts (Practice and Procedure) Rules that Basotho court practice and procedure should be regulated in accordance with Sesotho custom and law.[476]

The Wills (Execution) Ordinance of 1845 [477] provides that no will or other testamentary writing shall be valid unless it has both been signed by the testator [478] at the end thereof in the presence of two or more competent witnesses present at the same time, and such witnesses have attested and subscribed the will in the presence of the testator.[479]

The requirement of such formality for the making of wills is not only contrary to customary law, but also quite unsuitable to the circumstances of the Basotho people. Wills, accordingly, clearly remain valid according to customary law if they conform to the requirements of that law, regardless of the provisions of the Cape Ordinance.

The Law of Inheritance Act 1874 provides as follows: [480]

---

474. In § 22.

475. See ASHTON, *supra* note 191, at 239.

476. § 8. The Rules themselves are silent on the question of hearsay evidence.

477. Reprinted in LAWS OF BASUTOLAND VOL. VIII, 1963, at 509-10, § 3.

478. Or by some other person in the testator's presence and by his direction.

479. Notarial wills are however unaffected by the Act—see § 4.

480. Part II, § 5.

> Every person competent to make a will shall have full power by any will . . . to disinherit or omit to mention any child, parent, relative, or descendant without assigning any reason for such disinheritance or omission, any law, usage, or custom now or heretofore in force in Basutoland notwithstanding: and no such will as aforesaid shall be liable to be set aside as invalid, either wholly or in part, by reason of such disinheritance or omission as aforesaid.

This law poses very grave problems because of a conflict with customary law. It should first be pointed out that the word "Basutoland" was substituted for "Colony" by the Law Commissioner who undertook the 1960 revision of the laws, presumably because the word "Colony" originally referred to the Colony of the Cape of Good Hope. However Basutoland was still a colony in 1960 and there was no necessity to make such an alteration. The word "Colony" was retained in the same Act in the 1959 revision of the Laws of the Bechuanaland Protectorate despite the fact that that country was not a colony.[481]

In addition, the original Cape Act was clearly contemplating a reform of the Roman-Dutch common law. Under the old law a testator was bound to leave a certain portion of his estate, known as the legitimate portion, to his descendants and ascendants and in certain cases, to his brothers and sisters.[482] These explanations of the background to the wording of the statute are important since *prima facie* any contrary Sesotho law is abolished by the Act. Moreover there is a well-established rule of customary law to the effect that while wills are recognised they are only valid provided the heir according to Sesotho custom has not been deprived of the greater part of his father's estate.

---

481. Volume II, p. 1148 of the Law of the Bechuanaland Protectorate.

482. VOET 28, 2, 1-14.

This rule is to be found in section 14(1) of the *Laws of Lerotholi,* and was applied by the High Court in the case of *Mokorosi v. Mokorosi*[483] in 1954. The court thus held the will was only valid as to half of the estate; the other half devolved on the heir in accordance with customary law. Unfortunately, while upholding the decisions of three Basotho courts and the Judicial Commissioner's Court, the High Court did not advert to the problem raised by the Inheritance Act.

In view of the express wording of the Act, it is difficult to argue that the circumstances of the country do not permit its application without modification. However, perhaps it may be contended that the statute in referring to wills is only dealing with wills that are valid under the common law or statute and not customary wills. Thus, if a person executes a valid customary law will he will be bound by the rule that he cannot deprive the heir of the greater part of the estate. The *Mokorosi* case of course goes much further than this but the decision appears to have been given *per incuriam.*

B. The Enactment of Legislation

The enactment of legislation is now governed by section 63 of the Constitution,[483a] which provides that bills must originate in the National Assembly, usually be passed by both Houses[484] and then be assented to by the King. The bill is normally introduced by a Minister and is then read for the first time formally. A

483. [1954] H.C.T.L.R. 24.

483a. *See* Part II *infra* pp. 247-248. It should be borne in mind that since February 1970, legislative power has been vested in the Council of Ministers; *see* Preface, p. v.

484. § 65 specifies those occasions on which it is not necessary for the Senate to have passed a bill before it is presented to the King for his assent.

second reading is held later, and it is at this stage that Parliament debates the proposals contained in the bill. Before or after the second reading the bill may be sent to a select committee for its deliberations or, alternatively, the bill may be debated by the chamber in its committee stage. Next there is the report stage when the committee reports its conclusions to the House. Finally, the bill, which may by then have been substantially amended is read a third time, formally. If it is passed it then goes to the Senate. The Senate will then go through the same procedure as the Assembly with three readings. Unless it is sought to alter an entrenched section of the Constitution, a simple majority suffices to pass the bill.

Upon the King's assent, the bill becomes law and the King must thereupon cause it to be published in the Government Gazette as a law.[485] No law can come into force until it is published in the Gazette, but Parliament may provide for particular laws to come into operation at a date subsequent to their promulgation in the Gazette. Laws may also be made with retrospective effect.[486]

Annual volumes of legislation are published, but only in English, and there have also been two publications of volumes of the *Revised Edition of the Laws*, also only in English. The last was in 1960 and the one before that in 1949. Both the commissions entrusted with the task of consolidation were given wide powers to omit and alter laws provided no substantial amendments were made.[487] The Revised Edition of 1960 is conclusive proof of the statute law in force in the country on 5th March 1960 subject to certain specified

---

485. § 63(5) of the Constitution. *See* § 12(4) also.

486. *Id.* § 63(6).

487. *See, e.g.*, Law Revision Proclamation (No.12 of 1960), § 4.

omissions.[488] Thus any earlier statutes that do not appear in that Edition (or the specified omissions) have been impliedly repealed if this were not done so expressly.

The Law Revision (Reprinting and Correction) Law 1964 [489] provides for the publication of reprints of laws, together with amendments. Any such authorised reprint shall be deemed in all courts and for all purposes whatsoever to be the authentic law in force on the date of its publication.[490]

---

488. *Id.* § 14(2), applied in Mokotjomela v. R., [1963-66] H.C.T.L.R. 214. This provision has the effect of abolishing the old Roman-Dutch doctrine of abrogation of statutes by disuse. Any statute recognised by the Law Revision Proclamation or contained in the 1960 EDITION OF THE LAWS remains in force until it is repealed by legislation. Certain of the very old Roman and Roman-Dutch statutes (*e.g.*, JUSTINIAN'S CORPUS JURIS CIVILIS, the *Senatusconsultum Velleianum*, the *authentica si qua mulier*, the Political Ordinance of 1580 and the Octrooi of the Estates General of 10th January 1661) have, however, become embodied in the common law and different considerations therefore apply to them. South African law has long recognised the abrogation of a rule of the common law by disuse—see Green v. Fitzgerald, [1914] A.D. 88; Estate Heinamann v. Estate Heinamann, [1918] A.D. 84. The law can be rendered obsolete by contrary usage or by nonenforcement for a very long period in face of circumstances calling for its enforcement.

489. Law 4 of 1964.

490. *Id.* § 2(1).

PART II
THE CONSTITUTION

CHAPTER 1

THE GROWTH OF THE CONSTITUTION

A. The Constitutional Advance
B. The Constitution of 1959
C. The Constitution of 1965

After twelve years of Cape Colonial rule and nearly 86 years of British administration, the Basotho people on October 4, 1966, regained the independence their forefathers had decided to renounce in 1868 in preference to military defeat at the hands of the besieging Boers.

The outward sign of the renascent liberty of Lesotho was the promulgation of the Independence Constitution of 1966 by Order in Council dated September 20, 1966. By virtue of this Order of Her Majesty, Great Britain released Lesotho from its previous status of Crown Colony and, save for the retention of appeals of cases to the Judicial Committee of the Privy Council, severed its legal entitlement to rule. All rights, liabilities, and obligations of Her Majesty passed at the appointed day to the Government of Lesotho [1] and in the mandatory language of the first section of the Constitution it was established that "Lesotho shall be a sovereign democratic kingdom." Sovereign and democratic, Lesotho became an independent member of the British Commonwealth and the United Nations.

A. The Constitutional Advance

The roots of nationalism were never dormant during 98 years of foreign rule. Britain, at the behest of a people on the verge of capitulation, came reluctantly to the rescue in 1868, extending its political and

1. Lesotho Independence Order 1966, § 17.

military aegis to prevent a Boer conquest of Basutoland. Yet to the Basotho, though British protection was a sensible course in such perilous times, it was never meant to be permanent. As early as 1872 Letsie I, successor and son of Moshoeshoe, petitioned for representation in the Cape Parliament for the Basotho. In 1919 Paramount Chief Griffith requested that Her Majesty "extend still further steps in the direction of self-government to the Chiefs, Headmen, and people of the Basotho nation, in terms of the expressed wish of the late Chief Moshoeshoe when he sought the protection of the Government of Great Britain." [2] In a "steadily consistent way" requests for indigenous political autonomy emanated from Basutoland throughout the Colonial Era. For purposes of an account of constitutional development, however, the most important request emerged in 1955 as Motion 90 of the Basutoland National Council which resolved "that the Basutoland Council be given power to make laws in all internal matters, such laws to be confirmed by the Paramount Chief."

The Secretary of State's response to Motion 90 stated his willingness to hear proposals for a grant of law-making competence to the Council, yet this competence would clearly not extend "to matters affecting people other than the Basotho or countries other than Basutoland." Furthermore, he placed the burden of devising methods and policies of accommodation between the British administration and the Basotho administration upon the Council in the following terms:

> But before the Basutoland Council are given powers to pass laws, however, they will have to think how they should go about law-making and who is going to put the laws they pass into effect.

2. BASUTOLAND CONSTITUTIONAL HANDBOOK 48 (1960).

> The laws made by the Basutoland National Council will have to be administered by the Central Government and the Basotho Administration, and Councillors will have to consider how the Central Government and the Basotho Administration should be associated with the Council in the preparation and discussion of draft laws. The Basutoland Council must, therefore, submit its considered recommendations on these matters at the same time as it submits detailed proposals with regard to the scope of its law-making powers.[3]

In order to submit a detailed reply to the Secretary of State, the Council formed the Constitutional Reform Committee chaired by Councillor George Bereng.[4] The Committee was made up of one Councillor coming from each of the nine districts of the country, and in 1957 it invited Professor D. V. Cowen of the faculty of law at the University of Cape Town to serve as its constitutional advisor. By this time the Committee had already decided to work conjunctively with another committee of the Basutoland National Council, the Chieftainship Committee, which had been formed in 1956 to study the entire question of the place and function of the chiefs in the country. Because the role of the chiefs in the future constitutional structure was bound to be of cardinal importance,

> . . . it was unanimously accepted by both committees that the subject of constitutional reform was involved in the work of the Chieftainship Committee; . . . it soon became apparent that the tasks entrusted to the two committees were related and overlapped.

B. The Constitution of 1959

The work of the Constitutional Reform Committee and the Chieftainship Committee culminated in a

3. *Id.* at 9.
4. *Id.* at 11.

report submitted to the Basutoland National Council in July, 1958. This report, which was to be the detailed answer sought by the Secretary of State, gained unanimous approval by the Council. When presented in London by a special delegation from the Council it proved to be the basis, with slight exception, for the first Constitution of Basutoland in 1959.

The Constitution of 1959 reflected a concern with two troublesome issues. The first was a transitional matter, the proper share of indigenous power to be held by the Basotho as they strode toward an eventual independence as against the proper share of colonial power to be reserved by a British Government relaxing its grip yet concerned with the maintenance of order, the safeguarding of minority rights, and the political education of the Basotho. The second, as important as it was intractable, would prove to pose the permanent question mark: What ought to be the position of the traditional chiefs in the power structure established by the Constitution?

(1) DUAL LEGISLATIVE AND EXECUTIVE COMPETENCE

Generally speaking the Constitution resolved the first issue of temporary dual authority by the following means.

A newly constituted Basutoland National Council, consisting of 80 members, was established with the general power to legislate "for the peace, order, and good government of Basutoland." [5] This power or legislative competence, however, was subject to a reserved zone of legislative competence held exclusively by the High Commissioner with respect to which he

5. Lesotho Constitution, 1959, § 45(1). In connection, see Basutoland National Council Standing Orders, High Commissioner's Notice No. 16 of 1960.

also was empowered to make laws, styled "Proclamations," for the "peace, order, and good maintenance of Basutoland." The reserved zone—the "High Commissioner's matters"—specifically included the areas of External Affairs and Defence, Internal Security, Currency, Customs, Public Loans, Excise, Post, Television, Telephone, Broadcasting, Telegraph, Copyright, Trademark, Designs, Patent, and all matters concerning the Civil Service. Since it was recognised that there would perhaps be a certain amount of overlapping and that the Council and the High Commissioner would perhaps have concurrent competence that might lead to an undesirable amount of parallel legislation, provision was made for "hybrid" legislation. In such a case where a law was proposed in the Council which contained provisions in relation to the High Commissioner's reserved zone, the High Commissioner might signify his concurrence for its passage; and conversely, where a High Commissioner's Proclamation contained provisions in relation to the Council's zone of competence, the Council might by resolution concur in its passage.[6] The Council was granted the right to be consulted and to discuss beforehand any proclamation made by the High Commissioner save where its immediate passage was in his opinion necessary in the public interest.[7]

The right to consultation provided an avenue of appeal above the High Commissioner's office. Thus in cases where the Council objected that a proclamation dealt with subject matter outside of the "High Commissioner's matters" or that a proclamation was in effect discriminatory against any racial or religious community, it could require the High Commissioner

---

6. § 45(4).
7. § 46(1).

to submit the question to the Secretary of State. The Secretary's decision would be final.[8]

On the other hand the High Commissioner was vested with a *reserved power* which, irrespective of the apparent zones of competence established by the Constitution, enabled him to pass into law any bill or motion that the Council failed to pass in such form or within such time as he deemed reasonable or expedient, provided that in his opinion the bill was "expedient in the interests of public order, public faith, or good government." [9]

The dyarchy on the legislative level, which we have sketched, existed also at the executive level. The Constitution established an Executive Council comprised of eight members: the Resident Commissioner, three *ex officio* members (the Government Secretary, the Finance Secretary, and the Legal Secretary), and four members of the Basutoland National Council. Three of these four would be elected by ballot in the Council. The Executive Council was to be "the central policy-making body for Basutoland" similar in function to a cabinet, yet different in that it was not *responsible* to the legislature because it did not depend upon the legislature's confidence. Further, it differed from a cabinet in that its advice was not binding on the High Commissioner. The High Commissioner or the Resident Commissioner could act in opposition to the advice of the Executive Council whenever he considered it "right to do so," [10] though he was required to consult with the Executive Council unless the matter was too trivial, urgent, or secret.[11] The

8. §§ 46(2) and 46(3).

9. § 55(1).

10. § 22(1).

11. § 16.

Paramount Chief, however, was required to act in accordance with the advice of the Executive Council [12] unless the matter were trivial, urgent, or specifically placed in his discretion by section 18(2) of the Constitution. The Paramount Chief was entitled to be informed of the advice tendered by the Executive Council to the High Commissioner or the Resident Commissioner and could require that such advice be reconsidered at a subsequent meeting.[13]

Once a bill had passed through the Basutoland National Council it had to be presented first to the Paramount Chief for his assent and second to the High Commissioner. No bill could become law until the Royal Assent had been given. Concerning the powers of the Paramount Chief, it is clear that he possessed no power of veto. He was empowered, however, to delay the question of his assent. He was able to refer a bill back to the National Council for its reapproval and duplicate passage. If the National Council passed the *same* bill again after a delay of at least six months, then the Paramount Chief had no choice but to assent. It may be added that if in his opinion a bill was discriminatory against a racial or religious community the Paramount Chief could request that the bill be reserved for Her Majesty's signification.[14] At the next stage a bill which carried the Paramount Chief's assent was presented to the High Commissioner. Constitutionally he was not obliged to approve any measure. Bills that, in his opinion, contained objectionable features could be referred, together with a statement of objections, to the National Council for reconsideration, in which case all procedural stages were set at

---

12. § 23(1).
13. § 21(2).
14. § 56(2); § 58(2)(b)(iii).

naught.[15] It should be noted, however, that all laws, whether bills assented to or proclamations issued by the High Commissioner, remained subject to a power of disallowance of Her Majesty through a Secretary of State.[16] Furthermore, it was within the High Commissioner's discretion to reserve any bill for signification of the Queen's pleasure, and with respect to certain kinds of bills he was obliged to do so.[17]

The legislative and executive setting just de-

---

15. § 57.

16. § 60(1).

17. § 58(b). These included bills: (i) affecting provisions of the Constitution; (ii) relating to the privileges and immunities of the Basutoland Council or of its members; (iii) involving discrimination in favour or against any racial or religious community, if reservation were requested by Motlotlehi (the Paramount Chief); (iv) relating to entry into, and residence in, Basutoland; (v) varying the qualifications or disqualifications for voters in elections for District Councils.

Further the High Commissioner was under Royal Instructions not to assent to any of the following kinds of bills without the previous assent from Her Majesty:

(a) any bill for the divorce of married persons;
(b) any bill whereby any grant of land or money or other donation may be made to himself or to a Resident Commissioner;
(c) any bill affecting the currency of Basutoland or relating to the issue of banknotes;
(d) any bill establishing any banking association or altering the Constitution, powers, or privileges of any such association;
(e) any bill imposing differential duties;
(f) any bill the provision of which shall appear to him inconsistent with obligations imposed upon Us by Treaty;
(g) any bill affecting the discipline or control of Our naval, military, or air forces;
(h) any bill of an extraordinary nature and importance whereby Our prerogative, or the rights or property of Our subjects not residing in Basutoland, or the trade or transport or communications of any part of Our dominions or any territory under Our protection or in which We have for the time being jurisdiction may be prejudiced;
(i) any bill containing provisions to which Our assent has been once refused, or which have been disallowed by Us. *High Commission Territories Royal Instructions* H.C.N. 103 of 1959.

scribed is a complex and cumbersome scenario. Yet distribution of power is often more formal than substantial. As had been the case throughout the Colonial Era, here too, local government was left a wide orbit of practical autonomy which on the everyday level was the efficacious mode of rule while colonial government continued to hold dominant yet dormant jural powers.

> All the earlier stages of the history of Basutoland were characterized by the existence not merely of a marked line of demarcation between the matters controlled by the Administration and the matters which were left to the Basuto authorities, but by the unusual extent of the matters lying within the second category.[18]

The constitutional rearrangement of 1959 affected little the premises and workings of the system of "indirect rule." Indeed one may well take the view that the constitutional advance made in 1959 mainly accomplished the legal realisation of the *de facto* system of government.

(2) CONSTITUTIONAL REFORM OF THE CHIEFTAINSHIP

The future of a traditional system of political leadership based on hereditary prerogatives presented a dilemma to the Constitutional Reform Committee and Chieftainship Committee. On the one hand was the fact that the chiefs retained popular support and enjoyed prestige among the people of the nation.[19] That

---

18. V HAILEY, NATIVE ADMINISTRATION IN THE BRITISH AFRICAN TERRITORIES 133 (H.M.S.O. 1953).

19. This is not meant to imply that their support and prestige had not declined, for this seems axiomatic of the colonial condition. British rule in Basutoland as elsewhere in Africa tended to make the Chiefs responsible to the Government but not responsible to their people. JONES, BASUTOLAND MEDICINE MURDER CMD. No. 8209, at 69 (H.M.S.O. 1951). *See generally* BUSIA, THE POSITION OF THE CHIEFS IN THE MODERN POLITICAL SYSTEM OF ASHANTI (1951).

they were needed as "guardians of law and order" was a theory already heavily subscribed to by the British as evidenced by the introduction of the system of indirect rule in the Native Administration Proclamation of 1938. There could be little doubt that the chieftainship itself must be brought under greater institutionalised control and be made subject to law. Three areas in need of reform were those of disciplining, recognising, and remunerating the chiefs.[20] On the other hand reform of the chieftainship was not enough, for those concerned with hastening the political independence of the colony could not fail to recognise that given a certain pattern of colonial policy, London would have *a priori* objections to nondemocratic political institutions at independence. Lord Hailey had observed in 1953:

> However much the Native Authorities may insist on their claim to represent the Basotho nation, they are not likely to persuade the British Government to concede an advance in political status to Basutoland on terms which will transfer power to an oligarchy consisting of the Paramount Chief and a body of Chiefs of traditional standing. If there is anything in the principles which have hitherto regulated Colonial policy, such a status will only be conceded to a Government responsible to a suitably constituted and suitably powered Legislature.[21]

The Constitution of 1959 was not the place for radical innovations, but obviously some greater concessions to the electoral principle had to be made. The composition of the National Council had changed from the chiefly conclave of 1903 where the Paramount Chief nominated 95 out of 100 members. By 1958, 36

---

20. REPORT ON THE CONSTITUTIONAL REFORM AND CHIEFTAINSHIP AFFAIRS 51 (1958).

21. HAILEY, *supra* note 18, at 142.

out of the 100 members were indirectly elected by the nine district councils [22] and another six members were elected by sundry organisations in the community. Accordingly the decision was taken to make the National Council more representative of the people's will yet not so representative as to create an elected majority of members. The majority view of the report was that "at this stage of Basutoland's constitutional progress it would be premature to recommend an elected majority." [23] The Constitution of 1959 therefore widened the elected element to 40 members, still to be chosen indirectly by the district councils, which served as a kind of electoral college.[24] The nonelected membership was correspondingly set at 40 members comprised of an *official* element of four senior members of the Civil Service, a *traditional* element of 22 Principal and Ward Chiefs who would be *ex officio* members, and a *nominated* element of fourteen members selected by the Paramount Chief.

(a) Establishing the College of Chiefs

The solution to the problem of reforming the chieftainship which was advocated in the Report and adopted under the Constitution was the establishment of a body called the College of Chiefs. The College of Chiefs was designed to administer and police the chieftainship. Concerning the recognition of chiefs,

---

22. The composition of the district councils was not such as to deprive the "indirect elections" of popular participation. Each would include one elected member per 1,000 taxpayers together with each Principal and Ward Chief in the District, nominees of the Paramount Chief, representatives of African organisations, and the District Commissioner as chairman.

23. *Supra* note 20, at 62. A minority of the joint committees favoured the principle of an elected majority.

24. *See* Local Government Proclamation No. 52 of 1959 and District Councils Elections Proclamation No. 53 of 1959.

it was empowered to present for discretionary recognition by the High Commissioner a person deemed to be the Paramount Chief and to the Paramount Chief those to be mandatorily recognised as chiefs and headmen.[25] Its duties included the settlement of disputes as to hereditary successions to office, the delimitation and adjustment of chiefdoms, and the rights, duties, and powers of the chiefs conferred by Sesotho law and custom. Concerning the disciplining of the criminous, absent, or inefficient chiefs, the College was constituted to investigate such complaints and to recommend suspensions or removals by the Paramount Chief. The functions of the College already outlined were to be carried out by a standing committee of four members of the College elected by the rest. Under the 1959 Constitution the Standing Committee, as envisaged by the Report,[26] was to function as an administrative tribunal. Recommendations addressed to the Paramount Chief by the Standing Committee in these matters were binding on him subject to his right to refer a recommendation back to the Standing Committee for further consideration.[27] However, if the Standing Committee gave the same recommendation again or if their recommendation had been varied, confirmed, or reversed by the High Court, then the Paramount Chief was obliged to follow the recommendation of the Committee or of the Court, as the case might be. Decisions of the Standing Committee were reviewable by the High Court on grounds of *ultra vires* decision, bad faith, or serious irregularity in the proceedings.[28]

---

25. The power to grant recognition to the chiefs had been, under the Native Administration Proclamation of 1938, formerly accorded to the High Commissioner.

26. *Supra* note 20, at 98. There it is called the "Action Committee."

27. Lesotho Const. 1959 § 78(1).

28. § 79(1).

The Constitution of 1959 also "confirmed and declared" that the land in Basutoland was legally vested in the Paramount Chief in trust for the Basotho nation. The Paramount Chief and his chiefs, who under customary law hold a monopolistic control of land allocation and usage, retained their prerogative over the land by virtue of section 72(2):

> The allocation or grant of any right or privilege to occupy or use or in any way enjoy land to any person belonging to the Basotho nation, shall continue to be governed by Basotho law and custom for the time being in force. . . .[29]

C. The Constitution of 1965

The Constitution of 1959 was intended to be provisional. Its own draftsmen had described it as "a step out of a deep rut." And it became clear at an early date that the legal changes wrought by the Constitution were not sufficient for the now advancing tide of Basotho nationalism.[30] Furthermore, "a radical and really decisive step forward" was viewed as a precondition to the spontaneous release of energy and enthu-

---

29. The subject of land ownership, control, and tenure is discussed *infra*, pp. 254-268. Land reform is discussed *supra* pp. 172-189.

30. In part, this must have been a systemic disability of the document, for the increased powers of the Council and the widening of democratic representation galvanised political parties and articulated public issues in new degree. The inadequacies of the Constitution itself could not be immune from the effects of this healthy trend. The Basutoland Congress Party, which had won 30 out of the 40 elected seats in the 1960 elections, had almost from the very first rejected the Constitution and unequivocally called for speedy independence. The Paramount Chief, Bereng Seeiso, early identified himself as a nationalist. "Empiricism," a word he stressed, was a pejorative pun applied to the policies of British rule in Basutoland.

siasm required to ameliorate the misery, poverty, and subsistence condition of the Basotho people.

In September, 1961, the Basutoland National Council moved for the appointment of another Constitutional Commission whose terms of reference included:

(i) the improvement of the Constitution;

(ii) the introduction of responsible government; and

(iii) the addition of provisions protecting Human Rights and Fundamental Freedoms.

The Commission undertook to consult the views of the people about what kind of constitution they desired and between September and October, 1962, it extensively toured the country. Its report was completed in October, 1963. The proposals for constitutional change were significant and far reaching enough that when they were executed in the forthcoming Constitution of 1965 it could be assumed that Basutoland was politically and legally but a step from independence.

As with the 1959 Constitutional Report, the Report of 1963 was approved by the National Council and again served as the foundation for a new constitution, the Constitution of 1965. The merit of the Report had been to press for far-reaching constitutional measures while at the same time to convey with healthy impertinence the inadequacy of British colonial rule and the urgency of the situation. The Constitutional Conference held in London in 1964 produced not only an acceptance of the new constitutional advance, but a decisive statement about the timing of independence. The Secretary of State undertook that

> [I]f at any time not earlier than one year after the new elections the people of Basutoland, by resolutions of both Houses of the Basutoland Parliament (or, in the event of disagreements

between them by a majority of those voting on a referendum) should ask for independence, the British Government would seek to give effect to their wishes as soon as possible.[31]

Independence, then, was a possibility within two years. Certainly this would be an accelerated emancipation even by African standards.[32] The 1965 elections were the first mass elections in the history of the country. As of 1964 there was no elected majority in the Legislature. Six years is a short time to move from an official majority in the Legislature to cabinet government responsible to a purely democratic lower chamber. As we shall see, the independence progression would essentially be accomplished by the constitutional change in 1965 with the effect of eliminating, as a practical matter, an additional intermediary stage that the British traditionally employed in the transfer of power to a colony.[33] Thus, the 1965 Constitution produced fundamental changes in the division of power between Great Britain and Basutoland and in the internal structure of government, which must be explained in some detail.

(1) THE NEW DIVISION OF POWER

Under the 1959 Constitution the reserved zone of

---

31. REPORT OF THE BASUTOLAND INDEPENDENCE CONFERENCE 5 (1966).

32. *E.g.*, Ghana gained freedom in eleven years, Nigeria in eight. Lesotho negotiated the full route in seven.

33. It would have normally been the case after the 1959 Constitution to provide for a directly elected majority in the Legislature and a cabinet composed of elected and *ex officio* members presided over by the Governor (or British Representative). The stage featuring a prime minister, responsible cabinet, and directly elected lower chamber of Parliament would come later. This is the stage Lesotho reached in 1965 without going through the other. *See generally* JEFFRIES, TRANSFER OF POWER (Pall Mall, London 1960) and DE SMITH, THE NEW COMMONWEALTH AND ITS CONSTITUTIONS 38-76 (Stevens 1964).

Crown powers withdrawn from the legislative and executive competence of the Basotho placed a very small amount of legal power into the hands of the local institutions. Furthermore, the Basutoland National Council's zone of competence was subject to the Crown's powers of veto, certification, disallowance, and reservation. Obviously, with such elaborate external safeguards against the misuse of so little internal responsibility it was open to question by legal nationalists how the necessary political education for independence was to be developed. It could be shown, for example, that the field of external affairs, a reserved field, was in reality the field of internal affairs in a country with the unique geographical and economic disabilities of Basutoland.[34] The Commission remarked,

> If topics of this extent and importance, are to continue to be withdrawn from the competence of Basotho authorities it is idle, in our view, to talk of fitting the Basotho for genuine responsibility in government, let alone for independence.[35]

The recommendation of the Commission was to dispense entirely with the concept of a reserved zone of competence and in its place to insert in the Constitution a system of rule in which power was not di-

---

34. Besides San Marino, Lesotho is the only landlocked country in the world totally encircled by a single other country. With about 40% of its male adult working population living at any one time in South Africa and external sources of income comprising about 60% of the total government funds for expenditures, and its most significant internal income dependent on a customs agreement with South Africa, Lesotho's problems in the field of foreign affairs can hardly be overemphasised. The Report (*supra* note 31 at 33) noted that "Even the milk supply of the township of Maseru is a matter of external affairs, inasmuch as milk still has to be imported from the Republic." The geography and economy of Lesotho are fully discussed in the Introduction of this book.

35. *Supra* note 31, at 33.

vided but shared. To this new approach of governing the country was given the name "Condominium." Legislatively and executively the government of Basutoland was to have full competence on every matter except in the areas of defense, external affairs, internal security, public service, and finance. In these areas the British government would have concurrent but overriding powers of veto and certification.

(2) THE STATUS OF THE NATION AND OF THE PARAMOUNT CHIEF

The Report of the 1963 Constitutional Commission had strongly recommended that the Paramount Chief be recognised as the head of state under the style and title of King of Lesotho, and that Basutoland pass from the status of a Crown colony to that of a protected state or protectorate, as had always been the case in Bechuanaland and Swaziland. As a matter of British constitutional law, a colony is a dependency which has been annexed by the Crown. Its inhabitants are British subjects; its land is part of the Queen's dominions. A protected state or protectorate, on the other hand, is not an annexure at all. It is, technically speaking, a foreign country.[36] From 1884 onwards the head of state of Basutoland had been the monarch of Great Britain who ruled the country through the office of High Commissioners in residence in South Africa.

---

36. WIGHT, BRITISH COLONIAL CONSTITUTIONS 77 (O.U.P. 1947). The distinction in terms of legal power is purely a formal one since the passage of the Foreign Jurisdiction Acts of 1890 and 1913, 53 & 54 Vict., c. 37, and 3 & 4 Geo. 5, c. 16. Section one provides: "It is and shall be lawful for Her Majesty The Queen to hold, exercise, and enjoy any jurisdiction Her Majesty now has or may at time hereafter have within a *foreign* country *in the same and as ample manner* as if Her Majesty had acquired that jurisdiction by the cession or conquest of territory." (Italics added).

This constitutional relationship followed from the ordinary meaning of the Annexation Proclamation of 1868:

> From and after the publication hereof, the said tribe of the Basotho shall be and shall be taken to be, for all intents and purposes, British subjects; and the territory of the said tribe shall be, and shall be taken to be, British Territory.

At the constitutional discussions held in 1964, however, the British government decided not to alter the status of the country or to change its head of state. Basutoland would remain a colony until independence. Nevertheless some new and important provisions were introduced. The office of Motlotlehi (Paramount Chief) was formally established with sovereign immunities and Civil List (a tax-free allowance), and the designation of the rightful holder of that office was completely entrusted to the College of Chiefs acting in accordance with Sesotho customary law.[37] Previously, even under the 1959 Constitution, the High Commissioner possessed the discretion to recognise the Paramount Chief, and his choice need not have been in accordance with customary law.[38]

(a) Abolition of the High Commission Territory

The Constitution of 1965 also brought into force a long-overdue reform in the mode of British administration. Basutoland—one of the three High Commission territories—had throughout its history as a British colony been administered by a High Commissioner

---

37. Subject to an aggrieved heir's right to apply to the High Court to determine whether his claim under Sesotho law and custom was not superior to the designee of the College. *See* Lesotho Const., 1959, § 22(9).

38. Bereng Griffith v. 'Mantsebo Seeiso Griffith, [1926-53] H.C.T.L.R. 50, 79-84.

with offices in South Africa, who delegated authority and gave instructions to a Resident Commissioner stationed in Maseru.

It has been noted that this form of administration had unfortunate repercussions on Basutoland's development. The Office of the High Commissioner was made subject to the Commonwealth Relations Office rather than the Colonial Office because of the close relationship of the High Commission Territories with South Africa. As a result,

> [T]he territories were placed in the anomalous position of being worse off than other British Colonies and Protectorates inasmuch as these could theoretically evolve towards independence. The High Commission territories remained in a political limbo without prospect of change except in the direction of incorporation into South Africa. Even the development of local government was therefore twenty to forty years behind the times as compared with other British African territories.[39]

Furthermore, since 1930 the High Commissionership for the three territories was held simultaneously by the man who was High Commissioner for the United Kingdom in the Union of South Africa.[40] Dating from the withdrawal of South Africa from the Commonwealth in 1961 the High Commissioner continued his diplomatic duties under the new status of Britain's Ambassador to South Africa.

Here was a matter of good faith. How could one man perform "the often conflicting duties" of secur-

39. STEVENS, LESOTHO, BOTSWANA AND SWAZILAND 4 (Pall Mall, London 1967).

40. The latter was a diplomatic post in South Africa. No other High Commissioner in the independent states of the Commonwealth combined administrative and diplomatic duties. *See supra* note 36, at 78.

ing good relations with South Africa and at the same time carry out in the fullest degree the trust of the High Commission Territories? It might sometimes be true that a man could succeed in wearing two uniforms well, but the Basotho could with some justice complain that not only should their uniform be worn all the time but that it is nigh impossible to display both at once.[41] Yet, as the Commission would point out, this

> [E]ven if it were possible for a gifted man to combine these functions with full justice for all, we would emphasise that not only must justice be done, but it must manifestly be seen to be done. And, however good intentions or even practice may be under the present dispensation, the formal machinery, as seen by the ordinary citizen, does not, and cannot, inspire confidence.[42]

The thrust of this criticism led to the abolition of the post of High Commissioner in 1964,[43] and the Resident Commissioner was given a status equivalent to that of Governor.[44] The Constitution of 1965 created the office of the British Representative, who would reside in Basutoland and be directly responsible to the Secretary of State in London rather than to a High Commissioner in Pretoria.[45]

---

41. The metaphor is not farfetched: "The two High Commissionerships are at present held by the same office, but the offices are quite distinct even to the extent of having different precedence, *uniforms*, and office staffs." PALMER, CONSULTATION AND CO-OPERATION IN THE BRITISH COMMONWEALTH 31 (O.U.P. 1934). (Italics added).

was not the issue.

42. REPORT OF THE BASUTOLAND CONSTITUTIONAL COMMISSION 54 (1963).

43. The Basutoland, Bechuanaland, and Swaziland (High Commisioner) (Revocation) Order S. I. 1186 of 1964.

44. 1964 BASUTOLAND ANNUAL REPORT 6.

45. This was, after all, only a belated compliance with the original intention of Moshoeshoe when he in 1862 asked for British protection: ". . . What I desire is this—that the Queen

(i) Summary

The two constitutional changes just explained—the obliteration of the reserved zone of legislative and executive competence and the creation of the post of British Representative — permit a summary of the new constitutional position. Parliament was given the power to "make laws for the peace, order, and good government of Basutoland," which is the traditional legal formula conferring self-government. After a bill had passed both houses of parliament,[46] it would be presented to the British Government Representative who, under Section 56(5), might take one of two actions: submit it to Motlotlehi for assent, or after consultation with the Prime Minister, reserve it for signification of the Queen's pleasure. Bills could be reserved, however, only on the following grounds:

(i) where apparently prejudicial to the discharge of his responsibility for external affairs, defense, or internal security;

(ii) where apparently necessary to ensure proper financial administration or compliance with a condition attached to a financial grant made by the United Kingdom;

(iii) where apparently necessary to protect the terms of service of public officers;

(iv) where apparently prejudicial to the Royal prerogative;

(v) where purporting to amend or replace any provision of the Constitution.

---

should send a man to live with me, who will be her ear and eye and also her hand to work with me in political matters . . . . The man whom I ask from the Queen to live with me will guide and direct me . . . . When the agent and I agree as to what is right I shall carry it out . . . ." THEAL, 3A BASUTOLAND RECORDS (1862-1865) 143-144 (Struik, Capetown).

46. Passage through the Senate could be merely constructive. *See* Lesotho Const. 1965 § 58.

When a bill was presented for Motlotlehi's assent, he, acting on ministerial advice, would signify that he assented or withheld his assent. His prior power of referral of legislation back to the National Council or to the Executive Council under the 1959 Constitution was abolished.

The British Government Representative retained the power to legislate in certain areas, *viz.*, external affairs, defense, internal security, financial administration, and protection of the terms of service of public officers.[47] The implementation of his legislative power was, in the first instance, to take the form of a written request to the Prime Minister calling for its enactment. If his request were not fulfilled either in the specified form or within the specified period of time he was empowered to give the necessary orders for its enactment and publication in the *Gazette*.[48]

(3) THE LEGISLATURE

The unicameral Basutoland National Council, partly democratic, partly aristocratic, partly colonial, was laid to rest by the Constitution of 1965. In its place was established a bicameral legislature closely modeled upon the Parliament of the United Kingdom. The National Assembly, the lower house, was to be a democratic chamber comprised of 60 members, a speaker, and a deputy speaker. Its democratic character was settled by low minimum qualifications for its membership,[49] by the abolition of the indirect elections

---

47. § 59(1).

48. § 59(2).

49. To be qualified he needed only to be 21 years old, a British subject registered as an elector in a constituency and able to speak, read, and write either English or Sesotho well enough to be active in Parliament. (§ 37.) Because of Lesotho's high literacy rate this disqualified relatively few persons. With this may be compared Botswana's constitutional requirement

(which featured the Basutoland National Council), by the introduction of direct elections, and more importantly, by voter qualifications that rejected property and literacy criteria in favour of criteria simply based upon age, nationality, and residence.[50] Basutoland was divided into 60 constituencies, each entitled to elect one member to the National Assembly.

The establishment of the Senate can be seen, as indeed so many constitutional choices can be viewed, as yet another attempt to shape and to articulate an acceptable and progressive role for an hereditary chieftainship in a democracy. The experiment under the provisional Constitution of 1959 of having an indirectly elected and nonelected membership in the National Council was termed by the report "incompatible with the effective introduction of responsible government—the stage of development to which the Basotho now desire to advance."[51] Thus, in relegating the chiefs to a second chamber which in terms of power was truly secondary, the constitutional draftsmen ef-

---

(§ 62) that Members of Parliament must be able to speak and read English, a requirement that disqualifies the vast majority of the population.

50. Lesotho Const. 1965 § 36. Basutoland (Electoral Provisions) Order 1964; The National Assembly (Franchise and Registration of Electors) (Replacement) Regulations 1964 and (Amendment 2) 1964; *Registration of Electors* (Appeals to Magistrates) Rules 1964; G.N. 111, 1964; National Assembly (Conduct of Elections) (Amendment 2) Regulations 1965, amended by G.N. 28 of 1965.

51. *Supra* note 42, at 31. The commission endorsed three reasons for this view: (1) The voting power of the nonelected members contracts the responsibility of the elected members to a compass narrower than that of the well-being of the entire community; (2) Elected members are encouraged to engage in irresponsible behaviour that could be blamed on the hostility of the nominated members; (3) Nonelected blocs inevitably impede the growth of cohesive political parties.

fected the compromise of maintaining the chiefs in public life in a dignified body while at the same time discounting their political strength. The Senate was to consist of the 22 Principal Chiefs and Wards Chiefs (who also comprised the College of Chiefs) and eleven other Senators "for the time being nominated in that behalf by Motlotlehi." [52] Similar in power to the House of Lords after the reforms of 1911 and 1949, the Senate had powers merely of amendment and delay. Its concurrence was not essential in the passage of legislation. When a bill was passed by the National Assembly and brought before the Senate for its deliberations, amendments could be proposed by the Senate and submitted to the National Assembly, yet if such amendments were not accepted the bill pushed on regardless, subject to appropriate delays,[53] to the British Government Representative who would submit it to Motlotlehi for his signature.

(4) THE EXECUTIVE

One of the recognised defects of the 1959 Constitution was that the Executive Council was merely representative and not responsible to the National Council. The National Council was entitled to elect three members to the Executive Council; however, once elected they were irremovable and thus not "responsible" to that body.[54]

---

52. These words became the subject of an interesting suit in the High Court: Molapo v. Seeiso, [1963-1966] H.C.T.L.R. 150. (Discussed *infra*, pp. 299-300.)

53. The delay varied according to the declared nature of the bill (§ 58). Bills certified by the speaker as appropriation bills had to be disposed of in one day, those certified as money bills (other than appropriation bills) in thirty days, all other bills (*i.e.*, uncertified bills) in ninety days. The speaker's certification could not be questioned in any court.

54. Thus a member of the Executive Council might defect

This regime of representative government was abolished by the introduction of the British cabinet system of parliamentary government replete with a prime minister and cabinet ministers who "shall be collectively responsible to the two Houses of Parliament for any advice given to Motlotlehi by or under the general authority of the Cabinet and for all things done by or under the authority of any Minister in the execution of his office." [55] The intricate relationship between the Sovereign (or his agent) and the Cabinet, regulated by convention [56] in the United Kingdom, is written out in detail. We shall not outline it here for it is described separately below.[57]

(5) THE COLLEGE OF CHIEFS

The powers and responsibilities conferred upon the College by the 1959 Constitution were virtually all taken away in the 1965 Constitution.

It is not clear precisely why these powers were divested other than perhaps because it was thought that, being considerable and significant, they ought to be decentralized or were better placed in the hands of a more efficient or a more sufficiently detached authority than the College. A third possibility was that

---

from his party without losing his position. "With the subsequent defection of Khaketla from the B.C.P. the Executive Council remained a highly conservative force, closely identified with official British policy. As a result, the elected majority in the Legislative Council became the opposition without representation in the 'government,' and considerable tension developed between the two." STEVENS, *supra* note 39, at 69.

55. § 67(2). For the doctrine of "collective responsibility," *see infra*, pp. 253-254.

56. For the concept of "constitutional conventions," *see infra*, pp. 305-316.

57. *See infra*, pp. 306-311.

the chiefs desired to be relieved of some of their duties. This was the explanation offered by the Report for taking away the responsibility for disciplining the chiefs.[58] However, the task of recognising rightful chiefs was taken away from the College without comment in the Report and the matter is not dealt with in the 1965 Constitution. Similarly the Report was not explicit in its reasoning as to why the College should be relieved of the function of resolving disputes as to placings, rank, and boundaries. These responsibilities are all omitted from the provisions of the 1965 Constitution dealing with the College, but they are not affirmatively transferred to any other authority by any provision in the Constitution, though the Report recommended certain actions. Thus discipline would be dealt with by Motlotlehi in consultation with his Privy Council, and the recognition of chiefs would be decided by nomination of the family subject to an aggrieved claimant's right to bring the matter before the ordinary courts. After any and all disputes were settled the nominee would be presented to Motlotlehi for formal recognition. Boundary questions concerning the 22 principal chiefdoms would, where private discussion failed, be settled by Motlotlehi on the advice of a judicial commission. The question of headmen placings would be turned over to an appropriate Minister.

As a result, the functions left to the College were two. First, the College would maintain and safeguard the national archives. Second, the College would have the authority to determine in accordance with customary law the succession (including the designation of regent) to the Paramount Chieftainship. Its determination on the matter of accession to the Paramountcy

---

58. § 74(1)(e) 1959 Constitution. The Report (*supra* note 42) stated that the chiefs had found the task "embarrassing."

was reviewable by the High Court (subject to no appeal) upon the application of any aggrieved claimant.[59]

(6) PROTECTION OF FUNDAMENTAL HUMAN RIGHTS AND FREEDOMS

Chapter I of the 1965 Constitution contained provisions protecting civil and social liberties. For a number of reasons these provisions were noteworthy but since there is so little difference between them and the corresponding provisions of the Independence Constitution of 1966, we can await a detailed discussion of the latter provisions.[60]

---

59. Lesotho Const. 1965 § 22(11). These were the recommendations of the Report (*supra* note 42).

60. *See infra*, p. 317 *et seq.*

CHAPTER 2

THE INDEPENDENCE CONSTITUTION

A. The King
B. The Parliament
C. The Cabinet
D. Land

In the Commonwealth and elsewhere it is common to hear of Westminster models. This has been explained to mean

> . . . a constitutional system in which the head of state is not the effective head of government; in which the effective head of government is a Prime Minister presiding over a cabinet composed of ministers over whose appointment and removal he has at least a substantial measure of control; in which the effective executive branch of government is parliamentary inasmuch as ministers must be members of the legislature; and in which ministers are collectively and individually responsible to a freely elected and representative legislature.[61]

On this score the Lesotho Constitution is a Westminster model; it has received the essentials of British government embodied in the trinity of Monarchy, Cabinet, and Parliament. Further, there has been a reception of the principles, rules, and something of the spirit of the laws that regulate British government. There is, however, a danger in the use of this term, for it may tend to obscure the fact that the Lesotho Constitution straddles diverse worlds of law; that it is an eclectic, not merely an anglophile; an inventor, not merely an emulator. Provisions and ideas from a variety of settings such as Nigeria and the United States have been received. New strides for greater pro-

61. DE SMITH, *supra* note 33, at 77-78.

tection of the liberties of the individual have been taken. The Constitution represents a further step, a new synthesis, an object of interest in itself. And it must not be forgotten that the aim in the final analysis was an attempt to conform and adapt and originate a constitution true to the wishes of the Basotho and to the social conditions in which they live. The ultimate model was Lesotho itself.

A. The King

The King is the Head of State, his office a creature of the Constitution. Chapter IV of the Constitution contains nine sections devoted to the office, rights, and immunities of the King (who for the time being is Moshoeshoe II). As has been explained, not since 1868 has a Paramount Chief been in legal theory the Head of State; however, the office of the King is clearly the successor in title if not in power to the pre-eminent place held by Paramount Chiefs ever since Moshoeshoe I, the founder of the Nation. Succession to the throne is determined by customary law [62] which, in brief, holds that the first male child of the first wife married succeeds.[63] The designation of the rightful succession according to custom is entrusted to the College of Chiefs, their only significant function.[64] Claimants who are aggrieved by the designation of the College may within six months make an application to the Court of Appeals to vary it, subject to no appeal.[65] A regent

62. Lesotho Constitution (1966) § 33(1).

63. DUNCAN, SOTHO LAWS AND CUSTOMS 43 (O.U.P. 1960).

64. The College has already designated Moshoeshoe II's sons Khosana-Letsie David and Khosana Simeon as the heirs apparent in that order and as this was not contested within 6 months their sucession is now incontestable. G.N. 54 of 1967.

65. §§ 33(1) and 35(1) of the Constitution.

may also be designated, but this designation apparently cannot be questioned in any court.

The King is entitled to a Civil List, that is, an annual tax-free sum granted by Parliament for the expenses of the royal household and establishment.[66] Furthermore he enjoys sovereign immunities: from taxation,[67] from compulsory seizure of his property,[68] from criminal proceedings (in respect of either his private or official capacity),[69] and from civil proceedings (in his private capacity only).[70] These immunities, however, attach only for so long as the office is held. It should be stressed that the King is amenable to civil process for all things done or omitted to be done in his official capacity.[71]

The King exercises a number of important constitutional tasks and the Constitution requires that he be consulted and informed concerning the affairs of government and conditions in the country.[72] The King's Privy Council, his board of advisors, presumably is of assistance in such matters. It consists of three persons: the Prime Minister, an appointee of the Prime Minister, and an appointee of the King. The advice of the Council is not binding.

---

66. *Id.* at § 36(1). In 1967-68 the appropriation for the King's Civil List was R30,262. *See* the Appropriation Act 9 of 1967.

67. § 37(1) of the Constitution.

68. *Id.* at § 37(3).

69. *Id.* at § 38.

70. Prescription on claims against the King does not run during the period in which the King holds office. *Id.* at § 38(3).

71. Thus the King was made defendant in the case of Molapo and Four Others v. Constantinus Bereng Seeiso, In His Capacity as Paramount Chief of Basutoland, [1963-1966] H.C.T.L.R. 150 (1966) under section 24 of the Constitution of 1965 which is substantially the same as the present provision, section 38(1).

72. § 77 of the Constitution.

In order to understand better the *fiction* that the Head of State is the head of government, it is necessary to grasp that the Constitution contemplates royal functions of three varieties.

(1) AGENCY POWERS

First there are functions in which the King is merely an agent under instructions from a constitutionally authorized principal. This role is general unless the Constitution specifically provides to the contrary. The basis for this general rule is section 76(1) which provides as follows:

> Subject to the provisions of subsection (2) of this section the King shall, in the exercise of his functions under this Constitution or any other law, act in accordance with the advice of the Cabinet or a Minister acting under the general authority of the Cabinet except in cases where he is required by this Constitution or any other law to act in accordance with the advice of any person or authority other than the Cabinet.

The thrust of this general principle is that, absent an exception, the King must act in accordance with the advice of the Cabinet or, where designated, some other person. For instance, one cannot accept at face value the statement that "the King may at any time prorogue or dissolve Parliament,"[73] since in the exercise of the power to prorogue (adjourn) Parliament he must act in accordance with the advice of Cabinet, and to dissolve Parliament he is specifically directed to follow the advice of the Prime Minister.[74] On the same principle it is not to be thought that section 63(4) means literally what it says:

> When a bill has been presented to the King for

73. *Id.* at § 68(1).
74. *Id.* at § 68(4).

assent in pursuance of subsection (3) of this section, he shall signify that he assents or that he withholds assent.

The King has no power to veto legislation. Whenever he assents or withholds assent he is merely acting on orders from the Cabinet in accordance with the principle of section 76(1). Other important examples are that the King acting in accordance with the advice of the Prime Minister shall choose the members of the Cabinet from among the National Assembly and nominated members of the Senate,[75] and shall exercise the Prerogative of Mercy in accordance with the advice of the Pardons Committee.[76]

One is entitled to ask, what would be the legal effect of the failure of the King, either through neglect or recalcitrance, to follow the advice of his principal? The answer is that whenever it appears to the Prime Minister that such is the case he is empowered "to do that act himself and shall, at the earliest convenience thereafter, report the matter to Parliament; and any act so done by the Prime Minister shall be deemed to have been done by the King and to be his act."[77] Whether or not the King has received advice or acted in accordance with it, however, cannot be enquired into in any court.[78]

(2) POWERS SUBJECT TO CONSTITUTIONAL CONVENTIONS[79]

The second variety of royal function is one in which the King is not an agent but instead possesses a measure of discretion or autonomy but not beyond

75. *Id.* at § 72(3).
76. *Id.* at § 86(2).
77. *Id.* at § 76(4).
78. *Id.* at § 76(6).
79. Conventions are discussed separately *infra* p. 305 *et seq.*

the conventional discretion possessed by the constitutional monarch of the United Kingdom. The instances for the exercise of this discretionary power are exceptions to the general rule of section 76(1) and are exhaustively listed in section 76(2) in subsections (b), (c), (d), and (e). Thus subject to the relevant convention of the Constitution:

1. The King may disregard advice to dissolve Parliament if in his view it would not be in the best interests of Lesotho and the government could carry on without a dissolution; [80] on the other hand, he may dissolve Parliament without advice if following a resolution of no confidence by the National Assembly the Prime Minister has failed within three days thereafter to resign or advise a dissolution; [81] finally, he may dissolve Parliament without advice where the office of Prime Minister is not filled and he has no prospect of finding a majority leader within a reasonable time.[82]

2. He may choose as Prime Minister "the member of the National Assembly who appears to him to be the leader of the political party or coalition of political parties that will command the support of the majority of members of the National Assembly . . . ." [83]

3. He may remove the Prime Minister if following a resolution of no confidence the Prime Minister has failed within three days thereafter to resign or advise a dissolution; [84] or where owing to the results of a general election the King considers that when Parliament convenes the Prime Minister will no longer be the majority leader.[85]

---

80. § 68(4)(a) of the Constitution.
81. *Id.* at § 68(4)(b).
82. *Id.* at § 68(4)(c).
83. *Id.* at § 72(3).
84. *Id.* at § 72(4)(a).
85. *Id.* at § 72(4)(b).

4. He may appoint another Cabinet Minister to assume the duties of an ill or absent Prime Minister if it is impracticable to obtain the advice of the Prime Minister.[86]

(3) ABSOLUTE PREROGATIVE

The third variety of royal function is utterly subjective and in the nature of an absolute prerogative. Its exercise is subject neither to advice, convention, nor any objective standard save collateral restrictions imposed by the Constitution. Instances under this head are exhaustively listed in section 76(2) in subsections (a), (f), (g), (h), (i), and (j). Thus the King may appoint eleven Senators,[87] a Privy Councillor,[88] and three members of the National Planning Board.[89] He must concur in all appointments to his personal staff,[90] is the final arbiter of disputes concerning land allocations,[91] and subject to limitations prescribed by Parliament, may exercise those powers of discipline over the chiefs conferred under any law.[92]

B. The Parliament

The Parliament of Lesotho sits in Maseru, the capital of the country. Parliament in its strict sense

---

86. *Id.* at § 75(3).

87. *Id.* at § 41. A collateral restriction, however, is that his nominee must meet the qualifications for membership in Parliament. § 44.

88. *Id.* at § 80(2)(b). Only the King can call meetings of the Privy Council and may do so when he deems fit though he need not attend.

89. *Id.* at § 90(1)(a).

90. *Id.* at § 128(4).

91. *Id.* at § 99.

92. *Id.* at § 76(2)(j). The Chieftainship Act No. 22 of 1968 requires the King to follow the advice of the Minister concerning the implementation of decisions on disciplinary matters dealt with in the Act. (§ 18.)

consists of the National Assembly, the Senate, and the King.[93] Its life is five years unless sooner dissolved or extended during times of war.[94]

(1) LIMITATIONS ON POWER

Parliament's power to legislate is restricted both substantively and procedurally by the Constitution. The provisions respecting fundamental human rights are the clearest example of substantive restraints upon the range of permissible legislative topics. The provisions concerning the amendment to the Constitution establish certain procedural restraints which must be fulfilled before an amendment can be validly passed. Laws inconsistent with the Constitution are void.[95]

(2) SELECTION OF MEMBERS

The National Assembly, the elected chamber, consists of 60 members, one from each of the 60 single-member constituencies into which Lesotho is divided.[96] The Senate is comprised of 33 members, 22 of whom are permanent members. The latter are the Principal and Ward Chiefs set out in Schedule 2 of the Constitution. The other eleven members are nominated by the King.[97] The Assembly is presided over by a Speaker[98] and the Senate by a President,[99] both of whom are elected by their respective members from among themselves or from outside persons.

(3) QUALIFICATIONS

Membership in the National Assembly and Senate

---

93. *Id.* at § 40.

94. *Id.* at § 68.

95. Discussed *infra*, pp. 249-251.

96. § 42 of the Constitution.

97. *Id.* at § 41.

98. *Id.* at § 49.

99. *Id.* at § 47.

is confined to citizens of Lesotho [100] with the further requirement of members of the Assembly that they be qualified electors and able "to speak and, unless incapacitated by blindness or other physical cause, to read and write either the English or the Sesotho language well enough to take an active part in the proceedings . . . ." [101]

The permanent Senators and the Principal and Ward Chiefs may designate any other person to be a Senator in their behalf.[102] Any senatorial nominee of the King or senatorial designee of a chief or member of the National Assembly is disqualified if he is insane, under sentence of death, an unrehabilitated insolvent, holds in circumstances prescribed by Parliament an interest in government contracts, owes allegiance to a foreign power,[103] or has been convicted of an electoral offence.[104] The disqualifications do not apply to the Principal and Ward Chiefs of the Senate. No member of the Senate, however, nominated or permanent, is qualified to be a member of the National Assembly.[105] Any loss of the above qualifications curtails the right of nominated Senators and members of the Assembly to hold their seats.[106] Subject to section 45(2) and (4) their tenure is not otherwise terminated except by dissolution of Parliament.

(4) VOTERS AND CONSTITUENCIES

Lesotho practises universal adult suffrage, and every citizen over 21 years, subject to residence qualifications, is entitled to vote without reference to prop-

100. *Id.* at § 44.
101. *Id.* at § 44(2)(c).
102. *Id.* at § 41.
103. *Id.* at § 45(1).
104. *Id.* at § 45 and see the Electoral Act No. 23 of 1968.
105. § 45(5) of the Constitution.
106. *Id.* at § 46.

erty or literacy criteria.[107] The value of the individual vote is protected by a nonpolitical Constituency Delimitation Commission[108] which regularly reviews constituency boundaries.[109] The Constitution lays down the criteria for the Commission to follow—population density, community of interest, etc.—which are designed to avert the evils of gerrymandering.[110]

(5) DISTRIBUTION OF POWER

The Parliament of Lesotho is bicameral, but as at Westminster, real power lies in the lower house. Formally Parliament enacts laws (other than laws to amend the Constitution) when bills are passed through both houses and assented to by the King.[111] A bill is passed by a majority vote of those present and voting[112] subject to an objection for lack of quorum.[113] Bills can be introduced only in the National Assembly,[114] and once passed these cannot be amended by the Senate without the Assembly's concurrence.[115]

A striking feature of the Parliament of Lesotho is the debility of the Senate. This resulted from a decision originally made by the Constitutional Commission which had split over the dilemma of the chiefs. Having concluded that the presence of 22 aristocrats in a single chamber of otherwise elected members would produce unstable party government, the Commission was faced with the alternative of either excluding the

---

107. *Id.* at § 43(2) and see the Electoral Act No. 23 of 1968.
108. § 52 of the Constitution.
109. *Id.* at § 53(3).
110. *Id.* at § 53(2).
111. *Id.* at § 63.
112. *Id.* at § 60.
113. *Id.* at § 59.
114. *Id.* at § 63(2).
115. *Id.* at § 65.

chiefs altogether from the legislative process or accommodating them in a second chamber. The compromise reached was to seat the leading chiefs of the country (together with eleven persons chosen by the King) in a Senate or upper house but to restrict their powers to review and delay.[116] Accordingly, section 65 provides that where a bill is certified by the Speaker of the Assembly as an *appropriation* bill, it is introduced forthwith into the Senate and cannot be delayed for more than one day, whereupon it is presented to the King for assent together with any amendments made by the Senate and agreed to by the Assembly. Where a bill is certified by the Speaker of the Assembly as a *money* bill (other than an appropriation bill) the procedure is the same save that the period of delay in the Senate cannot exceed 30 days. Any bill that does not carry either of the certificates just referred to must be passed by the Senate within 90 days.

In keeping with ancient custom concerning the financial initiative of the Crown, there is provision that certain kinds of money bills cannot be taken up in either house without the consent of the Cabinet.[117]

Each house may regulate its own procedure and Parliament may prescribe the powers, privileges, and immunities of the members and committees of each house provided these do not exceed those enjoyed by the members and committees of the House of Commons of the Parliament of the United Kingdom.[118]

---

116. *Supra* note 42, at 30-33. The evidence demonstrates that the chiefs have rejected full participation in the Senate. Attendance has been consistently at quorum levels. Quorums have been maintained largely by the regular attendance of the nominated senators who, as a consequence, tend to influence the Senate disproportionately to their number.

117. § 64 of the Constitution.

118. *Id.* at § 66.

(6) AMENDMENT OF THE CONSTITUTION

Lord Bryce would no doubt have classified the Constitution of Lesotho as rigid, since its more important sections entail a special difficulty of amendment. Section 70 establishes for purposes of amendment three categories of sections which we may call the ordinary, entrenched, and specially entrenched sections.[119]

(a) Ordinary Sections

The ordinary sections of the Constitution can be altered or repealed as easily as the passage of an ordinary act. All that is required is the majority vote of those present and voting in the National Assembly, passage through the Senate subject to the requisites of section 65, and the assent of the King. The ordinary sections are the residuum formed by all sections that are not listed in subsections 3(a) and 3(b) of section 70. They number approximately 74 out of the 139 provisions of the Constitution.[120]

(b) Entrenched Sections

The entrenched sections set forth in subsection 3(b) cannot be amended unless certain requisite delays have passed and not less than two thirds of all the members of each house of Parliament have voted in favour. Twenty-six sections (or parts thereof) of the Constitution fall in this category.

(c) Specially Entrenched Sections

There are 46 specially entrenched sections (or parts thereof) of the Constitution listed in subsection

---

119. This is the terminology adopted by the REPORT OF THE BASUTOLAND INDEPENDENCE CONFERENCE 20-22 (1966).

120. The number is actually larger than this because many of the entrenched and specially entrenched sections are in fact entrenched only in certain of their subsections.

3(a). Notable inclusions are section 70 itself, the fundamental rights of Chapter II, the position of the King and the chieftainships, and the establishment and jurisdiction of the High Court and Court of Appeal. Amendment of specially entrenched sections requires the passage of the bill through Parliament by ordinary process and, subject to requisite delays, the approval of the majority of the people voting in a referendum. It would seem that the message revealed in *Collins v. Minister of the Interior* [121]—that in order to preserve the integrity of the entrenched sections all related sections must be entrenched—has been received and applied. Stratagems to circumvent substantive guarantees such as by "packing" the Courts and the Senate could not succeed without following the procedures for amending the entrenched sections.

Nevertheless the drafting has not been flawless on this point; for instance, section 76 is a crucial provision that essentially determines the role of the King in the system. According to the exhaustive list of the King's conventional and subjective functions in section 76(2), the King is entitled to exercise "the power to appoint the Prime Minister conferred on him by section 72(3) of this Constitution." Section 76 itself is specially entrenched but section 72, perhaps by oversight, is unentrenched. Section 72 therefore may be repealed by a mere majority vote in the National Assembly. In such a case, it is submitted, the power of the King to appoint the Prime Minister would no longer exist since nothing remaining would "confer" the power referred to in section 76(2). In similar fashion the King could be divested of his power to remove the Prime Minister under section 72(4), a fact which

---

121. [1957] 1 S.A. 552 (A.D.) discussed *infra*, pp. 297-298, note 209.

could upset the integrity of entrenched section 68(4) as well.

The provision for these various procedures of amending the Constitution is probably the result of a compromise between the fears of an over-rigid constitution and the desire to protect certain essential ideas from the vicissitudes of the momentary majority. On the other hand, it may be noted that although there is a procedural difference between what are here referred to as entrenched and specially entrenched provisions, it must not be assumed that an entrenched provision is always easier to amend than a specially entrenched provision. The depth of entrenchment may depend upon other matters as well. A referendum to the people may simply be more appropriate to the nature of the subject than a two-thirds vote of the houses of Parliament. For instance the question of the administration of land is made a specially entrenched prerogative of the King and the chiefs by virtue of section 93. If one wanted to insulate this prerogative against future change as securely as possible, it would have been logical to have entrenched but not specially entrenched these sections, since in the former mode the chiefs have predominant blocking power in the Senate while in the latter they have no voice at all. However, the choice of the founders of the Constitution to specially entrench these provisions rationally reflects the view—noted in the 1963 Constitutional Commission's Report [122]—that the whole system of land tenure was subject to reform in the future, an event nigh impossible were the Senate to possess a vote in the matter.

---

122. *Supra* note 42, at 67-69.

C. The Cabinet

What Bagehot described as "a *hyphen* which joins a *buckle* which fastens the legislative part of the state to the executive part of the state," [123] and what is the most significant English contribution to the art of government, is emulated without substantial variation in the Lesotho Constitution. Section 73 provides in part:

> 1. There shall be a Cabinet of Ministers, consisting of the Prime Minister and the other Ministers.
> 2. The function of the Cabinet shall be to advise the King in the government of Lesotho, and the Cabinet shall be collectively responsible to the two Houses of Parliament for any advice given to the King by or under the general authority of the Cabinet and for all things done by or under the authority of any Minister in the execution of his office.

The Cabinet is a board of control, the focal point of policy. Having determined a policy to follow, Cabinet instructs the department of the appropriate minister to carry it out either by administrative action within the prescribed limits of the law or by the drafting of proposed legislation so as to change the law. The Prime Minister, *primus inter pares,* must be a member of the National Assembly and, subject to convention, is selected by the King as the leader with the majority support of its members.[124] The Ministers of the Cabinet are chosen by the King upon the Prime Minister's advice from among the nominated members of the Senate and the elected members of the National Assembly.[125] The actual size of the Cabinet may be determined by Parliament though the Constitution pro-

---

123. THE ENGLISH CONSTITUTION 68 (Watts Ed. 1964).

124. § 72(3) of the Constitution.

125. *Id.*

vides that it cannot be smaller than seven.[126] The permanent Senators cannot be Cabinet Ministers.[127] All Ministers, whether nominated Senators or Assemblymen, are entitled to attend and take part (but not to vote) in all meetings and proceedings of the opposite house from which they are drawn.[128] The tenure of the Prime Minister and the Cabinet Ministers is covered below.[129]

The unity of the Cabinet and its susceptibility of effective criticism are furthered by the doctrine of collective responsibility, which Prime Minister Leabua Jonathan has defined for his own Cabinet as the duty:

(i) to support and vote with the Government in the National Assembly and in the Senate;

---

126. *Id.* at § 72(2). In 1966 the cabinet of Prime Minister Leabua Jonathan consisted of nine members including the Prime Minister. G. N. 2 of 1966. Since WWII British Cabinets have averaged from 16-23 ministers. WADE & PHILLIPS, CONSTITUTIONAL LAW 193 (7th ed. Longmans 1965.)

127. § 72(3) of the Constitution. This seems to be more than an expresssion of lack of faith in the qualification of the chiefs. It could hardly be maintained that of all the permanent senators now and in the future there might not be some whom a Prime Minister might wish to include in the cabinet. Of course the fact that the permanent senators also have many administrative duties that might suffer in view of the full-time responsibilities of a cabinet post may explain the decision in part. However, the decision would seem to reflect the original constitutional compromise reached on the advisability of an aristocratic chamber in the first place. This additional limitation on the influence of the Senate may have reduced certain fears of the advent to power of a party with a traditionalist philosophy and a cabinet composed of a number of permanent senators unresponsible *in spirit* to the lower chamber.

Compare the conventional practice in the United Kingdom of including members of both houses in the Cabinet. This practice is now mandatory because of the indirect effect of the Ministers of the Crown Act, 1937.

128. § 61 of the Constitution.

129. See *infra*, pp. 307-308.

(ii) to support (Government) policy both in public and in private; and

(iii) not to evade that responsibility by seeking to assign it to persons who are not Ministers.[130] Although the Cabinet is responsible to both houses of Parliament, it is the resolution of no confidence by the National Assembly alone that may provoke the resignation or dissolution of a ministry.[131]

D. Land

Chapter VIII of the Constitution states and protects rights that the people and the Chieftainship possess in land. From a broad constitutional standpoint, the task of the framers was to deal with the following three issues relating to land: residual ownership, rights of administration, and procedures of administration.

(1) RESIDUAL OWNERSHIP BY THE NATION

Although individual ownership as a European legal notion is alien to the land tenure system of the Basotho,[132] it is thought possible to speak of a residual ownership by the Nation. The Basotho have always expressed the uncontradicted view "that the Basuto Nation has a communal right to all the land of Basutoland, that is, that every member of the Nation has certain vested rights to the land." [133] Section 92 of the Constitution merely restates this when it says "all land in Lesotho is vested in the Basotho Nation."

---

130. G. N. 78 of 1967. The Prime Minister has also promulgated a manual of "do's and don'ts" for cabinet ministers.

131. § 68(4)-(5) of the Constitution.

132. Lesitsi v. Mafa, J.C. 84/1953 and see the discussion *supra*, at p. 172 *et seq.*

133. SHEDDICK, LAND TENURE IN BASUTOLAND 7 (H.M.S.O. 1954).

An important theoretical question, however, is to determine what rights in land are actually bestowed by this provision. Confusion arises because according to the Independence Order it was the Government of Lesotho and not the Nation which received title to all assets in the country formerly owned by the British.[134] If the British had title to Basutoland and transferred this to Lesotho's Government, what is the significance of saying that all land in Lesotho is vested in the Nation? The answer to this question becomes clearer upon an analysis of events in the preindependence era.

As a matter of British constitutional law, a colony such as Basutoland, as opposed to a protectorate, is territory annexed to the mainland; and its inhabitants become British subjects.[135] The title to its land, therefore, must ultimately vest in the Crown. Though it may be disputed whether such a result was ever intended by Moshoeshoe and the negotiators who dealt with him at the time of annexation, this seems to be the plain meaning of Proclamation 14 of 1868 which states that "the Territory of the said tribe shall be and shall be taken to be British Territory."[136] More-

---

134. If taken literally, § 92 of the Constitution seems to be directly contradicted by § 16(1) of the Independence Order which reads: "Any property or assets which before the commencement of this Order are vested in Her Majesty or, by or under the Basutoland Order 1965, in Motlotlehi or in the British Government Representative for the purposes of the Government of Basutoland, shall, from the commencement of this order, vest in the Government of Lesotho."

135. *Supra* note 36.

136. In HALSBURY, LAWS Vol. XI, § 251 (Butterworths), Basutoland was described as a "colony by cession." *Accord, Id.* Yet Moshoeshoe I himself said: "I could not according to the customs of my tribe alienate any portion of my territory without the consent of the people. It would be on my part introducing an unprecedented practice. The people I govern look upon me as being entrusted with the preservation of their country

over, it is to little avail to argue that Basutoland was properly a protectorate rather than a colony, for whatever difference may once have existed between the legal power of a soverign over colonies as distinct from protectorates has certainly evaporated since the Foreign Jurisdiction Acts of 1890 and 1913.[137] These provide that the power of the Crown in foreign countries (*e.g.*, protectorates) is "the same and as ample" as the power over territory acquired by cession or conquest (*e.g.*, colonies). In any event, certainly a complete exercise of ownership was invoked when Basutoland was ceded by the British to the Cape of Good Hope which annexed the country in 1871 [138] and later disannexed it in 1883 [139] after the Gun War.

From a practical point of view, however, three points were characteristic of the administration of land in Basutoland in the Colonial era.

(1) Never was land sold to any individual. The inalienability of land was a policy frequently sought and recognised. The South African Constitution, catering for the eventual incorporation of the territory, guaranteed it; [140] local traders tried unsuccessfully to avoid it; [141] but the law finally recognised it.[142]

---

and I would not forfeit or cede my right to any part of it without being considered as having robbed the community." THEAL, 1 BASUTOLAND RECORDS 1883, at 86.

137. 53 & 54 Vict., c. 37 and 3 & 4 Geo. 5, c. 16.

138. Act 12 of 1871.

139. Act 34 of 1883.

140. South Africa Act, 1909, Schedule § 14.

141. See Report *supra* note 20, at 21-22, and SHEDDICK, *supra* note 133, at 135-136.

142. Concessions Veto Proclamation No. 65 of 1922 (repealed); *see also* Paramount Chief's Circular Order No. 31 of 1946 (prohibiting allocations of fields to Europeans or ploughing on a half-share basis with Europeans); High Commission Territories Royal Instructions H.C.N. 103 of 1959 § 10 (prohibiting High Commissioner and Resident Commissioner from

(2) Consequently, foreign settlers were never attracted to or brought into the territory.

(3) Finally, colonial interference with the actual administration of land by the traditional authorities was kept to a minimum.[143] The regime of parallel rule, and later indirect rule, guided the country with a very light, if also neglectful, hand.[144]

In view, then, of the invincible popular belief that the land belonged to the Nation (a belief which lax colonial controls tended more to reinforce than to contradict) counterpoised against the unlimited legal power that in strictness the Crown potentially might wield, it is not surprising that doubt should have arisen as to the true owner of the soil. As Sheddick observed in 1954,[145] "There exists then, a situation in which the Crown and the Native Authority claim the supreme ownership of the Territory of Basutoland." In seeking an answer to this dispute, the Constitutional Reform Committee of 1958 urged a distinction between *sovereign* rights and *private* rights.[146] It argued that Britain's acquisition of Basutoland as a dominion did not disturb the Basotho Nation's *dominium* of the soil. The plenary powers of the Crown over the Colony did not create a change of private ownership unless private ownership was actually taken away. The mere ces-

---

any purchase of any building or land "as may belong to Us" without Secretary of State's permission).

143. *E.g.*, Chieftainship (Powers) Proclamation No. 61 of 1938. Section 9(1)(u) would confirm a chief's authority over land allocation and use. It empowered chiefs to issue orders which "by virtue of any African law or custom for the time being in force and not being repugnant to morality or justice, (he) has power to prohibit, restrict, regulate, or require to be done." (Now repealed by the Chieftainship Act, 1968.)

144. HAILEY, *supra* note 18, at 133-134.

145. *Supra* note 133, at 9.

146. *Supra* note 20, at 19-20.

sion of the country did not shift such ownership, but merely made it a possibility which, in accordance with British policy toward its Colony, was not fated to materialise. Later when the dominion called Basutoland achieved its independence, the *dominium* of the soil remained with the Nation. In respect of the Nation's rights in land, therefore, Parliament's power is limited. It cannot sell the Nation's land to individuals without amending the Constitution. On the other hand, section 92 is not a limitation on sovereign rights. Nothing there prevents the cession of Lesotho to a foreign power (Moshoeshoe did no less in 1868) so long as private rights are not disturbed.

This theory maintains that to vest the land in the Nation is to confer private but not sovereign rights. Fitting this distinction, however, to the realities of African land tenure requires caution and care. By nature, Lesotho's system of land tenure tends to blur sharp differences between what is private and what is sovereign. For instance the power of the chief or King under customary law to cede land to foreigners has always been actively debated. We know too that customary law denies to the private individual the incidence of full ownership. Nevertheless it is possible to state with a minimum of violence to Sesotho customary law that during colonial times the legal rights to land were divided. The Basotho Nation exercised a kind of present or actual title while the British Government held merely a potential title, that is, the unexercised but potential right to acquire or confer title to land when it saw fit.

This manner of viewing the ownership of colonial land has already gained the apparent approval of the Privy Council in *In re Southern Rhodesia* [147] and *Amo-*

147. [1919] A.C. 211 (P.C.).

du Tijani v. Secretary, Southern Nigeria.[148] In those cases their Lordships were asked to decide to what extent British presence in two different parts of Africa had uprooted the indigenous system of ownership and administration of land. The conquest of Southern Rhodesia by armed force, the intention of white settlers to gain private *dominium* over land there, together with, in the Board's view, the Matabele's undeveloped and imprecise legal conceptions of land tenure, all were said to show that any unalienated land in Southern Rhodesia would belong to the Crown rather than the original inhabitants. On the other hand, where the only avowed purpose of British settlement was to suppress the slave trade in Southern Nigeria, where the cession agreement conveying radical title to the Crown nevertheless required that the property rights of the inhabitants be fully respected, and where the system of communal tenure directed by the chiefs as trustees for the people seemed sufficiently recognisable to the Board,[149] it was found that the rights of the individual holders of land were sufficiently strong to warrant the payment of compensation when the land was taken from their use by the Administration. "A mere change in sovereign," said their Lordships, "is not to be presumed as meant to disturb rights of private owners."

The principle of these cases when applied to Lesotho indicates that questions of land ownership are not decided by mere reference to a radical or ulti-

---

148. [1921] A.C. 399 (P.C.).

149. Lord Hailey has said: "The apparent conflict between the decisions in the Southern Rhodesian and Southern Nigerian cases was due not to any variation in the principles followed by the Privy Council, but to the difference which, in its view, existed in the relations between tribesmen and chiefs in the two countries." AN AFRICAN SURVEY 802 (H.M.S.O. 1939).

mate title to land but as importantly by reference to the totality of the social, economic, and humanitarian relations between Crown and Colony. There is a difference between the sovereign's radical title and, to borrow a term of English constitutional law, the *conventional* title, for the latter is based upon the practice, understandings, purposes, and conditions which exist in the field rather than merely on the deed.

(2) THE CHIEFTAINSHIP'S RIGHT OF ADMINISTRATION

All rights in land in Lesotho may be seen from the point of view of either the administrators (King, Chiefs, and headmen) or the users (land dwellers, pastoralists, agriculturists).[150] Sections 93 and 94 of the Constitution, however, deal exclusively with the rights of the administrators, and the effect of these provisions may be condensed into the following points:

(1) The power to allocate land is vested in the King who in the exercise thereof acts as trustee[151] for the Basotho Nation (§ 93).

---

150. SHEDDICK, *supra* note 133, at 2 *et passim*; Crawford, *Land Shortage and Land Plenty: Land Tenure in Lesotho and Early Germany*" 84 S.A.L.J. 437, 441 (1967) and see *supra* p. 172 *et seq.*

151. The meaning of this word in the Constitution causes doubt. A trust is a legal conception unknown to customary law and therefore its accuracy as a legal term must suffer. In English and Roman-Dutch law (which deals with an *inter vivos* trust as a *stipulatio alteri*) a trust classically involves ownership vested in one person subject to conditions laid down for the benefit of another. As Solomon I.A. remarked in Estate Kemp v. McDonald's Trustee, [1915] A.D. 491, 508: "The underlying conception in these and other cases is that while the legal *dominium* of property is vested in the trustees, they have no beneficial interest in it but are bound to hold and apply it for the benefit of some person or persons or for the accomplishment of some special purpose." The Constitution, however, cannot mean that the King, as trustee, has legal *dominium* of the soil since it has already declared that the land is *vested* in

(2) The power to allocate is exercised by the chiefs as well as the King; however, this power is

---

the Nation. Secondly, the term "trustee" is employed only with reference to the power to allocate and revocate, which power would have to be the subject of the trust.

It is submitted that the term could be intended to mean one or all of the following: (1) A western lawyer's summary, analogical description of a chief or king's role in an African land tenure system. Thus Lord Sumner: "Lobengula's duties, if describable as those of a trustee, were duties of imperfect obligation." *In re* Southern Rhodesia, [1919] A.C. 211 (P.C.). Similarly Rayner C. J. "[The Chief] is to some extent in the position of a trustee." REPORT ON LAND TENURE IN WEST AFRICA (1898) quoted in Amodu Tijani v. Secretary, Southern Nigeria, [1921] A.C. 399 (P.C.). (2) A colonial sense of trusteeship over land which was transcribed by the British into the Constitution. Guardianship and trusteeship were words frequently bandied about in that era, as when Sir Henry de Villiers reported to the South African Constitutional convention that the Imperial Government "regarded itself in a special sense as a guardian and trustee of the Natives of South Africa." *See* HAILEY, THE REPUBLIC OF SOUTH AFRICA AND THE HIGH COMMISSION TERRITORIES 29 (O.U.P. 1963). (3) A fiduciary relationship (*uberimma fides*) between the King and the people. In this sense "trust" should be taken not in its technical legal sense but in the popular meaning of utmost good faith. This is most probably the sense in which the drafters were employing the word. Thus in a significant study entitled *Recommendations and Reflections on Some Problems of Land Tenure in Basutoland* (see *supra* p. 177 *et seq.*), prepared by four members of the University of Chicago (including Professor D. V. Cowen, the principal draftsman of the Lesotho Constitution) in 1963, the following statement was made: "With respect to all these (land) boards we recommend that the *trust principle* be expressed in law by providing that no person empowered to allocate land, or make official decisions concerning land allocation, or to advise on land allocation, *may allocate land directly or indirectly to himself, or advise on any land matter, in which he has a personal interest.* This embodiment in law should be accomplished by providing that (i) whenever personal interest is involved the person interested should be disqualified from taking part in the proceedings: (ii) a penalty should be imposed on a person who violates this trust principle." (At 11.) (Italics added.)

subject to the rights and duties conferred or imposed by the Constitution or any other law enacted in accordance with the Constitution (§ 93).

(3) Parliament may pass laws that determine and prescribe the nature of the rights in land which the King and chiefs have the power to allocate, as well as the "grounds" and "circumstances" in which their power should be exercised (§ 94).

(3) THE LIMITS PLACED UPON PARLIAMENT'S POWER

On first sight these sections appear to state a contradiction. If the King and the chiefs have the power to allocate rights in land, is it logical that at the same time Parliament is empowered to regulate the allocation of land? A contradiction in fact does exist if the King's "power to allocate" is a phrase meaning the traditionally held power of the Paramount Chief and his chiefs under customary law. Customary law itself has certain fixed rules that designate their powers.[152] If by proper interpretation of section 93 these customary rules have been incorporated, then they would not only remain in force but would receive all the safeguards of a specially entrenched provision of the Constitution. The contradiction would lie, therefore, in attributing a customary-law content to the words "power to allocate," while at the same time acknowledging that Parliament has the power to change the substance of that content without an amendment of the Constitution.

The Constitution, however, does not expressly say this. From the standpoint of the chiefs, section 93 does not guarantee *what* may be allocated but merely *who* shall do the allocating. While entrusting the King and the chieftainship with the administration of land,

152. *See* LAWS OF LEROTHOLI Part I § 7; SHEDDICK, *supra* note 133, chs. 9-10 and see *supra* p. 172 *et seq.*

section 93 also expressly subjects their power to the limitations imposed by other constitutional sections (including Parliament's regulatory power under section 94) as well as those imposed by any "other law." This latter exception would definitely embrace statutory, judicial, and customary law [153] and, of particular importance, those statutes of the Colonial Era that have amended in certain respects the customary rules.[154] Very clearly the purpose of the exception is not to entrench customary-law powers but to delimit a constitutional power by reference to customary law.[155] In light of these considerations, therefore, it is not proper to conclude that Parliament may regulate the substantive and procedural aspects of *what* may be ad-

---

153. § 139 of the Constitution. See *infra*, p. 335.

154. *See*, e.g., Chieftainship (Powers) Proclamation No. 61 of 1938 esp. § 9; Concessions Veto Proclamation No. 65 of 1922 (repealed, *see* Lesotho Independence Order, 1966, § 4(6)); Local Government Proclamation No. 52 of 1959 (conferring certain powers on District Councils previously exercised by chiefs); Precious Stones Order, 1961 (made under § 9(u) of the Chieftainship (Powers) Proclamation cited *supra*). For examples of post-independence limitations on their powers, *see e.g.*, Deeds Registry Act No. 12 of 1967 (esp. § 15 prohibiting registration of land titles conferring ownership); Land (Procedure) Act No. 24 of 1967; Mining Rights Act No. 43 of 1967 esp. § 6.

155. The 1963 REPORT OF THE BASUTOLAND CONSTITUTIONAL COMMISSION stated its intention in the following comment:

> We are firmly of the view that there should be inserted in the new Constitution a provision, alterable only by an affirmative vote at a referendum, laying down that the land of Lesotho is owned by the Basotho nation and, subject both to the provisions of the Constitution and to the provisions of any law for the time being in force is administered in trust for the nation by Motlotlehi and the Chieftainship. This entrenches the basic principle of land tenure in Lesotho which—though it undoubtedly admits of, and indeed calls for, improvement in *methods and details of application*—is still valued and strongly adhered to by the overwhelming majority of the Basotho people. (§ 110, at 60.)

ministered but cannot, short of an amendment to the Constitution, redefine *who* shall be the administrators?

This seems to be the basic distinction, but there may be specific problems in any attempt by Parliament to make far-reaching changes in the present land tenure system. To take the extreme example, should Parliament purport to enact under section 94 that all land lawfully allocated and presently under plough shall vest in absolute ownership in the name of the person to whom it was allocated, it will be evident that Parliament is changing more than the substance or procedure of allocable rights but is also taking away from the chieftainship all power to allocate such land for the future.[156] To make a power subject to regulation is one thing; to destroy it through "regulation" involves another. Furthermore, is it possible to continue to regard the King as trustee over land when the land has passed irrevocably from his control? The entrenchment of that power is vain if its efficacy can be totally extinguished by ordinary Act of Parliament. If this example serves to point out a limit to Parliament's power, it may also serve to indicate that there is some substantive meaning to the constitutional right of the chieftainship which exerts tension against the broad powers of section 94. How far Parliament's powers extend is uncertain, but certainly it is a matter of degree.

(a) An Example: The Mining Rights Act of 1967

The Mining Rights Act of 1967 is an interesting

---

156. A theoretical objection is that a grant of absolute ownership is inconsistent with the entrenched proposition that all land is vested in the Nation. (§ 92 of the Constitution.) However, as a practical matter this is not a serious problem. At English and American law freehold tenure signifies near absolute ownership despite ultimate title residing in the Crown or the State; see *supra* p. 186.

illustration of post-independence legislation in tension against the rights of the chieftainship. The Act created a Mining Board composed (for the time being) of the Cabinet.[157] All applications for mineral titles in the first instance must be made not to a headman or chief but to the Board which, after assessing the merits of the application, may recommend to a principal or ward chief in whose jurisdiction the land is that he grant the mineral title.[158] On the other hand the Board may refuse to recommend, in which case the application dies. Of course, while access to mineral resources traditionally formed a part of the administrative power of the chieftainship over land,[159] it may be argued that under the Act no power is really taken away from the chieftainship since a chief may refuse to follow a recommendation that has been made to him by the Board.[160] Yet the burden imposed by Parliament is that *all* applications are first screened by the Board so that the chieftainship's previous freedom to grant titles to all comers is considerably restricted. As formerly against the world, the chiefs now may say only yea or nay to preselected candidates. Is the Act constitutional?

The question invites a judgment perhaps not only of degree but of legislative intention. The courts might adopt the position that any degree of interference is constitutionally excessive if the purpose is purely and plainly *mala fide* toward the chiefs, while at the

157. Mining Rights Act, No. 43 of 1967, § 5(1).

158. *Id.* at § 6(3).

159. *See* the Precious Stones Order, 1961 (made under authority of section 9(u) of the Chieftainship (Powers) Proclamation, 1938) wherein it was affirmed that the minerals were held by the then Paramount Chief in trust for the Basotho Nation.

160. *Supra* note 157, at §§ 6(1), 6(4).

same time hold that no degree of regulation short of total extinction of the power is unconstitutional where that purpose is in good faith. But legislative intention is often said to be an impermissible judicial consideration and if the court will not look to the motive of the statute it must look to the degree of the derogation. Its attitude here may be one of indulgence, facilitated by a presumption of constitutionality measured to sympathise with the antinomy consciously embodied in the Constitution by the framers. It is submitted, however, that if the powers of sections 93 and 94 were deliberately set in tension against one another, the intention must have been to defer to the court the task of maintaining some sort of *reasonable balance* between them.

One measure of reasonableness open to the court would be to run a kind of "conventional title" analysis. Since the notions of national ownership of the land and the trusteeship of the chieftainship are not new ones but indeed were recognised in the Colonial Era, an examination of the legislative behavior of the Crown during that period might serve as a useful point of reference. Thus if a given proclamation encroached upon these principles to some extent but was nevertheless enforced by the British administration, then an act enacted by the Lesotho Parliament of the same content as the proclamation might be deemed valid, since it is reasonable to suppose that the extent of the conventional title to land owned by the British at independence was then transferred to the Lesotho government and became an embodied power under section 94. Ultimately, however, the question of a reasonable balance should be viewed in the light of conflicting social and economic realities which sections 93 and 94 symbolise: the opposition between traditional authority and privilege on the one hand,

and the necessary development and reform of the nation's greatest economic asset on the other. It will only be submitted here that judged under either of these approaches the Mining Rights Act would not be unconstitutional.

(4) PROCEDURES OF ADMINISTRATION

The procedure by which titles in land are allocated, revoked, or restricted is set forth in sections 95 through 101. These sections are not entrenched and may be revoked or altered by ordinary Act of Parliament.[161] Their detailed effect is well summarised in the Constitution, but several features of particular interest may be mentioned here. First, the power of administering land from the King on down to the headman permits the administrator in question to have complete discretion in regard to assessing the merits of an individual's case. On the other hand, a person aggrieved by a decision is entitled to several appeals as of right on the merits first to his chief, next to the principal chief, and finally to the King, each of whom has the power to uphold, reverse, or vary the decision. Finally, generally speaking, any statement or reason that is given as the basis of a decision on land is conclusive and cannot be questioned in any court; however, a limited right of appeal to the High Court is allowed in three procedural and two substantive instances. Procedurally, an order to quash a decision taken against the applicant may be granted if:

(a) prior consultation with advisory boards (in

161. The Mining Rights Act, No. 43 of 1967, repealed sections 95 through 101 of the Constitution insofar as they relate to rights to prospect and mine for any minerals on any land, and the grant of surface and water rights incidental to or in any way connected with prospecting or mining for minerals.

rural areas) or the local government authority (in urban areas) did not take place;[162]

(b) a written statement adequately explaining the grounds of the decision was not given;[163]

(c) appropriate principles of natural justice (*e.g.*, *audi alteram partem*) or procedures set up by Parliament under section 100 were not followed.

Substantively, a decision may be quashed if:

(a) *ex facie* or in substance it contravened a regulation established by Parliament under section 94; or

(b) it shows bad faith in intending to defeat, evade, or avoid a regulation of Parliament pursuant to section 94.

---

162. "Consultation" is of course sharply distinguished in the Constitution from the term "advice." The effect of the latter *must* be followed; that of the former need not. *See* § 139(11) of the Constitution.

163. The requirement is not that the reason be adequate but that the reason be adequately articulated and recorded.

CHAPTER 3

JUDICIAL REVIEW

To the lawyer a natural question to ask about the Constitution is whether it is enforceable in a court of law. The answer to this question may be to him of prior interest to its actual contents which, if unenforceable, may be considered merely precatory. His question is often phrased in terms of a hypothetical law passed by the legislature which contradicts a provision in the Constitution, and as a practical matter he is concerned to know which of the two, the act of the legislature or the Constitution, the courts will enforce. This simple question often evokes the most complex replies because it raises at once in the minds of constitutional lawyers a host of categories and problems, such as parliamentary sovereignty, judicial review, entrenched provisions, separation of powers, and others. These categories are, however, truly seamless and only become distinguishable for purposes of discussing the Constitution from various artificial standpoints such as the power of Parliament, the power of the courts, or the power of the executive. Though the following treatment focusses upon judicial review and the power of the courts, it would be neither accurate nor possible to leave these other important subjects out of the discussion.

Judicial review—the power of the courts to nullify the unconstitutional acts of the legislature and the executive—may be justified on one or more of three bases. One is a statement of express grant in the Constitution. A second is the view that judicial review inheres and is "essentially attached" to a written constitution. A third is the traditional power of courts to determine the validity of subordinate legislation.

A. The Literal Grant of Judicial Review

The overriding fact is that, with the exception of the fundamental human rights provisions, the Lesotho Constitution never declares candidly that the courts possess the duty or the power to nullify the unconstitutional acts of the legislature and the executive. Yet strong inferences are present that such was the design of the draftsmen. These inferences derive principally from an investigation of four provisions of the Constitution: sections 2, 110, 114, and 20.

(1) THE SUPREMACY CLAUSE

Section 2, one of the most vital provisions in the Constitution, reads:

> This Constitution is the supreme law of Lesotho and if any other law is inconsistent with this Constitution, that other law shall, to the extent of the inconsistency, be void.

This terse formulation contains two important thoughts. One is that by great juridical propulsion the Constitution is a law *supreme* above all others. The second is that all other laws must *conform*[164] to the standard of legality established by the Constitution or else be *void*. Yet is this mere sound and fury or has the Constitution provided some institutional procedure whereby its self-declared supremacy can be maintained? For it stands to reason that unless there is some agency vested with the authority to decide

---

164. All laws passed prior to the date of Independence are brought into conformity with the Constitution by § 4 of the Lesotho Independence Order in Council of 1966, Statutory Instrument No. 1172.

whether or not the inferior laws are consistent and possessed of the power to impose its judgment on the government as a whole, section 2 may signify nothing.

(2) UNLIMITED ORIGINAL JURISDICTION

It is natural, then, to ask whether the courts are not the organs of constitutional enforcement and in this connection it is necessary to examine their jurisdiction. The jurisdiction of the High Court is defined by section 110.

> (1) There shall be for Lesotho a High Court which shall have unlimited original jurisdiction to hear and determine any civil or criminal proceedings under any law and such jurisdiction and powers as may be conferred on it by this Constitution or by or under any other law.

The High Court, having original jurisdiction in proceedings "under any law," would appear to have in consequence jurisdiction to hear and determine cases under the Constitution itself, for the Constitution has already been declared "law" in section 2.[165] However, it cannot be maintained that section 110 confers the power of judicial review simply by stating that the court has jurisdiction of constitutional ques-

---

165. That the court's jurisdiction includes the Constitution itself is strongly implied by the various provisions in the Constitution which expressly deny to the court any jurisdiction in particular matters. For example, article 139(11) states as a proposition of general application that where the Constitution lays down that there should be consultation between any persons or authorities "the question whether such consultation was made shall not be enquired into in any court." Thus article 76(6) provides that no court shall enquire into whether the King has received or acted in accordance with advice or made consultation with any person or authority as required by the Constitution. Express deprivations of competence would not be necessary unless the Constitution as a general matter were to be a justiciable document.

tions. The power to adjudicate is not *a priori* the power to nullify. Section 110, therefore, cannot conclude the enquiry.

(3) THE POWER OF INTERPRETATION

The Constitution clearly confers the authority for its own "interpretation." Section 114 lays down:

> Where any question as to the interpretation of this Constitution arises in any proceedings in any subordinate court and the court is of the opinion that the question involves a substantial question of law the court may and shall if any part to the proceedings requests, refer the question to the High Court.

The term "interpretation" is also employed in three other contexts in the Constitution: the appeal of "interpretation" questions to the Court of Appeal, the application of the Interpretation Act of 1899 to the Constitution, and the general interpretation section.

Does the conferral of the authority to interpret the Constitution necessarily mean that the power of judicial review has been also conferred? Much depends upon the meaning of interpretation. In one sense, the interpretation of the Constitution connotes the testing of whether the terms of a law comport with the meaning of the Constitution, as when Lord Bryce described the exercise of judicial review in the United States by saying: "It is a question of *interpretation,* that is, of determining the true meaning both of the superior law and of the inferior law, so as to discover whether they are inconsistent." [166] In another sense the term may mean little more than the clarification of an ambiguity in a certain word, phrase, or provision of the Constitution in a dispute where the

166. 1 THE AMERICAN COMMONWEALTH 247 (Macmillan, New York 1921). (Italics added.)

litigants seek only this clarification.[167] In such a case neither side may be relying upon an act of Parliament or the executive so that the case is one purely of construing the Constitution and no other law.

Both uses of the term interpretation are probably sound. To accept the second sense over the first would seem unduly restrictive because for one reason it is fairly difficult to envisage a dispute that *solely* concerns the Constitution,[168] and because for another the jurisdiction of the court does not *prima facie* exclude cases that call for the court to determine the validity of an inferior law by interpreting the Constitution. In any case the authority to interpret the Constitution may permit judicial expression of what the Constitution says, but this does not carry us so far as to say that the court may declare the act in question void if it surpasses the bounds of the Constitution. The *interpretation* of the Constitution focusses only upon the court's role with respect to a case brought and disposed before it and not with respect to the question of the *binding* nature of its judgment in that case on the other departments of government. The power to interpret, however, takes on a sense of direction when it is read together with section 2. We have already noted that this power could, on one reading, import a power to declare inconsistent laws to be inconsistent. The thrust of section 2 is to equate inconsistency with voidness and the power to declare voidness. Strictly speaking one may say the courts determine when inferior

---

167. In order to discover the meaning of the constitutional language the court is directed to consult the Interpretation Act of 1889 which settles a number of potential verbal ambiguities, and lengthy section 139 of the Constitution, the general interpretation section.

168. Advisory opinions would almost always be of this nature but these are not permitted under the Lesotho Constitution. See *supra* p. 363.

laws are inconsistent, but the Constitution declares them void.[169]

(4) EXPLICIT JUDICIAL REVIEW: FUNDAMENTAL HUMAN RIGHTS

The competence of the High Court to declare that laws are inconsistent with the Constitution is specifically asserted by section 20, in reference to Chapter II of the Constitution. The duty of the court is to enforce the fundamental human rights contained in Chapter II, and at its disposal is the power to make orders, issue process, and give directions to accomplish that task. Acts of Parliament or the executive which are said by the court to contravene the guaranteed rights of the individual will clearly be rendered void by the force of section 2. It is logical to suppose that prior to a determination of contravention the provisions of Chapter II must to a certain extent be interpreted. Again this suggests that the authority to interpret the Constitution as envisaged by section 114 includes the authority to declare inconsistency with its terms.

(5) POSSIBLE OBJECTIONS

The case against judicial review on the literal level may be mentioned in passing. First is the obviously important point that the Constitution does not put the matter beyond controversy (which certainly would have been easy to do) and, however strong logical inference may be, a power of such magnitude should not be attributed unless the Constitution is crystal

---

169. "The task of the courts is to determine whether a law is inconsistent. Having found that it is, nothing more in strictness remains to be done because the Constitution has already declared that law to be void." Olawoyin v. Attorney-General, Northern Region, [1960] N.R.N.L.R. at 59-60.

clear.[170] Secondly, it may be asked why the courts seem to be given special powers under Chapter II. If the power to interpret the Constitution *is* a power to declare inferior laws inconsistent with the Constitution would not this general power have sufficed to safeguard individual liberties? One must either assume that section 20 is redundant (in that it repeats a power that the courts already possess) or that it bestows special powers relative only to Chapter II and not to the Constitution as a whole. The latter approach stresses the singularity of Chapter II, and is plausible if the notion "interpretation" be limited to cases of *pure* constitutional construction in which no other law is in issue. Indirect evidence that this was the intention of the draftsmen can be adduced from the careful dichotomy maintained between questions of *enforcing* Chapter II and questions of *interpreting* the Constitution. First it can be noted that the term "interpretation" is never employed in Chapter II. There the operative terms are "enforcement" and its *sine qua non,* "contravention." Second, in the provisions that have reference to appeals to the High Court, a clean line is drawn between those transfers and appeals with respect to enforcement under section 20 and those involving interpretation under section 114. The express design of the Constitution, it could be argued, is to secure the enforcement of Chapter II but not the rest of the Constitution.

B. Judicial Review Derived from Logic and Statutory Intention

Judicial review has often been justified by a kind of logical necessity, a justification easily restated in

170. It must be assumed that the constitutional draftsmen were aware of the long controversies generated by similar ambiguities in other constitutional systems.

terms of statutory intention. Thus it is asserted, for example by De Smith,[171] that the power is *implicit* in the principle that the Constitution is the supreme law and therefore "does not strictly need to be expressly stated." And Chief Justice Kania, in commenting on Article 13 of the Indian Constitution (a void-for-inconsistency clause similar to section 2 of the Independence Constitution) has observed:

> The inclusion of Article 13(1) and (2) in the Constitution appears to be a matter of abundant caution. *Even in their absence,* if any of the fundamental rights were infringed by a legislative enactment, the court has always the power to declare the enactment, to the extent it transgresses the limits, invalid.[172] (Italics added.)

(1) THE AMERICAN EXAMPLE

One classic exposition of a logical theory of judicial review, already worked out in its details by Alexander Hamilton,[173] was delivered by Chief Justice John Marshall in the great American case of *Marbury v. Madison.*[174] In that case Marshall determined

---

171. *Supra* note 33, at 109.

172. Gopalan v. State of Madras, [1950] S.C.R. 88, 100.

The same approach was taken by Judge Dosser in Liberia:

> It follows therefore from the most ordinary reasoning that if the Legislature passes a statute whose provisions infringe in the lowest degree what we have termed the *Highest Law,* that statute is *void ab initio;* because of its repugnancy to the Constitution. But it is equally obvious that to decide such points it was necessary that one of the three great powers of government should be invested with that function. While the Constitution does not in express terms confer that power upon the courts, yet from the very nature of such questions they fall under judicial observation, and we contend they are a proper subject for adjudication by the highest tribunal of the country. . . . *(In re the Constitutionality of the Act of the Legislature of Liberia,* approved January 20th 1914.)

173. THE FEDERALIST No. 78 (A. Hamilton).

174. 1 Cranch 137, 2 L. Ed. 60 (1803). William Marbury and others had been appointed federal judges by President John

that a law enacted by Congress, the Judiciary Act of 1789, which petitioner urged the Court to apply, was contrary to the Constitution. Two questions arose in his mind: If the statute contradicts the Constitution, is it void? If the statute is void, is it binding on the courts?

In answering his first question Marshall started with the proposition that there is an *original* right on the part of the people to establish in writing permanent fundamental principles by which governmental powers are assigned to departments of the government. The limits of these powers may be carefully de-

---

Adams in 1801 just before the expiry of the President's term of office. Their commissions, however, though signed and sealed, were never received by them because the Secretary of State, Mr. Madison, refused to make delivery. They instituted a petition for *mandamus* which asked the Supreme Court to compel the Secretary of State to deliver the Commissions. Though clear to the court that the petitioners had a right to possess the commissions which they sought, the logically prior question was whether the Supreme Court had power under the Constitution to issue a writ of *mandamus*. With the Judiciary Act of 1789 the Congress had passed a statute that purported to grant to the Supreme Court the Appellate jurisdiction to issue *inter alia* writs of *mandamus*. On the other hand, the Constitution in article III, section 2, carefully distinguished between the Supreme Court's original jurisdiction and its appellate jurisdiction:

> In all cases affecting Ambassadors, other public ministers and Consuls, and those in which a state shall be a party, the Supreme Court shall have original jurisdiction. In all other cases before mentioned, the Supreme Court shall have appellate jurisdiction . . . .

Chief Justice John Marshall argued that there was a clash between the Act of Congress and the Constitution. Writs of *mandamus* are not referred to in article III as among those cases in which the Supreme Court shall exercise its original jurisdiction yet the purport of the Judiciary Act is to bestow upon the court such a power. To be sure Congress had granted the power as part of the court's appellate jurisdiction, however the true nature of a *mandamus* was said to be an *original* and not an appellate action.

fined. Doubtless this is done with the intention to place limits upon the powers of these departments. Yet if these limits may be surpassed at will by the legislature then the distinction between a government of limited and unlimited powers is abolished, and written constitutions but "absurd attempts" that accomplish nothing. Rather, the *intentions* of the framers of written constitutions is that they shall be the fundamental law "and consequently the theory of every such government must be that an act of the legislature, repugnant to the Constitution is void." This theory, Marshall concluded, is "essentially attached" or inherently embodied in a written constitution.[175]

In framing the answer to his second question—the power of the courts—Marshall emphasised their function:

> It is emphatically the province and duty of the judicial department to say what the law is. . . . So if a law be in opposition to the Constitution, if both the law and the Constitution apply to a particular case, so that the court must either decide that case conformably to the law, disregarding the Constitution; or conformably to the Constitution disregarding the law; the court must determine which of these conflicting rules governs the case. This is of the very essence of judicial duty.

The choice for the courts may be clear, Marshall reasoned, but if the judge cannot consider the Con-

---

175. Hamilton expressed the matter in terms of agency principles:

> There is no position which depends upon clearer principles than that every act of a delegated authority, contrary to the tenor of the commission under which it is exercised, is void. No legislative act, therefore, contrary to the Constitution can be valid. To deny this would be to affirm that the deputy is greater than his principal; that the servant is above his master; that the representatives of the people are superior to the people themselves; that men acting by virtue of powers may do not only what their powers do not authorise, but what they forbid. *Supra* note 173.

stitution in court, that is, if the Constitution is not a justiciable instrument, would not this

> . . . subvert the very foundation of all written constitutions? It would declare that an act which, according to the principles and theory of our government, is entirely void, is yet, in practice, completely obligatory. . . . It would be giving to the legislature a practical and real omnipotence, with the same breath which professes to restrict their powers within narrow limits. It is prescribing limits, and declaring that those limits may be passed at pleasure.

Convinced that the courts were designated to guard and enforce the Constitution, Marshall exercised the power of judicial review and declared void a part of the Judiciary Act of 1789. As Marshall grasped, when we inquire whether any such power exists, we are necessarily asking no less than whether the Constitution itself has any legal force—whether the Constitution is to be an impotent, nonjusticiable set of directives or the vigorous paramount law that the framers and people proclaim it to be.

(2) ITS LIMITATIONS ABROAD

The logical ground for judicial review has been one of the most exportable of American constitutional doctrines. "One cannot fail to notice" wrote Durgah Das Basu, "how the Marshallian logic has been transmitted across the Atlantic to implement an organic instrument having a different phraseology." [176]

Yet certain objections may be posed against the doctrine and the advisability of its reception in a Commonwealth country such as Lesotho. It has already been mentioned that the Constitution must be taken literally and that its silence on this issue is a factor

---

176. 1 COMMENTARY ON THE CONSTITUTION OF INDIA 159 (Sarkar, Calcutta 1955).

of real importance. This argument is the more persuasive when applied to the lengthy Westminster Constitutions which, unlike the compressed United States Constitution, strove for the completeness of an elaborate code of fundamental law. *Expressio unius est exclusio alterius.*[177] Secondly, even assuming that the guardian of the Constitution is a logical necessity, nevertheless he need not be a court. The Constitutions of the Fourth and Fifth French Republics are both written and paramount yet the guarding of the constitution against legislative transgression is entrusted to a nonjudicial "Constitutional Council" which passes scrutiny during the legislative process.[178] Thirdly, it is open to doubt whether Marshall's rolling chain of reason, which began with the democratic assumption that the people have a right to establish basic principles for their own governance, starts on the right foot in places where the Constitution emanates not from the people but from the British Parliament.[179] Thus one is

---

177. Perhaps one must not forget the counter rule of validation,

> For centuries it has been an accepted canon in interpretation of documents to interpolate into the text such provisions, though not expressed as are essential to prevent the defeat of the venture at hand; . . HAND, THE BILL OF RIGHTS 14 (Harvard Univ. Press 1958).

178. CONSTITUTION OF THE FIFTH REPUBLIC Article 61. Decisions of the Constitutional Council are not subject to appeal. (Article 62.) *Compare* the work of the Rhodesian constitutional council (§ 73) under the 1961 Constitution. For details *see* Crawford, *The Working of the Rhodesian Declaration of Rights,* 83 S.A.L.J. 337 (1966).

179. Alexander Hamilton argued that the power of judicial review was not undemocratic because it upholds the Constitution and the Constitution is the overriding will of the people. Besides the danger of accepting such a statement (*e.g.,* the will of *which* people, those who *historically* consented or those who now can only express themselves, short of amendment, through their elected representatives?) it is difficult to judge to what extent it is applicable to Lesotho. In theory the

hesitant to conclude that draftsmen schooled in the constitutional law of Great Britain, where parliamentary sovereignty is termed the "dominant characteristic" of the political system and the notion of judicial review both waxed and waned all in the Seventeenth Century,[180] would regard the purpose of the Lesotho Constitution frustrated and the will of the demos defeated if the courts could not rescind the excesses of the legislature. Indeed the available evidence does not suggest that Westminster draftsmen are concerned with the problem of judicial review.[181]

Constitution of Lesotho is not a document with a democratic origin yet a significant attempt was made to tailor its provisions to the needs and aspirations of the people. The Constitutional Commission made an extensive tour of the country, interviewed 330 witnesses whose oral and written evidence swelled to four volumes. The range of discussion, however, was mainly limited to the chieftainship (including the position of the King) and the question of land which are by no means the entirety of the Constitution. Furthermore it is questionable whether this system of interviewing was equivalent to a referendum on these issues. On the other hand the Independence Constitution was thoroughly debated in the Basutoland Parliament which was democratically powered. Still, where the choice is starkly posed between independence and colonial rule the reality of the consent to the constitutional trappings of independence is not above doubt. In addition, as Paul and Clapham note from African experience elsewhere, especially Ghana, popular referendums may reflect such antithetical and vacillating views as to challenge their claim to be a "solemn compact" intended to bind later generations of voters. ETHIOPIAN CONSTITUTIONAL DEVELOPMENT 180-181 (O.U.P. 1967).

180. Dr. Bonham's Case, 8 Co. Rep. 107a (1610). *See* MCILWAIN, HIGH COURT OF PARLIAMENT AND ITS SUPREMACY Ch. 4 (New Haven 1910), and CORWIN, THE "HIGHER LAW" BACKGROUND OF AMERICAN CONSTITUTIONAL LAW (Cornell Univ. Press 1965).

181. The inclusion of the supremacy clause in the Lesotho Constitution was brought about by the specific request of the

(3) NOVEL USE OF SEPARATION OF POWERS DOCTRINE

Recently, however, in *Liyanage v. The Queen*[182] the Privy Council has concluded that there is a limited sphere of judicial review even for those courts in written constitutional systems that have not established "visible" fetters over Parliamentary power, such as by means of a bill of rights or express provision for judicial review. This sphere relates to the separate departments of government established by the Constitution as against Parliamentary attempts to tamper with their constitutionally intended functions. It is asserted that the separation of powers embodied in a constitution may form another source of judicial power quite apart from, though more limited than, the source of power relied upon in *Marbury v. Madison.* This theory was asserted as far back as 1952 in the second *Harris Case*[183] where the Appellate Division of South Africa, under legislative siege, held invalid the High Court of Parliament Act,[184] part of a parliamentary plan[185] to overcome the ruling in the first *Harris Case*[186] by constituting the Parliament as an ultimate court of appeal in all cases where the Appellate Division declared an act invalid. In discussing the

---

Basotho. Furthermore the Botswana Constitution, a recent example of Westminster drafting, contains no supremacy clause and, in general, leaves the issue of judicial review on a more insecure textual footing than is the case even in the UNITED STATES CONSTITUTION OF 1787.

182. [1966] 1 All E.R. 650 (P.C.), noted 1966 MOD. L.R. 420.

183. Minister of Interior v. Harris, [1952] 4 S.A. 769 (A.D.).

184. Act 35 of 1952.

185. *See infra* note 209.

186. Harris v. Minister of Interior, [1952] 2 S.A. 428 (A.D.).

invalidity of the statute, Justice van den Heever stated —[187]

> From the second preamble to the South Africa Act it is clear that the authors of our constitution had in mind the doctrine of the *trias politica* and the existence of some judicial power to enforce the constitutional guarantees. That seems to follow by necessary intendment. . . . We have had many kinds of courts; we have had trial by battle, by fire, and by flood. . . . In this respect the Legislature has absolute freedom of action and it is not for the existing courts to criticise the wisdom or equity of a measure passed in the exercise of that power by a comparison of the court established with courts answering to some preconceived standard. All this however, is subject to one limitation which follows by necessary implication and has no relation to the character or competence of the new creation: it must be a court.

In substance, there can be no separation of powers when the court is only a term meaning Parliament in disguise.

Liyanage v. The Queen[188] came before the Privy Council on appeal from Ceylon. On January 27, 1962, an overthrow of the Government of Ceylon was successfully thwarted and the conspirators were arrested. To ensure that a "deterrent punishment of a severe character . . . be imposed on all those who are guilty of this attempt . . ." the Government undisguisedly embarked upon "a legislative plan *ex post facto* to secure the conviction and enhance the punishment" of the conspirators. A new penal statute was enacted which retroactively "legalised their imprisonment while they were awaiting trial. It made admissible their statements inadmissibly obtained during that period. It altered the fundamental law of evidence so

187. *Supra* note 183, at 792.
188. *Supra* note 182.

as to facilitate their conviction. And finally it altered *ex post facto* the punishment to be imposed on them." As the trial court observed:[189]

> The Act removed the discretion of the court as to the period of the sentence to be imposed, and compels the court to impose a term of ten years' imprisonment, although we would have wished to differentiate in the matter of sentence between those who organised the conspiracy and those who were induced to join it. It also imposes a compulsory forfeiture of property.[190] These amendments were not merely retroactive: they were also *ad hoc*, applicable only to conspiracy. . . .

Eleven defendants were convicted under the Act and appealed to the Privy Council attacking the validity of the legislation.

The basis for the attack was not readily apparent, for the Ceylonese Constitution, like the South African Constitution, contains neither a bill of rights nor express provision for judicial review. In short, it ostensibly contained no express fetter on the power of Parliament. Despite these appearances the Privy Council held that this particular statute violated the Constitution. The reason was not that the statute was *ad hominem* and lacked generality, which was true, nor that it was an act of attainder with retrospective force, which again was true. The particular basis of their Lordships' opinion was that the Act violated the intent of the Constitution to establish a separation of powers, that is, "a separate power in the judicature which under the Constitution as it stands cannot be usurped or infringed by the executive or the legislature." Of course Parliament had the power to amend the Constitution, but this required a two-thirds ma-

---

189. Quoted from Government White Paper of Feb. 13, 1962.

190. *Cf.*, art. 1, § 9, U. S. CONSTITUTION.

jority with a certificate of the Speaker and had not been obtained in the case of the legislation in question. Though no power was expressly vested in the judiciary by the Constitution, the Board reasoned that in Ceylon, where the courts had been functioning since 1833, the change of sovereignty at independence produced no apparent effect on the courts. As a consequence "there was no compelling need . . . to make any specific reference to the judicial power of the courts . . ." and relying upon the general structure of the Constitution, the Board was prepared to imply the existence of this power and to say that the principle of separation of powers was intended to be judicially enforceable.

Their Lordships had no doubt that the impugned Act violated the principle of separation of powers.

> These alterations constituted a grave and deliberate incursion into the judicial sphere. Quite bluntly, their aim was to ensure that the judges in dealing with these particular persons on these particular charges were deprived of their normal discretion as respects appropriate sentences. They were compelled to sentence each offender on conviction to not less than ten years' imprisonment and compelled to order confiscation of his possessions, even though his part in the conspiracy might have been trivial.

Fearing that "the judicial power could be wholly absorbed" or gradually "eroded" if such acts were deemed valid, the Board declared the Act *ultra vires* the Constitution.

The importance of the decision in *Liyanage* may be limited to situations in which the legislative intention is clearly to victimize particular individuals by any process of law, and if this is true then it probably will not disturb accepted constitutional theory to any great degree. Parliament's role is to make the law, the courts' to interpret and apply it, and therefore if Parliament passes a law that is really a criminal sentence, Parliament has usurped the part allotted to the courts. However, if *Liyanage* is not strictly limited to its facts, the decision has wide implications. For if the courts may nullify *ad hominem* legislation which is a "grave and deliberate incursion into the judicial sphere" then *a fortiori* they may nullify *in rem* legislation that invades the judicial sphere. The Privy Council's reasoning seemed based on the premise that because Parliament could not abolish the courts outright without a proper constitutional amendment, Parliament could not indirectly accomplish the same by destroying or fundamentally altering the legal rules that the courts apply. Otherwise the courts become but empty shells. This theory to some extent marries the constitutional meaning of a court to many of the subordinate rules regulating the functioning and framework of the court. This is not to say that a statute is automatically void that abolishes judicial appeals, or trial by jury, or the use of assessors, or restricts the presence of lawyers in court. Coupled with legislative *mens rea* any one of these might be sufficient, whereas without it the line is difficult to draw. Apparently, however, there is a point beyond which even a legislature in good faith could not go.

C. The Judicial Review of Subordinate Legislation and Acts

Judicial power in Great Britain is inferior power. Rather than a co-equal department of the government armed with judicial review, the British courts exercise a power of administrative review whereby they serve to ensure that Parliament's statute is carried out in conformity with its letter. If the actions of the executive exceed the power granted to it by an act of Parliament then the function of the courts is to declare such action *ultra vires*. The courts serve as checks on defective *administration* of the law; however, it is not in the power of the courts to nullify or void the law itself. This restricted function of the courts is a corollary of the English doctrine of parliamentary sovereignty which, as described by Albert Venn Dicey, meant in a *positive* sense that Parliament might make laws on a boundless range of subjects, and in a *negative* sense that there was a thorough absence of any competing legislative competence from such quarters as the Queen, the individual Houses of Parliament, the actions of the electors, or the courts. In the legal (but of course not in the political) sphere Parliament is capable of anything—even impossibilities—[191] subject perhaps to Lord Bryce's modification that with all its putative omnipotence it cannot bind its successor[192] and as well to the rather recent view that

---

191. DeLolme's celebrated opinion "that Parliament can do everything but make a woman a man, and a man a woman" is trenchant but inaccurate. Parliament does not have to live in a real world. It may do as it pleases with the sexes.

192. *Supra* note 166, at 243 n. 1. The Westminster Parliament cannot bind itself even as to the form of subsequent legislation. Ellen Street Estates v. Minister of Health, [1934] 1 K.B. 590. On the other hand it has been held by the Privy Council that the Parliament of a state of a dominion could bind its successor to follow an extraordinary procedure in order to amend an act. Attorney-General for New South Wales v. Trethowan, [1932] A.C. 526. It could be noted that with the term "omnipotence" lawyers are only experiencing difficulties that the theologians have entertained for a long while, as when they ask: "Can God make a stone so heavy he cannot pick up?" Curiously Dicey held that while Parliament could not bind its successor, it could abdicate or share its powers. INTRODUCTION TO THE STUDY OF THE LAW OF THE CONSTITUTION 68 (10th ed. Macmillan, London 1959). Bryce, however, held that it could not. 1 STUDIES IN HISTORY AND JURISPRUDENCE 207 (O.U.P. 1901.)

it cannot create valid laws except in accordance with the established procedural rules, written or unwritten, that identify its authority (see below).

The great difference between British and American courts is that the latter possess the authority to set themselves against and to defeat the concerted authority of the Congress and the Executive while the former envision themselves as the agents of Parliamentary will "whose function it is to enforce that will not to question it."[193]

Possibly, as Dicey suggests,[194] the American theory of judicial review with its apparently different theory of judicial power was inspired by and is but a logical extension of the power of administrative review. In this respect it is necessary to see a resemblance between the American government and a subordinate authority with law-making powers, for example a British municipal council. Under the council's charter it may have the power to enact bylaws for certain purposes and if in a suit it is shown that the council has enacted a bylaw that exceeds its chartered purposes then the British courts, in keeping with their mandate to effectuate Parliament's will, have the competence to declare the bylaw *ultra vires*. Dicey argued that in the American context the government itself is but analogically a chartered, subordinate authority situated at the feet of the sovereign people, and that if the courts may vitiate unconstitutional laws it is because of a power akin to administrative review.

(1) THE SOUTH AFRICAN EXAMPLE: CONSTITUTIONAL CRISIS OF 1952

To those like Jennings who view such analyses

---

193. Ndlwana v. Hofmeyr, [1937] A.D. 229, 237 per Stratford A.C.J.

194. DICEY, *supra* note 192, at 94-99.

as "adventures in metaphysics" it should be pointed out that on such theories questions of overweening importance can depend in the courts. This was graphically shown in the great question put to the South African Appellate Division in *Harris v. Minister of the Interior.*[195]

(a) The Problem

In the South Africa Act of 1910, the Independence Constitution of the Union, a safeguarding provision, section 35, was included to preserve the previous right of the Cape coloured to exercise the franchise. This provision was "entrenched," meaning its terms could not be amended except by an extraordinary procedure that entailed passage of the amendment by a two-thirds majority of the total membership of Parliament at a joint sitting of both houses. For the amendment of any other provision of the Constitution or legislation upon any other subject Parliament functioned bicamerally in the same manner as the British Parliament. This amending requirement was again repeated in section 152 of the South Africa Act, the general amendment section. The efficacy of these provisions was directly questioned by the claimed passage of the Separate Representation of Voters Act of 1951, which, while attempting to disqualify coloured voters through the establishment of separate parliamentary representation for Europeans and non-Europeans in the Cape of Good Hope, passed through the House of Assembly and the Senate sitting separately and by simple majority rather than by the special procedure stated in sections 35 and 152.

The mode of enactment of the Act of 1951 would have seemed a blatant illegality; however, the govern-

195. *Supra* note 186.

ment had strong reason to believe in the law's validity.[196] Prior to 1931 there was no doubt that the Parliament of South Africa was bound strictly by the provisions of the South Africa Act. In 1931, however, Great Britain enacted the Statute of Westminster [197] which repealed the Colonial Laws Validity Act of 1865,[198] declared that no act of a Dominion parliament

---

196. The Nationalist Government even took counsel's opinion from a leading constitutional lawyer, Professor E. C. S. Wade of Cambridge University who advised that the entrenched clauses were no longer binding. Published in the *Cape Times*, March 24, 1952.

197. The relevant provisions of the Statute of Westminster are as follows:

> 2. (1) The Colonial Laws Validity Act, 1865, shall not apply to any law made after the commencement of this act by the Parliament of a Dominion.
> 2. (2) No law and no provision of any law made after the commencement of this act by the Parliament of a Dominion shall be void or inoperative on the ground that it is repugnant to the law of England, or to the provisions of any existing or future act of Parliament of the United Kingdom, or to any order, rule or regulation made under any such act, and the powers of the Parliament of a Dominion shall include the power to repeal or amend any such act, order, rule or regulation in so far as the same is part of the law of the Dominion.
> 3. It is hereby declared and enacted that the Parliament of a Dominion has full power to make laws having extra-territorial operation.
> 4. No act of Parliament of the United Kingdom passed after the commencement of this act shall extend, or be deemed to extend, to a Dominion as part of the law of that Dominion, unless it is expressly declared in that act that that Dominion has requested, and consented to, the enactment thereof.

198. The Colonial Laws Validity Act provides in part:

> 2. Any Colonial law which is or shall be in any respect repugnant to the provisions of any act of Parliament extending to the Colony to which such law may relate, or repugnant to any order or regulation made under authority of such act of Parliament, or having in the Colony the force and effect of such act, shall be read subject to such act, order, or regulation, and shall, to the extent of such repugnancy, but not otherwise, be and remain absolutely void and inoperative.
> 3. No Colonial law shall be or be deemed to have been void or inoperative on the ground of repugnancy to the

should be void for repugnancy to the law of England or an act of the United Kingdom Parliament, declared that Dominion parliaments should henceforth have extraterritorial legislative competence, and prohibited the application of acts of the United Kingdom Parliament to the Dominions without their request and assent. It was contended that by virtue of this act the South African Parliament had gained the sovereignty possessed by the British Parliament and that the constitutional restrictions imposed by the South Africa Act were inefficacious and were amendable by an ordinary bicameral act of repeal.

Furthermore, in 1937 in *Ndlwana v. Hofmeyr* [199] this interpretation was officially endorsed by the Appellate Division. There it was claimed that an act establishing separate voter registration for Africans in the Cape was *ultra vires* section 35 [200] of the South

---

law of England, unless the same shall be repugnant to the provisions of some such act of Parliament, order, or regulation, as aforesaid.

4. No Colonial law, passed with concurrence of or assented to by the Governor of any Colony, or to be hereinafter so passed or assented to, shall be deemed to have been void or inoperative by reason only of any instructions with reference to such law, or the subject thereof which may have been given to such Governor by or on behalf of Her Majesty, by any instrument other than the letters patent or instrument authorising such Governor to concur in passing or to assent to laws for the peace, order, and good government of such Colony, even though such instruments may be referred to in such letters patent or last-mentioned instrument.

199. *Supra* note 193.

200. Section 35 provides:

(1) Parliament may by law prescribe the qualifications which shall be necessary to entitle persons to vote at the election of members of the House of Assembly, but no such law shall disqualify any person . . . in the Province of the Cape of Good Hope who, under the laws existing in the Colony of the Cape of Good Hope at the establishment of the Union, is or may become capable of being registered as a voter from being so registered in the province of the Cape of Good Hope by reason of his race and colour only . . ., unless the Bill . . . be passed by both Houses of Parliament sitting

Africa Act. The Appellate Division held that it had not the power to inquire into the validity of the act because the Statute of Westminster had made Parliament sovereign.

> Parliament's will, therefore, as expressed in an Act of Parliament cannot be questioned by a court of law whose function it is to enforce that will not to question it. In the case of subordinate legislative bodies courts can of course be invoked to see that a particular enactment does not exceed the limited powers conferred. It is obviously senseless to speak of an act of a Sovereign law making body as *ultra vires*. There can be no exceeding of power when that power is limitless.[201]

(b) The New View of Sovereignty

Despite the strong pronouncement of the court in *Ndlwana's Case,* the Appellate Division in the first *Harris Case* declared that the Separate Representation of Voters Act was invalid. The court's main argument was that the Statute of Westminster had not abrogated the South Africa Act of 1910. First, there was no express repeal of the entrenched sections by the Statute of Westminster and a repeal by implication is not favoured or presumed. Second, when the Statute of Westminster declared that no act of a parliament of a Dominion should be void or inoperative on grounds

together, and at the third reading be agreed to by not less than two-thirds of the total number of members of both Houses. A Bill so passed at such joint sitting shall be taken to have been duly passed by both Houses of Parliament.
(2) No person . . . who at the passing of any such law is registered as a voter in any province shall be removed from the register by reason only of any disqualification based on race or colour.

201. *Id.* at 237. The court rejected the precedent of an earlier Appellate Division case, Rex v. Ndobe, [1930] A.D. 484, which unequivocably asserted the Court's power to hold an act of the legislature *unconstitutional.* The reasoning was that R. v. Ndobe was decided prior to the Statute of Westminster of 1931, and would not be decided in that way again.

of repugnancy to any act of the Parliament of the United Kingdom, this did not mean that the Union Parliament was free to contravene sections 35 and 152, for it must be assumed that the term "Parliament of a Dominion" in South Africa's case meant Parliament constituted relevantly in either its bicameral or unicameral form. Since the South Africa Act itself established and defined the "Parliament" of South Africa, that act must be consulted in order to interpret and understand the import of the Statute of Westminster. And the South Africa Act defined the "Parliament" which could amend sections 35 and 152 in a special way. The court reasoned that the true intent of the Statute of Westminster was not to disinter the entrenched clauses but to grant the Union Parliament a competence that it never possessed before—that is, the competence to enact other kinds of legislation repugnant to an act of the British Parliament, such as the repeal of the British Merchant Shipping Statute insofar as it applied to the Union. Thus the bicameral "Parliament," by virtue of the Statute of Westminster, was accorded the legal power to pass laws repugnant to all acts of the United Kingdom Parliament save one, namely the South Africa Act, which for purposes of the relevant amendment, defined Parliament as a unicameral body.

The line adopted by the court, presaged by Professor D. V. Cowen,[202] did not ask *what can Parliament do*; instead it asked *who is Parliament.* Rules of identification of the sovereign are logically prior to questions of his competence. It is not illogical for a court to admit that acts of the Union Parliament cannot be judicially questioned while at the same time

---

202. PARLIAMENTARY SOVEREIGNTY AND THE ENTRENCHED SECTIONS OF THE SOUTH AFRICA ACT (Juta, Capetown 1951).

insisting that the body which passed the act was *not* Parliament. As Latham wrote,[203]

> It is, therefore, an incomplete statement to say that in a state such and such an assembly of human beings is sovereign. It can only be sovereign when acting in a certain way prescribed by law. At least some rudimentary manner and form is demanded of it: the simultaneous incoherent cry of a rabble, small or large, cannot be law, for it is unintelligible. The minimum would be rules prescribing some sort of majority—simple, plurality, absolute majority, unanimity, or some arbitrary portion—coupled with rules for the election of a chairman.

Thus where the Ceylonese Parliament purportedly passed an act at variance with the Constitution, lacking a constitutionally required endorsement of the Speaker that it had been passed by the necessary two-thirds majority for an amendment, the Privy Council in *The Bribery Commissioner v. Ranasinghe*[204] declared the act invalid, Lord Pearce there saying—[205]

> [A] legislature has no power to ignore the conditions of law-making that are imposed by the instrument which itself regulates its powers to make law. . . . The proposition which is not acceptable is that a legislature, once established, has some inherent power, derived from the mere fact of its establishment, to make a valid law by the resolution of a bare majority which its own constituent instrument has said shall not be a valid law unless made by a different type of majority or by a different legislative process.

---

203. Latham, *What Is An Act of Parliament?* 1939 KING'S COUNSEL 152 quoted from HEUSTON, ESSAYS ON CONSTITUTIONAL LAW 8 (2d ed. Stevens 1964).

204. [1964] 2 All E.R. 785.

205. *Id.* at 792. "The fact remains," said Justice van den Heever "that the South Africa Act is our constitution and apart from that constitution there are no organs of state and no powers." The second Harris Case, *supra* note 183.

(c) Implied Use of Administrative Review

The tacit theory which justified the court's jurisdiction in the first *Harris Case* was clearly that of administrative review. This power was impliedly recognised by government counsel's argument:

> Prior to the passing of the Statute of Westminster, the Union Parliament was a nonsovereign, subordinate Colonial Legislature. Its subordination rested solely upon the fact that Courts of Law could declare laws made by the Union Parliament invalid by reason of their being repugnant to an act of the British Parliament.[206]

Since the court held that the Statute of Westminster did not disturb the South Africa Act, this power of review was still in effect. Only through the repeal of the South Africa Act would the courts no longer be the guardians of the Constitution.[207]

---

206. *Supra* note 186, at 441.

207. McWhinney faults this analysis because "it no longer seems possible politically to justify their (commonwealth constitutions') continued binding force in those terms alone. . . ."

Instead he would suggest that the South African Constitution (and no doubt he would say the same of the Lesotho Constitution) had "local or popular roots." Though admitting that this conception has some elements of a "legal fiction," McWhinney argues that it nevertheless comes closest to explaining political realities. (JUDICIAL REVIEW IN THE ENGLISH-SPEAKING WORLD 100 (2nd ed. Toronto Univ. Press 1960). Accepting *arguendo* the necessary fiction, one could question to what extent such comment would be valid in Lesotho. Do the jural links to the United Kingdom represent political realities or do the local roots of the Constitution reflect political realities? The answer may be that they both do. It has already been stated that too great a confidence could not be placed in the democratic origins of the Lesotho Constitution. *See supra* note 179. Secondly, there is a great economic dependence upon Great Britain which is likely to continue for the foreseeable future. The "political" sovereignty of Lesotho must take into account its economic vassalage to foreign aid. Thirdly, there is no serrated antipathy

It was of course necessary for the Appellate Division to reject *Ndlwana's Case* in its decision, for to have deemed it a controlling precedent would have deprived the court of all jurisdiction in the case. The paradox of the first *Harris Case* is that the court succeeded in exercising the power of judicial review only because the result was to enforce the South Africa Act and to deny the traditional view of parliamentary sovereignty. It was scarcely intimated that if the South African Parliament had been liberated by the Statute of Westminster the court would have had no jurisdiction in the first place.

The court's taciturnity about the essential question of its own competence is difficult to explain in terms of any other theory of judicial review. As we have seen in *Marbury v. Madison,* it was an exertion for the court to explain the theoretical necessity of such a power in the face of a constitution that made no express grant to the Supreme Court. The South Africa Act is silent on the matter as well. On the other hand the Appellate Division with good reason need not have advanced Marshall's theory that judicial review is a power "essentially attached" to a written constitution, for the two constitutions manifested an essential difference. The American Constitution was an indigenous expression of fundamental law that proceeded from the people. The South Africa Act of 1910, on the other hand, sprang into existence by virtue of an act of the British Parliament, and therefore the Union of South

---

toward Great Britain in Lesotho such as was sharpened by South Africa's Nationalist regime. The strength of local roots is in some degree a function of the vigour with which they are asserted. Finally, the Lesotho Constitution contains a number of express open-ended ties with English constitutional law. This law is a source for Lesotho's constitutional development and is itself a root that must be taken into account.

Africa, its Parliament, and its courts depended for their legal legitimacy upon an external Parliamentary will. Strictly speaking, all acts of the Parliament of South Africa were subordinate legislation of the British Parliament authorised by a charter.[208, 209]

---

208. This point seems not to have been fully appreciated by Chief Justice Centilivres when it was raised by counsel:

> Mr. Beyers then contended that no country which, like the Union, emerged from a colony into a Dominion within the framework of the British Constitution can be a sovereign state unless it has a sovereign parliament functioning bicamerally in the same manner as the British Parliament and that if this is not so in the case of the Union, it cannot be a sovereign state unless it breaks completely with its past and abolishes the monarchy. I cannot agree with this contention. It seems to me to be based on the fallacy that a Dominion Parliament must necessarily be a replica of the British Parliament despite the fact that all Dominion Parliaments have constitutions which define the manner in which they must function as legislative bodies. . . . A State can be unquestionably sovereign although it has no legislature which is completely sovereign. *Supra* note 186, at 463-64.

The Chief Justice was correct in noting that legal sovereignty does not depend upon bicameralism in the legislature, however Counsel seemed to be making at least the legitimate point that the Union Government, from the legal point of view, will forever be subordinately linked to the British Parliament. This parasitic position is to some extent a derogation from complete legal sovereignty, though this is not to disagree with Heuston that "the decision in no way denies the sovereignty of the Union of South Africa as a state in international law." (*Supra* note 203, at 16.) *And see* Cowen, *Legislature and Judiciary*, 15 MOD. L.R. 282, 292-296 (1952).

209. The epilogue to the first Harris Case is one of the saddest vignettes in South African history. Frustrated in its attempt to remove coloured voters from the common rolls by the Appellate Division, the Nationalist Government embarked upon a series of "legal" stratagems.

(a) It passed the High Court of Parliament Bill by majority vote at a bicameral sitting that purported to establish a High Court of Parliament composed of all the members of Parliament and provided that where any act of Parliament was invalidated by the Appellate Division that judgment was to be brought in review before the High Court. The judgment in

(2) ADMINISTRATIVE REVIEW IN LESOTHO

In Lesotho, as in South Africa, the exercise of administrative review could be employed as an accurate description of the source of the power in the courts to sustain the Constitution against parliamentary encroachment. Because Lesotho's independence is derived not from revolution but from legal conferral, the present courts in theory retain the power they historically possessed in the Colonial Era to review the inferior laws.[210] This power of review could be explicitly mentioned in the text of the Constitution, yet to fail to do so is not fatal, for it is a traditional function of the courts which would be retained unless expressly excluded. Under the High Court Proclamation of 1938[211] the High Court was granted jurisdic-

---

the first Harris Case was reviewed and overruled. However in the second Harris Case, *supra* note 183, the Appellate Division held the High Court of Parliament Act to be invalid mainly on the grounds that the High Court was really not a court but simply Parliament in disguise.

(b) It passed in a bicameral sitting in 1955 the Appellate Division Quorum Act which required eleven (instead of the usual six) judges to sit in appeal of a case that involved the constitutional validity of an act of Parliament. Soon afterwards it passed in like form the Senate Act which enlarged greatly the size of the Senate, granted to the bigger provinces of the Union greater representation, and provided for elections by simple majority rather than the previous system of proportional representation. In the 1955 elections the government captured 77 out of 89 seats in the Senate. Now heavily armed with a "packed" Senate and Appellate Division, the government pushed through (by a ⅔ majority in a joint sitting) the South Africa Amendment Act which revalidated the Separate Representation of the Voters Act of 1951. The validity of the Amendment Act and the Senate Act was subsequently tested before the newly constituted Appellate Division in Collins v. Minister of the Interior, *supra* note 121, which upheld both of them by a majority of 10 to 1, Schreiner, J.A. courageously dissenting.

210. *Supra* note 182.

211. Proc. 57 of 1938, 1 LAWS OF BASUTOLAND, Ch. 3, 148, (1949).

tion "in all causes and proceedings whatsoever, both civil and criminal" arising in the Territory of Basutoland. This grant of unlimited jurisdiction conferred on the High Court the same jurisdiction as the Supreme Court of South Africa.[212] The High Court Proclamation of 1954[213] did not disturb this grant, which was confirmed by the Constitution of 1959[214] and the Constitution of 1965.[215]

(a) Distinction Between National and Parliamentary Sovereignty

Yet to treat the government of a nation that proudly professes its independence as no more than a subordinate authority with legislative competence usually raises an objection: Is not subordination incompatible with the sovereignty of the nation?

The answer is that here lies a confusion between national sovereignty and the legal theory that binds together the internal system of justice. For purposes of international law the independence or sovereignty of a nation is judged in political terms. The basic criterion is the absence of external interference in a country's affairs. The presence of dormant jural links is clearly no denigration of sovereignty in this sense of the word. However, because the independence of Lesotho and the establishment of its government are, legally, the product of an order in Council, the legal validity of its internal institutions and acts thereunder can be judged only in terms of that statutory instrument. To expect the courts to apply to those insti-

---

212. The power of judicial review had been recognised in 1930 in South Africa in R. v. Ndobe, *supra* note 201.

213. Proc. 18 of 1954.

214. § 65(2).

215. § 105.

tutions some other standard of legal validity [216] is to expect their allegiance to shift from that organic instrument to some other basis. Such a shift, of *grundnorm* if you wish, will normally require more compulsion or cogency than the theoretical objection that the internal standard of legal validity is a foreign statute.[217] Lesotho is not legally the "sovereign" of its legal system, for that "sovereignty" hinges on the pleasure of the British Parliament which theoretically could,[218] but as a practical matter would not, repeal the Independence Constitution.

(b) A Lesotho Example: The Case of the Five Senators

This source of power may explain the judicial re-

---

216. Both sections 65(2) and 105(1) of the Constitutions of 1959 and 1965 respectively grant the High Court unlimited original jurisdiction.

217. As van den Heever J.A. remarked,

> [T]he fact that our constitution is the creature of the British Parliament seems to me a fortuitous circumstance which is quite irrelevant; so too is the fact that we have a written constitution. I would have been of the same opinion if it had been framed by a constituent assembly, made by Solon, or extracted from the laws of Hammurabi.

Harris v. Minister of the Interior, *supra* note 183, at 791.

218. The existence of this theoretical power was denied by Stratford A. C. J. in Ndlwana v. Hofmeyr, who stated in an *obiter dictum* the view that the British Parliament lost its power to legislate for a colony once a colony became independent because "Freedom once conferred cannot be revoked." This of course is not a legal but merely a political remark. *See* Dixon, *The Law of the Constitutions*, 51 L.Q.R. 611. Lord Sankey was being strictly logical in British Coal Corporation v. The King, [1935] A.C. 500, 520 when he said that as an "abstract" proposition the British Parliament could repeal the Statute of Westminster expressly or by passing legislation inconsistent with it. It must be kept in mind, however, that in lacking legal autochthony Lesotho is not unlike virtually every member of the commonwealth whose legal lifelines converge on Westminster. *See generally* ROBERTS-WRAY, COMMONWEALTH AND COLONIAL LAW 289-301 (Stevens 1966).

view exercised in *Molapo v. Constantinus Bereng Seeiso,*[219] which was decided in 1966 under the Constitution of 1965. Motlotlehi[220] had made eleven nominations to the Senate under his prerogative granted by section 34 of the Constitution, but when five of these eleven, the applicants, voted in favour of independence for Basutoland, which Motlotlehi opposed, Motlotlehi removed them and appointed five other senators in their place. The constitutionality of this removal depended upon the proper meaning of section 34:

> The Senate shall consist of the 22 Principal Chiefs and Ward Chiefs and eleven other Senators for the time being nominated in that behalf by Motlotlehi.

The precise question was whether the phrase "for the time being" meant that the nominated senators held office at Motlotlehi's pleasure, that is, an agency relationship terminable in his absolute discretion, or whether it meant that a nominated senator, as opposed to an *ex officio* senator, held office only for the duration of Parliament but nevertheless at least for the duration of Parliament.

The Court was persuaded that on the correct construction Motlotlehi had the power only to nominate but not the power to revoke a nomination. The main support for this reading was that section 71(2), which purported to list exhaustively the discretionary powers of Motlotlehi, did not contain mention of a power to revoke Senate nominations; and section 39(1), which listed the reasons and circumstances under which a member of Parliament other than a permanent member should be disqualified from holding his seat, also failed to mention revocation of a nomination.

---

219. *Supra* note 52.

220. The Paramount Chief's title under the 1965 Constitution.

The absence of mention of this type of removal or disqualification created a strong inference that none was intended, on the theory *expressio unius est exclusio alterius.*

The strongest argument advanced by Motlotlehi was based upon section 130(13), which is as follows:

> Without prejudice to the provisions of section thirty-two (3) of the Interpretation Act 1889 . . . where any power is conferred by this Constitution to make any order, regulation or rule or pass any resolution or give any direction or make any declaration or designation, the power shall be construed as including the power, exercisable in like manner and subject to the like conditions, if any, to amend or revoke any such order, regulation, rule, resolution, direction, declaration or designation.

It was argued that this general rule of interpretation clearly indicated that Motlotlehi had the power to revoke at will a senatorial nomination. But the court replied that the power to nominate is not mentioned in section 130(13), and further that there is a difference of meaning between a designation and a nomination.

Interrupting here, both the court and the parties appear to have overlooked section 76(2)(c) which apparently employs the phrase "for the time being" in a sense inconsistent with the court's holding. It states:

> (2) Motlotlehi's Privy Council shall consist of . . . .
>
> (c) One other person for the time being nominated in that behalf by Motlotlehi.

It could hardly be maintained that Motlotlehi could not dismiss his Privy Councillor, for a Councillor has no stated term of office. Furthermore, the court's reliance on the distinction between "nomination" and "designation" is not borne out by the implications of section 76(2)(c).

In conclusion, the court supported its interpretation of section 34 with the observation that it would indeed be extraordinary to discover, in a state at the penultimate stage of constitutional development toward a sovereign democracy, that Motlotlehi could exercise such control over a member of Parliament. Such a conclusion could strike both at the principle of freedom of speech in the Senate and at collective responsibility in the Cabinet.

The High Court declared the executive act of removal of the applicants and appointment of five new senators by Motlotlehi to be null and void. The power of the court to vitiate an act of the executive, however, is nowhere expressly stated in the 1965 Constitution. Moreover, there is neither a section in that constitution that declares that the Constitution is the supreme law, nor a provision stating that laws inconsistent with its tenor are void.

On what ground, then, could the court nullify Motlotlehi's act of removal and appointment? Counsel for the applicants pointed out to the court that it was empowered *inter alia* by section 47 with jurisdiction to hear and determine any question whether:

> (a) any person is for the time being validly nominated or designated as a senator under section thirty-four of this Constitution; . . .

Section 47 is an express grant of jurisdiction over the subject matter before the court but, as has been explained earlier, jurisdiction is not equivalent to the power of judicial nullification of the unconstitutional acts of the other departments of government without an additional power that declares that the court's interpretation of what the Constitution says is legally superior to the executive's interpretation of the Constitution. On the theory of administrative review, however, the court simply effectuates the intention of the statute in question not by reason that it has superior power over the legislature and the executive, but simply because the Constitution is in legal theory the creation of the British Parliament which is legally superior to the legislature, the executive, and the courts. The role of the courts is to defend Parliament's will against the excesses and corruptions of maladministration.

D. Résumé

From this brief enquiry into the sources of judicial review under the Lesotho Constitution certain points are clear. First, the power of judicial review is demonstrably granted; the issue is simply to what extent. Textually, the grant is express in terms of the court's power and duty to protect fundamental human rights. Some doubt exists, however, as to whether the other parts of the Constitution are as expressly justiciable, for two possible readings can be given to those provisions which recognise a judicial power to *interpret* the Constitution.

A wide reading of that term—which would permit the comparison of legislative and executive acts with the Constitution—may be doubted, but it is submitted that the case against it is not as strong as the inferences in favour of it. Second, putting to one side the letter of the Constitution, there is a substantial body of doctrine and case law that justifies judicial review on the ground of logic and statutory intention or by analogy to administrative law. From a survey of two such theories it would appear that there is ample authority for the assertion that the entire Constitution of Lesotho, save those provisions that are expressly excluded, is subject to the power of judicial review.

CHAPTER 4

CONVENTIONS IN THE CONSTITUTION

A. The Legislature
B. The Executive
C. The King
D. Enforcement in the Courts

One of the distinctly English contributions to the Constitution of Lesotho is the transplantation of many of its constitutional conventions into the corpus of the instrument.

Though the term "convention" has a precise meaning in English constitutional theory, it is apt to mislead the civilian who may confuse it with contract and the international lawyer who may take it for treaty. Mill described British conventions as the "unwritten maxims of the Constitution," [221] while Dicey characterised them as judicially unenforceable rules, "understandings, habits, or practices which, though they may regulate the conduct of the several members of the sovereign power, of the Ministry, or of other officials, are not in reality laws at all since they are not enforced by the courts." [222] Jennings found them to be "rules for effecting . . . co-operation" that are designed "to make the legal constitution work." [223]

Some conventions are of such an institutional importance that it would no doubt shock a foreign observer to learn that they are indeed no more than conventions, such as the rules that the Queen cannot veto any bill passed by the two Houses of Parliament, that the Cabinet must resign office when it ceases to

---

221. MILL, CONSIDERATIONS ON REPRESENTATIVE GOVERNMENT 87 (1st ed. London 1865).

222. *Supra* note 192, at 24.

223. JENNINGS, LAW AND THE CONSTITUTION 80-81 (3d ed. Univ. of London Press 1948).

command the confidence of the House of Commons, that the Prime Minister is chosen by the Queen as the man best able to command the support of the House of Commons, or that Parliament must be convened at least once a year. That these conventions both appear to be and are in fact unshakeable dogmas of the English Constitution points out that, while perhaps they are judicially unenforceable, they are in fact as binding as if they were. Furthermore, conventions are neither strictly British constitutional phenomena nor exclusively the by-product of a partially written constitution, but are associated with many other countries that have written constitutions.[224] It is therefore to be expected that over a period of time one may note the growth of unwritten conventions in the Lesotho Constitution as well.

The reception of British conventions into the Lesotho Constitution may be viewed, with some overlap, under three headings: those relating to the Legislature, the Executive, and the King.

A. The Legislature

Two conventions of importance are seen in the Constitution in the field of legislative procedure. Under section 64, money bills that are charges on public revenue or on the people cannot be proceeded upon by

224. Thus in the United States it would appear to have been a convention, with the exception of the administration of Franklin Delano Roosevelt, that no president should serve more than two consecutive terms in office. This is now codified by the 23rd Amendment. Similarly the Constitution grants the President the authority to appoint federal judges, but by convention he chooses those who are suggested by a Senator from the state in question. The self-imposed restraints by the Supreme Court on its power of judicial review (*e.g.*, that it does not decide "political questions," or will face a constitutional question only if it is unavoidable) could be viewed as conventions.

Parliament without the assent of the Cabinet. This is in keeping with the ancient practice of the financial initiative of the Crown [225] expressed in the rule that "a demand from the Crown invariably precedes a grant by the Commons." [226]

Secondly, under section 65, the Lesotho Senate is restricted to powers of debate, amendment, and delay [227] and cannot veto bills that have passed through the National Assembly. This provision embodies the essence of the British convention now statutorily enacted in the Parliament Acts of 1911 and 1949, that the House of Lords cannot indefinitely oppose the House of Commons whenever it is clear that the latter represents the will of the Nation.[228]

B. The Executive

There are a number of importations now reduced to writing in the realm of cabinet affairs. Corresponding to Westminster convention, the cabinet is chosen bv the sovereign on the advice of the Prime Minister from among the upper and lower houses, though with the difference that in Lesotho the permanent members of the Senate—the principal and ward chiefs—are ineligible to serve.[229] Similarly, the Prime Minister is chosen by the sovereign only from among the members of the National Assembly. Cabinet positions are

---

225. Now codified in Standing Order 82.

226. COCKS, ERSKINE MAY'S PARLIAMENTARY PRACTICE 719 (17th ed. Butterworths 1964).

227. *One day* for speaker-certified appropriation bills, *thirty days* for speaker-certified money bills other than appropriation bills, and *ninety days* for all uncertified bills.

228. Hypothetically the House of Lords still retains a small range of veto power on certain kinds of bills.

229. § 72(3). Thus only the nominated members of the Senate can be cabinet ministers.

vacated [230] whenever the holder suffers the loss of his parliamentary seat otherwise than by a dissolution (*e.g.*, upon electoral defeat, death, or disqualification),[231] dismissal at the hand of the Prime Minister, or collapse of the ministry signalled by the resignation, removal, or appointment of a Prime Minister. The Prime Minister's office becomes vacant whenever the Prime Minister loses his seat in the National Assembly other than by reason of dissolution.[232]

Throughout their tenure in office all ministers are bound by the rule of collective responsibility to the two houses of Parliament.[233] A minister unprepared to defend a cabinet decision must resign and if he does not resign he is responsible. As Jennings observes:

> From the minister's point of view it means only that he must vote with the Government, speak in defense of it if the Prime Minister insists, and that he cannot afterwards reject criticism of his act, either in Parliament or in the constituencies, on the ground that he did not agree with the decision.[234]

C. The King

The most difficult set of conventions surrounds the exercise of the King's prerogative. As has been explained, few areas remain matters of true prerogative because of the general principle established by section 76 that, subject to explicit exception, the King shall act in accordance with the advice of the cabinet or, where required, some specified authority. Thus in the main the King functions as an agent, as in regard

---

230. § 72(6).
231. § 46.
232. § 72(5).
233. § 73(2).
234. JENNINGS, CABINET GOVERNMENT 278 (C.U.P. 1965).

to the appointment of cabinet ministers, the assent to legislation, and the like.[235] Were the King to neglect or decline to carry out a function *required* by another's advice under section 76(4), the Prime Minister is empowered to disregard and overreach by performing the act himself. In such cases, courts have no competence to question whether the King received the advice or acted in accordance with it.[236]

Certain decisions with reference to the dissolution of Parliament and the appointment and removal of the Prime Minister form specific exceptions to the general rule of section 76 and are reserved for the King's "own deliberate judgment." These discretionary powers are found in four provisions of the Constitution referred to in section 76(2):

(i) section 68(4):

> In the exercise of his power to dissolve Parliament, the King shall act in accordance with the advice of the Prime Minister:
>
> Provided that—
>
> (a) if the Prime Minister recommends a dissolution and the King considers that the government of Lesotho can be carried on without a dissolution and that a dissolution would not be in the interests of Lesotho, he may refuse to dissolve Parliament. . . .[237]

---

235. *See supra* at pp. 239-244 for discussion of the King's agency, conventional, and prerogative powers.

236. § 76(6).

237. As to when and why a sovereign may refuse a dissolution, *see* JENNINGS, *supra* note 234, at 420-428; WILSON, CASES ON CONSTITUTIONAL AND ADMINISTRATIVE LAW 21-26 (C.U.P. 1966). As to lack of confidence in the government, *see* JENNINGS, *supra* note 234, at 492-497. It is to be noted that under the Lesotho Constitution a vote of no confidence is only effective if it is accompanied by a proposal of the name of the new Prime Minister. § 68(5).

(ii) section 72(3):

The King shall appoint as Prime Minister the member of the National Assembly who *appears to him* to be the leader of the political party or coalition of political parties that will command the support of a majority of the members of the National Assembly and shall, acting in accordance with the advice of the Prime Minister, appoint the other Ministers from among the members of the National Assembly or from the Senators who are nominated as Senators by the King under section 41 of this Constitution: . . .[238] (Italics added.)

(iii) section 72(4):

The King may remove the Prime Minister from office—

(a) if a resolution of no confidence in the Government of Lesotho is passed by the National Assembly and the Prime Minister does not within three days thereafter resign from his office or advise a dissolution of Parliament; or

(b) if at any time between the holding of a general election to the National Assembly and the date on which the Assembly first meets thereafter, the King *considers* that, in consequence of changes in the membership of the Assembly resulting from that election, the Prime Minister will no longer be the leader of the political party or coalition of political parties that will command the support of a majority of the members of the Assembly.[239] (Italics added.)

(iv) section 75(3):

The powers of the King under this section shall be exercised by him in accordance with the advice of the Prime Minister: Provided that if the King considers that it is impracticable to obtain the advice of the Prime Minister owing to his absence

---

238. Regarding the choice of the Prime Minister, *consult* JENNINGS, *supra* note 234, at 20-58; WILSON, *supra* note 237, at 16-21.

239. For the basis of the Prime Minister's removal following a general election, *see* JENNINGS, *supra* note 234, at 490-92.

or illness he may exercise those powers without that advice.[240]

Two points are important to note. The judgment involved in these decisions is not utterly subjective because the proviso clause to section 76(2) declares that "the King shall in the exercise of the said functions act, so far as may be, in accordance with any constitutional conventions applicable to the exercise of a similar function by Her Majesty in the United Kingdom." Second, since a decision of this kind is to be truly the King's own and not on the advice of another, it is not within the competence of the Prime Minister to overreach the King by performing the act himself.[241]

---

240. On the replacement of an absent or ailing Prime Minister, *see* JENNINGS, *supra* note 234, at 26-28.

241. This is admittedly only one interpretation but, it is submitted, the one that is justified by the text. The powers of the P.M. to overreach the King do not vest in any other instance than the King's failure to act when he is "required by this Constitution to do any act in accordance with the advice of any person or authority. . . ." In the circumstances under discussion, however, the King is clearly not required to follow anyone else's advice. There is one instance of potential controversy. Should the Prime Minister advise a dissolution and the King refuse to order a dissolution on the grounds given in section 68(4)(a), the Prime Minister might take the view that the King was behaving unconventionally and, hence, unconstitutionally. If the Prime Minister were right about the relevant convention then he would appear entitled to order the dissolution himself, for ordinarily the King must follow advice where he is required by the Constitution. The dispute between them would be in essence whether the decision to be made by the King falls within the proviso clause to section 68(4) or not. On the other hand if the Prime Minister makes a *bona fide* error about the meaning of the relevant convention he would not be entitled to order the dissolution. It should not be assumed, however, that the Constitution intended this critical question of royal prerogative to rest upon the Prime Minister's knowledge of conventions, but rather upon the King's. Therefore it is more logical to assume

D. Enforcement in the Courts

Incorporated by reference, British conventions become justiciable standards of constitutional behaviour for the King to follow.[242] It would have been open, of course, to redact with precision the conventional standards applicable to Her Majesty, but this path may have been rejected in the interest of flexibility and in recognition of the great practical difficulties in codifying the conventions on such matters as the dissolution of Parliament and the dismissal of ministers.[243] Flexibility is inherent in the conventions themselves, whose open-textured content, ever uncertain and changing, will allow for honest division of opinion about their meaning. Further flexibility is engendered, however, by the inclusion of the phrase "so far as may be" (*mutatis mutandis*), a phrase familiar to a country that survives on imported law. One can only sympathise with a monarch who must make tripartite decisions: what is the meaning of the relevant convention, to what extent is it altered by the changed conditions of Lesotho, and how is it to be applied in the particular case.

Nor is the problem of certainty any easier for the court. While a court must administer a farrago of unwritten practises and habits that have vague and even vanishing margins, it must at the same time decide a controversy of national importance. Such con-

---

that the Prime Minister has no such competence to overreach the King.

242. Roberts-Wray is critical of this approach because "the [King] and the Courts may become involved in a political controversy" and because of the general difficulty of elucidating "precisely what the conventions are." *Supra* note 218, at 327-28. Evatt, however, favours justiciable conventions. THE KING AND HIS DOMINION GOVERNORS 289 (Cass 1936).

243. Clearly we will no longer be able unqualifiedly to say with Dicey that conventions are not enforced in the courts.

troversies will place greater pressure than is usual upon the court to give an aura of certainty and rightness that of course may only be illusory. If a court is to decide such difficult cases, clearly it stems from the nature of the law to be administered and the magnitude of the cause that it cannot choose between competing *dicta* about conventions.[244] The King must be accorded a latitude of legality that extends to the edges of English conventional practice. Only in a case of a clear mistake, that is, where there is no support for his position, should the court declare his act unconstitutional. Here, perhaps more so than in any other area of constitutional litigation, the court should extend a strong presumption of constitutionality. This course is dictated not only by a need for certainty, but by the exacerbation that the King and perhaps also the court may be in severe confrontation with another department of the government, such as the executive. Thus, if the King violates convention and chooses the wrong person to be Prime Minister, it is in effect the court's task to name the true Prime Minister or even to order the installation of a new Prime Minister. Perhaps the past acts of the putative Prime Minister are retrospectively invalid because they were not executed by the true Prime Minister. These are not results that can be supported with marginal reasons.

To raise these doubts, however, is not to argue that the reference to British conventions is ill-advised.

---

244. One is tempted to speculate to what extent, in a country whose courts regularly administer customary law, it would be possible to successfully resist using customary-law criteria for the recognition of conventions. (One is also tempted to ask whether incorporation by reference precludes indigenous constitutional growth of conventions. Does the foreign model remain static as of the year 1966 or does it continue to export its conventions thereafter?)

The wisdom of excluding it from the Constitution would have to be judged in light of the Nigerian case of *Adegbenro v. Akintola.*[245] In May, 1962, the Governor of the Western Region of Nigeria removed the then Premier, Chief Akintola upon receipt of a letter signed by 66 of the 124 members of the House of Assembly, that stated that they no longer supported Chief Akintola, although there had been no adverse vote in the House. Under the Constitution of the Western Region of Nigeria, the Governor had the right to remove the Premier from office whenever it "appear[ed] to him" that the Premier no longer commanded the support of a majority of the members of the House of Assembly.[246] Though the provision in question was a written facsimile of an unwritten practice of the Constitution of the United Kingdom, there was no express proviso (as in Lesotho) that the Governor would also be bound by comparable constraints on the British Sovereign in exercising the power.

The question of the constitutionality of the Governor's act was referred to the Federal Supreme Court, which answered that the Governor, analogous to the limitation upon the British sovereign, could not remove the Premier except in consequence of proceedings on the "floor" of the House, such as a vote of no confidence, a defeat on a major measure, or a series of defeats on measures of some importance. The Privy Council, however, reversed the Federal Supreme Court by adopting a strict construction. In their Lordships' view of the provision, whatever the political dangers of permitting the Governor to gather his evidence of nonsupport from another quarter, rather than strictly from the Parliamentary floor, this is what the Con-

---

245. [1963] A.C. 614.
246. § 33(10).

stitution literally envisions in the words "appears to him." A contrary intention would have been expressly stated. The act of removal, therefore, was a political question that was not subject to judicial review.

The difficulty with the decision of the Privy Council, however, is that it never decides whether the nature of the Governor's discretion is really subjective or objective. If purely subjective, then he may remove the Premier upon acquisition of any evidence which he sincerely credits, regardless of its utter lack of probity or relevance.[247] The Board, however, did not endorse this position, nor would it seem to be a proper or workable rule in a democracy. If, on the other hand, the discretion must be exercised somewhat objectively (as the Board implied),[248] the question was whether the letter signed by the 66 members of the House was in fact reasonable and sufficient evidence that the Premier had lost the support of the majority, but the Board never addressed itself to this question.[249] Indeed it asserted that the act of removal was not reviewable by a court of law which, to bring us full circle, implies that the Governor's discretion is utterly subjective.

The express proviso in the Lesotho Constitution resolves this troublesome question in *Adegbenro v.*

---

247. *E.g.*, at one extreme Calpurnian dreams and rumors.

248. In argument counsel for respondent presumed that the Governor must have some evidence. *Supra* note 245, at 622.

249. Counsel for appellant did argue this question, pointing out that even in the case of a letter signed by the 66 members it may well be that in a debate in the House certain factors that they did not know about would win them over. Furthermore the letter might have been obtained by a misstatement of the person who obtained the signatures. He noted too that a substantial proportion of those who signed the letter afterwards voted in favor of Chief Akintola. *Supra* note 245, at 623-624.

Akintola. It establishes an objective guide for the King and political participants to follow, as well as a reviewable standard for the courts to apply. It should also be borne in mind that although court enforcement of conventions may not be the rule in the United Kingdom today, neither are serious disputes about the constitutional powers of the Queen. In newly independent states such as Lesotho, where only recently the Monarch was accustomed to more than titular power, there is value in defining power as explicitly and precisely as the subject matter will permit. It does not seem that the purpose or the effect of the proviso would be to foster constitutional imbroglios, but it might help to resolve or mitigate a crisis that may already exist.

CHAPTER 5

FUNDAMENTAL HUMAN RIGHTS

A. Constitutional Methods and Procedures for Enforcement
B. Constitutional Standards for Enforcement

Just government is the wise distribution of rights granted to society as a whole as against those retained by the individual. Though the Constitution grants collective power to the Parliament, it also grants freedom to each person. The mission of Chapter II of the Lesotho Constitution is to preserve or create a just equilibrium between the competing claims of the individual and the state. Thus the 1963 Constitutional Commission said:

> In advocating a Bill of Human Rights and Freedoms, we do not contemplate a dismembered society of self-sufficient individuals, where all the emphasis is on the rights of each, without regard to social duties and the establishment of a just social order. On the contrary, we would like to see established in Lesotho a polity in which the rights and obligations of individual citizens one to the other, and the rights and obligations of the community to which they belong, are reconciled in a stable social order, and preserved from the abuse of power in any of its forms. And such a social order can, in our view, best be encouraged in the manner which we suggest.[250]

Fundamental rights, however, are not primarily the product of a cool-headed intelligence; to us they seem the total claim of many individuals of diverse nationality in a sweep of historical opposition to arbitrary state power. The history of individual rights,

---

250. Report of the Basutoland Constitutional Commission 83 (1963).

Holmes might agree, has not been logic but an experience as deeply rooted as Magna Carta of 1215, the Bill of Rights of 1689, the American Bill of Rights of 1791, the Declaration of the Rights of Man of 1791, and the Universal Declaration of Rights of 1948.

It is clear, however, that the fundamental human rights to which the people of Lesotho are constitutionally committed do not spring unassisted from the experience of the Basotho Nation. The eulogised free speech of the traditional *pitso* (public meeting) is of a different quality from that now desired and envisaged for a democratic society with universal adult suffrage.[251] The old paternalistic laws of discrimination, meant to protect the Basotho from themselves and others, are no longer suited nor perhaps sanctioned by the principles now erected by the Constitution.[252] Independence and the Constitution have conspired to introduce into the mainstream of Basotho society radical principles that seem unheralded and unforged by the historical forces permitted to clash in 98 years of colonial rule. Nevertheless the Constitution clearly represents a plateau of just social relations which the Basotho seek as their own.

Yet if the study of other societies demonstrates

---

251. *"C'est toute en liberté"* Father Dieterlen enthusiastically wrote about the *pitso*. LIVRE D'OR 32-33 (Maison des Missions Evangeliques, Paris, 1912). Eugene Casalis said that he witnessed the "greatest freedom and plainness of speech." THE BASUTOS 293 (James Nisbet & Co., London 1861). But Widdicombe noticed an important limitation: "Anyone may speak, but the common people rarely do so, leaving the oratory to their superiors. As a rule, they content themselves with endorsing or dissenting from the remarks made by the chiefs or their counsellors." FOURTEEN YEARS IN BASUTOLAND 42 (Church Printing Co., London 1891).

252. *See infra,* Excursus: Background to Discrimination, at p. 419.

anything it is that the quality of freedom for the individual depends not upon the excellence of its documents but upon the excellence of its people. The firmest constitutional guarantees to the individual can be circumvented by a people determined not to live with them, as in South Africa,[253] whereas no formal guarantees are needed if the people are determined to protect them, as in Great Britain. The essence of the matter resides in the character of the people, who, with their own values, decide whether the paper guarantees are to come to life.

In one sense the Constitution does not establish specific values, for it places a great reliance on future interpretation. The meanings of crucial words such as "reasonably" and "necessary" are inevitably of an open content which is to be filled by the government, the society, and the courts at some later time when the needs and circumstances arise to interpret and test their meanings. It may even seem to some that the provisions on fundamental rights are neutral principles, neither agents of good nor evil, which represent merely a postponement of the difficult question of balance and adjustment between man and men. Certain persons may be discouraged by the manner in which the provisions are drafted. Much freedom seems to be undeniably given to the individual if one fastens the eye exclusively on the first subsection of every right, but just as much seems to be taken back again the farther one reads on. This ambivalent mode of stating two things at once, of writing down and erasing simultaneously, has tempted some observers to conclude that the inclusion of fundamental rights in constitutions is fruitless. "Rights," said Professor Wheare, "cannot be declared in a constitution except in absolute and un-

---

253. *As in* the Harris case, *supra* note 186.

qualified terms, unless indeed they are so qualified as to be meaningless." [254]

This, it is submitted, is not altogether true. If Professor Wheare is voicing the well-known allergy of the English lawyer to general principles, his observation is colourably provincial, since general principles are the familiar tools of the civilian and, increasingly, of the common lawyer as well. One can submit with Professor Schwelb that

> . . . general principles embodied, and general phraseology used, in a basic document sometimes have a decisive effect on subsequent legal history. The constitutional law of the United States might be different if the Fifth and Fourteenth Amendments had not prohibited deprivation of life, liberty, or property "without due process of law," or if general expressions such as "the privileges and immunities of citizens" and "equal protection of the laws" had not been used.[255]

Furthermore there is a distinction between "guarantees" coupled with saving clauses such as "save as the law permits"—which Professor Wheare may have in mind—and genuinely crafted rights such as are found in the Lesotho Constitution.[256] The rights found there are not absolute, for the government is permitted to apply restrictions. On the other hand this is not to say that the rights thereby become meaningless, for the permissible amount of that restriction is strictly limited. Further, it is something more than meaningless to require the government to show that the restric-

---

254. MODERN CONSTITUTIONS 71 (O.U.P. 1951).

255. HUMAN RIGHTS AND THE INTERNATIONAL COMMUNITY 54 (Quadrangle 1964). *See also* the REPORT OF THE WILLINCK COMMISSION 97 (H.M.S.O. 1958).

256. *See* COWEN, FOUNDATIONS OF FREEDOM 127-128 (O.U.P. 1961).

tion on the right is valid.[257] Indeed the question for the future may be not whether these rights prove to be useless but whether they do not prove to be too effective, that is, whether the stringent claims of the individual Mosotho can be reconciled with the task posed to the government of one of the poorest countries in Africa, geographically isolated within a racial tinderbox.

It is clear why the draftsmen were not satisfied with an uncritical importation of the prototypal Nigerian Bill of Rights. The Nigerian Constitution of 1960, in its treatment of fundamental rights, was the precursor and model for the constitutions of other African states besides Lesotho, such as Sierra Leone, Uganda, Kenya, and Botswana. It led the way in setting forth not merely a set of rights comparable to the United States' Bill of Rights, but in enumerating in great detail much that the United States' document did not state. In the Lesotho Constitution important changes in the model were made, however, which no doubt owe their origin or inspiration to the special situation of the country, subject as it is to the restrictions levied by illiteracy, mass poverty, and an unfortunate dependence on encircling South Africa.

It has been said that the constitution that will not bend will break; but the Lesotho Constitution is capable of bending with the realities of the times. Incursions on individual liberties are disfavoured only when they cannot be tangibly justified. The future need not unfold that the rights were a straitjacket for Parliament or, as Mr. Justice Jackson once put it,[258] a "suicide pact" with the people. Of course any strict standard involves a certain risk of its own re-

257. *See infra* pp. 344-348.

258. Dissenting opinion in Terminello v. Chicago, 337 U.S. 1 (1949).

jection, but we would submit that if Lesotho is to provide an example of liberty in Southern Africa it will accept such risks and dedicate itself to the exercise and maintenance of fundamental human rights.

A. Constitutional Methods and Procedures for Enforcement

(1) MATTERS OF STRUCTURE AND FORM

Certain broad features of structure may be stressed at the outset by way of understanding the logical process by which the courts of Lesotho must come to decisions in questions of fundamental rights.

Generally in every section that sets out a fundamental right, the first subsection always makes a sweeping statement that seems to establish an absolute right. Any law, or act in pursuance of law, that falls short of this absolute right constitutes *prima facie* a denial of the right. The ensuing subsections, however, always qualify the broad statement of right initially established; these subsections are sometimes known as "saving clauses" because they expressly *save* or retrieve the validity of laws and subsidiary acts that would otherwise have contravened the absolute right. This dichotomous structure represents a recognition of the dialectical claims of the individual and the state, and indeed it would not be improper to label the first as the *individual's* clause and the second as the *state's* clause. On the other hand, from the standpoint of drafting technique, one may describe them as the *civilian's* clause and the *common lawyer's* clause, for they represent a clash between civilian and common-law legal method, the one inclined to generalise a right or principle without exceptions, the other tending to state numerous exceptions or specific rules which only imply the existence of a general right.[259]

---

259. For a description of the methodological clash in the

To the first generalisation that we have noted—the dichotomous structure of the rights—it must be added that the various rights show great diversity in terms of their wording, standards, and structure.[260] In order to explain this diversity more fully it may be of benefit to classify the rights.

(a) Rights Classified

There are various ways of classifying the rights in the Lesotho Constitution. One distinction is according to the *persons* to whom they are available. Thus all the rights are entrenched guarantees for all persons, citizens and aliens alike, with the exception of sections 7 (Freedom of Movement) and 17 (Freedom from Discrimination) which are entrenched guarantees to citizens alone and not aliens.[261] Another classification is formed by those rights that are *positively* worded in that they establish a freedom "of" or "to" something, such as sections 5, 6, 7, 11, 12, 13, 14, 15, and 18, as against those that are *negatively* worded in that they guarantee noninterference "from" something, such as sections 8, 9, 10, 16, and 17.[262] Again

---

drafting of the European Convention (1950), the ancestor of the Fundamental Rights of the Lesotho Constitution, *see* ROBERTSON, HUMAN RIGHTS IN EUROPE 17-18 (Manchester Univ. Press 1963).

260. "Standards" are those formulae that are employed to direct the judge in assessing the validity of an action or law restrictive of a protected right or rights. *See* Appendix B for an analysis of standards to be applied to the Lesotho Constitution. It is to be noted that the application of these standards is normally made in conjunction with a constitutional directive that the challenged law or action be held invalid "to the extent" that the standard is not satisfied. The incidence of other standards not expressly invoking reasonableness or democratic values (*e.g.*, "to such extent as may be necessary in the execution of a lawful order . . . ," § 6(i)) has not been recorded.

261. Discussed *infra*, pp. 409-410.

262. The classification refers only to the matter of wording.

one can classify the rights according to their subject matter. Thus some relate mainly to a *fair criminal process, e.g.*, sections 10 (Freedom from Arbitrary Search or Entry) and 12 (Right to a Fair Trial). Others are more immediately concerned with *human dignity, e.g.*, sections 8 (Freedom from Inhuman Treatment), 9 (Freedom from Slavery and Forced Labour), 11 (Right to Respect for Private and Family Life), and 17 (Freedom from Discrimination). Still others appeal to the *rational nature of man, e.g.*, sections 13 (Freedom of Conscience), 14 (Freedom of Expression), and 15 (Freedom of Assembly and Association).

The final classification discussed here is that based upon the nature of the saving clauses. In general the rights display saving clauses that fall into three types:

(i) *Rights which either have precise saving clauses or lack saving clauses altogether.* This is illustrated by section 8:

> 1. No person shall be subjected to torture or to inhuman or degrading punishment or other treatment.
> 2. Nothing contained in or done under the authority of any law shall be held to be inconsistent with or in contravention of this section to the extent that the law in question authorises the infliction of any description of punishment that was lawful in Lesotho immediately before the coming into operation of this Constitution.

The significant feature of this type of right is that its exceptions have a rigid quality that admits of some precision. It is a relatively simple task to con-

---

Though the distinction between positive and negative rights can be one of *substance*, the rights in the Lesotho Constitution are essentially always negative restrictions against governmental interference which, however, are sometimes worded as if they were positive rights.

sult the books to determine which forms of punishment were authorised before the Constitution came into force. Statutes in existence prior to the Constitution are not required to conform to clause 1. Clause 1 is prospective in that by explicit exception only statutes or subsidiary acts after the Constitution can be tested. In such cases the decision for the court is not to concern itself with a complex saving clause but instead with the meaning of the first clause in its use of such words as "torture," "inhuman," and "degrading." The exceptions are clear but the right may not be. Rights in this category are sections 8 and 18.[263]

(ii) *Rights with semi-precise saving clauses.* An example of this type of right is section 9:

> 1. No person shall be held in slavery or servitude.
> 2. No person shall be required to perform forced labour.
> 3. For the purposes of this section, the expression "forced labour" does not include:
>
> (a) any labour required in consequence of the sentence or order of a court;
>
> (b) any labour required of any person while he is lawfully detained that, though not required in consequence of the sentence or order of a court, is *reasonably required* in the interests of hygiene or for the maintenance of the place at which he is detained:
>
> (c) any labour required of a member of a disciplined force in pursuance of his duties as such or, in the case of a person who has conscientious objections to service as a member of a naval, military, or air force, any labour that that person is required by law to perform in place of such service;
>
> (d) any labour required during any period when Lesotho is at war or a declaration of emergency under section 21 of this Constitution is in force or in the event of any other emergency or

263. § 18 has no saving clause.

> calamity that threatens the life or well-being of the community, *to the extent that the requiring of such labour is reasonably justifiable* in the circumstances of any situation arising or existing during that period or as a result of that other emergency or calamity, for the purpose of dealing with that situation; or
>
> (e) any labour *reasonably required* by law as part of reasonable and normal communal or other civic obligations. (Italics added.)

The important feature of this second type is that while some of the exceptions are about as precise as words can be—such as clause 3(a)—other exceptions depend for their meaning upon broad standards of *reasonableness*—such as clause 3(b). Thus in section 9, labour that is "reasonably required" or "reasonably justifiable" will in some circumstances not be considered forced labour. Particular care must be made to distinguish the meaning of these differing standards of reasonableness from each other as well as from other standards of ambiguous import that appear in other sections classed of this type. At some places the relevant standard is "to such extent as may be necessary."[264] At others it is "reasonably justifiable in a democratic society."[265] The rights that can (with some arbitrariness) be placed in this category are sections 5, 6, 9, and 17.

(iii) *Rights with imprecise savings clauses.* Section 14 may serve as a representative of the third type:

> 1. Every person shall be entitled to, and (except with his own consent) shall not be hindered in his enjoyment of, freedom of expression, including freedom to hold opinions without interference, freedom to receive ideas and information without interference, freedom to communicate ideas and

264. *E.g.*, section 6(j) and similarly 5(2).

265. *E.g.*, section 17(4) (e).

> information without interference (whether the communication be to the public generally or to any person or class of persons), and freedom from interference with his correspondence.
> 2. Nothing contained in or done under the authority of any law shall be held to be inconsistent with or in contravention of this section to the extent that the law in question makes provision—
> (a) *in the interests* of defence, public safety, public order, public morality, or public health; or
> (b) *for the purpose* of protecting the reputations, rights, and freedoms of other persons or the private lives of persons concerned in legal proceedings, preventing the disclosure of information received in confidence, maintaining the authority and independence of the courts, or regulating the technical administration or the technical operation of telephony, telegraphy, posts, wireless broadcasting, or television; or
> (c) for the purpose of imposing restrictions upon public officers.
> 3. A person shall not be permitted to rely in any judicial proceedings upon such a provision of law as is referred to in subsection 2 of this section except to the extent to which he satisfies the court that that provision or, as the case may be, the thing done under the authority thereof does not abridge the freedom guaranteed by subsection (1) of this section *to a greater extent than is necessary in a practical sense in a democratic society* in the interests of any of the matters specified in paragraph (a) of subsection (2) of this section or for any of the purposes specified in paragraph (b) or paragraph (c) of that subsection. (Italics added.)

The reason why the saving clauses of the rights of this type are called imprecise is twofold. On the one hand there are two [266] imprecise standards of constitutionality to which legislation and acts thereunder

---

266. The standard "for the purpose of" we do not consider as important as the two others as a matter of classification. *See infra* note 407.

must conform. First, in clause 2(a) laws may constitutionally derogate from the *prima facie* right provided they are *in the interest* of defence, public safety, public order, public morality, or public health. Second, in clause 3 it is said that a permissible derogation from the *prima facie* right must not abridge it *to a greater extent than is necessary in a practical sense in a democratic society.* Controversy is inevitably associated with the vagueness of these terms. What extent is a necessary extent? And what further limitation is imposed by "practical sense"? What, as a practical matter, is necessary in a democracy? What is a democracy and to which democracies are we referring? [267] Framed in a flexible way with sundry open-ended questions, the exceptions to such rights clearly both permit and require greater judicial discretion, more interpretation and elaboration, and admit of less precision. On the other hand the imprecision engendered by these flexible standards extends throughout the right. In this third type of right the meaning of the entire saving clause depends upon such flexible standards. Whatever precision the words of any part of the saving clause have is jeopardised by the imprecise standard by which they are modified. The rights that may be classified in the category under discussion are found in sections 7, 10, 11, 13, 14, and 15.[268]

(b) Strict Construction

It follows from the detailed nature of the saving clauses that there is no judicial discretion to read in other exceptions than are present. For example in the rights that we have termed "imprecise," the saving

---

267. These problems are explored at pp. 398-401.

268. Section 16 does not conveniently lend itself to category (ii) or (iii), for it contains the significant elements of both. It has therefore been omitted in the list.

clauses systematically refer to the great heads of defence, public safety, public order, public morality, and public health as justifications for departure from the *prima facie* right. The courts could not accept, however, the validity of a law that derogated from a freedom on the justification of public *happiness* or *civic-mindedness*. This is the position taken in India [269] where it is said no other exception can be introduced short of an amendment to the constitution. *Expressio unius est exclusio alterius*. For structural reasons a strict construction of the great heads of authority and loose construction of the first subsection is the most favourable to the rights of the individual; however, individual liberty would not appear to suffer even if a strict construction were applied throughout. For the broad language of the *prima facie* right is often shaped inclusively rather than exclusively. Thus in regard to the "imprecise" rights there is no attempt to define the content of the right but rather to provide nonexclusive illustrations of it.[270]

The principle of strict construction, however, is relevant not only in construing the constitutional provision but also in construing an impugned statute. Ostensibly the title and wording of a statute may not disclose a restriction of a fundamental right, but its pith and substance may nevertheless have that effect.

---

269. BASU *supra* note 176, at 550.

270. Thus section 14 speaks of Freedom of Expression as "including" the freedom to hold opinions, receive and communicate ideas, etc., without information. With this one may contrast by way of example the corresponding section in the Botswana Constitution which makes it clear that the instances of the freedom just mentioned (*i.e.*, to hold opinions, receive and communicate ideas, etc.) are definitional of the concept rather than merely illustrative of a broad principle. CONSTITUTION OF BOTSWANA, § 12 (1966).

The court should not be bound by the statutory characterisation fashioned by the legislature if the law is in fact a derogation of a fundamental right uncountenanced by the saving clause, for otherwise the legislature could by conscious or unconscious misnomer circumvent the guarantees altogether.[271] Thus an act with the seemingly innocuous purpose to prevent unfair newspaper competition by regulation of the price, number of pages, and allocation of advertising space of newspapers was struck down in *Sakal Papers Ltd. v. Union of India* [272] as a substantive infringement of freedom of expression and the press which was not preserved by anything in the saving clause of that guarantee. On the other hand it is equally obvious that the court cannot strike down every law which *in some way* infringes a fundamental right for, as was pointed out in *Gopalan v. Madras*,[273] every lawfully detained inmate of the gaols could raise the cry *inter alia* that his freedom of expression was being restricted by his detention. If it is clear that the legislature had no *mens rea* to abridge a fundamental right, the preferred approach is to measure the directness of the abridgement. Thus in *Express Newspaper Ltd. v. Union of India* [274] an act to regulate the wages of journalists and their conditions of service was challenged as an unconstitutional invasion of freedom of expression and the press on the grounds that it might among other things lead to curtailment of newspaper circulation and loss of the independence of the press. The court, however, ruled that these were not direct or inevitable but remote consequences and in the ab-

---

271. Dwarkadas Shrinivas v. The Sholapur Spinning & Weaving Co., [1954] S.C.R. 674.

272. [1962] S.C.R. 842, 847.

273. *Supra* note 172.

274. [1958] S.C.R. 578.

sence of ulterior motive on the part of the legislature characterised the measure as only one that "affects the press." [275] This result logically follows from the observations of Chief Justice Kania in *Gopalan v. Madras:*

> If there is legislation directly attempting to control a citizen's freedom of speech or expression, or his right to assemble . . . peaceably and without arms, etc., the question whether that legislation is saved by the relevant saving clause of article 19 will arise. If, however, the legislation is not directly in respect of any of these subjects, but as a result of the operation of other legislation, for instance, for punitive or preventive detention, his rights under any of these sub-clauses is abridged, the question of the operation of article 19 does not arise. The true approach is only to consider the directness of the legislation and not what will be the result of the detention, otherwise valid, on the mode of the detenue's life.[276]

(2) THE GUARANTEE OF REDRESS

Redress is itself a guarantee. It is the role of section 20 to enforce the fundamental rights of Chapter II, and the High Court is the prime vehicle of redress. It is broadly empowered under section 20 to make orders, issue process, and give directions that it considers appropriate to secure the enforcement of the rights. It seems clear that the court need not feel oppressed by the niceties of the forms and writs of Roman-Dutch and English law. Rather it is at liberty to utilise, fashion, or create an arsenal of arrayed remedies appropriate to the circumstances. This is not

---

275. *Id.* at 618.

276. *Supra* note 172, at 100. It is submitted that this question is not very different from the question of direct and indirect burdens on freedom of conscience as stated in the United States, *see infra* at pp. 395-397.

to overlook, however, that convenient use may be made of orders similar to the English prerogative orders of mandamus, prohibition, *certiorari,* and *quo warranto,* and the writ of *habeas corpus.*[277]

(3) THE EFFECT, APPLICATION, AND SCOPE OF THE RIGHTS

(a) Laws Void for Inconsistency

The Constitution declares in section 2 that laws inconsistent with its tenor are void. A basic distinction should be observed between the laws that are enacted *after* the Constitution and the laws already in force *before* the Constitution.

(i) The Post-Constitutional Laws

The effect of a declaration of voidness on a law enacted after October 4, 1966, may be analyzed in two respects: its prospective effect and its retroactive effect. With regard to the prospective effect, once an inconsistent law has been declared void, it ceases to be valid and to operate in the future. It does not seem appropriate to follow the qualified language of the Indian [278] or Pakistan [279] courts in describing the effect as the "hibernation" or state of "eclipse." Rather, as Mr. Justice Field once observed:

> An unconstitutional act is not a law; it confers no rights; it imposes no duties; it affords no pro-

---

277. Section 5 of the High Court Act of 1967 provides: "The High Court shall have full power, jurisdiction, and authority to review the proceedings of all subordinate courts of justice within the Territory, and if necessary to set aside or correct the same." For a clear exposition of *certiorari* and *prohibition see* WADE, ADMINISTRATIVE LAW 96-100 (Clarendon 1961); BASU, *supra* note 176, Vol. III 495 *et seq.*

278. GLEDHILL, INDIA: THE DEVELOPMENT OF ITS LAWS AND CONSTITUTIONS 181 (Stevens 1964).

279. Maudoodi v. W. Pakistan, P.L.D. 1964 S.C. 673 at 735. "It is really more a state of hibernation than one of death."

tection; it creates no office; it is, in legal contemplation, as inoperative as though it had never been passed.[280]

What effect a declaration of voidness has *retroactive* to the court's ruling raises several considerations. There is something to be said for the view that a statute inconsistent with the Constitution is void *ab initio* because section 2 declares an unconstitutional law to be "void" rather than "voidable" in the sense of valid until declared void.[281] Hence it could be argued that a court has no power to accord any prior validity to such a law. On the other hand, there seem to be weightier reasons in favour of the view that we must give a flexible construction to the word "void" in section 2 if the result is to be reasonable. It is a recognised disadvantage of the system of judicial review that it is a haphazard check upon legislative excess subject to indeterminate time lag. In the interim between the passage of a law and the ruling of the court there may have been time for rights in good faith to have been vested and general reliance to have been placed on the law leading to settled transactions. To declare that a law has been void from the very date of its inception is an approach that may produce fundamental unfairness to parties who have acted in good faith.

A further trouble is that this rigorously logical approach may also place the court in conflict with other sections of the Constitution. Thus, for example,

---

280. Norton v. Shelby County, 114 U.S. 425, 442 (1886). Chicot Country Drainage District v. Baxter State Bank, 308 U.S. 371, 374 (1940).

281. It is of course always open to argument that the confusion of Roman-Dutch law surrounding the use of the term "void" is such—witness the chaos in the Law of Persons—that "voidable" was indeed intended.

to rescind *ab initio* a statutory amendment that licensed certain persons to engage in an activity statutorily prohibited as to all other persons might transform any prior "lawful" dealings into *ex post facto* criminal offences, a result in conflict with section 12(4). The ruling may also divest those persons of certain property without compensation, an invasion of right under section 16. Retroactive invalidity in all cases may not only be unfair but apparently unconstitutional as well.

This view follows the principle that the state cannot restrict one fundamental right even for the purpose of guaranteeing better a different fundamental right,[282] since that ground of authority is not to be found in the saving clauses. Even so, it is open to question whether the rigorous approach would not in any event be a greater restriction than is necessary in a practical sense, a standard applicable to the courts as well as to the legislature and the executive. For these reasons, therefore, it is submitted that the court has the discretion to limit the retroactive application of its declaration of voidness whenever that is necessary in order to prevent injustice, uphold the security of transactions, and avoid collision with other rights guaranteed by the Constitution. It is true, as Chief Justice Hughes has observed, that "an all-inclusive statement of a principle of absolute retroactive invalidity cannot be justified." [283]

(ii) The Preconstitutional Laws

The laws in force before the Constitution came

---

282. As Justice Mudholkar has written: " . . . the state cannot make a law which directly restricts one freedom even for securing the better enjoyment of another freedom. All the greater reason therefore for holding that the State cannot directly restrict one freedom by placing an otherwise permissible restriction on another freedom." Sakal case, *supra* note 272.

283. *Supra* note 280.

into effect are as liable to be declared void for inconsistency as any law enacted after the Constitution. This much is clear from section 4, which stipulates that the "existing law" must be read in conformity with the Constitution. Section 4(5) explains that:

> For the purposes of this section the expression "existing law" means any proclamation, law, rule, regulation, order, or other instrument made or having effect as if it had been made in pursuance of (or continuing in operation under) the existing Order . . . and having effect as part of the law of Basutoland immediately before the appointed day . . . and includes the customary law of Basutoland and any other unwritten rule of law so having effect.

This is also made clear by the meaning of the phrase "law which is inconsistent" to be found in section 2, for the meaning of the word "law" wherever it is used in the Constitution is inclusively defined by section 139 as

a. any instrument having the force of law made in exercise of a power conferred by a law; and

b. the customary law of Lesotho and any other unwritten rule of law. It follows from this that section 2 operates to conform every aspect of the legal pyramid including not only the laws to be found in the statute books and case reports but the Sesotho customary law, the imported South African common law (and custom), and the conventions and practices of the Constitution (imported or indigenous) as well.

In considering the effect of a declaration of voidness upon the preconstitutional laws, however, a distinction must be drawn between the validity of the law itself and the validity of specific instances of its application,[284] sometimes broadly referred to as "trans-

284. The Indian position with respect to fundamental rights

actions." The existing laws became subject to modification on and after October 4, 1966, but transactions past and completed before that date did not. The Constitution does not meddle with the past, for otherwise obligations long established or discharged and sentences lawfully imposed and long since served might stand on reviewable bases. However, if the transaction is uncompleted before the Constitution takes force and "if a right which arose prior to the Constitution is still subsisting after the coming into force of the Constitution and is guaranteed thereunder, then a continuing infringement thereof may be redressed . . . ."[285] There may be difficulty, however, in determining when a transaction is actually past and completed. An Indian court, for example, has held that in circumstances where a preconstitutional order of dispossession of a homeowner was carried into execution after the Constitution brought into effect the guaranteed right to acquire and dispose of property, there was no redress even though the order was inconsistent with the Constitution since the dispossession was only a consequence of a right to possession which was lost earlier.[286] Similarly, where the Constitution came into force during a criminal proceeding involving charges of violating a statute restricting free speech and expression, the court held that the Constitution had no effect since the liability had "accrued" prior to the Constitution.[287] It is submitted, however, that to ex-

---

stems from a reading of Article 13 of the Constitution which gives textual support to the distinction. *See* GLEDHILL, *supra* note 278, at 39 and BASU, *supra* note 176, at 248.

285. *Supra* note 279.

286. Nabhirajiah v. State of Mysore, [1952] S.C.R. 744, reprinted in BASU, II CASES ON THE CONSTITUTION OF INDIA 2 (Sarkar, Calcutta 1956).

287. Neshavan v. State of Bombay, [1951] S.C.R. 228, reprinted in BASU, *Id.* Vol. I at 2.

clude the enforcement of a law or to exclude the judicial proceedings for the determination of guilt under a law from a definition of what occurs when a law is *applied* is indeed narrow and unnecessary. Perhaps in recognition of this has the limitation been laid down that the foregoing position applied only to substantive and not to procedural guarantees.[288]

When a statute is declared void, it must not be assumed that it is struck from the statute books. Though inoperative and lacking all force, it is not in the same position as if it had been repealed by Parliament. A subsequent reversal by the Court of a lower court's decision or of its own previous decision would revive the statute on the theory that the Constitution, correctly interpreted, does not negate the law.[289] Since in strictness it is the Constitution in section 2 that declares voidness, it further follows that the law is void not just as between the parties before the court but may be counted upon as void by the world at large. Parties to future transactions and litigants in subsequent cases may treat the statute or a relevant part as void.[290]

(iii) Severability

The Constitution declares a law void to the extent of its inconsistency with the Constitution. If all of

---

288. Lachmandas v. State of Bombay, [1952] S.C.R. 710, reprinted in BASU, *supra* note 286 at 89.

289. In this instance alone would the expressions "eclipse" and "hibernation" be in order. But where a law has been declared by the Constitution to be void and the legislature subsequently amends the Constitution so as to remove the impediment to the law's validity, it is clear that the statute is not revived but must be reenacted. *See* BASU, *supra* note 286, at 252-53.

290. This is the position taken in India which Basu believes "marks an advance over American constitutional jurisprudence in so far as it would prevent harassing prosecutions and unnecessary litigation." *Supra* note 286, at 251.

the law is inconsistent, then the whole must fall. If only part of the law is inconsistent, then the rest may still be operative subject to the rules concerning severability.

As a general matter, if the inconsistent words and clauses are integral to the sense of the entire law so that what is left after severance is meaningless, then severance cannot take place and the whole act is declared void. The essential criterion is whether "what remains is so inextricably bound up with the part declared invalid that what remains cannot independently survive." [291] Yet even where the consistent sections have an independent meaning and can stand on their own feet, the court must consider whether the legislature, if it had been aware of the voidness of the other sections, would have enacted the valid parts separately. This is a determination that requires not only a review of the history and object of the legislation but an assessment of whether the remainder of the statute is not so carved and truncated and different in substance that the legislature could not have intended it to stand alone.

(b) Protection of "Persons" and "Citizens"

Section 4 declares that "every person in Lesotho is entitled, whatever his race, tribe, place of origin or residence, political opinions, colour, creed, or sex, to fundamental human rights and freedoms . . . ." [292] The meaning of the word "person" embraces every human being within Lesotho. "Person" also includes a corporation [293] and, perhaps, a child *en ventre sa mère*.[294] By

291. Attorney-General Alberta v. Attorney-General of Canada, [1916] A.C. 597.

292. *Cf.* the Constitution of India, which restricts the protection of fundamental rights to citizens.

293. § 139(15) Interpretation Act of 1889.

294. It is an established principle of Roman-Dutch law that

specific exception, however, the freedom of movement and freedom from discrimination are not guaranteed to every person but only to citizens.[295] It is strongly doubted whether a corporation can ever become a citizen.[296]

(c) Protection Against Private and State Action

The Constitution of Lesotho protects the rights of the individual not merely from the action of the state and its officers but also from private persons. Section 4(2) provides:

> For the avoidance of doubt and without prejudice to any other provision of this Constitution it is hereby declared that the provisions of this chapter shall, except where the context otherwise requires, apply as well in relation to things done or omitted to be done by persons acting in a private capacity (whether by virtue of any written law or otherwise) as in relation to things done or omitted to be done by or on behalf of the Government of Lesotho or by any person acting in the performance of the functions of any public office or any public authority.

The protection, then, of the fundamental rights provisions consists of a legal shield not merely against the unconstitutional acts of the state, but also, "unless the context otherwise requires," against unconstitutional invasions of liberty by individuals within society. Although the Constitution does not specifically define

---

a child in the womb is deemed to have legal personality whenever that fiction operates to its advantage. *See* Pinchin v. Santam Insurance Co., [1963] 2 S.A. 254(W).

295. §§ 7(3)(c) and 17(4)(a), respectively. However, in these instances all persons would receive protection at least until a law to the contrary is validly enacted.

296. Chapter III of the Constitution entitled "Citizenship" focusses upon the rights of natural persons, and it is settled in India that rights are guaranteed only to natural persons who are citizens.

the particular variety of context to which it is referring, it would seem basically it refers to the *verbal* context contained in the constitutional language of the relevant right. We shall discuss by way of example the meaning of the verbal context.

In India [297] as well as in the United States [298] individuals are merely guaranteed that their liberties will not be invaded by the state. For example, an agreement for the sale of a house between a vendor and a purchaser of the same race that the latter will never resell the house to a third person of a different race is considered a mere *private* agreement. No third person could gain redress if he were prejudiced by this discriminatory pact. If, on the other hand, the purchaser were to break his agreement and sell the property to a third person of a different race, the vendor could neither collect damages against the purchaser for breach of promise nor evict the new owner from the property, for to enforce his agreement in the court

297. BASU, *supra* note 286, at 546.

298. In the United States, however, the once black-letter distinction between "state" and "private" action can no longer be inscribed with any certainty. Increasingly, as state authority reaches deeper and consciousness of social problems mount, the view is gaining ground that private action is actually different from state action only in degree. To be free to do what is "private" depends less upon the effect of an individual decision by the discriminator than community decisions which allow to him that form of freedom. According to recent evidence the United States Supreme Court is fast drawing this conclusion. *See* Mulkey v. Reitman, 387 U.S. 369 (1967); Jones v. Alfred H. Mayer Co., 392 U.S. 409 (1968). The innovative language of section 4(2), hedged somewhat by the question of "context," may be seen as an attempt to accommodate this far-reaching conclusion if and when Lesotho cares to adopt it. *Generally, see* Lewis, *The Meaning of State Action,* 60 COLUM. L. REV. 1083 (1960) and Black, *Forword: The Supreme Court 1966 Term,* 81 HARV. L. REV. 69 (1967).

of the state would amount to state enforcement of discrimination.[299]

Now, while the constitutional distinction between private and state acts may be obliterated in the Lesotho Constitution, the verbal context of the above example precludes a remedy against the purely private discriminator, because "the context [of the relevant right] otherwise requires." In section 17 on Freedom from Discrimination, it is clearly asserted in subsection 1 that "no *law* shall make any provision that is discriminatory either of itself or in its effect." In that context the protection would seem to be only against state action since only the state can make laws.[300] Vary the example, however. A person is refused service at a hotel on account of his race. Under section 17(7) "No person shall be treated in a discriminatory manner in respect of . . . hotels, (and) beer halls. . . ." In the context of discriminatory treatment in hotels as described in section 17(7), the right extends its protection not simply where an individual enters a state-owned hotel but where he enters a privately owned hotel as well.

In the usual case, however, the verbal context establishes no restriction whatsoever. In the Freedom of Expression (and in other rights with "imprecise" saving clauses), the context of the first clause is characterised by the unqualified broadness of the individual's right and its indifferent effectiveness against both

---

299. Shelley v. Kraemer, 334 U.S. 1 (1948); Barrows v. Jackson, 346 U.S. 249 (1953).

300. However, the reader's attention should be drawn to the considerations mentioned *supra* in footnote 298. If the context discloses that private discrimination indeed is infected with state support in unacceptable degree, the courts may indeed take the view that such discrimination is unconstitutional state action.

forms of interference. Furthermore its saving clause speaks of permissible derogations in limited instances by "laws," but no mention at all is made of any permissible derogations by private acts. This context, far from "requiring" nonprotection, speaks eloquently in its favour. The slightest derogation of Freedom of Expression by private act is *prima facie* unconstitutional since no authority for it can be found in the saving clause.[301]

It would be tempting to ask at this point whether, aside from verbal contextual restrains, the factual or *situational* context should not also be examined, for there may be invasions emanating from the private sector which are deemed too minor to deserve protection or too indirect or exotic to receive primary regard. For example, a court could feel that noisemaking and jeering during a political speaker's delivery constituted a mere *de minimis* violation of his right to free expression. It may similarly feel that the illegal detention of an individual, although it prevented free communication with the outside world and thus violated the right of free expression, was nevertheless a mere incidental effect of the primary restraint on Freedom of Movement or Freedom from Arbitrary Search and Seizure. If the situational context may in some cases circumscribe the impractical reach of a right, the courts would then be given the discretion to apply a kind of "rule of reason" test. Private infringements would be generally actionable unless in context the violation were too indirect, insubstantial, or impracticable to remedy.

---

301. Perhaps, however, in reference to the definitional section of the right, the court will be tempted to read in a certain amount of reasonable interference as not being interference with "expression" as constitutionally defined.

However, this attention to situational context in section 4(2) was probably unintended by the draftsmen, if only because it seems to stretch the ordinary meaning of the context. More importantly, the essential problem is later dealt with by the workings of section 20(2). (See below.) An example may clarify this point. Suppose *A* locks the door to a student's room to which there is no other exit, *A* will have committed the Aquilian delict sometimes called false imprisonment. At the same time, however, *A* has unconstitutionally restricted the student's freedom of movement. Should the student's remedy be in delict or in constitutional law? Theoretically it could be either and thus the draftsmen have bestowed discretion on the High Court in section 20(2) to decline to exercise its Constitutional jurisdiction where "it is satisfied that *adequate means of redress* for the contravention alleged are or have been available to the person concerned under any other law." The exercise of this discretion should depend in part upon the situational context. Under the circumstances the nonconstitutional remedy may adequately redress the incidental constitutional injury. On the other hand, if the nonconstitutional remedy does not exist or is inadequate, clearly the court can take jurisdiction under Chapter II, and this may represent a substantial increment of freedom from injurious acts in the private sector that fall short of delict [302] and are enforced in contract,[303] and are not considered criminal.[304]

---

302. *E.g.*, verbal abuse or vilification of one's race.

303. *E.g.*, subject to the doctrine of abuse of rights, eviction by one's landlord simply because of one's political views or religion. *See* Scholtens, *Abuse of Rights*, 75 S.A.L.J. 39 (1958).

304. It is possible for certain injuries to be remedied under the heads of delict, crime, contract, and fundamental right, all at the same time.

(4) THE BURDEN OF PROVING A VIOLATION OF FUNDAMENTAL RIGHT

A most significant feature of the fundamental rights provisions for both lawyers and constitutional connoisseurs is the striking innovation introduced on the question of burden of proof. Just as success or failure in a delict or contract case is often determined by judicial rules as to the placing of the burden of proof, so too in constitutional law the placing of the burden of proving contravention either upon the individual or the state (or anyone claiming a right under a statute) will have an important bearing on the effectiveness of enforcing or resisting claims.

(a) The Proof May Rest upon the Government

In the constitutional systems of the United States, India, and Nigeria, it is the litigant alleging the contravention who must prove his case. Perhaps this is still so in Lesotho with respect to seven out of the fifteen fundamental rights, namely sections 5, 6, 8, 9, 16, 17, and 18. In seven of the remaining eight,[305] however, the burden of proof is imposed not upon the person who alleges contravention but upon the adversary party (usually the Government), who relies upon the validity of the impugned law. This reversal of the customary burden of proof is accomplished by the following language from one of those rights:

> *A person shall not be permitted to rely in any judicial proceedings upon such a provision of law as is referred to in subsection (2) of this section except to the extent to which he satisfies the court* that that provision or, as the case may be, the thing done under the authority thereof does not abridge the freedom guaranteed by subsection (1) of this section to a greater extent than is

305. These are §§ 7, 10-15.

> necessary in a practical sense in paragraph (a) of subsection (2) of this section or for any of the purposes specified in paragraph (b) or paragraph (c) of that subsection. (Our italics).

The import of this language is to reverse the entire focus of the dispute. It is not a question of the applicant's claiming that the law or act thereunder is unconstitutional, but instead a question of the respondent's satisfying the court that the law or subsidiary act *is* constitutional. The revolutionary aspect of this can hardly be overemphasised. In other systems where judicial review flourishes, no principle is more clearly fixed than the presumption in favour of constitutionality,[306] and its corrollary, that the challenger of a law must bear the burden of proving his claim. This burden is particularly difficult since the presumption, curiously, is often laid down in terms as if the legislature must be proved guilty beyond a reasonable doubt.[307] And reasonable doubts will normally still hover in judges' minds whenever rational relationships can be *conceived* or when a *possible* construction of the statute will reconcile it with the Constitution. To de-

---

306. In Maluleke v. Minister of Law & Order, [1963] 4 S.A. 206 (S.R.) Chief Justice Beadle substituted the maxim *omnia praesumuntur rite esse acta* to express the presumption, "The presumption which I consider would be made in cases such as this is no more than that the legislature intends every act to be read 'subject to the Constitution.' If every possible presumption should be made in favour of the validity of a law, the presumption set out above is one which in the circumstances I think can reasonably be made." (At 212.) On the other hand a clear inconsistency with the Constitution cannot be presumed away by the Courts. *See* Nkomo v. Minister of Justice, [1965] 1 S.A. 498 (S.R., A.D.) (invalidation of Preventive Detention (Temporary Provisions) Amendment Act, 1964).

307. In a different analogy it has also been suggested that the court's rational probe of the legislature's mind resembles the proceedings of a lunacy commission.

cree a presumption of unconstitutionality, a presumption of guilt until innocence is proved, is somewhat Copernican.

Preferred Freedoms. Perhaps the inspiration for the innovation we have been discussing derives from a debate in American constitutional law about the so-called "preferred freedoms" of the First Amendment. A persistent strain in American legal thought insists on the primacy of the First Amendment and holds that freedom of expression is the greatest liberty of all. Mr. Justice Cardozo is by no means alone in describing freedom of expression as "the matrix, the indispensable condition, of nearly every other form of freedom."[308] Though Justice Frankfurter has expressed his opinion that "preferred freedom" is a "mischievous phrase, if it carried the thought . . . that any law touching communication is infected with presumptive invalidity,"[309] Professor Black of Yale University has advocated just such a "mischief":

> Some people think—and I am one of them—that the court, once it takes note that a challenged statute prohibits or in some way penalizes free speech, ought to shift from a *general* presumption of constitutionality to a specific presumption of unconstitutionality. . . .[310]

If this inference of unconstitutionality is not rebutted by the party relying on the law's validity, the decision may be cast in favour of the applicant. Of course,

---

308. Palko v. Connecticut, 302 U.S. 319 (1937). For an apotheosis of free speech, *see* MEIKLEJOHN, FREE SPEECH AND ITS RELATION TO SELF GOVERNMENT (1948) and his essay in AALS, SELECTED ESSAYS ON CONSTITUTIONAL LAW 600-617 (West 1963).

309. Kovacs v. Cooper, 336 U.S. 77, 90 (1949) (concurrence).

310. THE PEOPLE AND THE COURT 217 (Macmillan 1960).

without a close study of the particular law in its factual setting, there is no means of foretelling how great or small the reliant's burden will be. Likewise, no assessment of the strength of a presumption in favour or against constitutionality can be made without specific regard to the particular test of constitutionality laid down in the saving clause in question. For example, because the burden of proof is beneficially shifted in the preferred rights they may always appear to be more easily enforceable by the individual against the state than the nonpreferred rights of Chapter II of the Lesotho Constitution. But it should be noted that the preferred rights generally carry imprecise saving clauses while the nonpreferred rights often carry precise or semi-precise saving clauses.[311] The individual's ease of detecting and demonstrating a violation of the latter may in some cases be equal to his procedural advantage over the state in the former because there is always the possibility that an imprecise standard may receive a judicial interpretation very favourable to the state.

The Rhodesian Constitution of 1961 formally establishes an explicit allocation of the burden of proof which offers an interesting contrast to the position in Lesotho. In Rhodesia the burden of proof switches shoulders not less than three times before resting upon the Government. Justice Beadle outlined this procedure in *Maluleke v. Minister of Law and Order*[312] in the following steps.

1. The complainant must show that there has been some infringement of his right.

2. If the Minister then submits a certificate to the

---

311. The classification of saving clauses into the precise, semi-precise, and imprecise is treated *supra* at pp. 324-328.

312. *Supra* note 306, discussed in Crawford, *The Working of the Rhodesian Declaration of Rights*, 83 S.A.L.J. 337 (1966).

court signifying that the law is necessary, the law is deemed presumptively valid.

3. The complainant may then prove that in a society with a proper respect for such a right the infringement cannot be accepted without proof.

4. The Minister must then prove that the law is in fact necessary, failing which it will be declared *ultra vires*.

It will be noticed that this procedure places greater burdens upon the individual than under the Lesotho Constitution. Though under both procedures the Government is in the final analysis called upon to prove the validity of its enactment, under the Lesotho Constitution the individual's burden terminates simply after step one of the procedure necessary under the Rhodesian Constitution.

The Lesotho Constitution displays a choice to adopt and expand the notion of preferred freedom. The eight freedoms of Movement, nonarbitrary Search or Entry, Respect for Private and Family Life, Conscience, Expression, Assembly and Association, and nonarbitrary Seizure of Property have been accorded a preferred place that similar rights do not enjoy, to the authors' knowledge, in any other constitution in the world. Here is the sign of a value judgment deeply entrenched in the instrument tending to weight the scales in favour of the individual as against the state.

(b) Burden of Proving Nonpreferred Freedoms

It has been said in passing that in respect of the remaining rights (nonpreferred) one should presume that the burden of proof remains upon the applicant. This view is prompted by the lack of explicit mention of the question in the provisions themselves. On the other hand, the silence of the Constitution could well be construed as an implicit deferral of this question to the courts, so that they might develop procedural rules that fairly distribute the burden in a manner suggested by their structure and purpose.

In India the courts have held that once the applicant succeeds in pointing out that the law in question violates *prima facie* the absolute right, the burden of proof shifts to the respondent to show that the *prima facie* violation falls within one of the great heads of the saving clause, *e.g.*, defence, safety, or health. If the respondent discharges this burden, then the burden falls again upon the applicant to show that the restriction is unreasonable.[313] The basis for this badminton approach is justified on the theory that the main purpose of the Constitution is to guarantee to the individual the right of the first subsection. The primary object is not to ensure that the state should be permitted to restrict that right in accordance with the saving clause.

> To say otherwise would mean that the citizen has a fundamental right to be subjected to restrictions in the exercise of the fundamental rights solemnly declared and embodied in a written constitution to be protected against legislative inroads.[314]

This division of proof appears to be both fair and logical and may recommend itself to the Lesotho courts as appropriate in dealing with the sections on fundamental rights that are not explicit on the matter.[315]

(5) PROCEDURES FOR THE PRESENTATION OF A CLAIM

There are four basic procedures by which a case involving a constitutional question is presented before the High Court. The first two of these procedures are specifically geared to cope with fundamental rights

313. BASU, *supra* note 176, at 559.
314. BASU, *supra* note 176, at 560.
315. *E.g.*, § 9(3)(b).

questions. The third is designed to handle questions both of fundamental rights and constitutional interpretation. The fourth deals only with questions of interpretation. We will briefly list and then discuss all four.

(i) Direct application to the High Court by an aggrieved person or citizen under section 20(1) to remedy a completed or threatened fundamental rights violation.

(ii) Transfer of a fundamental rights question under section 20(3) from a subordinate court to the High Court at the instance of one of the parties or the person presiding in the subordinate court.

(iii) Presentation of a case to the High Court by appeal as of right in questions of constitutional interpretation of fundamental rights in accordance with section 123.

(iv) Transfer of a substantial question of constitutional interpretation under section 114 from a subordinate court to the High Court at the instance of one of the parties or the court itself.

(a) Direct Application under Section 20(1)

Direct application is a fundamental right that ensures access to the High Court. A person or a citizen is entitled to a hearing whenever his freedom has been violated or is in jeopardy of violation. Rules concerning standing to sue and the ripeness of the case may be expected to be construed in light of the court's power to protect the applicant from anticipated breaches. In this respect the court's power and function are of a different sort than that conferred under sections 110 and 114 for the adjudication of questions of constitutional interpretation.

Though access is a guaranteed right, the determination of the question by the court is not mandatory. The court may decide to decline jurisdiction where it is satisfied that "adequate means of redress" are or have been made available to the applicant under "any other law." Adequate redress may be afforded in many instances by remedies sounding in delict, contract, property, and the criminal law. Furthermore, there are other means of access to the courts aside from those in Chapter II (*viz.*, sections 114 and 123), and the phrase, "under any other law" may be referring to the means of redress that can be obtained by pursuing them. Thus it is important to recognise that the means of redress mentioned in section 20(2) can refer to an adequate nonconstitutional remedy or an adequate constitutional remedy.

If the vindication of the constitutional right is the chief concern, the High Court's discretion to refuse jurisdiction may pivot upon factors related to supervision of the court system. Hence the decision might be influenced by the novelty of the question, the clarity of the jurisprudence, the size of both dockets, fair distribution of labour within the courts, unfair delays to the other party, and perhaps most importantly, the High Court's confidence in the subordinate court's capacity to make the correct constitutional judgment.

The important aspect of the phrase "under any other law" is to point the way beyond the Constitution to the private-law sphere. Both Sesotho customary law and Roman-Dutch law presume a certain degree of individual liberty. Though capable of modification by Parliament, the actions presently available in those systems are often able to maintain the liberties granted by the Constitution especially in regard to *private* rather than *state* action. (See above.) To illustrate, an act of racial discrimination by a hotel in refusing access to a traveller because of his race may sometimes be adequately redressed in delict by the *actio injuria-*

rum in a subordinate court without the necessity of a direct application to the High Court on account of the violation of section 17. Or, on the other hand, adequate redress may once have been available to the applicant in the form of a private-law remedy that has been prescribed [316] or even by virtue of a statutory exception in his favour of which he failed to take advantage. Arguably, the right of direct access to the High Court is not intended to give applicant's cause a second life.

In determining the adequacy of a nonconstitutional form of relief, however, the court may be of the opinion that if the remedy can be granted only after the injury has already occurred, it is not adequate in all cases to preserve the constitutional right. Thus, were a man to know that he must first suffer outrage, imprisonment, or physical injury in order to practise his fundamental right, he may be persuaded or obliged by the risk to forego it. For an individual in the grip of such choices, the only adequate remedy may be preventive relief under section 20, *e.g.*, through the use of interdict and declaratory judgment.[317] Nevertheless, despite the importance of the question of whether or not jurisdiction will be exercised in terms of section 20, the High Court's ultimate decision appears to be final and not subject to an appeal to the Court of Appeal or the Judicial Committee of the Privy Council.

The right of direct access may be circumscribed further in cases where a constitutional claim has already been settled on the merits by a subordinate court. The Indian Supreme Court has held in such

---

316. GLEDHILL, FUNDAMENTAL RIGHTS IN INDIA 9 (Stevens 1955).

317. *See infra* at pp. 366-367 for further discussion of preventive relief.

cases[318] that a fresh application under the direct procedure of the fundamental rights provisions is barred by *res judicata* so that the aggrieved party can only pursue his claim to the High Court by way of appeal. Such an appeal, however, would lie as of right and may even be direct.[319]

(b) Transfer of the Question under Section 20

The transfer of a question of a fundamental right is also a guarantee of section 20(3). There are several factors of interest in this provision.

First, one should note that the case pending in a subordinate court is not transferred, but only the "question" of fundamental right. Even where the question is not really ancillary to a cause but forms the substance of the cause it is more accurate to say that the question transfers but the case remains lodged below, for, as is provided in section 20(4), it is the subordinate court that ultimately disposes of the case in accordance with the High Court's decision on the question.

Second, it is also important to note that transfer may be provoked by either party to the proceedings or by the person presiding. The person presiding has no discretion to refuse a referral requested by a party unless the question is in his opinion merely *frivolous* or *vexatious*. Both adjectives suggest a point without merit; however, the outlook of the party raising it may differ: in one case without hope or pretence of being seriously considered, in the other with the strategical hope of delaying, abusing, or wearying one's opponent or the court. The High Court again has the discretion to decline jurisdiction of a transferred ques-

318. Daryao v. State of U.P.A., [1961] S.C. 1457; BASU, *supra* note 176, at 195.

319. § 123 Lesotho Constitution.

tion where adequate means of redress exist, and there would seem to be no appeal from a decision to refuse to take jurisdiction.

Where the High Court accepts jurisdiction and decides the point, this decision on the question is susceptible of appeal by right to the Court of Appeal and to the Judicial Committee, in which case the proceedings below are stayed until a final decision is given.

Third, a question involving a fundamental right may be transferred from any "subordinate" court. A subordinate court is defined by the Constitution as any court other than the Judicial Committee, Court of Appeal, High Court, or a court-martial.[320] Thus the transfer may arise from a Resident Magistrate's court, first-, second-, and third-class subordinate courts, the Judicial Commissioner's Court, as well as the central and local courts. The purpose of this procedure is both to relieve an untutored bench of the burden of such complex issues and to hasten their determination in a higher and, generally, more competent court. What remains significant, however, is the implied recognition that all such subordinate courts are competent to adjudicate questions of fundamental rights that are not transferred. Certainly no set of courts could be less equipped to decide matters of public law than the central and local courts: scarcely a judge has formal training, their civil jurisdiction is restricted to the application of Sesotho law and custom, and lawyers are not even permitted to appear in civil causes.[321] In this light the transfer of questions under section

320. § 139(1).

321. Central and Local Courts Proclamation 62 of 1938, § 20. In criminal cases, however, the Proclamation permits lawyers to appear (*Id.*) and in fact a criminal accused has a constitutionally guaranteed right to counsel (at his own expense) in criminal cases. (§ 12(2) of the Constitution.)

20(3) is not merely an interesting efficiency but a procedure that is indispensable.

Yet, with all respect, the subordinate courts may not even be adequate to the task of framing constitutional questions with the proper conciseness and relevance that is so essential to the procedure. It would seem rare that a problem inadequately understood could in turn give rise to an adequate question. Apparently this has been the experience with the Nigerian lower courts working under a similar system, and a certain amount of difficulty should be anticipated in Lesotho as well.

(c) Appeal as of Right under Section 123

Appeals of cases from subordinate courts involving questions of fundamental right or constitutional interpretation come before the High Court as of right. The appeal is not direct unless there is no further appeal as of right to a higher subordinate court and any appeal by way of leave to a higher court has actually been withheld. It is important to stress the difference between the *appeal* of such questions (which contemplates the existence of a finalized proceeding in a subordinate court), as opposed to direct application or the transfer of a question (which does not require a prior or completed proceeding in a subordinate court).

The appeal of such cases would not include those appeals from decisions of lower tribunals in which questions of fundamental rights or constitutional interpretation have already been transferred to the High Court. This limitation is necessary in order to prevent a redundant decision by the High Court, and the Constitution rightly provides that an appeal does not include cases in which questions have been "referred" to the High Court pursuant to the transfer machinery of sections 20(3) and 114(1). Does this mean, however, that an appeal cannot lie where the High Court has declined to take jurisdiction pursuant to section 20(3) because it was satisfied that adequate means of redress were or had been available?[322] The answer depends upon an interpretation of the word "referred." On the literal level attempts to interpret it may be inconclusive. However, three points may be considered. Both sections 20(3) and 114(1) provide for transfer, yet only section 20(3) involves a discretion to refuse jurisdiction on grounds of extraneous adequate redress. Therefore when a question is "referred" in terms of section 113(1) it must be meant that it was in fact transferred. Secondly, if the provision were intended to prevent a duplicated effort by the High Court, no duplication need be feared by allowing the appeal. Thirdly, the reasonableness of an appeal from a refusal to accept jurisdiction should depend in any event upon the motive for the refusal. For instance, if the refusal were motivated by a lack of confidence in the capacity of the subordinate court to render adequate redress, it might be fairer to the parties, and in keeping with the importance of constitutional litigation, to permit a review of the subordinate court's decision by the High Court as of right rather than merely by leave.

(d) Transfer of the Question under Section 114

Cases involving constitutional interpretation that are in the jurisdiction of subordinate courts are subject to the referral of a substantial question of interpretation to the High Court. Again the transfer may be provoked by either party or the court. The subordinate court has no discretion to refuse a transfer unless it is of the opinion that the question is not substantial. Once a substantial question is put to the High

322. No such declinatory discretion is granted by section 114.

Court it must accept jurisdiction. Section 114(2) says it "shall" give its decision on any question submitted from the subordinate court; whether or not a question is substantial seems unimpugnable since the subordinate court seems to be given complete discretion in this determination. Subsequently the case must be disposed of by the subordinate court in accordance with the High Court's decision on the question.

(i) Meaning of "Substantial Question"

The meaning of a "substantial question" of law may be taken in both a generic and technical sense. Substance, from a technical point of view, is related to the rules of precedent. A question that has been long settled by the highest court is not substantial. There must be doubt or difference of opinion as to what the law is, such that arguments in favour of more than one interpretation can reasonably be adduced.[323] By "settled," however, we may mean something more than binding under the rules of precedent; it refers as well to the maturity and incontestability of the binding precedent in question. Basu has observed, "A question ceases to be substantial if it is so explicitly foreclosed by previous decisions as to leave no room for real controversy." [324]

In Lesotho, where two stages of appeal in the court hierarchy exist beyond the High Court, it may require a certain amount of judicial activity and lapse of time before any question may be regarded as insubstantial from the standpoint of precedent. A question for the future is whether any matter is "explicitly foreclosed" without at least a prior ruling by the Court of Appeal.

On the other hand, substance in the generic sense refers to the importance of the question as a matter

323. Olawoyin v. A-G.N.R., [1961] 1 All N.L.R. 269.
324. BASU, *supra* note 176, at 177.

of constitutional interpretation. Thus a matter of substance would certainly be a question of "great general or public importance" as is referred to in section 122(3). Some matters—let us take the constitutionality of racially segregated schools in the United States as an example—do not apparently cease to be of substance though settled by precedent for over half a century. There would be an understandable tendency for the courts of Lesotho at first to regard every constitutional question as substantial where two positions can be maintained plausibly and no prior ruling exists. On the other hand, a question of substance in the generic sense may be defined not only in terms of the public importance of the matter but with reference to its intramural importance to the outcome of the litigation. A question of great general interest may be of no relevance where other issues in the case are dispositive. This follows from the general rule that constitutional issues are decided only as a last resort.[325] Thus in *Gamioba v. Esezi II*[326] the lower court referred a question of constitutional interpretation to a High Court in Nigeria at the joint request of the parties without ever having seen the pleadings. The High Court remanded the case to the lower court on the ground that before a matter can be referred it must be determined whether or not it must necessarily be decided. Since this step had not been taken, the question was *prima facie* insubstantial.

(6) RESTRAINTS ON ENFORCEMENT OF FUNDAMENTAL HUMAN RIGHTS

(a) Express Restraints

(i) Jurisdiction

There are certain provisions in the Constitution

---

325. *See infra* at pp. 374-375.
326. [1961] All N.L.R. 584.

in which the original or appellate jurisdiction of the courts has been either specifically limited or expressly withdrawn. Thus the effect in some is to preclude judicial enquiry only partially, in others to preclude it entirely. Any matters arising under the latter, therefore, are essentially political not judicial questions.

1. No court is competent to enquire into:

(a) a certificate given by the Speaker of the National Assembly pursuant to section 65. (Section 65(7).)

(b) whether the King, in cases where he is obliged to follow the advice of another, has received the advice or acted in accordance therewith. (Section 76(6).)

(c) the substantive grounds upon which decisions as to land allocation in terms of sections 95, 96, 97, 98, and 99 are made, subject to exceptions in sections 101(2) and 101(3). (Section 101(1).)

(d) the exercise of the power to appoint the replacement of an officeholder unable to carry out his functions. (Section 139 (9).)

(e) whether a person required or authorised to consult with some other person before exercising a function has consulted as required or authorised. (Section 139(11).)

2. No court, save the Court of Appeal pursuant to section 35, has jurisdiction to decide disputed claims to the throne.

3. No court, save the High Court pursuant to section 54, has jurisdiction to decide questions as to the membership of Parliament.

4. The various deprivations of original and appeal jurisdiction described by sections 20, 110, 114, 115, 121, 122, and 123.

(ii) Declaration of Emergency and State of War:

The Prime Minister may by proclamation published in the Gazette declare that a state of emergency exists.[327] The effect of this declaration under section 19 is to permit derogations from the rights of personal liberty,[328] freedom from discrimination, and the equal protection of laws [329] by taking measures under existing Acts of Parliament that are "necessary in a practical sense in a democratic society for dealing with the situation that exists in Lesotho during that period." A declaration lapses at the end of fourteen days unless it is approved by resolutions in both Houses of Parliament.[330] Such a resolution then becomes the underlying legal basis for the declaration and remains in force for six months or such shorter period as may be prescribed. A resolution may be extended, but not for more than six months dating from the renewal of the resolution.[331] During times of war similar powers are authorised without a declaration of emergency.[332] Nothing would seem to oust the jurisdiction of the courts to assess whether such derogations are necessary in a democracy under the circumstances.[333]

(b) Implied and Semi-Express Restraints

In addition to the preceding instances where the Constitution has expressly precluded judicial review, there are other restraints that limit the jurisdiction of the court. According to the doctrine of separation of powers, the province of a court is not to make law. Nor is it to test the law *mero motu.* From ancient times its institutional function has been to resolve disputes brought before it by parties. This *raison*

---

327. § 21(1).
328. § 6.
329. §§ 17 and 18.
330. § 21(2).
331. § 21(5).
332. § 19.
333. § 19(1).

d'être, viewed within a constitutional scheme of government, was once elucidated in a classic description.[334]

> The functions of government under our system are apportioned. To the legislative department has been committed the duty of making laws; to the executive the duty of executing them; and to the judiciary the duty of interpreting and applying them in cases properly brought before the courts. The general rule is that neither department may invade the province of the other and neither may control, direct, or restrain the action of the other. . . . We have no power *per se* to review and annul acts of Congress on the ground that they are unconstitutional. That question may be considered only when the justification for some direct injury suffered or threatened, presenting a justiciable issue, is made to rest upon such an act. Then the power exercised is that of ascertaining and declaring the law applicable to the controversy. It amounts to little more than the negative power to disregard an unconstitutional enactment, which otherwise would stand in the way of the enforcement of a legal right.

Once the inner logic of this is appreciated, it follows that in order to avoid encroachments upon the powers of another department, the "negative power" of judicial review cannot be exercised unless first there is an adversary proceeding before the court. A proper case is a *sine qua non* to review.

To recognise the proper case, however, may call for, in Justice Frankfurter's words, "the expert feel of lawyers" trained in the tradition of "the business of the Colonial Courts of Westminster." [335] But the question is more than historical or institutional. The Constitution of the United States grants jurisdiction

334. Massachusetts v. Mellon, 262 U.S. 447, 488 (1923) per Mr. Justice Sutherland.

335. Joint Anti-Fascist Refugee Committee v. McGrath, 341 U.S. 123 (1951) (concurrence).

to the Supreme Court only when there is a "case" or "controversy" before it. The Constitution of Lesotho, while it uses perhaps more liberal terminology, states certain requirements that, by implication, exclude other possibilities. According to section 110, the High Court has jurisdiction over civil and criminal "proceedings." With particular reference to fundamental rights, it has jurisdiction when an individual alleges that a right has been or is "likely" to be violated "in relation to him." Such wording, whatever its ultimate meaning, suggests that the courts of Lesotho do not possess a *carte blanche* to interpret the Constitution at will even in instances that do not fit these descriptions. Yet, on the other hand, in reaching a final appreciation of the meaning of these terms and its own authority, the High Court cannot ignore that the powers given to it to preserve fundamental rights were intended to be something more than traditional. As the exclusive watchdog of Chapter II, it must somehow use every power it has and do everything it can to make those liberties a reality rather than a vain dream.

The following is but an adumbration of certain rules that are derived from the experience of other constitutional systems in the exercise of judicial review. In the interest of space, they can receive only summary mention here. Nonetheless, the subject must be raised because the Lesotho courts will undoubtedly desire to consider them, subject always, of course, to the specific commands found in the provisions of the Constitution.

(i) Feigned and Moot Controversies

Courts hear and determine litigation that is adversary and controversial. This means that the parties must be truly antagonistic and that the subject of the dispute be a live issue. Thus *feigned* [336] or collusive

---

336. Feigned: U.S. v. Johnson, 319 U.S. 302 (1943), re-

cases in which the parties have simply agreed to test the state of the law or *moot* [337] cases in which the issues have already evaporated will not provoke the court into making a constitutional decision.

(ii) Advisory Opinions

Though expressly permitted in some constitutional systems, it seems clear that in Lesotho the court does not furnish mere legal advice either to the Government or a private party. The constitution does not authorise the court to advise other departments of government. The court is only authorised to take jurisdiction of "proceedings" under section 110 and to redress contraventions or threatened contraventions of fundamental rights under section 20. Thus if the Government, wishing to ascertain the constitutionality of a bill in Parliament before its passage, asked the court for such a ruling, the court might respectfully decline, for a court of law can take cognisance only of laws already in force and then only in a factual case brought before it rather than in the abstract.

---

printed in HART AND WECHSLER, THE FEDERAL COURTS AND THE FEDERAL SYSTEM 114 (Foundation) (suit between tenant and landlord to test constitutionality of Maximum Rent Regulations paid for entirely by landlord, tenant merely affording use of his name): Chicago and Grand Trunk Ry. v. Wellman, 143 U.S. 339 (1892), reprinted in HART AND WECHSLER 117 (friendly suit between ticket purchaser and railroad to test statutory railroad rates).

337. Moot: California v. San Pablo & Tulare R.R., 149 U.S. 308 (1893), reprinted in HART AND WECHLSER 119 (suit to recover state taxes where tender of payment had already been made and amount owing deposited to the state's account); U.S. v. Munsingwear, Inc., 340 U.S. 36 (1950), reprinted in HART AND WECHSLER 121 (price regulations repealed during suit brought for their violation); St. Pierre v. U.S., 319 U.S. 41 (1943), reprinted in HART AND WECHSLER 124, (sentence for contempt already served by petitioner by the time *certiorari* granted).

(iii) Ripeness of the Controversy

It is often said that a case is not justiciable controversy until it is *ripe,* that is, until the factual posture of the case reveals that an actual collision of interests has already taken place between the plaintiff and the defendant. For instance in *United Public Workers v. Mitchell* [338] the petitioners, employees of the U.S. Government, and their union sought a declaratory judgment that the Hatch Act of 1940 was void and unconstitutional as a restriction *inter alia* on their freedom of expression. The Hatch Act provided:

> No officer or employee in the executive branch of the Federal Government . . . shall take any active part in political management or in political campaigns.

None of the petitioners, save one, had engaged in political campaigns or management in violation of the Act, but their desire was to do so without enforcement of the Act and subsequent loss of their employment. On the principle that "concrete legal issues, presented in actual cases, not abstractions, are requisite," the Supreme Court refused to grant a declaratory judgment under these facts with the following observation:

> The power of the courts, and ultimately of this court, to pass upon the constitutionality of acts of Congress arise only when the interests of litigants require the use of this judicial authority for their protection against actual interference. A hypothetical threat is not enough. We can only speculate as to the kinds of political activity the (petitioners) desire to engage in or as to the contents of their proposed public statements or the circumstances of their publication. It would not be in accord with judicial responsibility to adjudge, in a

338. 330 U.S. 75 (1947), reprinted in DOWLING & GUNTHER, CASES AND MATERIALS ON CONSTITUTIONAL LAW 91 (Foundation Press 1965).

> matter involving constitutionality, between the freedom of the individual and the requirements of public order except when definite rights appear upon the one side and definite prejudicial interference upon the other.[339]

Thus in a Rhodesian case Chief Justice Beadle queried:

> [C]an the complainant say he has been illegally hindered in the enjoyment of his rights before any attempt has been made to hinder him, and before there is any indication whatsoever that any such attempt will ever be made to do so? . . . I think the answer is that so long as nothing whatsoever has been illegally done by the Minister which actually interfered with the complainant's rights, it does not lie in his mouth to say: "He [*sic*] has been hindered in the enjoyment of his rights." [340]

This statement seems to be in accord with the position of the Roman-Dutch common law on declaratory judgments as found in Lesotho,[341] Rhodesia,[342] and South Africa.[343] "After all," wrote Chief Justice Innes,

---

339. DOWLING & GUNTHER 93. *Cf.* Adler v. Board of Education, 342 U.S. 485 (1952), reprinted in DOWLING & GUNTHER 94-95. It should be explained that declaratory judgments are not necessarily beyond the court's power in the U.S. In fact the Federal Declaratory Judgment Act 28 U.S.C. 2201-02 specifically allows them, but the statute requires that the case present an "actual controversy." The constitutionality of this statute was unanimously upheld in Aetna Life Insurance Co. v. Haworth, 300 U.S. 227 (1937), reprinted in HART AND WECHSLER 136-138.

340. *Supra* note 306, at 213-214.

341. Motsamai Pholo v. Principal Chief of Mokhotlong, [1963-1966] H.C.T.L.R. 188 (1966).

342. Bulawayo Municipality v. Bulawayo Indian Sports Ground Committee, [1956] 1 S.A. 34 (S.R.).

343. The common-law position in South Africa was changed by the General Law Amendment Act No. 46 of 1935.

> Courts of Law exist for the settlement of concrete controversies and actual infringements of rights, not to pronounce upon abstract questions, or to advise upon differing contentions, however important. And I think we shall do well to adhere to the principle laid down by a long line of South African decisions, namely that a declaratory order cannot be claimed merely because the rights of the claimant have been disputed, but that such a claim must be founded upon an actual infringement.[344]

An important *caveat* must be stated at this point. Though the above remarks may reflect the probable position that will be taken by the Lesotho judiciary on questions of constitutional "interpretation," a vital distinction must be observed with respect to fundamental rights. Under section 20 a party may complain not only of past and completed contraventions of his fundamental rights but of contraventions "likely" to infringe his rights as well. Consequently an individual may seek a preventive remedy against threatened or imminent violation. The degree of proximity between the threat and the foreseen infringement described by the term "likely" is redolent of the "probable" cause standard for obtention of a warrant in search and seizure questions. It seems at least to convey the notion that the infringement, given a set purpose of enforcement by the Government and motions in that direction, will on an average take place more times than not. In coping with their mandate to protect against likely infringement the courts may be expected to employ a repertoire of remedies, not the least of which are interdict and declaratory judgment. It may be added here that the benefit of declaratory relief lies not merely in the prevention of enforce-

344. Geldenhuys and Neethling v. Beuthin, [1918] A.D. 426, 441.

ment of an unconstitutional law but in extricating the individual from the dilemmatic choice between the perils of his own interpretation of his fundamental rights and the abandonment of those rights out of fear of incurring serious injury, *e.g.*, a term of imprisonment or loss of employment. For the above reasons the Courts of Lesotho may find the dissenting opinion of Justice Douglas in *United Public Workers v. Mitchell* (*supra*) more in accord with the Constitution. Having noted that the petitioners would most certainly be dismissed by the Civil Service Commission if they engaged in political activities, Justice Douglas concluded by saying:

> Declaratory relief is the singular remedy available here to preserve the status quo while the Constitutional rights of these appellants to make these utterances and to engage in these activities are determined. The threat against them is real not fanciful, immediate not remote. The case is therefore an actual not a hypothetical one.

(iv) Standing

In the present context, standing differs from the concept of *locus standi in judicio* at Roman-Dutch law. The latter means an incapacity to sue or be sued in court, such as in the case of an unemancipated minor or a wife subject to marital power. As a constitutional requirement, however, standing signifies generally that the party who assails a law has been injured by operation of it. As expressed in *Baker v. Carr* [345] the underlying purpose of this rule is "to assure that concrete adverseness which sharpens the presentation of issues upon which the court so largely depends for illumination of difficult constitutional questions."

There are in reality two separate and distinct as-

345. 369 U.S. 186, 204 (1962).

pects of the requirement that may be formulated as subrules. First, the injury must be substantial. Second, the injury must be personal not vicarious. We shall refer to each subrule in turn.

a. The Injury Must Be Substantial. The party impugning the law must have a sufficient *interesse* or litigable interest in the action. His injury must be substantial, not miniscule, incalculable, or remote. The classic illustration is *Frothingham v. Mellon.*[346]

Mrs. Frothingham, in her capacity as a national taxpayer, brought suit to challenge the constitutionality of the Maternity Act of 1921 which apportioned certain funds from the national treasury among those states of the Union which would comply with the provisions of the statute so as to reduce infant mortality and protect mother and child health. Her contention was that the effect of the apportionment of funds to a state would increase future taxation and thereby take away her property unreasonably. The merits of the case were never reached. While carefully reaffirming the standing of a municipal taxpayer to challenge the illegal use of public moneys on the ground that this interest is direct and immediate,[347] the court declared that a national taxpayer lacked standing.

> His interest in the moneys of the treasury—partly realised from taxation and partly from other sources—is shared with millions of others, is comparatively minute and indeterminable, and the

346. *Supra* note 334.

347. But the court has not always recognised standing even where municipal taxpayers have sued. Doremus v. Board of Education, 342 U.S. 429 (1952) (standing denied for lack of financial injury where municipal and state taxpayers challenged state statute requiring verses from Old Testament to be read in public schools). *But see* Wieman v. Updegraff, 344 U.S. 183 (1952).

> effect upon future taxation, of any payment out of the funds, so remote, fluctuating and uncertain, that no basis is afforded for an appeal to the preventive powers of a court. . . .[348]

Despite the authority of the *Frothingham* case, it seems proper to interject the cautionary note that there is little reason to believe that a citizen of Lesotho would lack standing to assert a fundamental right in his capacity as national taxpayer. Having an overall population of only one million, and a unitary rather than a federal form of government, Lesotho compares in such features to the states of the United States. The Lesotho taxpayer should therefore have a standing comparable to the well-recognised standing of state or municipal taxpayers to challenge the unconstitutionality of state or municipal laws.[349] Furthermore, in the recent case of *Flast v. Cohen*,[350] the Supreme Court sharply circumscribed the *Frothingham* case and recognised a national taxpayer's standing to attack the validity of a federal statute. In *Flast* the Court held that a national taxpayer possessed standing if there is both (1) a "logical link" between the

---

348. *Supra* note 334, at 487. Not far removed from the Court's mind was the consideration that to hold otherwise would be to recognise an astronomically large class of plaintiffs. "If one taxpayer may champion and litigate such a cause, then every other taxpayer may do the same, not only in respect of the statute here under review, but also in respect of every other appropriation act and statute whose administration requires the outlay of public money, and whose validity may be questioned." *Id.* It should further be noted that although Frothingham's case denied standing to challenge a treasury expenditure, the court has recognised standing where the defendant was *resisting the collection* of an unconstitutional tax. U.S. v. Butler, 297 U.S. 1 (1936).

349. *Taxpayers' Suits: A Survey and Summary*, 69 YALE L.J. 895 (1960).

350. 392 U.S. 83 (1968).

status of taxpayer and the type of enactment under attack, and (2) a nexus between the status of taxpayer and the "precise nature" of the infringement. Finally, in the United States the requirement of standing is not enforced overstrictly in any event in questions involving fundamental rights, such as freedom of speech, religion, or protection from racial discrimination. This explains in part the turnabout in the *Flast* case, which concerned freedom of religion, and indeed the generalisation is warranted by a wide range of cases that corroborate to some extent the theory of preferred freedoms.[351] Given the hierarchy of constitutional values, the preference for individual liberty should tend to triumph over implicit restrictions related to the convenience of the judicial task.

The requirement of substantial injury was applied by the Federal Supreme Court of Nigeria in 1961 in *Olawoyin v. Attorney-General, Northern Region*.[352] Plaintiff sought a declaratory judgment that Part VIII of the Children and Young Persons Law of 1958 was contrary to sections 7, 8, and 9 (protecting Private and Family Life, Freedom of Conscience, and Freedom of Expression, respectively) of the Nigerian Constitution of 1954. The act, in brief, prohibited those under sixteen from participating in politics and laid down penalties for violation of its terms. Plaintiff, who was an adult and had not violated the act, failed originally to plead in what way the law was a restriction of his rights, though his counsel maintained in argument that plaintiff had children

351. *E.g.*, Thornhill v. Alabama, 310 U.S. 88 (1940); Terminiello *supra* note 258; Kunz v. New York, 340 U.S. 290 (1951); McCollum v. Board of Education, 333 U.S. 203 (1948); Everson v. Board of Education, 330 U.S. 1 (1947).

352. 1961 F.S.C. 269.

whom he wished to educate politically.[353] Concerning the sufficiency of standing to sue, counsel urged the proposition that the enactment of a law creating an offence against that which a person is constitutionally entitled to do is a sufficient interest to enable any citizen to seek a declaration in court. Following Indian, American, and Australian authorities in point, Justice Unsworth rejected this contention, dismissing the application with the following observation:

> It seems to me that to hold that there was an interest here would amount to saying that a private individual obtains an interest by the mere enactment of a law with which he may in the future come in conflict; and I will not support such a proposition.[354]

b. The Injury Must Be Personal. In essence the party cannot complain of an injury to someone other than himself.[355] Ordinarily, one does not have standing to assert *jus tertii.*[356] Thus, if a statute applies constitutionally to the party before the court, he will not acquire standing to challenge merely by pointing out that it applies unconstitutionally to some person not before the court. The wording of the Lesotho Constitution substantiates this restriction. Under section

---

353. Counsel revealed on appeal the significant fact that the plaintiff was the secretary of a political party, but the court would not consider this because it was not raised below in the High Court.

354. *Supra* note 352, at 271. An earlier attack on the impugned statute failed on the merits in Cheranci v. Cheranci, [1960] N.R.L.R. 24 (Bate J.).

355. One notable exception is the case of a detained individual under section 12. In that instance any other person, seemingly even a complete stranger, may make application for his release.

356. For a scholarly discussion, which makes note of important exceptions to this rule, *see* Sedler, *Standing to Assert Jus Tertii in the Supreme Court*, 71 YALE L.J. 599 (1962).

20 an individual is only entitled to complain of violations "in relation to him." The phrase "in relation to him" describes the proper assailant, the person with a sufficient relationship to the violation to assert or resist on the basis of a constitutional right.

It is interesting to note that a comparable principle operates in the private-law sphere. Thus in a delictual claim for personal injury, the plaintiff cannot build upon the duty of care owed to another.[357] Likewise, apart from *stipulatio alteri,* a stranger to a contract can claim no breach thereunder as the ground of recovery for his own injury.[358]

The constitutional rule under discussion is well instantiated by *Tileston v. Ullman.*[359] A physician sought a declaratory judgment of unconstitutionality against a state criminal statute that prohibited the use of drugs or instruments to prevent conception, and the giving of assistance or counsel in their use. He alleged that three of his patients had health so poor as to be endangered by childbearing and that the

---

357. Bourhill v. Young, [1942] 2 All E.R. 396.

358. HAHLO AND KAHN, UNION OF SOUTH AFRICA: THE DEVELOPMENT OF ITS LAWS AND CONSTITUTION 487 (Stevens 1960).

359. 318 U.S. 44 (1943), *supra* note 336, reprinted in HART AND WECHSLER, at 156. In Griswold v. Connecticut, 381 U.S. 479 (1965), reprinted in FREUND, CONSTITUTIONAL LAW 199 (Little, Brown & Co. 1966 Supplement), a doctor who gave counsel and assistance in the use of contraceptives was found guilty of being an accessory to the crime under the same statute in Tileston v. Ullman. In a successful appeal against the constitutionality of the statute the doctor's standing was held to be sufficient. The court distinguished Tileston v. Ullman on the ground that petitioner there sought declaratory relief whereas in the case before it the appellant had been already convicted. "Certainly the accessory should have standing to assert that the offense which he is charged with assisting is not, or cannot constitutionally be, a crime."

statute would forbid his offering professional advice to protect their health. The Supreme Court held that the plaintiff had no standing to sue. The attack on the statute had been characterised in terms of deprivation of life, but the physician's life was not in danger. "His patients are not parties to this proceeding and there is no basis on which we can say that he has standing to secure an adjudication of his patients' constitutional right to life which they do not assert in their own behalf." [360] Thus in the analogous case of *Charanjit Lal v. Union of India,*[361] pursuant to a statute designed to bring efficiency to a spinning and weaving company the elected directors were replaced by directors appointed by the Government. The petitioner, owner of a single share in the company, sought a declaration that the statute was void for inconsistency to the fundamental rights to hold property and to enjoy equal protection of the laws. Starting from the proposition that a corporation has a personality distinct from those of its shareholders, the court said that the corporation was the proper party (through the old directors) to assert a constitutional infringement in relation to itself. "It would not be open to an individual shareholder to complain of an act which affects the fundamental rights of the company except to the extent that it constitutes an infraction of his own rights as well." [362]

---

360. Tileston v. Ullman, *Id.* at 46.

361. [1950] S.C. 499.

362. But *contra,* the principle of direct and individual injury are two important cases. In Pierce v. Society of Sisters, 268 U.S. 510 (1925), a statute to take effect in several years required parents to send their children only to public schools. It was held that the appellee, a Roman Catholic institution, from which parents were withdrawing their children in anticipation of the coming to force of the new law, had standing to enjoin the statute's future enforcement. In Barrows v. Jackson,

The rules of judicial restraint that have been discussed thus far—adversary litigation, ripeness, standing—have been received as sensible rules in many countries where judicial restraint is exercised.[363] Significantly they have been received under the Constitution of Nigeria from which Lesotho is direct constitutional heir and beneficiary. Their place in the Constitution of Lesotho, however, is secured by more than mere emulation of constitutionalism abroad. Nor is the doctrine of separation of powers the only reason. Rather it is the words of the Constitution more than anything else that require them. Thus, as explained in preceding paragraphs, a "likely" violation of a fundamental right suggests the ripeness of the issue, the correct stage for a judicial determination to be beneficially rendered. "In relation to him" describes the party truly injured and therefore truly interested in a vigorous adversary encounter. It is primarily in the elucidation of the various meanings and policies behind such constitutional language that foreign experience may make its lasting contribution.

(v) The Doctrine of Last Resort

A corrollary of the proposition that the courts do not seek jurisdiction is that the courts will not decide a question of constitutionality except out of strict necessity. Where two or more grounds exist for the

---

supra note 299, the defendant breached a term of a land contract in which he agreed not to sell the land to Negroes. On a suit for breach of contract it was held that defendant had standing to resist the claim on the basis that it denied equal protection of the laws to Negroes even though he himself was not a Negro. These cases may show that the court has either abandoned or relaxed the rule when it considered greater values were at stake.

363. *E.g.*, Australia (Crouch v. Commonwealth, 77 C.L.R. 339); India (BASU, *supra* note 176, at 182); Nigeria (*see supra* note 352).

decision of the case of which one is a constitutional ground, the courts will not consider the constitutional questions unless all other grounds urged have been disposed of. Nor will a constitutional question be disposed of if a construction of a statute is fairly possible by which the question may be fairly avoided. Furthermore constitutional issues will not be formulated and decided in broader terms than is required by the precise facts of the case to which the decision is to be applied.[364]

B. Constitutional Standards for Enforcement

The fundamental rights of the Constitution contain a mozaic of differing standards of doubtful import. It would in truth be beyond the scope of this work to explore all of them, but it is thought necessary at least to sketch the principles of the ones that seem the most important.

(1) THE CONCEPT OF REASONABLENESS

Before entering upon a close discussion of the particular language of the Lesotho Constitution it is appropriate to provide some introduction to the concept of *reasonableness* as the master standard because every particular formulation of the standard is but a variation of it. Each variation, depending upon the verbal formula, may be designed to heighten or lower, widen or narrow the criteria and scope of the flexible standard of reasonableness, which is the objective standard of delict, contract, and crime, indeed of every field of law. The vintage of the concept is old, and its roots go down very deep. "He who bids the law rule,"

---

364. THE CONSTITUTION OF THE UNITED STATES OF AMERICA, ANALYSIS AND INTERPRETATION 630-631 (Small & Jayson 1964).

said Aristotle,[365] "bids God and Reason alone rule." And in a famous case Lord Coke declared,[366] "When an Act of Parliament is against common right and reason . . ., the common law will controul it, and adjudge such Act to be void." Thus modernly, Justice Harlan can refer us to a "rational continuum" which broadly includes a freedom from all substantial arbitrary impositions and purposeless restraints.[367]

In the constitutional jurisprudence of the United States, what is reasonable is posed in terms of what affords "due process of law" and "equal protection of the law." In India an act is deemed reasonable if it is "in the interests of" a permissible end, while in Nigeria constitutional acts are those that are "reasonably justifiable in a democratic society in the interests of" a goal authorised by the Constitution. For Botswana and Malawi, on the other hand, the act must be "reasonably required in the interests of" a constitutional head of authority. Then again the Lesotho Constitution poses the problem in substantially different phraseology. Thus, simply to equate reasonableness with constitutionality is to oversimplify matters, for what is *constitutionally* reasonable varies from constitution to constitution owing to the particular modification of meaning created by the individual standard.

It is usual to divide the concept of reasonableness into two parts: substantive reasonableness and procedural reasonableness. These we shall briefly discuss in turn.

(a) Substantive Reasonableness

Reasonableness describes a just relationship be-

---

365. POLITICS III, XIV, 5.

366. Dr. Bonham's Case, 8 Co. Rep. 113b (1610).

367. Poe v. Ullman, 367 U.S. 497, 543 (1961) (dissent).

tween means and ends. Almost everyone agrees that a man who heads only south to reach the North Pole, who burns his house to roast a pig, or who purchases a rifle to hunt unicorn is going about things in an unreasonable fashion. Such acts are deemed unreasonable because there is a bad relationship between the means and the end. Sometimes it is possible to state categorically that the *means* cannot accomplish the end (as by going only south to reach the north), or that the end is not possible (to kill a unicorn), or that the means chosen (burning a house) are too radical and disproportionate (merely to roast a pig).

(i) There Must Be a Rational Connection

It is the concern of the courts as guardians of the constitution to judge whether Parliament has acted reasonably. There must be *some* rational relationship between the measure passed by Parliament and the object Parliament desires to achieve. Thus though Justinian [368] believed that homosexuals caused earthquakes, a law banishing or exiling all homosexuals for that reason could not be valid in Lesotho. To pick another absurd but clear example, if Parliament passed a law prohibiting the sale of pink shirts that stated in its preamble the avowed purpose of curbing the spread of narcotics and drug addiction, the law would be patently unreasonable because there is manifestly no rational or efficacious relationship (absent other facts) between pink garments and the drug trade. In *Schware v. Board of Bar Examiners,*[369] petitioner was denied a license to practise law in New Mexico because his past membership in the Communist Party prevented satisfaction of the "requisite moral character." Justice Black said such political affiliation could not raise

---

368. NOVELS 77.

369. 353 U.S. 232 (1957), reprinted in LOCKHART, CONSTITUTIONAL RIGHTS AND LIBERTIES 454 (1st ed. West).

"substantial doubts" about his present good moral character. The connection could not be rationally justified. Concurring justices wrote that

> . . . to hold as the [state] court did, that communist affiliation for six to seven years up to 1940, fifteen years prior to the court's assessment of it, in and of itself made the petitioner a person of questionable character is so dogmatic an inference as to be wholly unwarranted.

(ii) The Connection Cannot Be Too Remote

It is not enough, however, that a statute possess *some* efficacious relation to its designated objective or purpose. A statute may be considered unreasonable because the relationship is remote or simply hypothetical rather than proximate. For example the possibility that a university student who is exposed to Doestoyevsky's *Crime and Punishment* will be inspired to commit a philosophical crime is just conceivable, yet a law that banned the book for that reason would without doubt be void. The relationship between the suppression and the foreseen danger is merely hypothetical and therefore unreasonable.

When a measure is proximately related to its purpose, however, admits of honest division of opinion. Here a distinction may be made between the private-law and the constitutional-law meaning of remoteness. In the fields of delict and contract, for example, the court usually has the benefit of hindsight in deciding whether certain completed damage caused by the defendant was remote under the particular facts of the situation. In constitutional law, however, the "damage" is not always a completed fact. Because "damage" to the state is a foreseen possibility, prior restraint on the exercise of a certain liberty may be sought to be imposed. Consequently the court must engage in the perils of predictive causation to determine whether the foreseen event is too remote or not.

(iii) The Restriction Cannot Be Disproportionate

A statute may be both reasonable in the sense of *efficacious* or *proximate* and yet be such a drastic restriction on freedom that it is unreasonble. In *Butler v. Michigan*,[370] for example, the state criminal law forbade the sale of all books that tend to corrupt the morals of youths. The Supreme Court struck down the statute because of its disastrous breadth.

> We have before us legislation not reasonably restricted to the evil with which it is said to deal. The incidence of this enactment is to reduce the adult population of Michigan to reading only what is fit for children.

The same consideration is illustrated by *Nandan v. State*.[371] The crime of sedition in the Indian Penal Code, under which appellant was convicted, did not include as an element of the offence an incitement to violence or an apprehension of violence by the authorities. Such a law was unreasonably restrictive because it could be used to suppress speech having only the slightest tendency to disrupt public order. Justice Desai observed that:

> . . . even an intimate conversation, or a conversation with a person who is not at all likely to disturb public order, is punishable. A speech to the wife, or to a minor, or to a paralytic person, or to a life convict, or to an alien, or to a Government servant, is punishable even though there can be no apprehension of any public disorder from the wife, the minor, the paralytic person, the life convict, the alien, or the Government servant.[372]

370. 352 U.S. 380 (1957).

371. [1959] A.I.R. 101.

372. *Id.* at 107; it is interesting that a similar penal provision in the Nigerian Penal Code was declared constitutional in DPP v. Obi, [1961] All N.L.R. 186, with no attention paid to the fact that the unnecessary scope of the crime might restrict speech that posed no threat to public order.

(iv) The End Must Be Possible and Lawful

A statute of Parliament, no matter how appropriate or related to some end, is inherently defective if that end is impossible or unlawful. DeLolme's remark that even Parliament cannot turn a man into a woman only serves to remind that Parliament cannot defy established laws of science. But Parliament not only may be incapable of turning a man into a woman, it has no legal right to try. For even where the purpose for a law can be achieved by that law it will be void if the Constitution has not granted or has forbidden such a purpose. To illustrate, in *Lochner v. New York*,[373] a state statute prohibited bakery employees from working more than sixty hours in a week or ten hours in one day. Asserting that bakers are subject to no greater hazards to health than a doctor or a lawyer,[374] the court voiced an economic philosophy of true *laissez-faire* (now discredited) and declared the act beyond the rightful *power* of the state. In its approach to governmental restraints on liberty of action as well, the Supreme Court has invalidated the regulation of a school board's compelling school children to salute the flag on the ground that such attempts to promote national solidarity and patriotism are not within the police power.[375]

(v) Courts Do Not Choose Between Rational Means

It is an established principle that where various

373. 198 U.S. 45 (1905), overruled by Bunting v. Oregon, 243 U.S. 426 (1917), which, however, need not destroy the decision's usefulness as an example of the principle of substantive reasonableness.

374. Much of the court's argument also contends there was little or no *proximate relationship*: "The connection, if any exist, is too shadowy or thin to build any argument for the interference of the legislature."

375. West Virginia State Board of Education v. Barnette, 319 U.S. 624 (1934).

alternative means have a rational basis the one preferred by the court cannot be substituted for the one chosen by the legislature. This is consonant with a general presumption of constitutionality and respect for the legislature's determination. On this principle Chief Justice Marshall wrote:

> Let the end be legitimate, let it be within the scope of the Constitution, and *all means which are appropriate,* which are plainly adopted to that end, which are not prohibited, but consistent with the letter and spirit of the Constitution, are constitutional.[376] (Italics added.)

Thus the use of the court's veto as a means of imposing its own political or economic philosophy constrained Mr. Justice Holmes to remark in dissent in *Lochner v. New York*:[377]

> But a constitution is not intended to embody a particular economic theory, whether of paternalism and the organic relation of the citizen to the state or of *laissez-faire.*

And as he reminded the court that, "the 14th Amendment does not enact Mr. Herbert Spencer's Social Status," so Mr. Justice Black would later observe:

> Whether the legislature takes for its textbook Adam Smith, Herbert Spencer, Lord Keynes, or some other is no concern of ours.[378]

This limitation upon judicial power follows from the desire for democratic government, both that the people, speaking through their representatives, should have a right to choose amongst rational means and, that the legislature is in a better position than the

---

376. McCulloch v. Maryland, 4 Wheat. 316 (1819), reprinted in DOWLING & GUNTHER, 185, at 193.

377. *Supra* note 373, and 198 U.S. 45 (1905), reprinted in LOCKHART, *supra* note 369, at 20.

378. Ferguson v. Skrupa, 372 U.S. 726 (1963).

court to understand and appreciate the solution to the problem at hand.[379] And thus Chief Justice Sastri spoke for a guarded use of the court's power (even while the Indian Supreme Court invalidated a statute as being an unreasonable restraint on freedom of association):

> . . . It is inevitable that the social philosophy and the scale of values of the Judges participating in [a] decision should play an important part, and the limit to their interference with legislative judgement in such cases can only be dictated by their sense of responsibility and self-restraint and the sobering reflection that the Constitution is meant not only for people of their way of thinking but for all, and that the majority of the elected representatives have in authorising the imposition of the restrictions considered them to be reasonable.[380]

(b) Procedural Reasonableness

A traditional concern of governments, whether aristocratic, theocratic, democratic, or totalitarian, is to establish a ruling process, a system of administering people and resources. However, if this process is carried out secretly, arbitrarily, capriciously, and sometimes retroactively, it would appear to be unreasonable, even grotesquely so. Prompted by this disquieting possibility, the common law or the Constitution may have explicitly given to the individual certain procedural guarantees. In the criminal law, for example, there are fundamental rules, now guaranteed by the Lesotho Constitution,[381] about the right to confront and cross-examine witnesses, to legal representation, and to a presumption of innocence and prohi-

---

379. *See* Hamdard Dawakhana v. Union of India, 1960 A.I.R. 554.

380. State of Madras v. Row, [1952] A.I.R. 196, 200.

381. § 12.

bitions against double jeopardy of life and limb, *ex post facto* legislation, and compulsory self-incrimination. These historic notions of fairness inhere in the concept of *fair trial*. Much of it was central to Dicey's formulation of the "rule of law."

In civil matters, on the other hand, the two great principles of "natural justice" are the touchstones—but not the final elaboration—of the concept of procedural reasonableness. First, a court must be impartial and unbiased. Therefore no one ought to be the judge of his own case. (*Nemo debet esse judex in propria causa.*) Second, no man ought to be condemned unheard. (*Audi alteram partem.*) Hence it is essential that the accused be given adequate notice of the case against him and ample opportunity to answer and raise relevant defences. The reasonable law, said Daniel Webster,[382] is "a law which hears before it condemns; which proceeds upon enquiry, and renders judgment only after trial."

Procedural reasonableness, however, has more general dimensions. The principles outlined in regard to substantive reasonableness equally apply. Thus, if the government jeopardises a substantive right through a procedural restriction, then there must be shown to exist a rational nexus between the chosen administrative means and the permissible administrative end. Such means cannot be remote or disproportionate without conditioning the value, even the existence, of the substantive right. For example, assuming a law restricting the sale of pornography is substantively rational, it may nevertheless be procedurally irrational in laying down a legal presumption that any person in mere possession of pornography, such as a bookdealer, entertained the necessary

382. The Trustees of Dartmouth College v. Woodward, 17 U.S. 518, 581 (1819).

mens rea to possess pornography. Similarly, a law restraining the free movement of citizens may be reasonably related to a particular danger in the community, such as a smallpox epidemic or a planned *coup d'etat,* yet where a citizen's movement is restrained without notice, hearing, or court review, whenever the executive is subjectively satisfied that such dangers exist, the procedure may subsume a despotism that the Constitution cannot digest.[383]

Since the two illustrations just discussed are of particular pertinence to constitutional law on the Southern African scene, it is proposed to take a closer look at each of them.

(i) Unfettered Executive Discretion

Restraints on fundamental rights that are laid down at the subjective discretion of a member of the executive are inherently unprincipled. If the reasonableness of restraints cannot be judged objectively [384] in the courts, fundamental liberties may then depend upon the state of the relevant minister's digestion.[385]

---

383. Professor Fuller would describe these two problems as questions of *procedural morality.* Enactments that lack rudimentary procedural structure he would not classify as "laws." MORALITY OF LAW Ch. II (Yale 1964).

384. The Constitution, it is submitted, is naturally hostile to the "subjective" approach adopted by the House of Lords in Liversidge v. Anderson, [1942] A.C. 206. *Cf.* Nakkuda Ali v. v. Jayaratne, [1951] A.C. 66 (P.C.).

385. It may be said in this connection that the vesting of pure discretion in the executive may result from an unconscious act on the part of Parliament as well as by express conferral. Statutes that lay down unusually vague rules may offend notions of substantive (*see supra* at pp. 375-382) and procedural reasonableness. Procedurally, their vagueness may neither afford to the individual an ascertainable standard of criminal guilt or civil liability, nor to the executive an objective guide of application. Thus vague statutes are generally antithetical to the requirements of notice and nonarbitrary application. *See*

The evils of this scarcely need illustration. Seldom since Torquemada's Inquisition has more terrifying power been "legally" wielded by arbitrary hand than under South Africa's General Law Amendment Act of 1963. Though nothing close to this extreme exists in Lesotho, there have been worrisome tendencies. For instance section 30 of the Public Order Proclamation of 1964 (now repealed)[386] at one time vested in the executive the utterly subjective power to outlaw a society for reasons of public order or security into which no court could enquire.[387] Today, under section 20 of the Constitution, however, this statutory ouster of jurisdiction would have been void, for the individual has the entrenched right under that provision to bring to court any violation of a fundamental right.[388] Further it would have to be shown by the state to the court's satisfaction that the vesting of pure discretion in the executive is the kind of restriction that is a practical necessity in a democracy.

In the United States the position is that such laws are *prima facie* unconstitutional[389] while in India

---

generally Amsterdam, *The Void for Vagueness Doctrine:* SELECTED ESSAYS ON CONSTITUTIONAL LAW 560 (A.A.L.S. 1963).

386. Repealed by the Internal Security (Public Meetings and Processions) Act No. 15 of 1966.

387. *Cf.* Botswana Penal Code § 48 (granting to the President of the Republic absolute discretion to declare prohibited publications); *Cf.* Rhodesia, *e.g.*, Law and Order (Maintenance) Act of 1960, Ch. 39, § 18(1) (Governor may prohibit any publication which in his opinion is contrary to public safety or security).

388. Indeed this principle extends to any law that encroaches upon *any part* of the Constitution. If the legislature could oust the jurisdiction of the court merely by inserting a clause to that effect, the legislature would thereby be entitled to deprive the court of its power of judicial review whenever it pleased. This the legislature cannot do.

389. *See, e.g.*, Kunz v. New York, *supra* note 351 (license to speak on public streets granted or denied at subjective dis-

complete executive discretion has been held unconstitutional as to basic rights,[390] but in other areas it has been said to depend upon "the nature of the right and the circumstances calling for the restriction." [391] In Pakistan in *Hossain v. Government of East Pakistan*,[392] the court gave its approval to a statute vesting complete executive discretion to prohibit newspaper publication for a thirty-day period (renewable) of any subject or class of subjects for the purpose of securing public order or safety, with provision for review by the executive (not the courts). Petitioner's newspaper was banned by executive order from the publication of any matter relating to the strikes, meetings, and agitation of students. Adopting a Lilli-

---

cretion of commissioner of police); Niemotko v. Maryland, 340 U.S. 268 (1951) (permits for the use of public park issued by Park Commissioner without standards); Cantwell v. Connecticut, 310 U.S. 296 (1940) (solicitation for religious, charitable, or philanthropic causes forbidden without approval of a state officer); Sweezy v. New Hampshire, 354 U.S. 234 (1957) (investigating committee given such a broad frame of reference as to grant it arbitrary discretion of picking subjects and questions to pursue).

390. *Supra* note 380; "The formula of subjective satisfaction of the Government or of its officers, with an Advisory Board thrown in to review the materials on which the Government seeks to override a basic freedom [of association] guaranteed to the citizen, may be viewed as reasonable only in exceptional circumstances and cannot receive judicial approval as a general pattern of reasonable restrictions on fundamental rights."

391. BASU, *supra* note 176, at 589. *See* Khare v. State of Delhi, [1950] S.C.R. 519 (upholding statute permitting externment in interest of public safety on subjective decision of the Executive).

392. [1965] P.L.D. 68. The case is only illustrative and is not meant to state the prevailing position in Pakistan. *Cf.* Maudoodi v. W. Pakistan, *supra* note 279 (law struck down that permitted Provincial Government on executive discretion to outlaw any association).

putian's view of judicial power, the court stressed that it, unlike the executive, was not an appropriately informed body to judge the gravity of social conditions. And reckoning that the purpose of the act was to permit prompt preventive action by the executive, the court both conceded the need for subjective discretion as well as for dispensing with a prior hearing. A subsequent hearing under the circumstances satisfied the requirement of *audi alteram partem* even though the subsequent review was by the executive and not by the courts, for

> . . . the provision could [not] be otherwise as the Government is in possession of all relevant materials and would be the best judge if any change in the situation or the attitude of the party concerned demands modification or possession [*sic*] of the order.[393]

With respect, one could agree that the executive is the appropriate body to execute the law without being illogical in also maintaining that the law must set forth a reviewable standard and the aggrieved party is entitled to an expeditious judicial hearing. To admit that the executive has better machinery for the collection of facts than does the court may entitle the executive to place a *prima facie* prohibition on news dissemination but does not *a priori* prevent the presentation of the factual basis of that decision in a speedy hearing.[394] It is submitted that above all, what cannot

---

393. *Id.* Hossain case at 79.

394. In terms of accomplishing the same *desiderata* by less restrictive means, Pakistan could have installed in the act machinery permitting the executive to obtain an *ex parte* injunction on certain classes of news subjects *pendente lite* the quick resolution of the reasonableness of a thirty-day restriction. *See* the procedure of New York's anti-obscenity statute set forth in Kingsley Books, Inc. v. Brown, 354 U.S. 436 (1957), reprinted in LOCKHART, KAMISAR, & CHOPER 538 ff.

be conceded is that executive decision-making is an arcane process beyond the ken of the court, for if it is, it has no right to be, especially where it makes serious inroads on freedom of expression.[395]

Constitutional issues of this kind, it is submitted, were overlooked in *Lerotholi v. Blake*.[396] The Vice-Chancellor of the University of Botswana, Lesotho and Swaziland temporarily excluded certain students from the University without a prior hearing pursuant to Statute 5(5) of the University Charter.[397] Charges against the students were then pending before a disciplinary committee of the University for alleged participation in a student strike which had expressed dissatisfaction and grievances against the University.

The court took the view that the procedural rule of *audi alteram partem* was dispensable in an emergency and gave conclusive weight to the Vice-Chancellor's own characterisation of the situation as an emergency. As Johnstone, A. C. J. expressed it,

> I can see no good reason why the court should not accept the Vice-Chancellor's assessment of the

---

395. At the African conference on the rule of law, Lagos 1961, the following minima were laid down: AFRICAN CONFERENCE ON THE RULE OF LAW 17-18 (International Commission of Jurists, Geneva 1961).

(a) that the full reasons for the action of the executive be made known to the persons aggrieved; and

(b) that the aggrieved person shall be given a fair hearing; and

(c) that the grounds given by the executive for its action shall not be regarded as conclusive but shall be objectively considered by the court.

396. [1963-1966] H.C.T.L.R. 174 (1966).

397. Statute 5(5) reads: "The Vice-Chancellor may refuse to admit any person as a student without assigning any reason and may suspend any student from any class or classes and may exclude any student from any part of the University or its precincts. He shall report every such suspension or exclusion to the Council and the Senate at their next meeting."

situation and its possible developments as grave. What the Vice-Chancellor had to contemplate was a situation in which certain students wished to pursue their studies without interference and the possibility that a return to the campus of the persons against whom disciplinary charges were being investigated would lead to further disturbances, unrest or interruption to the academic activities of the University. In my view the Vice-Chancellor and the Senate of the University are in a far better position than this court to assess the gravity of the situation at the University, and in the absence of convincing evidence to the contrary, I accept the Vice-Chancellor's view that exceptional circumstances, in the nature of an emergency have existed at the University since 9th September, 1966.

Since the right to protest is a basic aspect of free expression, however, it is a pity that the court did not mention the applicability of the constitutional guarantee of freedom of expression.[398] At the very least it fell to be decided whether the Vice-Chancellor's power under Statute 5(5) of the University Charter was procedurally reasonable, that is, whether Statute 5(5), *ex facie* or "as applied," did not restrict freedom of expression "to a greater extent than is necessary in a practical sense in a democratic society."

(ii) Statutory Presumptions

An onerous presumption ranged against the individual in court may so escalate his burden of proof as to make a public hearing an empty formality and thus breaching indirectly the principle of *audi alteram partem*. The recognition of this kind of breach of fair

398. The cause of action in Lerotholi's case arose prior to the promulgation of the 1966 Constitution and thus would have had to be dealt with under the 1965 Constitution. This would have made no substantive difference, however, since the provisions in regard to fundamental human rights in the two constitutions are in every material respect identical.

play may have prompted the repeal of sections 8 and 9 of Lesotho's Public Order Proclamation of 1964 [399] which had not only imposed strict criminal liability on attending or addressing an unlawful assembly, but placed the burden on the accused to show that the assembly in question was not unlawful. In short, the statute rebuttably presumed every essential of guilt.

As in all questions of reasonableness the essence is in the rational connection. Thus in *Tot v. U.S.*[400] a Federal statute made it

> . . . unlawful for any person who has been convicted of a crime of violence . . . to receive any firearm or ammunition which has been shipped or transported in interstate or foreign commerce.

One of the presumptions of the statute was that the possession of a firearm or ammunition by such a previously convicted person should give rise to a presumption that it had been received after being shipped in interstate or foreign commerce. In striking down the legislation the court declared:

> Under our decisions a statutory presumption cannot be sustained if there is no rational connection between the fact proved and the ultimate fact presumed, if the inference of the one from proof

---

399. The relevant sections were repealed by the Internal Security (Public Meetings and Processions) Act No. 15 of 1966, which, however, in section 12 reasserted the standard of strict criminal liability.

400. 319 U.S. 463 (1943). *See also* Bailey v. State of Alabama, 219 U.S. 219 (1911) (unconstitutional presumption that labourers' breach of contract was *prima facie* evidence of intent to defraud employer of salary advances); Schware, *supra* note 369 (unconstitutional presumption that because of past membership in Communist Party petitioner not morally fit to practice law); Manley v. Georgia, 279 U.S. 1 (1929) (unconstitutional presumption that every bank insolvency shall be deemed fraudulent).

of the other is arbitrary because of lack of connection between the two in common experience.

On this principle one may venture to doubt the soundness of the kind of presumptions illustrated in Swaziland's Societies Proclamation.[401] Section 13 lays down *inter alia* that a society is rebuttably presumed to be unlawful if proceedings are brought against it and section 14 *inter alia* rebuttably presumes that if books, insignia banners, and the like of an unlawful society are found in the defendant's possession he is one who assists in the management of the society. It is submitted that these presumptions are manifestly irrational. First, the unlawfulness of a society has nothing in fact or reason to do with the decision to prosecute, for the latter rests on the subjective judgment of the executive. Second, the possession of banners or books may create a remote inference of membership in a society but surely not of being a manager, no more than the possession of a manufactured product argues that one is a partner in the firm of manufacturers.[402]

Where a fact is to some extent rationally inferred from the existence of a proven fact, the court may assess whether the width of the inferential gap is a reasonable restriction under the circumstances of the case. Thus the magnitude of the social evil—gold smuggling in India—was held to make reasonable a rebuttable statutory presumption that the seizure of goods was in fact supported by the agent's reasonable

---

401. No. 33 of 1963. The Lesotho Public Order Proclamation of 1964, at § 34 rebuttably presumes that the possessor of such materials is a member and a manager of the unlawful society.

402. Unregistered partnerships would be unlawful societies under the proclamation. *See* § 9(1) and § 2.

belief that they were smuggled.[403] On the other hand, where there is no palpable danger to the community, it seems clear that the following presumptions would be unreasonable restrictions: (1) attendance at a meeting of an unregistered (and therefore unlawful) organisation presumes guilty knowledge that the meeting was unlawful; [404] (2) perusing a book relating to an unlawful (because unregistered) organisation presumes the reader a member; [405] and (3) a bookdealer's possession of a book presumes his guilty knowledge of its contents.[406]

(2) THE PARTICULAR FORMULA: "TO A GREATER EXTENT THAN IS NECESSARY IN A PRACTICAL SENSE IN A DEMOCRATIC SOCIETY IN THE INTERESTS OF" [407]

By far the most important and prevalent formulation of substantive and procedural reasonableness in Lesotho's fundamental rights is the phrase to be found in the rights with "imprecise" saving clauses. The foregoing introductory summary of the con-

---

403. Collector of Customs v. Sampathu, [1962] S.C. 316, cited and discussed in BASU, *supra* note 176, at 598-599.

404. *E.g.*, § 22, Lesotho Societies Act, No. 20 of 1966; § 11, Societies Act, Laws of Swaziland 1963; Botswana Penal Code § 67.

405. *E.g.*, § 9(1)(b) of Southern Rhodesia's Unlawful Organisations Act No. 38, 1959 *and see* Musururwa v. Attorney-General of Southern Rhodesia, 1963 R & N 565.

406. Botswana Penal Code § 45 *and see* Hafagee v. State, Criminal Appeal 16, (1967). Such a provision was declared unconstitutional in Smith v. California, 361 U.S. 147 (1960).

407. The test is actually longer. One omitted section of it that may be of importance in regard to certain constitutional questions is the phrase "for any of the purposes specified." No attempt to explore its possible meanings (which on investigation, it is submitted, may prove rather complex) has been made here.

cept of reasonableness now permits a discussion of its meaning. In the following discussion this standard will be dissected for purposes of convenient analysis. We do not propose to forget, however, that the test is integral and that the meaning of each section depends on the whole.

(a) "To a greater extent than is necessary in a practical sense . . ."

To grasp the meaning of this phrase, one may start with the following passage from the *Report of the Basutoland Independence Conference of 1966:* [408]

> The Constitution provides for a court-enforced Bill of Rights, including several features which combine to afford an exceptionally strong safeguard for individual freedom; among these being a requirement having the effect that in most cases where governmental or legislative action curtails a protected right or freedom, it is for the government to establish in the courts if challenged that, where there are several reasonable ways of achieving a legitimate governmental objective, *the means least restrictive of human freedom must be chosen.* (Italics added.)

Subject to the limitations on the use of *travaux préparatoires* by the courts, the original intention as found by the Report was to adopt a constitutional standard of "the least restrictive means." This is a rewording, however, which is not entirely satisfactory, for it leaves out at least three important ideas: *necessary, practical,* and *democratic society.* We can postpone consideration of "democratic society" for the moment and center on "necessary" and "practical."

The constitution does not command Parliament to employ the "least restrictive means" but to employ the least restrictive of necessary means, necessary un-

408. At 4.

derstood from the practical point of view. For, if a restriction cannot exceed what is necessary then all unnecessary restriction, subject to severability, is void. The measuring rod of constitutionality then is the least restriction necessary. And to determine what is necessary one is forced to consider what is practical. In this connection it seems correct that if two measures are equally capable of achieving a desired objective, then as a *practical* matter they are the same though from the standpoint of individual liberty one may restrict it much more than the other. The one that is the more restrictive may be thought "necessary" on account of, let us say, secondary aesthetic or cultural advantages yet perhaps these are not practical necessities. Or the more restrictive measure may be considered necessary because it affords certain conveniences of enforcement or administration, yet if the inconvenience caused by their absence does not thwart the main aim of the measure perhaps they should not be deemed necessary. Again the more restrictive measure may have the virtue of accomplishing completely the legislative aim, yet if that aim can accommodate incomplete though *substantial* fulfillment by a less restrictive measure perhaps the first should not be considered necessary. Finally, and without pretension of exhaustiveness, a more restrictive and widely phrased measure may be thought necessary not in terms of the everyday requirements but for the reserve power to meet contingencies or rare occurrences. But restrictions that cater for the remote are, arguably, not practical necessities.

It has been said earlier that under other constitutions courts are, and perhaps should be, chary to choose between competing reasonable means. A self-imposed rule restrains them to respect the judgment of the legislature. The Lesotho Constitution, however, has thrust upon the courts the task of making these difficult and vexing choices. A number of examples may make this clearer.

In the field of freedom of expression, let us suppose that the state wishes to prevent children under twelve from viewing certain kinds of motion pictures that make a great display of sex. Rather than banning such films altogether, in which case the restriction would be excessive,[409] the state enacts that this variety of film can only be shown on a weekday on the rational supposition that schoolchildren, as a rule, attend the cinema during weekends. Some restriction on freedom of expression remains however, in that adults and children over twelve are deprived of viewing during weekends what (to them) is constitutionally protected expression. The burning issue in Lesotho would be to determine whether the legislature has chosen the least restrictive of necessary (and rational) means. Thus it might be pointed out[410] that the state could have chosen the simpler path of prohibiting by criminal sanction the entry of and sale of tickets by theatre owners to children under twelve. This method not only efficiently excludes the very persons who perhaps ought not to see such films but does not unnecessarily infringe the freedom of those who have a constitutional right to do so.

Or again, in the realm of freedom of conscience, it has been held in certain countries that the non-invidious "indirect burdens" on the freedom are constitutionally acceptable.[411] Thus stores may be closed

---

409. Perhaps the closest analogy is Butler, *supra* note 370, discussed *supra* at p. 379.

410. But whose burden is it to suggest alternate and less restrictive means, the applicant or the respondent? Is this a matter the court may even raise of its own motion?

411. *See* Braunfeld v. Brown, 366 U.S. 599 (1961), (re-

by law on Sundays though Jewish storeowners, who must in conscience close also on Fridays, are financially disadvantaged.[412] Or national elections may be set on a Saturday, though Seventh Day Adventists cannot in conscience vote on their day of absolute rest.[413] Or the state may decline unemployment compensation to those who have refused "available employment" entailing Saturday work out of religious scruples.[414] Given the goals of the legislation, has Parliament chosen the least restrictive path? Concerning the rights of the Jewish storeowner, clearly a law would be less restrictive if statutory exceptions provided that Jewish stores may remain open on Sunday. The state might argue, however, that this exceptional activity may thwart the goal (thought to be necessary) of one day of complete rest for everyone. However, if the legislature is not empowered to restrict more than is practically necessary, is it entitled to seek complete compliance or is substantial realisation of its goal its only legitimate constitutional alternative?

Referring now to the second example, again there is little doubt that an electoral law would be less restrictive if national elections were held on a neutral day so that even Seventh Day Adventists could vote. On the other hand, electoral experience may conclusively establish that, given the general pattern of business and social behaviour in the nation, more people

---

printed in LOCKHART, KAMISAR & CHOPER 618; McGowan v. Maryland, 366 U.S. 420 (1961), reprinted in LOCKHART, KAMISAR & CHOPER 609.

412. Braunfeld v. Brown, *supra* note 411.

413. Ojiebe v. Ubani, [1961] 1 All N.L.R. 277. The facts of the case are used purely for illustrative purposes. The holding cannot be said to permit indirect burdens.

414. Sherbert v. Verner, 374 U.S. 398 (1963). Again the case is not cited for its holding (which disagrees with the text) but for its illustrative facts.

will in fact exercise the franchise on Saturday than on any other day. Tuesday may be a neutral day, but Saturday is best. However, if in rejoinder it were pointed out to the court that a simple exception to the electoral law could go between the restricting horns—*e.g.*, that Seventh Day Adventists could be allowed to vote (similar to absentee-voting procedure) either beforehand or afterwards—then it would appear that the state had not chosen the least restriction necessary after all.

Finally, where religious scruples prevent Saturday work and thereby disqualify an applicant for unemployment compensation, clearly an exception carved into the statute would soften its impact. But on the state's behalf it could be said that such an exception might encourage the filing of fraudulent claims by "unscrupulous claimants feigning religious objections to Saturday work" in which case the compensation fund would be diluted and employers prevented from accomplishing necessary Saturday work. Yet is this degree of restriction "necessary in a practical sense" where there is no proof of fraudulent claims to warrant such fears?[415] Restrictions imposed to cope with speculative evils do not seem to us to be necessary in a practical sense.

Though parallels drawn from the sphere of private law are to a certain extent rightly viewed with diffidence by students of constitutional law, it is instructive to note a thoroughly similar judicial standard employed in the field of delict. In delict, where

---

415. The court in Sherbert, *Id.* said that unproven fears could not justify the restriction. But even if such fears were warranted "it would plainly be incumbent upon the appellees to demonstrate that no alternative forms of regulation would combat such abuses without infringing First Amendment rights. . . ."

the legislature has granted by statute the authority to defendant to carry out certain functions, the courts will not recognise the defence of statutory authority —that the legislature intended to abridge rights normally protected by the law of delict—unless it is shown that "all possible methods of exercising the power will cause invasion of plaintiff's rights." [416] Thus for example, a municipality's authority to establish a garbage site is not a good defence to an action for nuisance where it can be shown that there are other sites of equal suitability that would not produce damage to landowners.[417] Hence, it is considered "negligent" to have chosen "a bad method, in that there was another method 'reasonably practicable' which would, if adopted, have caused less or no injury." [418] Thus, the delictual standard applied to private acts authorised by statute, like the constitutional standard applied to those acts of the legislature authorised by the Constitution, is an attempt to restrict governmental interference to that minimum consistent with governmental effectiveness. The tendency of both is to maximise the freedom of the individual.

(b) ". . . In a Democratic Society . . ."

Democracy is not a neat term and as a constitutional standard it suffers from several deficiencies. First courts may experience difficulty in applying the term in the scientific sense, *i.e.*, popular government, for thoughts immediately run to the tyrannies of pure and nominal democracy. It would indeed be a grotesque conclusion to learn that what is necessary in a practical sense is the expedient guillotine of Revolutionary

---

416. Bloemfontein Town Council v. Richter, [1938] A.D. 195, 231.

417. Tobiansky v. Johannesburg Town Council, [1907] T.S. 134.

418. *Supra* note 416.

France. On the other hand, perhaps the term is intended to convey an impression of the rule of law and libertarian values historically associated with certain, but by no means all, democratic societies. If so, perhaps it would have been better to refer to those values or those societies.

In any event it is submitted that the criterion of "democracy" should tend to look in two directions. It should be introspective because Lesotho too is a democracy, and its real or imagined needs for the circumscription of individual liberties become a datum as valid as the experience of any other democracy. From this point of view it is an understandable tendency to reword the standard to read "in [our] democratic society." [419] In tension, however, against undue introspection are the steadying values to be extracted from other democratic societies. It would be captious to demand precision from an overall view of democratic societies but, as has been suggested, the benefit may be to provide some notion of the lowest common denominator of democratic behaviour.[420] In this sense it may serve as a kind of objective index to the visceral reactions of democratic countries. Here one is reminded of Cardozo's language: is there

> . . . a hardship so acute and shocking that our policy will not endure it? Does it violate those "fundamental principles of liberty and justice which lie at the base of all our civil and political institutions"? [421]

Such mind-channeling phrases may to some extent

419. As Chief Justice Ademola did in DPP v. Obi, [1961] All N.L.R. 186.

420. COWEN, THE FOUNDATIONS OF FREEDOM 128-129 (O.U.P. 1961). The more mundane effect of the standard may be to put a *prima facie* stamp of persuasiveness or nonpersuasiveness on cited comparative materials.

421. Palko, *supra* note 308.

place in relief a question of preventive detention or academic freedom.

One is tempted to add, however, that the superficial use of a comparative standard—the quick scan of the legal horizon—is almost worse than none at all, is positively misleading and destructive. Cases are but glimpses. Not only must one not go lightly into the reports, one must go beyond them to interpretive works, not the least of which is history. In this context one can only note as disingenuous the comparative approach of Hathorn J. in *Musururwa v. Attorney-General of Southern Rhodesia.*[422] Labouring with the question whether laws against sedition are to be found in a society that has a "proper respect for the individual," Judge Hathorn discovered that sedition was a punishable offence at English, Scottish, and Roman-Dutch common law and also an offence in the United States though not called sedition. Deeming this discovery "of greatest importance in the present inquiry," Hathorn J. concluded there was no case for going behind the Minister of Law and Order's certificate that stated that the law was necessary in the interests of public safety and order.

With respect, this will not do. First, it was dubious to characterise the Unlawful Organisations Act[423] as a law against sedition, for as Judge Hathorn's own research in the Shorter Oxford English Dictionary's definition of sedition should have demonstrated, an act empowering the declaration of unlawful organisations on grounds so divergent and vague as endangering public safety, prejudicing tranquility and good order, and promoting feelings of ill-will or hostility between

422. *Supra* note 405 and [1963] 4 S.A. 720 (S.R.).

423. Act 38 of 1959, as amended by Act 9 of 1963, recompiled as Unlawful Organisations Chapter 81, Volume II STATUTE LAW OF SOUTHERN RHODESIA (revised edition, 1963).

the races does not fall *proprio vigore* under a criminal classification of "a concerted effort to overthrow an established government." The first requisite of accurate comparison is accurate characterisation of the ground of reference. Second, it is not enough to decide without explanation which societies have a proper respect for the individual and then fasten upon the narrowest indicium of the quality of that respect, a common-law crime or a statute, as good evidence that proper respect tolerates laws against sedition. If the phrase "proper respect for the individual" is not to provoke a game of labels, some effort must be made to understand the substantive meaning of seditious behaviour in foreign countries in contexts of stress and nonstress and in light of any procedural restrictions (such as the minister's certificate). Such an effort is, to some extent, at the mercy of available library resources and materials, especially in financially embarrassed parts of Africa; yet perhaps this should only serve to increase the need to avoid dogmatic assessments. In any event such an approach may help one to avoid the trap of believing that there is no substantive difference between sedition in the United States and sedition in Southern Rhodesia.

(c) ". . . In the Interests of . . ."

This section of the test is a phrase with a wide ambit of connotations. It is found in numerous constitutions but never arranged in the precise fashion we find in the Lesotho Constitution. Its unique setting should make us wary of uncritical importation of foreign precedents.

It is apparent that if this phrase were to be construed simply on its own terms it would present the usual range of questions concerning substantive and procedural reasonableness. The recurrent question is, as usual, this: In what form and for what reasons will a restraint upon a fundamental right be "in the interests of" defence, public safety, public health, public morality? In some constitutions, notably the Indian, there is no other standard of reasonableness. Thus under the Indian Constitution it is said that for a law to be "in the interests of" one of the great heads postulates a rational and proximate relationship between the two. Yet the degree of rational connection is put on an indefinite footing by the breadth of meaning inhering in the term *interest,* a breadth that can only be increased through the use of the plural of that word. There is an *obiter dictum* in one Indian case that the phrase may have a wider meaning than "for the maintenance of" and should include anything that even indirectly helps to realise one of the great heads.[424] It follows that the legislature is authorised to take measures to curb at an early stage tendencies that it perceives will bring about harm at a later time subject to the requirement of some proximate relationship.[425] As Justice Gurtu observed:

> Some limited meaning must necessarily be given to the words "in the interests of public order" and, in my view, a restriction to prevent an imaginary chance of disturbance of public order or a chance of disturbance of public order in the remote future or an infinitesimal present chance of disturbance in the immediate future could not be justified in the "interest of public order." [426]

Were this to be the accepted approach under the Lesotho Constitution it would set at naught the stringent concept of practical *necessity* which is also a prominent part of the constitutional standard under

---

424. *Supra* note 371, at 104.
425. BASU, *supra* note 176, at 552, 574-575.
426. *Supra* note 371, at 114.

discussion. It is puzzling that whereas necessity imposes a heightened test of rational and proximate nexus, "in the interests of" seems to reduce the whole to a lower level. When faced with this tension between the parts of the overall standard it seems wrong to attempt to eliminate the tension by concluding that "in the interests of" is not a test of reasonableness at all but simply a verbal conjunction leading into the saving heads of authority. On this theory the true problem would only be the determination of what laws pursuant to the saving heads of authority are practical necessities in a democracy. On the other hand, assuming that there is a tension between two standards of differing constitutional rigidity, it would seem equally wrong to impute to one a priority over the other and in that way to resolve the difficulty.[427] Our reason is that the Constitution gives us no other indication than that the test is integral, that "in the interests of" has a contributive meaning that ought to be taken into account, and that there is no ostensible priority established save those *created by the words themselves*. The proper construction, it is submitted, is that an impugned law is judged from both a wide and narrow view of constitutionality and that it must succeed under both in order to be valid. Though many things are "in the interest of" say, public safety, not as many can be said to be necessary in a democracy and perhaps fewer still can be said to be practical necessities in a democracy. On this view the court need not choose between tests, but only allow the tests to function according to their literal rigidity or flexibility. If this means that

427. It would also be out of place to maintain that "necessary in a practical sense" modifies the restriction and "in the interests of" modifies the saving heads. The more probable construction would be that every word following "necessary" is a modifier of it.

the narrow view, like Occam's razor, is the more efficient, this is because the Constitution, and not its interpreters, has chosen it.

(d) ". . . Defence, Public Safety, Public Order, Public Morality, and Public Health."

These five great heads of authority appear in all imprecise saving clauses in the Constitution. It would be virtually impossible to categorise the exhaustive potential in each; however, it may suffice to illustrate their general meanings.

Defence. The interest in defence implies protection from external attack upon the realm and the authority to anticipate and prepare for this event by the financing and development of land and air defence forces.

Public Safety and Public Order. The interest of society in public order expresses itself mainly through the peace-keeping provisions of the criminal law. Public order, in this sense, is germane to public safety because safety is a by-product of public peace. This may explain why laws grounded respectively in each, such as the Internal Security Act of 1967 and the Public Order Proclamation of 1964,[428] seek to regulate or proscribe much the same kinds of activities. Thus both safety and order underwrite the existence of the police and its various powers and duties of patrol, surveillance, control over public movement in the street, the granting of protection, prevention of violence, and the apprehension of criminals. They likewise support the function of a fire department and the regulation of street parading, public gatherings, military drilling in public, and the like.[429] Public safety more than anything else, however, would seem to be the chief justi-

428. Repealed by the Printing and Publishing Act of 1967.

429. *E.g.*, Internal Security (Public Meetings and Processions) Act of 1966.

fication for many preventive regulations typically found in statute books, such as fire ordinances, industrial safety equipment, building codes, and highway speed limits. It is clearly foremost in the quarantining of public disease, and the purification of foods and drugs.

Public Health. Public health may be hazarded by the activities, the possessions, and the physical condition of each person in society. Harmful activities such as the pollution of air and streams, the consumption of narcotics and liquor, and the smoking of dagga may be interdicted on the ground of public health. The ownership or possession of diseased livestock, infected plants and trees, and slum property may also fall into this category. The same public interest may circumscribe an individual's bodily freedom or integrity, such as marital prohibitions between close kin, sexual sterilisation of the congenitally feebleminded, prescribed hygienic burial procedures, and the sequestration of carriers of communicable diseases.

Public Morals. Legislation connected with public morals usually relates to gambling, liquor, vice, and fraudulent or dishonest practices. Additionally all varieties of lascivious conduct, sexual perversions, and illicit intercourse would fall under this rubric, not to mention the control of cruelty to animals and brutal or sadistic sports.

It is characteristic of these five heads of authority that they embody an exceedingly broad range of permissible legal ends that overlap in many cases. For example, if there is an injurious activity within the kingdom, it may be in the interest of both safety and public order to bring it under control. Likewise, many measures that relate to public health may as well relate to public safety, such as compulsory vaccination and the institutionalisation of the insane.

To acknowledge the broadness of these concepts, however, is not to say that they have no terminal points. The law may exist that cannot conceivably fall under one of them. The word "public" may be an important boundary marker wherever it is used. Public morality, for example, suggests the antithesis of private morality. For those persuaded by the Wolfenden Report, homosexual relations between consenting adults is a question for private conscience and is not within the domain of public morality. Similarly, the Basotho, though increasingly Christian monogamists in modern times, have consistently disappointed the ecclesiastical authorities with their refusal to treat the practice of polygyny as a moral question. Indeed it requires invincible hubris to expect that they should.[430] For the same reason the distinction between the public and private spheres of safety, order, and health could also present troublesome questions for the future.

It is an elementary point that the great heads of authority are constitutional sources of authority not criminal standards of liability. Constitutional guides for Parliament, the executive, and the courts are emphatically too broad and vague to serve as critical standards restricting individual liberty. This fundamental distinction, however, has not always been recognised by the draftsmen of Lesotho's statutes.

An unfortunate example is the Printing and Publishing Act of 1967. It makes criminal the printing, publishing or possession of any statement that is a "clear and present danger [431] to public safety, public order, public morality, or fundamental human rights and freedoms . . . ." This mode of drafting attempts

430. *Cf.* Reynolds v. U.S., 98 U.S. 145 (1878).

431. The first four words quoted from the statute are the celebrated test of Justice Holmes in Schenck v. U.S., 249 U.S. 47 (1919).

to overcome the necessity of enumerating any specific offences, some of which were repealed by the Act's provisions, such as the well-known crimes relating to obscenity, sedition, subversion, and libel,[432] others of which hitherto have not been recognised or declared to be criminal.

Due to its vagueness, this statute fails to warn. "Men of common intelligence," in Justice Frankfurter's words, "must necessarily guess" at its meaning.[433] The vice of vagueness also encroaches upon a most vital principle of the rule of law: "that no man is punishable or can be lawfully made to suffer in body or goods except for a distinct breach of law." [434] We know too that all this is not "necessary in a practical sense," for greater precision was already achieved by the earlier statutes repealed by the act. The Constitution is not content with generality where specificity is known to be possible. "[P]recision must be the touchstone of legislation so affecting basic freedoms." [435] Furthermore, though the statute's vagueness fails to provide warning, its very overbreadth manages to have a chilling deterrence upon the exercise of expression in Lesotho.[436] This master crime consists of all derogation authorised by the saving clause, and the perilous burden of deciphering the potential subdivisions of crime camouflaged within its nebulous terms is placed upon the individual.

---

432. Respectively the Obscene Publications Proclamation of 1912, Public Order Proclamation of 1964 (in provisions relating to sedition and subversion), and the Newspaper Regulation Proclamation of 1917 (in provisions relating to seditious libel).

433. *See* references *supra* note 385.

434. DICEY, *supra* note 192, at 179.

435. NAACP v. Button, 371 U.S. 415, 438 (1963).

436. *Cf.* Aptheker v. Secretary of State, 378 U.S. 500 (1964).

(3) INTERRELATED STANDARDS: DISCRIMINATION AND THE EQUAL PROTECTION OF LAW

(a) Discrimination: The Contour of the Standard

The Constitution of Lesotho in section 17 requires over 650 words in order to establish freedom from discrimination. Sixty percent of this represents extensive savings. If this wordiness means anything, it is a warning that Lesotho's problems with discrimination are not clear cut. Before passing to its interrelation with the guarantee of Equal Protection of Law, it may be helpful to see in outline the main features of this lengthy provision.

(i) What Is Discrimination?

Subsection (1) decrees that "no law shall make any provision that is discriminatory of itself or in its effect." This last phrase "of itself or in its effect" means a law discriminatory by its very terms ("on its face") or in its execution or application ("as applied"). This aside, what does "discriminatory" mean? The Constitution in subsection (3) says:

> In this section the expression "discriminatory" means affording different treatment to different persons attributable wholly or mainly to their respective descriptions by race, tribe, place of origin or residence, sex, political opinions, colour, or creed whereby persons of one such description are subjected to disabilities or restrictions to which persons of another such description are not made subject or are accorded privileges or advantages which are not accorded to persons of another such description.

With that definition in mind, we may merely underscore certain of its significant criteria to which we can return later. First, the treatment afforded must be *different* from that which others receive. Second, the reason for the different treatment must be *wholly* or mainly due to a description by race, colour, creed, etc. Third, "different treatment" may be negative or positive. It may consist of disabilities imposed upon the complaining party or of privileges conferred upon a third person.

(ii) Who Is and Is Not Protected by the Right?

It may at once be noted that citizens alone are protected against discriminatory laws.[437] Parliament therefore may pass by ordinary act a law that discriminates against aliens, corporations,[438] and perhaps foundations. Yet until such laws are passed, all persons, citizens or not, enjoy the same protection. Furthermore all persons are entitled to be *treated* in a nondiscriminatory "manner" by all public servants whose entitlement to act is pursuant to written law.[439] No person, therefore, need tolerate discriminatory abuse or insults from a member of officialdom, for such conduct treats the individual in a "discriminatory manner." However, if a law itself discriminates against aliens, obviously the application of that law, within its terms, to aliens by an official should be distinguished from treatment in a "discriminatory manner." Finally, with respect to access to public accommodations, all persons, citizens and aliens alike, receive constitutional protection against treatment in a "discriminatory manner." Public accommodations would comprise shops, hotels, lodging houses, public restaurants, eating houses, beer halls or places of public entertainment as well as any place of public resort maintained wholly

437. § 17(4) (a). Discussed *supra* at pp. 338-339.

438. Though a corporation is considered a juristic "person" (see Interpretation Act, 1889 pursuant to section 139(15)), it is strongly doubted that a corporation can be a "citizen." In India it is settled that a corporation cannot be a citizen. BASU, *supra* note 176, at 546.

439. § 17(2).

or partly out of public funds or dedicated to the public use. Not only is access a constitutional right but even where granted it must not be done in a "discriminatory manner." It may also be noted that the constitutional right extends even against purely private acts of discrimination by individuals—acts that are unsupported by any form of state action or participation.[440]

(iii) What Is and Is Not Protected by the Right?

There are five classes of laws that are expressly saved no matter how discriminatory their effect may be. The first and most important of these is the customary law of Lesotho.[441] It will never be deemed discriminatory when it is applied to those persons who are subject to it.[442] For instance the rules of customary law relegating women to an inferior status are not subject to attack because of their discriminatory effect. Second, the "personal law" of an individual, that is, laws relating to marriage, divorce, burial, devolution of property on death, and the like, may be applied without being considered discriminatory.[443] This pro-

440. Section 4(2) makes it clear that fundamental rights protect against private or state interference, unless the context of the provision in question requires otherwise. Discussed *supra* at pp. 339-343. Compare the position in India which guarantees solely against "state action": Shamdasani v. Central Bank of India, [1952] S.C.A. 36, reprinted BASU, *supra* note 286, Vol. I at 68-70.

441. § 17(4)(c).

442. The constitutional language saves the validity of customary law when applied to "persons who, under that law, are subject to that law." It is therefore to customary law that one must look to answer the question, "Who is subject to customary law?" This sets up a choice of law question of great complexity, especially where customary law is not clear about the extent of its application. It is only clear that a law, not in accordance with custom, that subjects a citizen to customary law may be unconstitutional if the custom in question is discriminatory.

443. § 17(4)(b).

vision is perhaps wider than the first in its application to diverse sets of peoples. It would seem to save the validity not only of the personal law of different customary systems [444] but the law of persons in the Roman-Dutch system which may well contain certain discriminatory aspects, especially in the realm of marriage. Third, an act of Parliament that appropriates public revenues or funds cannot be impugned for discrimination.[445] Such a law does not of course impose taxes or remit debts but merely earmarks *accrued revenues* to be spent for specific purposes.[446] Fourth, a law is not to be deemed discriminatory which sets up qualifications for employment in public service, local government, or the police so long as these qualifications do not *specifically relate* to description by race, sex, colour, creed, etc.[447] For instance a qualification requiring that members of the police be able to lift 150 pounds of dead weight may have the effect of excluding all women from their ranks, though the law would not specifically relate to sexual discrimination but to physical ability. Fifth, a law that imposes restrictions judged valid in respect of certain other fundamental rights [448] cannot be held to be discriminatory under

444. This provision does not seem likely to be as important in Lesotho, which is a culturally and legally unified nation, as in some other African countries that comprise various tribes and encounter frequently the phenomenon of interpersonal conflict of laws. *See* Cowen, *Africa Legal Studies—A Survey of the Field and the Role of the United States*, AFRICAN LAW 18-23 (Oceana 1963). Under section 17 the application of personal-law *A* to plaintiff and personal-law *B* to defendant will not amount to discriminatory treatment on the part of the court.

445. § 17(4)(d).

446. This distinction is recognised in § 65.

447. § 17(5).

448. *These are:* freedom of movement (§ 7), freedom from arbitrary search and seizure (§ 10), right to respect for private and family life (§ 11), freedom of conscience (§ 13), freedom of

section 17.[449] Thus if an entire village's freedom of movement is restricted (say) in the interests of public health owing to a raging epidemic, then such a restriction is not incidentally discriminatory.

(iv) The Validity of Laws Not Specifically Saved

If one puts aside the various laws just referred to in (iii), it remains to be considered what is the constitutional test for the validity of other laws that can be said to violate the *prima facie* guarantee of freedom from discrimination. The general test is whether, having regard to the nature of the disability or privilege in question and to any special circumstances pertaining to those persons affected, such a disability or privilege is "reasonably justifiable in a democratic society." Thus even where a law affords different treatment wholly or mainly because of a person's description by (say) race and is in consequence clearly discriminatory within the meaning of the first subsection, the law may still be valid if on account of the nature of the restriction or special circumstances it is reasonably justifiable in a democracy. This may seem curious. It is difficult to conceive how a law can be wholly or mainly based on race if at the same time there are special circumstances or reasons that make the law "reasonably justifiable." The Constitution will tolerate a rational classification based upon special circumstances and the nature of the disability but it is still to be pointed out how such a rational classification could ever be considered attributable wholly or mainly to race in the first place.

The answer may lie in one of two directions. One path is to say that the Constitution recognises the pos-

---

expression (§ 14), and freedom of assembly and association (§ 15).

449. § 17(8).

sibility that a law, the embodiment of sheer prejudice, may nevertheless sometimes be justifiable in a democracy for certain reasons. What reasons there are to overcome what one would have thought was a grotesque result, are not known to the present writers. The other path is to say that the aim of the definition of discrimination in subsection (3) is to define the term as broadly as possible so that subsection (1) affords a broad protective coverage. The error of the first approach is to engage in a substantive analysis to the exclusion of a formal analysis. Thus in deciding to what the words "different treatment" and "wholly or mainly attributable" to a prohibited description refer, should we not accept them as referring not only to purely formal attributions but also substantive attributions to a person's description as well? Thus any law that expressly employs a prohibited description to classify one group differently from another is *prima facie* suspect even though the classification may be proved rational and considered by the court to be reasonably justifiable in a democracy.

For example a law that expressly discriminated according to "place of origin" by reserving a set quota of places at the university for candidates from certain mountain villages would *prima facie* violate the freedom. On examination, however, the discrimination might prove to be reasonable because these particular villages had a special history of educational deprivation and lack of public care. On the other hand, laws that do not expressly employ a prohibited description must nevertheless be pierced and brought within the ambit of the definitional section, for their substantive effect may be discriminatory.

Thus, to vary the above example slightly, a law might require the university to reserve a similar amount of places for candidates who receive their sec-

(b) The Relationship to Equal Protection

Every person shall be entitled to equality before the law and to the equal protection of the law. (Section 18.)

That the law must not discriminate nor deny the equal protection of the laws are companion precepts. Each is concerned to ensure that persons indistinguishably situated do not receive distinguishable treatment under the law. The constitutional command that the law cannot disable some and privilege others sheerly on the basis of "description" merely illustrates the wider principle that equal protection of the laws requires the same treatment for everyone unless there is some good reason for the contrary. This has been well explained by Chief Justice Muhammed Munir:

> [As a broad proposition] equal protection of the laws means that no person or class of person shall be denied the same protection of the laws which is enjoyed by other classes in like circumstances in their lives, liberty, and property and in pursuit of happiness. . . . [It] requires that all persons shall be treated alike, under like circumstances and conditions, both in the privileges conferred and in the liabilities imposed. In the application of these principles, however, it has always been recognised that classification of persons or things is in no way repugnant to the equality doctrine provided the classification is not arbitrary or capricious. (sic), is natural and reasonable and bears a fair and substantial relation to the object of the legislation.[451]

The concept of equal protection of the laws has not the same meaning as the concept of equality before the law. The latter derives from the English doctrine of the rule of law that Dicey said meant that

451. Jibendra Kishore v. The Province of East Pakistan, P.L.D. 1957 L.C. (Pak.) 9.

> . . . every man, whatever be his rank or condition, is subject to the ordinary law of the realm and amenable to the jurisdiction of the ordinary tribunals.[452]

This means that there is fair and equal administration and universal subjection to law from king down to peasant. It does not guarantee "the equal protection of equal laws," for as Lord Wright has said, "All are equally subject to the law, though the law as to which some are subject may be different from the law to which others are subject." [453]

Because the concept of equal protection of the laws is a broader formulation of the principle that underlies the Freedom from Discrimination, it would seem to follow that every contravention of section 17 will be a violation of section 18, though every violation of section 18 need not necessarily violate section 17.

This essential difference lies in the phraseology and formulation. The negative command to Parliament and the executive, that discrimination cannot be instituted, complements and also contrasts with the positive right of every person that the laws shall be equal. Furthermore apart from its negative formulation, section 17 restrictively defines discrimination in relation to a set number of categories, to wit: race, tribe, place of origin or residence, sex, political opinions, colour, or creed. Thus if an applicant to the High Court alleges that a certain statute imposes a capricious classification, discriminatory to him on the basis of his *vocation* in life or his ownership of immovable property or his amount of yearly income, the attack cannot proceed under section 17 but must be brought as a question of the equal protection of the laws because such "descriptions" are not strictly to be found in section

452. *Supra* note 192, at 193-194.
453. (1945) CAMB. L.J. 4.

17. On the other hand section 17, while it places a broad ban on discrimination, also preserves a certain amount of it through its saving clauses. No such saving clause attaches to section 18, however, and if, as section 17(10) declares, the generality of section 18 is not prejudiced by the specificity of section 17, it would follow that an unsuccessful application under section 17 against a law expressly saved or judicially approved as "reasonably justifiable" could succeed under section 18.

Section 17(10), were it to have intended any other result, would have decreed that the generality of section 18 *was limited* by the provisions of section 17. Phrased in a different fashion, it could have declared that a law that is nondiscriminatory could, despite this fact, be a denial of the equal protection of the laws. For example, if Parliament passed a law that declared that all aliens living in Lesotho must pay a basic tax of R5 a year, there is no doubt that under section 17 Parliament would have the power by ordinary act to enact the measure into law. Since, however, equal protection of the laws is guaranteed to every person—citizens, corporations, and aliens alike—why should not such a law violate section 18? Perhaps the answer is that section 17(10) intends merely that the individual protection found in section 17 is neither exclusive nor preemptive and that claims for discrimination in *other* areas may be brought under section 18. It would therefore not intend interference with the logical requirement that the remedies of section 17 should be exclusive *within* their own sphere of operation and that the prescribed definitions and limitations recognised therein must be employed where appropriate. This would mean for example that a claim alleging racial discrimination must be brought under section 17 while another claim alleging discrimination on the basis of profession must be brought under section 18. In sum, the scope of section 17 should be *subtracted* from that of section 18. Thus to the extent that "saved" discrimination would ordinarily be an unjustifiable encroachment upon the principle of equal protection, that discrimination is in effect saved under section 18 as well.

A second source of difficulty, however, is created by the absence of any savings in section 18. When dealing with rights with saving clauses, the courts are prone to follow a principle of strict construction whereby savings not specifically made cannot be introduced by implication, a rule favourable to individual liberty.[454] Should the same approach be taken when no savings are present? Since no power to derogate from the equal protection principle is expressly granted to the state, then no power to make rational classifications can be read in. On this view the right to equal protection of the laws would be subject to the provisions of section 17, an absolute ban against the slightest infringement. This is certainly not an indefensible conclusion, for the purpose could have been to allow rational classifications only with respect to the selected area set out in section 17. The meaning of section 17(10) would then be perfectly clear: the derogations permitted by section 17 are without prejudice to an absolute right protected in other areas by section 18, though section 17 must always be applied to questions with which it specifically deals.

It is highly probable however, that if another reasonable interpretation existed the courts of Lesotho would follow it, for it is not usual to fetter government power so absolutely. First, in construing saving clauses, the principle of strict construction serves the

---

454. Discussed *supra* at pp. 328-331. *See also* Sakal Papers v. Union of India, 1962 S.C. 305, 315. BASU *supra* note 176, Vol. I, 550.

purpose of controlling a power that is already expressly recognised. Where no savings are present the principle need not be applicable. Secondly, since the equal protection guarantee is a right adopted from the American Constitution in its original phraseology and structure, the implied power of the state to classify rationally, which is so thoroughly recognised there, was adopted also. The Indian Constitution also imported the equal protection guarantee and significantly the implied power has been received there and American precedents utilised persuasively.[455] Further, the Indian Constitution in sections 14 and 15 contains somewhat parallel provisions to sections 17 and 18 in the Lesotho Constitution and no problems of the sort hitherto mentioned appear to have troubled the courts.[456]

(c) Excursus: Background to Discrimination in Lesotho

In 1961 the Basutoland National Council appointed a Select Committee on Discriminatory Legislation to investigate the nature, extent, and remedies for discrimination in the laws. This was an understandable expression of concern by the Council, for if the statute books of Lesotho are opened at around the year 1960, one is at first sight struck by the parallels with South Africa. The laws then were rife with racial terminology, racial classifications, and differences of treatment pivoting upon the racial terms "European," "native," and "African." On first impression the principle of such laws would appear to be no worthier than plain racial prejudice.

Such an impression, however, is not entirely ac-

---

455. BASU, *supra* note 176, at 444.
456. *Id.* 505-506.

curate or fair and to explain why, one could divide the laws under three main headings:

1. Laws designed to favour or protect the Basotho.
2. Laws employing racial terminology as description.
3. Laws that may contain invidious discrimination.

(i) Paternalism

British legislation in Lesotho in the 20th Century contains a strong streak of paternalism. Some of this no doubt is owing to the particular form of colonialism practised by the British. Much of it seems explained, however, by the circumstances surrounding the original annexation: a natural sympathy for the beleaguered condition of the country, the latter's straightforward trust in the Queen, and the danger of military defeat by the Orange Free State. Later there may have been a fear of repeating the unfortunate "generosity" of Swaziland in ceding through concession agreements the ownership of much of the nation's land. Later still, as South Africa crystallised its racial policy and concomitantly stepped up its demands on Britain for cession of the High Commission Territories, that cession, though once fully planned, became increasingly incompatible both with original understandings and the Foreign Office's developing sense of trusteeship over Basutoland.[457] General reasons such as these, we submit, together with particular exigencies explain a certain amount of legislation containing racial terms. Thus the *Prohibition of Deposits and Barter Proclamation*, No. 24 of 1942 made it a criminal

457. J. A. Hobson for one believed that Basutoland was the best illustration of a "true" imperial policy. IMPERIALISM 245-246 (3d ed. Allen and Unwin 1938), *but see* ROBINSON, THE DILEMMAS OF TRUSTEESHIP 68-70 (O.U.P. 1965).

offence for a European trader to engage in credit transactions with Africans in which money or security was received as a deposit, though no such offence would be committed by an African trader who was party to a similar transaction. All deposits in the possession of non-African traders had to be returned to the African debtors. The legislation seemed designed to restrict the advantages of trade where there is great inequality of bargaining power between Africans and Europeans. The *Medicine Men and Herbalists Proclamation,* No. 44 of 1948 provided *inter alia* that, "any African who for gain practises as a diviner or as a rain doctor or lightning doctor, or professes a knowledge of witchcraft or of the use of spells or charms, or advises any person to bewitch or injure persons or property, or supplies any person with the pretended means of witchcraft, shall be guilty of an offence," despite the fact that the white missionary movement would have been stillborn if the same terms *mutatis mutandis* had been applied to it. One cannot help but react to the conceit instanced in such a law. The purpose did not appear to be to grant a monopoly to white missionaries [458] as much as to protect the Basotho from the real or supposed dangers of their own (but not European) superstitions.[459] Perhaps a last example [460]

---

458. Though one could plausibly argue this since other sections of the Proclamation require medicine men and herbalists to be licensed, to renounce the European title of "doctor" or "chemist" or "dentist," to deal only in "African medicines" and only in accordance with "Basotho custom."

459. The high incidence of ritual murders (*Diretlo*) in Basutoland, moreover, indicates also that the measure was an attempt to deal with that public order question. *See* JONES *supra* note 19. According to the figures in the report, in 1942 three ritual murders had taken place and the same number had occurred the year before.

460. Examples are numerous. *See* the Game Preservation Proclamation 33 of 1951 (Empowering the Resident Commis-

which if not blatantly discriminatory is certainly the most clearly paternal, is the *Concessions Veto Proclamation,* No. 65 of 1922.[461] It rendered void and unenforceable any prior or future concession or grant of any rights in land by a chief unless approved by Her Majesty's Secretary of State, though this did not disturb the power to grant permission, with the approval of the Resident Commissioner, to any person to occupy land as a site for a mission station, school, store, dwellinghouse, or garden. The purpose was to place stringent external controls over the alienation of land

sioner to licence the hunting of game in Basutoland, but Africans need not acquire such licences); Basutoland Entry and Residence Regulations H.C.N. 38 of 1958 (Requiring fewer forms and documentary information from Africans than non-Africans, *see* 1st Schedule); Protection of Fresh Water Fish Proclamation 45 of 1951 (Allowing Africans, but not non-Africans, to take and possess certain kinds of fish in or out of season without licences by means of certain, otherwise prohibited, modes, though Africans on Government Reserves are not defined as Africans for these purposes); Basuto Courts Proclamation 23 of 1958 (*e.g.*, the rule that no lawyer may appear and act for any party (§ 30) exists presumably in order to protect the court and unrepresented parties from excessive legal niceties. This proclamation incidentally never came into force.) Trading Proclamation 72 of 1951 (Restricted traders licence issuable only to Africans, see Schedule, item 17); Liquor Proclamation 58 of 1948 (outlawing sale of liquor to non-Europeans subject to certain exceptions) later amended by Law 1 of 1962.

461. The proclamation was brought into effect when it was learned that several chiefs were contemplating alienations to Europeans. BUELL, THE NATIVE PROBLEM IN AFRICA 172 (Cass 1965). The proclamation was not exactly discriminatory because no one, not even a Mosotho, was entitled to ownership as understood in the Roman-Dutch law. On the other hand traders, missionaries, or anyone other than a Basotho required the approval of the Resident Commissioner in order to receive a land allocation, which does seem discriminatory. The proclamation was specifically repealed by the Order to the Independence Constitution, § 4(6).

to outsiders while allowing the missions and traders to continue to operate. To a point the statute only enforced Basotho law and custom, which says that all land is inalienable. However the statute goes beyond that custom in that it also acknowledges the fact that grants and concessions with the approval of the Secretary of State would be valid.

(ii) Racial Terminology

Some laws recognise racial classification but do not afford different treatment on that account. Racial terms are used without *practical* or discriminatory consequence, though they nonetheless amount to a form of legislative insult to the individual. Merely to expunge the record of the odious terms usually cures the defect of the law. Thus for instance the *Stamp Duties Proclamation,* No. 16 of 1907 defined "Government employee" to mean "any person, whether European or native . . . employed by the Basutoland Government," and defined "teacher" as "any person, whether European or native, employed as a teacher . . . ." Similarly in the Concessions Veto Proclamation of 1922 one reads:

> No concession or grant of any property or rights of any nature whatsoever heretofore or hereafter made by any Native Chief having authority shall be recognised by any Court of Law. . . .

To remove the word "native" or "European" in such statutes can hardly be said to change the sense or application of the proclamation. The Select Committee on Discriminatory Legislation in its review of the laws systematically deleted these distinctions, one would think because they offend rather than because they have discriminatory effect. Their work shows that one of the minor yet regrettable aspects of the colonial heritage is that the word "native" has lost its legitimacy in the English language. But though its use may excite disgust, laws containing it are not necessarily discriminatory.

(iii) Invidious Discrimination

To the present day observer who looks back upon the pre-independence laws, the validity of some *vis à vis* the Constitution may seem dubious. Their uneven impact, tested by a principle of equality, may appear to have no other apparent rationale than prejudice or invidious purpose. Yet within the context of colonial government an historical motive may have existed which, while nonetheless perhaps invalid or inappropriate today, need not have had a racial root.

To be sure, the colonial mind was not disposed to concern itself greatly with the question of discrimination in any event. The natural consequence of suzerainty is class privilege. Differentiation between the amenities and privileges afforded to the European administrator and the African population may have followed so freely from the premises of the former's presence as to have been accomplished with minimal pain and reflection. Discrepancies bothered the lawgiver then perhaps less than today when economic distinctions between locals and expatriates are nevertheless blithely perpetuated. Indeed the problem of discrimination in the colonial mind may have surfaced only when it did not directly affect him, that is, when class legislation was proposed to apply within the same racial or tribal group rather than between himself and the indigenous world. Thus it was probably not thought extraordinary or unfair to establish segregated schools in Basutoland for the sole education of European children.[462] But to establish compulsory education for the sons of chiefs as a means of strengthening the basis for indirect rule, *this* could be termed im-

462. European Education Rules, G.N. 18 of 1950.

permissible class legislation,[463] an outlook resting on the double-edged proposition that indigenous peoples are entitled to the equal protection of the laws only where European and African interests do not collide.

On the other hand certain forms of class legislation may have been caused by the mechanics of "indirect rule." [464] Since the object was to rule *through* traditional leaders whose powers, though largely unchanged in scope, were given a statutory basis, such statutes would naturally exempt from their authority those persons residing in the country who were not normally subject to the traditional authorities.[465] To take but one example, in the administration of justice, a prerogative traditionally held by the chieftainship, the "native" courts held civil and criminal jurisdiction over causes in which all the parties were "natives." [466] They possessed no jurisdiction over Europeans and the latter received separately administered justice in the High Court and subordinate court system. This classification may appear racial yet its origin may lie not only in the requirements of European pride but in the dictates of a principle of administration. Of course once one moves away from laws dealing principally

---

463. As in Southern Nigeria. *See* BUELL *supra* note 461, at 722.

464. *See* LUGARD, THE DUAL MANDATE Chs. X and XI (Cass 1965); BUELL *supra* note 461, at 717-27; Bull, *Indirect Rule in Northern Nigeria 1906-1911*, ROBINSON AND MADDEN, ESSAYS IN IMPERIAL GOVERNMENT (1963).

465. *See* Chieftainship (Powers) Proclamation No. 61 of 1938. Now repealed and replaced by the Chieftainship Act No. 22 of 1968.

466. *See* the Native Courts Proclamation No. 62 of 1938, §§ 6 and 7. This proclamation has been greatly amended by Proclamation 4 of 1964 and Regulation 10 of 1965; *see* reprint in Vol. 10 (1965) at 1860. *See also* Proclamation 23 of 1958 which, however, has never come into effect. For a complete discussion of the jurisdiction of these courts *see* pp. 127-133 *supra*.

with traditional administration—such as land allocation, dispensation of justice, and maintenance of law and order—then this historical explanation loses most of its force. Context cannot always reprieve what was ugly and wrong. For example, history does not persuasively explain why Europeans should have been able to purchase and drink liquor without legal restriction but Africans as a class were unable to do so unless in possession of a permit from the District Officer.[467] Nor why the High Court should have been authorised by proclamation to pay witness fees on a racial criterion, that is, payment in graduated descending amounts to Europeans, Coloured, and "aboriginal Africans"; [468] or why European policemen, whatever their rank, were empowered to detain imported or exported articles,[469] to admit an accused to bail,[470] and to enter certain

---

467. Liquor Proclamation No. 58 of 1948, § 23, the racial reference later amended by Law 1 of 1962, *but see* reprint LAWS OF BASUTOLAND Vol. VII (1962) stating that § 23 is repealed. By an ordinance of 1854, Moshoeshoe had prohibited any importation of spirituous liquors into the country, but the measure was not discriminatory in its effect on different races. But "the system of permits and exemptions" wrote the Select Committee on Liquor Proclamation in 1961 "is one of the most discriminatory in the Liquor Proclamation since it applies only to one section of the population. . . . The tide is changing and your Committee feels it would be sheer fantasy to assume that the Basuto (*sic*) shall tolerate to remain in their present plight to placate the stupid resistance of a fanatic, selfish, and racialistic European minority that does not want the Basuto (*sic*) to assert their right to freedom and human dignity in their own homeland." *Report of the Select Committee*, p. IV (1961).

468. Witnesses Allowances Proclamation 9 of 1925, H.C.N. 78 of 1925, § 1. A "station of life" test could be applied to raise basic rates, but the basic rates discriminated according to race.

469. Exportation and Importation Restriction Proclamation 61 of 1921, § 10(1).

470. Criminal Procedure and Evidence Proclamation No. 58 of 1938, § 114(2).

premises [471] while no African policeman, regardless of rank, was empowered to do so. *In consimilii casu* should it have been a crime to incite Africans but not Europeans to rebellion? [472] Why should the births and deaths of all persons *other than Africans* be recorded if this placed every other race on a higher footing? [473] Such discrimination does not dissolve upon historical analysis unless imaginary explanations are provided.

What is essential to realise, however, is that since independence classifications based upon "colonial reasons," whether those be racial or rational in context, have ceased to be valid unless they are rational in the new context of democratic freedoms. If changing times have sapped their *raison d'être,* history cannot cure their present evil, for the Constitution would conform such existing laws to the standard of section 17.

(d) Laws not "Reasonably Justifiable in a Democratic Society"

In an analysis of a case concerning discrimination under section 17 of the Lesotho Constitution, there are three questions of particular significance. What is meant by "different treatment"? When is different treatment *attributable wholly or mainly* to an individual's description? What discrimination is reasonably justifiable in a democratic society? The first two

---

471. Obscene Publications Proclamation No. 9 of 1912, § 4, racial reference later amended by Law 6 of 1962. Employment of Women and Children Proclamation No. 71 of 1937, § 1. Wheat and Wheaten Products Control Proclamation 64 of 1941, § 3, racial reference later amended by Law 4 of 1963.

472. § 2 Proclamation 18 of 1899, now incorporated as § 7 of Sedition Proclamation 44 of 1938, racial references deleted by Law 2 of 1962.

473. Registration of Births and Deaths Proclamation No. 17 of 1947.

questions have been dealt with earlier, and the following discussion will center on the third.

Certainly it cannot be maintained that discrimination can *never* be "reasonably justifiable" in a democracy, for otherwise restrooms could not be partitioned according to the sex of the users nor pacifists be exempted from military combat on the basis of their religious beliefs. The Constitution without doubt acknowledges a power to make such rational classifications as long as they do not clash with domestic values. But when is a classification rational and when does it overstep the limits of democratic tolerance? Would a special tax on all Europeans in Lesotho be reasonable on the basis of being a kind of surcharge for alleged abuses of the Colonial Era? Some of the resident Europeans may have had no hand in the alleged abuses; however, could the law's overly broad classification still be maintained in the interests of convenient administration? Still, what kind of prospective guarantees are afforded the Europeans if past and putative sins can be resurrected; or is the answer that the past is buried but at present great inequalities exist between "advanced" and "backward" segments of the population, which must be reduced? Would it still need to be shown that all Europeans are "advanced" and no Basotho are other than "backward"?

Consider the problem of alcohol. It seems to be thought in some quarters that North American Indians, Eskimos,[474] and the Basotho [475] are seduced more easily than others by the intoxicating effects of liquor. In the unlikely event that the Parliament of Lesotho were to outlaw the sale of liquor to Africans but not

474. DOUGLAS, WE THE JUDGES 399 (1956).

475. Liquor Proclamation No. 58 of 1948, § 23; *see supra* note 467.

to Europeans on the justification that the former possess this "special trait," would the law be reasonable? We would want to know, would we not, what proof there is that *all* Basotho share this "special trait" and what proof that *no* European is similarly handicapped. It seems highly unlikely that such generalisations are true or required unless we accept the answer that though there are exceptions to the rule in both classes, it would be too difficult for Parliament to provide administrative machinery to account for them.

Suppose that Parliament without a word of explanation, reinstituted a separate schooling for European and African schoolchildren in Maseru.[476] Would this be reasonable? Under the right circumstances certain rational motives could be imputed to Parliament's collective purpose which the court would no doubt mention: Sharp language differences might make separate classes more efficient; cultural differences can be said to require teachers and books responsive to the special needs of each set of students. But in Lesotho today it is neither the case that the Basotho speak no European languages, nor that all Europeans have a common tongue. Culturally many Basotho have adopted European "modes of life" and some Europeans may be said to have adopted a "Basotho way of life." Even aside from this, would separate schooling be justified if it is true that

> . . . to separate them from others of similar age and qualification solely because of their race generates a feeling of inferiority as to their status in the community that may affect their hearts and minds in a way unlikely ever to be undone.[477]

Questions such as those posed above cannot be

---

476. *Cf.* European Education Rules G.N. 18 of 1950.

477. Brown v. Board of Education, 347 U.S. 483 (1954).

answered without taking into account at least three points.[478]

First, a law that is reasonable must rest on empirical evidence; a rational classification is a question of fact. Further it ought to affect not necessarily all persons but only those which, rationally, it ought to affect.

Second, the law must additionally be justifiable in a democracy. No doubt the racial laws of the Third Reich were defended "rationally" by their proponents, but to a democrat they violated every sense of fairness.

Third, the two requirements just listed may become distorted to a certain extent by the process of judicial review. Two points are often stressed here: the limited fact-finding powers of a court, and the presumption of constitutionality. The court may accept the principle that classifications should be empirical while at the same time plead that it is not a research team or an investigating committee of the Assembly and therefore cannot prove or disprove what the legislature says is fact. On the other hand, while accepting the veracity of the evidence that the legislature credits, the court is entitled to question the reasonableness of any legislative conclusions drawn from that evidence. With respect to the presumption of constitutionality, the court may show due respect for the legislature's good judgment and pure motive. Where the legislative purpose is unclear, the court may, in all deference, attribute a constitutional purpose if one exists that is plausible and reasonable. Of course if no good purpose can even be imagined, then there is no recourse other than to invalidate the law as unjusti-

---

478. *See generally* the lucid treatment of ten Broeck and Tussman reprinted in SELECTED ESSAYS, *supra* note 308, at 789.

fied. Somewhere in the midst of such considerations, the court may listen to the claim that the legislature possessed the *mens rea* deliberately to punish, insult, or abuse one segment or individual of the population. Such a motive is forbidden, but clear detection of its existence is not easy. Legislation inherently is shaped by a variety of motives and special interests. Further, the court must virtually charge the Parliament with lack of integrity and bad faith, and may have to maintain that Parliament masked its guilty intent with red-herring rationales couched in the act or inserted in the debates. To add to its confusion, the court may find that though a forbidden motive is present, an unintended rational purpose exists and is in fact a good one. In spite of these difficulties, there are situations—and South Africa and parts of the United States are examples—where a ruling class wears prejudice on its sleeve, and in such a case the court need hardly be said to "discover" an evil intent, for it is impressed by such intent at every turn.

(i) Discrimination Coupled with an Equality

In connection with the foregoing discussion, it will be helpful to discuss the instructive South African decision of *Minister of Posts and Telegraphs v. Rasool.*[479] The question was whether the order of the Postmaster-General to establish separate rooms in the Pietersburg post office for Europeans and non-Europeans was reasonable or not in terms of his powers under Act 10 of 1911 to establish, maintain, and abolish post offices and "issue such instructions as he may deem necessary for the conduct and guidance of offi-

479. [1934] A.D. 167. This case is properly classified as an administrative law decision. However if South Africa's Constitution contained a bill of rights it would have been a constitutional case. *See* INNES, JUDICIAL REVIEW OF ADMINISTRATIVE TRIBUNALS IN SOUTH AFRICA 219-21 (Juta 1963).

cers in carrying out the provisions of the Act." The underlying legal principle that the court felt bound by was that the legislature cannot have intended to give authority to make unreasonable rules.[480] It was common cause that the amenities and services in the segregated facilities were equal. Nevertheless the Transvaal Provincial Division had held, following a liberal line of its own cases,[481] that the order was unreasonable and void. In the Appellate Division, Stratford A. C. J. noting that the discrimination was coupled with equal services refused to hold that classification by race is unreasonable, unless it is

> . . . absurd or obviously designed to serve no useful purpose as for example a classification upon the colour of one's hair. But a division of the community on differences of race or language for the purposes of postal services seems, *prima facie*, to be sensible and make for the convenience and comfort of the public as a whole, since appropriate officials conversant with the customs, requirements, and language of each section will conceivably serve the respective sections.[482]

---

480. As in all cases involving bylaws, the court relied upon the principle enunciated by Lord Russell of Killowen in Kruse v. Johnson, [1895-1899] All E.R. 105, [1898] 2 Q.B. 91: "If, for instance, they were found to be partial and unequal in their operation as between different classes, if they were manifestly unjust, if they disclosed bad faith, if they involved such oppressive or gratuitous interference with the rights of those subject to them as could find no justification in the minds of reasonable men, the court might well say Parliament never intended to give authority to make such rules and that they are unreasonable and *ultra vires*."

481. Moses v. Bcksburg Municipality, [1912] T.P.D. 659 (discriminatory housing of "natives and coloureds"). Williams & Adendorff v. Johannesburg Municipality, [1915] T.P.D. 106 (separate trams for Europeans and Coloureds); Swarts v. Pretoria Municipality, [1920] T.P.D. 186 (discriminatory cab service).

482. *Supra* note 479, at 175.

Justice de Villiers, concurring in a separate opinion, posed the hypothetical case of a public office where persons with names beginning with the letters A-to-M are required to transact business in one room and those from N-to-Z in another. Provided this is a discrimination "coupled with equality" it cannot be held unreasonable *per se*. On the same score one cannot condemn outright a division based on colour. However, if the Postal Department ordered that blue-eyed customers must transact in a special room and everyone else in another this would be almost on its face unreasonable. Here he reasoned that

> . . . the ground of unreasonableness would be its gratuitousness. In the language of Lord Russell it would "involve an oppression or gratuitous interference with the right of those subject to it." The position is quite otherwise in the case of discriminations on the grounds of initial letters of names, or on grounds of race or colour, for many reasons may be conceived upon which such discriminations might justly and reasonably be made.[483]

Justice Gardiner made telling points in dissent. First he noted as a practical matter that the Indian population shares a common language not with Africans but with Europeans. Therefore it was in his opinion still to be explained by the majority how their racial classification was rational. More importantly, however, he stressed what the majority ignored, the motive behind the order. The prejudices of the Europeans of South Africa towards the other races are a matter of public history evidenced in numerous discriminatory acts of the legislature creating different statuses for the various races. The common law, on the other hand, recognises two countervailing elements: the principle of the equality of man and the protected

483. *Id.* at 182.

interests of personality expressed in the legal concept of *dignitas*. Entertaining no doubt that "this relegation of Indians to a non-European counter is humiliating treatment," Justice Gardiner continued

> I cannot shut my eyes to the fact that the instruction in question is actuated by the circumstances that a large number of Europeans object to being brought into contact in public offices with non-Europeans, and that they regard the latter as being of a lower order of civilisation.[484]

He therefore concluded that such treatment being an impairment of individual *dignitas,* it could only be brought about by legislative action.

The argument between the majority and minority opinions in *Rasool's* case concerns several themes of general importance. First, does "different treatment" describe or pertain to tangible differences alone or is it ever proper to consider the intangible and psychological effects on the human personality? Is the damage which "different treatment" causes to the individual a real or patrimonial loss only, or does it also comprise intellectual damage for *injuria*? The majority said that discrimination coupled with equality cannot work an inequality or produce damage, presumably neither patrimonial nor intellectual. Such a partition is therefore reasonable provided there is a conceivably rational explanation for it. The dissent asserted that partition causes humiliation to one race and not to the other, and in this sense there is a patent inequality. Second, to what extent should the "real" motives behind the law, however unreasonable, be taken into account or disregarded if the court can impute "rational" motives? Justice Gardiner could not "shut [his] eyes" to the racial purpose of the law but the majority ap-

484. *Id.* at 190.

parently showed greater willingness to impute good motive, an imputation actuated on a principle similar to the presumption of constitutionality.

(ii) Separate but Equal

It is agreed by all hands that where a racial classification is established by law, wherein services and facilities of discrepant quality or quantity are consistently afforded to one race, that this amounts to a discrimination which is unreasonable or, if you will, not justifiable in a democracy. Such a form of "different treatment" is almost invariably unconstitutional. On the other hand, some would argue—but the writers do not—that where a racial classification prescribes for different races separate services and facilities that are of equal quality, that though the treatment be different it is nevertheless reasonable if some rational explanation can be adduced in its support. This proposition found expression in the United States in the phrase "separate but equal" and in South Africa in the phrase "discrimination coupled with an equality." It is said that in either case there is no *tangible* discrimination though there may be intangible discrimination. A word here is necessary to explain these terms for it is submitted they may be taken in various senses.

Tangible vs. Intangible Discrimination. In the first place tangible and intangible discrimination may refer to the causes or to the effects of discrimination. A tangible cause may be one perceptible with the naked eye, touched with the hand, or scientifically ascertained. The focus is upon some external object that is a cause of discrimination, for instance where the state provides some schoolchildren with 1000-calorie lunches and other schoolchildren with only 500-calorie lunches. In contrast, an intangible cause of discrimination is very difficult to measure if it is measurable at all. Here the focus is placed upon the objectified state of mind and feelings of the plaintiff, the defendant, and (perhaps) the legislature. Where *X* refuses to associate with *Y*, for example, whether this is an intangible cause depends upon what *X* intends or means and what *Y* reasonably feels, taking into account such possibilities as *X's* absolute political power, *X's* established public history and public policy of race prejudice, and *Y's* clear susceptibilities and low resistence to feelings of insult. A tangible effect, on the other hand, may have a tangible or intangible cause. It would seem to mean some scientifically *measurable* injury to the plaintiff as a result of discrimination, such as where low-calorie lunches produce nutritional deficiencies in children or where induced feelings of inferiority produce retarded educational development.[485] An intangible effect, which also may result from a tangible or intangible cause, is an effect on the state of plaintiff's mind, perhaps producing lesions of outrage or humiliation, the extent of which cannot be verified with accuracy, as where plaintiff to his humiliation is excluded from a public swimming pool on account of his race.[486]

This terminology, when used in the context of the courtroom, takes on a specialised direction. Lawyers may employ the terms to refer in an oblique fashion to the question of the burden of proof and persuasion, for this burden is no doubt lighter where the discriminatory cause or effect is tangible. They may also have in mind the question of plaintiff's *locus standi* on the theory that intangible damage is not a sufficient *interesse* in the cause of action.[487] In a more significant

---

485. *Supra* note 477, and LOCKHART 660.

486. Mehta v. City of Salisbury, [1962] 1 S.A. 675 (S.R.) (F.S.C.).

487. *Compare* the parallels found in South African administrative law, INNES, *supra* note 479, at 21-31.

sense, lawyers use these terms, again obliquely, to refer to the nature of the damage the plaintiff has suffered. Tangible discrimination may be thought to be associated with patrimonial loss, accrued or prospective, capable of pecuniary assessment. Intangible discrimination, in contrast, may be thought to be identified with intellectual forms of damage impairing the plaintiff's personality on a clear analogy of the interests protected and redressed by the *actio injuriarum*. The extent of damage to the *dignitas* is always a matter of rough judgment. Furthermore the analogy to delictual damages will take into account that non-patrimonial or intellectual damage may result as a consequence of tangible or intangible discrimination. The maxims "separate but equal" and "discrimination coupled with an equality" lay stress on the point that the plaintiff has not suffered patrimonial loss. To the extent that these maxims are deemed to articulate a standard of reasonable treatment, they exhibit that the court is not willing to take into serious account intellectual damage. On the other hand, even though the court professes its willingness to take intellectual damage into account, the problem remains that such damage is difficult to prove.

(iii) The Demise of "Separate but Equal"

Twenty years after *Rasool's* case the historic decision of *Brown v. Board of Education* [488] decided that segregation in the public school system of the United States was a denial of the equal protection of the laws to Negro children. In this decision the Supreme Court distinguished its earlier decision of *Plessy v. Ferguson*,[489] the transatlantic counterpart of *Rasool's* case, wherein an act of the Louisiana legislature re-

---

488. *Supra* note 477.
489. 163 U.S. 537 (1896).

quiring all railway companies to provide "equal but separate accommodations for the white and coloured (sic) races . . ." was deemed to afford equal protection of the laws. The *Plessy* decision resembles *Rasool's* case in its overall approach, but with respect to the question of legislative motive, it made the following remarkable observation:

> We consider the underlying fallacy of the plaintiff's argument to consist in the assumption that the enforced separation of the two races stamps the coloured race with a badge of inferiority. If this be so, it is not by reason of anything found in the act, but solely because the coloured races choose to put that construction upon it.[490]

But of course, said Judge Harlan in dissent, what other construction is possible when

> Everyone knows that the statute in question had its origin in the purpose, not so much to exclude white persons from railroad cars occupied by blacks as to exclude coloured people from coaches occupied by or consigned to white persons . . . . No one would be so wanting in candour as to assert the contrary.[491]

In *Brown v. Board of Education* the Supreme Court totally rejected the proposition of "separate but equal" in the field of public education. The Court's decision proceeded on the theory that education is an experience of crucial importance to an individual's development. Yet racial partition of children causes this experience to be unequal not because Negro children *choose* to construe the situation in an unfavourable light but because unconsenting minors do view the situation unfavourably and with harmful results. Said Chief Justice Warren:

---

490. *Id.* at 655.
491. *Id.* at 656.

> To separate them from others of similar age and qualifications solely because of race generates a feeling of inferiority as to their status in the community that may affect their hearts and minds in a way unlikely ever to be undone.

But the decision does not only rest upon inferiority harboured in the mind or damage through insult to personality. While recognising these intangible factors, the Court also attempted to concretise the effects of such psychological damage through the use of materials from the social sciences to show that "a sense of inferiority affects the motivation of a child to learn. Segregation has a tendency to [retard] the educational and mental development of Negro children . . . ." As a result the court could declare that "separate educational facilities are inherently unequal."

Though the decision in the *Brown* case did not expressly overrule *Plessy v. Ferguson* and though it purported to pronounce a doctrine relevant only to public schools and problems with children of tender years, nevertheless it came to be seen that the back of "separate but equal" was broken for good as subsequent cases extended its *ratio* by analogy into numerous spheres of public life.[492] Racial classification itself had finally been deemed inherently unreasonable.

From the foregoing discussion it is abundantly clear that enlightened opinion regards the doctrine of "separate but equal" to be an unacceptable legal stan-

---

492. Mayor of Baltimore v. Dawson, 350 U.S. 877 (1955) (public beaches and bathhouses); Holmes v. City of Atlanta, 350 U.S. 879 (1955) (municipal golf courses); Gayle v. Browder, 352 U.S. 903 (1956) (seating on busses); New Orleans City Park Improvement Ass'n v. Detiege, 358 U.S. 54 (1958) (public parks and golf course); State Athletic Comm'n v. Dorsey, 359 U.S. 533 (1959) (athletic events); Turner v. Memphis, 369 U.S. 350 (1962) (airport restaurant); Johnson v. Virginia, 373 U.S. 61 (1963) (courtroom seating).

dard. Though still persisting in South Africa,[493] significantly it has been repudiated by dicta in Rhodesia in *Mehta v. City of Salisbury*[494] where Chief Justice Beadle rejected *Rasool's* case and accepted in principle the *Brown* decision. It is submitted that the doctrine cannot be considered appropriate to Lesotho and is not tolerated by section 17 of the Constitution.

---

493. *See, e.g.*, R. v. Pitje, [1960] 4 S.A. 709 (A.D.), where acting under the statutory authority to control the courtroom for the convenience of all, a magistrate's order to an articled clerk who was an African to sit at a segregated non-European table set up by the magistrate was *held* reasonable and a conviction of contempt of court by refusing to obey the order was affirmed. It was considered that the articled clerk was as well seated at one table as at another.

494. *Supra* note 486.

PART III

THE COURTS AND THE LEGAL PROFESSION

THE COURTS AND THE LEGAL PROFESSION

A. The Courts
B. The Judiciary and the Magistracy
C. The Legal Profession
D. Law Reporting

A. The Courts

The structure of the judicial hierarchy appears in diagram form in Appendix D. At the base lie the Central and Local Courts, administering the customary law. Above them stand the High Court, the Court of Appeal, and the Privy Council.* In an intermediate position sit the Subordinate Courts and the Judicial Commissioners' Courts. The various courts will be discussed in turn.

(1) The Judicial Committee of the Privy Council

At the apex of the judicial system stands the

* The High Court, Court of Appeal, and Privy Council were all regulated to a large extent by the 1966 Constitution, and its suspension in 1970, therefore, had a direct impact upon them. Following the *coup d'état* the Chief Justice returned to the Republic of South Africa and refused to hold sessions of the High Court on the ground that its position was uncertain as a result of the suspension of the Constitution. Three months later a new High Court and a new Court of Appeal were established by the Court of Appeal and High Court Order, No. 17 of 1970 and sessions were resumed.

Many of the provisions establishing and regulating those two courts are the same as those contained in the 1966 constitution and the judges themselves continued to hold office in the successor courts. The jurisdiction of the courts was, however, altered in two important particulars. First, appeals to the Judicial Committee of the Privy Council were abolished and thus judgments and orders of the Court of Appeal are now final. Secondly, original and appeal jurisdiction in constitutional interpretation and application have disappeared as a consequence of the suspension of the constitution.

Judicial Committee of the Privy Council. The tendency in recent years has been for former British dependencies to abolish appeals to the Judicial Committee either upon independence or soon afterwards.[1] One of the arguments for keeping such appeals is that the Committee can take, perhaps, a more detached view of the case, especially in constitutional matters where local feelings may run high. On the other hand it may equally be argued that the Committee, sitting in London, thousands of miles away from the country where the case originated cannot hope to grasp the local issues and give a realistic decision which will take these into account.[2]

Whatever the respective merits of these arguments may be, Lesotho retained appeals to the Judicial Committee upon independence and has at the time of this writing taken no steps to abolish them.

(a) Regulation of Appeals

Appeals are governed by the Basutoland, Bechuanaland Protectorate, and Swaziland (Appeals to

1. The following countries abolished appeals to the Privy Council upon independence or soon afterwards: Tanganyika, Ghana, Uganda, India, Pakistan, Cyprus, Kenya, Zambia, Malawi, and Nigeria.

The Privy Council still hears appeals from the following independent Commonwealth countries—Australia (subject to limitations imposed under the Commonwealth of Australia Act 1900, § 74), New Zealand, Ceylon, Malaysia, Jamaica, Trinidad and Tobago, Singapore, Malta, the Gambia, Sierra Leone, Botswana, Swaziland, Barbados, and Guyana.

2. *See, e.g.*, the criticism of Privy Council decisions in appeals from Canada in SCHMEISER, CIVIL LIBERTIES IN CANADA 16-17 (O.U.P. 1964); for some views on its contribution to Nigerian law, see EZERA, CONSTITUTIONAL DEVELOPMENTS IN NIGERIA 275-78 (C.U.P. 1964), NWABUEZE, MACHINERY OF JUSTICE IN NIGERIA 201-06 (Butterworths 1963), and PROEHL, FOREIGN ENTERPRISE IN NIGERIA 55-58 (U.N.C.P. 1965).

Privy Council) Order in Council 1954 [3] as amended by the Basutoland, Bechuanaland Protectorate, and Swaziland (Appeals to Privy Council) (Modification) Order 1965,[4] and the Independence Order in Council 1966.[5]

Appeals may go to the Judicial Committee as a matter of right, or with the special leave of the Committee, or in pursuance of the leave of the Court of Appeal. These three avenues of appeal are treated in turn.

(i) Appeals as of Right

The Constitution provides for such appeals from decisions of the Court of Appeal in respect of:

a. Final decisions in any civil or criminal proceedings on questions as to the interpretation of the Constitution;

b. Final decisions given in exercise of the jurisdiction conferred on the High Court by section 20 of the Constitution (which relates to the enforcement of fundamental human rights and freedoms);

c. Final decisions of the High Court in the determination of any of the questions for the determination of which a right of access to the High Court is guaranteed by section 16 of the Constitution (which relates to the right of persons whose property is compulsorily acquired); [6]

d. Final decisions in any civil proceedings where the matter in dispute on the appeal is of the value of R1,000 or upwards, or where the appeal involves directly or indirectly a claim to or question respecting property or a right to the value of R1,000 or upwards;

---

3. S.I., 1954, No. 1370.
4. No. 132 of 1965.
5. S. I. 1966, No. 1172.
6. § 121(1).

e. Final decisions in proceedings for dissolution or nullity of marriage;

f. Such other decisions in civil proceedings as may be prescribed by Parliament.[7]

In an appeal from Nigeria in the case of *Adegbenro v. Akintola* [8] the Privy Council had to interpret the expression "final decisions" used in a similar context in the Nigerian Constitution.[9] A case involving the interpretation of the Constitution had come before the court of first instance which had referred various issues to the Federal Supreme Court for its determination. An appeal against the decision of the Federal Supreme Court came before the Privy Council and there it was contended for the respondent that the determination by the Supreme Court of issues referred to it by a lower court did not fall within the category of "final decisions." The argument ran that the proceedings that had commenced in the lower courts had not yet been terminated by a final decision. The Privy Council held, however, that the Supreme Court had given *its* final decision, and therefore an appeal did lie to the Privy Council.

The Lesotho Constitution provides for references by a lower court to the High Court of questions involving the interpretation of the Constitution in similar terms to the provisions in the 1960 Nigerian Constitution.[10] Moreover the draftsmen of the Lesotho Constitution seem to have been apprised of the point raised in *Adegbenro v. Akintola,* for the Constitution expressly provides that decisions given in pur-

7. § 122(2).

8. [1963] 3 All E.R. 544.

9. § 114 of Nigeria (Constitution) Order in Council 1960 (S. I. 1960 No. 1652).

10. § 114.

suance of these references are included within the meaning of the expression "final decisions." [11]

It is appropriate at this juncture to mention briefly Rule 2 of the Judicial Committee Rules [12] which might appear to affect appeals as of right. The rule reads:

> All appeals shall be brought either in pursuance of leave obtained from the courts appealed from, or, in the absence of such leave, in pursuance of special leave to appeal granted by Her Majesty in Council upon a petition in that behalf presented by the intending applicant.

At first sight, this provision would seem to outlaw appeals as of right, but it was held in *Chikwakwata v. Attorney-General,*[13] a Rhodesian case, that appeals as of right still lie, but it is necessary to go through the formality of obtaining the "leave" of the court appealed from. "Leave" here does not mean that this court has any discretion in the matter, and thus it is really a misleading use of the word. The court merely has to confirm that an appeal does lie as of right so as to relieve the Privy Council of the burden of reaching this decision.

(ii) Appeals with the Special Leave of the Judicial Committee

The Constitution provides that such appeals shall lie from a decision of the Court of Appeal in any civil or criminal matter.[14] The only exceptions relate to succession to the throne and the appointment of a Regent.[15]

---

11. § 121(2).
12. S. I. 1957 No. 2224 (reprinted in LAWS OF BASUTOLAND, VOL. X, 137 at 142 (1965).
13. 1965 R.L.R. 324.
14. § 122(4) of the Constitution.
15. *See*, § 35 of the Constitution and p. 239 *supra*.

Special leave of the Judicial Committee will always be necessary in criminal cases (except those involving questions as to the interpretation of the Constitution), since the Court of Appeal has no right to grant leave in such cases and such appeals do not lie as of right. In addition, special leave will be needed in civil cases if the Court of Appeal has refused its leave to appeal.

(iii) Appeals with the Leave of the Court of Appeal

The Constitution provides that such appeals shall lie in two classes of cases:

a. decisions in any civil proceedings where, in the opinion of the Court of Appeal, the question involved in the appeal is one that by reason of its great general or public importance or otherwise ought to be submitted to the Privy Council; and

b. such other decisions in civil proceedings as may be prescribed by Parliament.[16]

A cursory perusal of Rule 2 of the Judicial Committee Rules might leave one with the impression that the Court of Appeal has the power in all cases to give leave to appeal. However, that this is not the true position is clear from a communication from the Lord Chancellor of England to Beadle C. J.,[17] adopted by the Appellate Division of Southern Rhodesia in *Chikwakwata v. Attorney-General.*[18] The Court of Appeal only has power to give leave where provision is made for the granting of such leave by a Lesotho statute. Since no Lesotho statute, including the Constitution, gives such power in criminal cases, these can only reach the Privy Council pursuant to the grant of spe-

---

16. § 122(3).
17. Reprinted in 1965 R.L.R. 330-31.
18. *Supra* note 13.

cial leave. The Rules are only procedural and do not give a right to appeal where none exists independently.

(b) The Present Legal Position of the Judicial Committee

It is not correct to speak of the Judicial Committee as an English judicial body since its English jurisdiction is limited to a few extremely specialised fields.[19] Nowadays it is almost exclusively concerned with hearing appeals from independent Commonwealth countries, although it does indeed have its roots in the colonial past. Its jurisdiction originated in the royal prerogative, *i.e.*, the fact that the British Sovereign had the special right of being the supreme tribunal of justice in the British Empire. The Judicial Committee was, therefore, in theory at least, merely a body of men who had the function of advising the British Monarch on those judicial matters that were submitted to them. In reality, the Committee's proceedings were and still are strictly judicial proceedings [20] and the Committee is made up of those who presently hold or have held high judicial office in the United Kingdom or Commonwealth.[21] It is current

---

19. *E.g.*, to hear appeals from medical and dental practitioners whose names have been struck off the register by Disciplinary Committees of their respective professions, and also in prize cases.

20. *See generally*, Ibralebbe v. R., [1964] A.C. 900 (P.C.), [1964] 1 All E.R. 251, an appeal from Ceylon; Hull v. McKenna, [1926] I.R. 402; and WADE AND PHILLIPS, CONSTITUTIONAL LAW Ch. 33 (Longmans).

21. The Judicial Committee is made up of the Lord President of the Council (who does not usually sit), the Lord Chancellor, the nine Lords of Appeal in Ordinary (who are members of the House of Lords), the Lords Justices of Appeal (who do not usually sit as they are members of the English Court of Appeal where they are fully occupied), and such other judges or ex-judges of the superior courts of the Commonwealth as are

practice for a majority of "the Board" (which is the expression used to describe a session of the Committee) to consist of judges who presently sit in the House of Lords. However, even its theoretical foundation, being based on the concept of Empire, is now no longer acceptable, and as a result appeals from Lesotho go to the Judicial Committee as a court in its own right [22] —indeed as the highest appellate court for Lesotho. A decision of the Committee is to be enforced in the same way as if it were a decision of the court appealed from and there is a provision in the Constitution to this effect.[23] Thus the old idea that a decision of the Committee was merely the advice of its members to the British Sovereign has, at any rate so far as Lesotho is concerned, passed away. In keeping with its new role based on similar provisions in the laws and constitutions of other newly independent states, the Privy Council is now able to give its judgments in a manner more consonant with a court of law. Whereas formerly only one judgment could be given on the basis that advice to the Sovereign should be unanimous and not contradictory, dissenting opinions have now been introduced.[24]

It should be borne in mind that the Judicial Committee sits in London and not in Lesotho and thus

---

Privy Councillors—Judicial Committee Act, 1833 (3 & 4 Will. 4, c. 41), Judicial Committee Amendment Act 1895 (58 & 59 Vict., c. 44); Appellate Jurisdiction Acts 1908 (8 Edw. 7, c. 51) and 1913 (3 & 4 Geo. 5, c. 21), and the Administration of Justice Act 1928 (18 & 19 Geo. 5, c. 26). Membership at present includes judges from Australia, New Zealand, and Trinidad and Tobago.

22. As opposed to Her Majesty in Council. This follows the practice adopted by Kenya on independence—*See* ROBERTS-WRAY, COMMONWEALTH AND COLONIAL LAW 450 (Stevens 1966).

23. § 124(1).

24. *See* the Judicial Committee (Dissenting Opinions) Order in Council of 4th March 1966.

there is likely to be considerable expense in taking an appeal to it. However, provision exists for special leave to appeal to the Committee *in forma pauperis* where the petitioner is not worth £100 in the world.[25]

When the Judicial Committee hears a case brought to it from a country administering Roman-Dutch or South African law it will naturally apply that law and not English law [26] and in the past it used to have one member who had had judicial experience of that law.

This is well illustrated by the case of *Nkau Majara v. R.*[27] where the Committee was composed of Lord

---

25. Judicial Committee Rules, S. I. 1957 No. 2224, § 2. The petition must be accompanied by an affidavit from the petitioner stating that he is not worth £100 in the world excepting his wearing apparel and his interest in the subject-matter of the intended appeal, and that he is unable to provide sureties. A certificate of counsel must also be sent stating that the petitioner has a reasonable ground of appeal, though this will not automatically mean that the Privy Council has to grant leave to appeal *in forma pauperis*—*see* Nelson v. East African Newspapers (Nation Series), Ltd., [1963] 3 All E.R. 812. If the appeal is not *in forma pauperis* the costs are likely to be high, since an English Q.C. will often lead and commonly be assisted by a junior from the country of appeal. In addition, 30 copies of a party's case must be printed and bound.

26. *But see* the amazing revelation in Lerotholi v. R., [1926-53] H.C.T.L.R. 149, 156 (P.C.), that in the earlier case of Tumahole v. R., [1926-53] H.C.T.L.R. 123 (P.C.) (Basutoland) it was argued for the appellants and not disputed by Counsel for the Crown that, from 1884 onwards, English law and practice had been applicable in Basutoland save insofar as superseded by legislative enactment. That such an error could go unnoticed in the High Court as well as before the Privy Council can only be explained by the colossal incompetence and lack of interest of those responsible for the legal affairs of the country at that time. For further discussion of these two Privy Council decisions *see* pp. 466-467 *infra*.

27. [1954] H.C.T.L.R. 38. *See also* Jayawickrema v. Amarasuriya, [1918] 20 N.L.R. 289 on appeal from Ceylon.

Goddard (then Lord Chief Justice of England), Lord Reid (also a member of the House of Lords), and Mr. L. M. D. de Silva (who formerly held high judicial office in Ceylon).

In that case a headman had, contrary to his duty, refrained from arresting the culprits on his arrival at the scene of a ritual murder. In this way, and also by his subsequent conduct in failing to report the murder and give prompt assistance to the police, he had assisted the murderers by giving them an opportunity to escape from justice. The question was whether or not his conviction as an accessory after the fact by the Basutoland High Court should be upheld. Under English law a person can be convicted of being an accessory after the fact only if he actively assists the principal offender and not if he only stands by passively and omits to do something. It was argued for the appellant that the term "accessory after the fact" had to be given a meaning under South African law identical to its meaning in English law, since it was originally an English legal term of art. The Privy Council held that this was not necessarily so and stated,

> No doubt it would retain much of the connotation which it possessed under English law but its meaning in the country of its adoption could naturally and properly be influenced by the system of law prevailing in that country, namely the Roman-Dutch law. This was almost inevitable as the term had to be used in relation to, and in the course of administration of, that law. . . . In their Lordships' opinion an authoritative view of the true position is to be found in the following passage in the judgment of Innes C. J. in the case of *Rex v. Mlooi*[28] . . . : "He who intervenes[29] to assist

28. [1925] A.D. 131.

29. The use of the expression "intervenes" is confusing

a criminal after the event may conveniently be called an accessory after the fact—not in the technical and restricted sense in which that term is used in English law, but in an extended sense applicable to crimes in general. So used, its meaning is well understood. . . ." [30]

The Committee reached the conclusion that to constitute a person an accessory after the fact under the law of Basutoland (as it was then), it is sufficient to establish that assistance was given to the principal offender in circumstances from which it would appear that the giver "associated" himself with the offence committed. South African law makes no distinction for this purpose between giving passive assistance and giving positive assistance. Applying this law and not English law, the Committee dismissed the appeal.

Nearly all the cases that have so far come before the Judicial Committee on appeal from Lesotho have concerned criminal matters and it is as well to state the true position of the Committee in relation to such appeals. The Committee is not a court of criminal appeal [31] and it does not have the wide powers that such

---

here since Nkau Majara v. R. was concerned with passive assistance. R. v. Mlooi was not concerned with this problem but with whether or not an accessory after the fact is a *socius criminis*.

30. *Supra* note 27, at 44.

31. *See generally* ROBERTS-WRAY, *supra* note 22, at 437 and Nadan v. R., [1926] A.C. 481, 495. In Tadeyo Kwalira v. R. an appeal from Malawi (No. 38 of 1963), the Board reiterated the view of its function in criminal appeals which it laid down in Arnold v. King Emperor, [1914] A.C. 644, [1914-15] All E.R. 779, 781-82 (P.C.) as follows:

> This Committee is not a Court of Criminal Appeal. It may in general be stated that its practice is to the following effect: It is not guided by its own doubts of the appellant's innocence or suspicion of his guilt. It will not interfere with the course of criminal law unless there has been such

a court would have. It will disturb a decision in the court below only where there are strong grounds for doing so. The rule laid down by the Committee in *In re Dillett*[32] is that there must have been some clear departure from the requirements of justice, and an appeal will not be allowed unless it is shown that by a disregard of the form of legal process, or by some violation of the principles of natural justice, or otherwise, some substantial and grave injustice has been done. Such irregularity was uncovered by the Committee in the case of *Tumahole Bereng v. R.*[33]

> an interference with the elementary rights of an accused as has placed him outside the pale of regular law, or unless, within that pale, there has been a violation of the natural principles of justice so demonstratively manifest as to convince their Lordships, first that the result arrived at was opposite to the result their Lordships would themselves have reached, and secondly that the same opposite result would have been reached by the local tribunal also, if the alleged defect or misdirection had been avoided.

In civil cases, special leave will only be given by the Privy Council "where the case is of gravity involving a matter of public interest or some important question of law, or affecting property of considerable amount, or where the case is otherwise of some public importance or of a very substantial character."—Prince v. Gagnon, [1882] 8 App. Cas. 103, 105.

32. [1887] 12 App. Cas. 459, 467.

33. *Supra* note 26. *See also* Mahlikilili Dlamini v. R., [1942] A.C. 583 (P.C.), [1934] 1 All E.R. 463, a case from Swaziland where a failure to hold the whole of the proceedings in public in accordance with the law was held *prima facie* to amount to a disregard of the forms of justice. The Judicial Committee allowed the appeal because the opinions of the assessors on matters of custom had been given privately to the judge instead of in open court as required by the relevant proclamation. For other examples of appeals allowed by the Privy Council where a disregard of the forms of justice occurred see Ras Behari Lal v. The King Emperor, [1933] 102 L.J. (P.C.) 144 (member of jury did not understand the language in which the trial was conducted) and Knowles v. R., [1930] A.C. 336 (judge in Ashanti sitting without jury, sentencing to death for murder without considering the possibility of manslaughter).

Here the administrative officer who sat with the judge at the trial pursuant to the relevant statutory provisions, had acquainted himself before the trial with certain material aspects of the Crown case in the company of a number of Crown witnesses and had interrogated one of the accomplices of the accused in connection with several important aspects of his evidence. The Committee held that his subsequent participation in the trial was highly irregular and therefore set aside the conviction for murder. In the words of the judgment:

> As has been so often said, justice must not only be done but must manifestly be seen to be done. In their Lordships' opinion [the administrative officer's] conduct was such as to cause doubt in the public mind as to the complete impartiality of the proceedings in which he subsequently took part. . . . [I]t might well have been thought, when his activity became known, that he had come to Court with a biased mind in the sense of having formed a definite view as to what had occurred or as to the credibility of the witnesses whom he had observed or questioned. . . . All this, of course, is in the realm of conjecture, but when the irregularity complained of may reasonably engender suspicions of this nature it cannot be left out of account, particularly when, as here, the opinion of the Officer could have been communicated to the judge in private.[34]

It remains to advert to a doctrine that has been established by the Privy Council, that it will not normally disturb concurrent findings of fact in the courts below, more especially in cases relating to customary law.[35]

---

34. Tumahole case, *supra* note 26, at 141.

35. Kwamin v. Kufuor, [1914] P.C. (1874-1928); Devi v. Roy, [1946] A.C. 508. The practice of the Board is to decline to review the evidence for a third time where two local courts have

(c) The Authority of Privy Council Decisions

It is certain that decisions of the Privy Council in cases that have come to it on appeal from Lesotho are binding on all other courts in Lesotho, since it is the highest court for the country. The binding effect of Privy Council decisions given in cases originating from other countries is much more doubtful.† It may be said at the outset that decisions applying English law cannot even be relevant unless the common law in force in Lesotho and the English common law agree on the point or unless the two systems of law are otherwise identical, for instance if they possess statutes *in pari materia*. Clearly, decisions applying Roman-Dutch or South African law in South Africa, Botswana, Swaziland, Rhodesia, and Ceylon are entitled to great respect in the Lesotho courts, but the question that does arise is whether or not they are binding.

(i) Two Theories

The authority to be attached to Privy Council decisions is a problem that has given rise to a number of conflicting theories.[36] One of these states that the

---

reached the same findings of fact. Dissents by individual members of those courts do not affect the position. In order for the Board to depart from this practice there must be some miscarriage of justice or violation of some principle of law or procedure. The Board will always be reluctant to depart from the practice in cases that involve questions of manners, customs, or sentiments peculiar to the country or locality from which the case comes, whose significance is specially within the knowledge of the courts of that country. *See also* Chua Chee Chor v. Chua Kim Yong, [1963] 1 All E.R. 102.

† In terms of the Court of Appeal and High Court Order, 1970 extraneous Privy Council decisions given after 8th May 1970 will not be binding on courts in Lesotho—see footnote asterisk on p. 443 *supra*.

36. *See* the discussion in ROBERTS-WRAY *supra* note 22, at

Privy Council is not one body hearing appeals from all over the Commonwealth, but a separate entity for every country for which it is the highest court of appeal. Therefore, it is argued, decisions on appeal from one country can only be binding in that country and not elsewhere.[37] This theory may be buttressed by two practical considerations. First it may be questioned whether a Privy Council decision in a case coming from, *e.g.*, Southern Rhodesia should be allowed to alter the law of Lesotho without discussion of the existing law of Lesotho. Thus counsel, briefed on the decisions in the courts of Lesotho, would have to be heard in argument before a decision affecting the law of Lesotho could be given. Secondly, how can decisions of the Lesotho High Court or Court of Appeal be said to be overruled by decisions on appeal from, *e.g.*, Ceylon, since "overruling" implies that the decision has been considered and set aside?[38]

The defect of this theory, however, is that it fails to take account of the reality of the Committee's operations. It is staffed by a relatively constant board of judges and it has a standard procedure and body of rules that are followed in all appeals, irrespective of origin. Moreover, it is predictable that if the Board gives a particular ruling in country *A* it will give the same ruling later in country *B* if the same legal system exists in both countries.[39]

Another theory is that decisions of the Privy

572-75; DANIELS, THE COMMON LAW IN WEST AFRICA 186-190 (Butterworths 1964); and Allott, 1968 J.A.L. 3, 7-9.

37. In Negro v. Pietro's Bread Co., Ltd., [1933] O.R. 112, the Ontario Court of Appeal refused to be bound by the Privy Council decision in the Australian case of Victorian Railway Commissioners v. Coultas, [1888] 13 App. Cas. 222.

38. *See* Pesona v. Babouchi Baas, [1948] 49 N.L.R. 442 Ceylon).

39. *See* Allott, *supra* note 36, at 9.

Council *are* binding in all countries where that body is the highest court of appeal for the simple reason that courts in practice decide cases on that assumption.[40] Thus one finds the following statement in the judgment of the Privy Council in *Fatuma binti Mohamed bin Salim Backhshuwen v. Mohamed bin Salim Backhshuwen*[41] a case from Kenya:

> In *Said bin Muhammed v. Wakf Commissioner*[42] . . . the experienced judges of the Court of Appeal for Eastern Africa did not doubt that on a question of Mohamedan law decisions of the Privy Council in appeals from India must bind them in appeals from the High Court of Zanzibar. Their Lordships are of opinion that this was clearly the correct view and that it must prevail also in appeals from Kenya.[43]

Thus here the Privy Council was expressing the view, albeit in an *obiter dictum,* that their decisions are authoritative beyond the country from where the appeal comes.[44] This view receives support from the widely held belief, endorsed by the courts, that Privy Council decisions on important matters of constitutional law are of general application and not limited to the country of origin. Thus the Swaziland case of *Sobhuza II v. Miller*[45] has long been accepted as au-

---

40. In Onogen v. Leventis & Co., Ltd., [1959] G.L.R. 105, 115, a Ghanaian judge held himself bound by a decision of the Privy Council on appeal from India.

41. [1952] A.C. 1.

42. [1946] 13 E.A.C.A. 32.

43. *Supra* note 41, at 14.

44. The Privy Council took the same view in Tzamburakis v. Rodoussakis on appeal from Tanzania (P.C. appeal No. 5 of 1957 reported in 1958 J.A.L. 186) as to the binding effect of their decision in the Indian appeal of Tricomdas Cooverji Bhoja v. Thakur, I.L.R., 44 Cal. 759.

45. [1926-53] H.C.T.L.R. 1; (1926) A.C. 518. The facts of the case were as follows. Mbandzeni, who was the Paramount

thority for the principle that if the jurisdiction conferred upon the British Sovereign by the Foreign Jurisdiction Act 1890 is exercised, then it cannot be called in question by the courts. The courts will rely on the representatives of the Crown to know the limits of its jurisdiction and to keep within these limits. As soon as the jurisdiction has been exercised, it is unchallengeable. Thus in the *Sobhuza* case the Judicial Committee accepted the validity of an Order in Council without question. It has never been suggested that this case was only authoritative for Swaziland. Indeed it has been followed time and again throughout the Commonwealth. Similarly, decisions such as that in *In re Dillett*[46] on the jurisdiction of the Committee in

---

Chief of Swaziland from 1875 to 1889, had granted numerous concessions including one to the predecessors in title of the respondents. Under the concession the grantees bound themselves not to interfere with the rights of the Swazi inhabitants. The appellant claimed that the first respondent had trespassed on the existing rights of Swazi occupants and had caused them to be ejected from the land they occupied. A convention had been made in 1894 between Great Britain and the South African Republic which, apart from giving the latter rights of legislation, jurisdiction, and administration, guaranteed the grazing and agricultural rights of the Swazis and contained a proviso that no law thereafter made in Swaziland was to be in conflict with the guarantees given to the Swazi people in the convention. This was followed by an Order in Council which disregarded the proviso and the guarantees, and gave the High Commissioner power to make grants of lands which he promptly did, including one to the respondents. Since the grant was one of full ownership, the respondents evicted the Swazi occupants. The Privy Council held that the Crown could not, except by statute, deprive itself of freedom to make Orders in Council even when these were inconsistent with previous Orders such as the 1894 Convention. Thus the principle of the Crown's unfettered power to extend its jurisdiction was established, and its right to make an inconsistent Order in Council was accepted without question.

46. *Supra* note 32, at 10.

criminal appeals are thought to be of worldwide application.[47]

(ii) Some Judicial Views on the Question from Roman-Dutch Jurisdictions

Before hazarding a conclusion on this question it may be useful to examine briefly some of the judicial pronouncements on the subject in jurisdictions administering Roman-Dutch law.

In South Africa it is possible to find conflicting statements on the authority of decisions of the Privy Council on matters of Roman-Dutch law on appeal from Ceylon. Thus in *Hare v. Trustee of Heath*,[48] Lord de Villiers C. J. remarked:

> The case of *Tatham v. Andree* [49] was decided by the Privy Council in 1863 on appeal from the Supreme Court of Ceylon where the Roman-Dutch Law also prevails; but I ought here to observe that if the decision of the Privy Council in that case had been inconsistent with the rules laid down and recognised in this Court for half a century, and if those rules appeared to me to carry out the true principles of the Roman-Dutch Law, I should not consider the decision of the Privy Council as binding upon this Court in the present case.[50]

However the decision of the Privy Council in *Le Mesurier v. Le Mesurier* [51] on appeal from Ceylon was held to be absolutely binding in both *Ex parte Kaiser* [52] and *Murphy v. Murphy*.[53] Both *Tatham v. Andree* and

---

47. It was applied, *e.g.*, in Fakisandla Nkambule v. R., [1955] H.C.T.L.R. 1 (P.C.) (Swaziland).

48. [1884] 3 S.C. 32.

49. 1 M.P.C.C. (N.S.) 386.

50. *Supra* note 48, at 33.

51. [1895] A.C. 517 (P.C.).

52. [1902] T.H. 165.

53. [1902] T.S. 179.

Le Mesurier v. Le Mesurier were decisions on the Roman-Dutch common law.

Turning to decisions interpreting statutes we find a more consistent approach being developed. In *de Waal N.O. v. North Bay Canning Co., Ltd.*,[54] the South African Appellate Division held itself bound in construing a South African statute to follow the Judicial Committee's interpretation of identical wording in a foreign statute. A proviso was later added in *Estate of Wege v. Strauss* [55] that there should be nothing in the Roman-Dutch common law requiring a different interpretation. In Southern Rhodesia the courts have taken the same view. Thus in *R. v. Nkala* [56] the Federal Supreme Court in construing a clause in the Sedition Act held it was bound to follow the decision of the Privy Council in *Wallace-Johnson v. R.*[57] (an appeal from the Gold Coast, as it then was). Beadle C. J. said:

> Whether or not, therefore, the decision in *Wallace-Johnson's* case is binding on the High Court depends on whether or not any difference which there might be between the common law of Southern Rhodesia and the Gold Coast might affect the interpretation to be placed on the Southern Rhodesia Act and the Gold Coast Act respectively. That there may be a difference in the common law of the Gold Coast and of Southern Rhodesia, I will concede, for the purposes of this enquiry. But the ordinary grammatical meaning of the wording of the two Acts seems to me to be so plain that I cannot see how any difference in the common law of the two countries could affect their interpretation. It is clear also that the decision in *Wallace-Johnson's* case was arrived at purely on considera-

---

54. [1921] A.D. 521.
55. [1932] A.D. 76.
56. [1961] 4 S.A. 177 (F.C.).
57. [1940] 1 All E.R. 241.

tion of the words of the statute itself, and that the interpretation placed on the word "disaffection" by the Privy Council was not influenced in any way by what the common law of the Gold Coast might or might not have been.[58]

R. v. Nkala is instructive in showing that on the pure interpretation of the words of a statute, a Privy Council decision from a basically English law jurisdiction was held binding in a basically Roman-Dutch law jurisdiction. Apart from differences in the common law that may affect the position where they are relevant, there are also *dicta* to suggest that the surrounding circumstances may on occasion play a significant part. This is an element to be taken into account in the interpretation of statutes generally, but it may be especially important in view of the wide differences that exist between conditions in the white-dominated part of Southern Africa and those prevailing in nonracial independent African states like Lesotho.

As recently as 1962 Beadle C. J. in the Southern Rhodesian case of *City of Salisbury v. Mehta*[59] was distinguishing the racial conditions in South Africa from those in Southern Rhodesia. The question was whether or not the city of Salisbury could differentiate between the races in municipal swimming baths, and the South African picture was painted as follows:

> It stands to reason that in a country whose statute book is honeycombed with differential legislation as between white and coloured, and in which colour distinction in churches, schools, sports, places of amusement, and in society generally are carefully observed, it can scarcely be said that in delegating legislative powers to municipalities, the Legislature could not possibly have contemplated

58. *Supra* note 56, at 182-83.
59. [1962] 1 S.A. 675 (S.R.).

> that these subordinate law-making bodies would follow its own example as well as the settled social and colour differentiation.[60]

Beadle C. J. then went on:

> Interpreting a South African statute against this background it might well be right to infer that the South African Legislature when it gave a subordinate authority certain general authority, intended also to give it the authority to "differentiate" between the races. In considering a statute made in a country whose racial policies are quite different from those of the Republic of South Africa, it might, however, be quite wrong to draw a similar inference.
>
> For example it would surprise me if the Courts of England would hold that when the English Parliament gave the Birmingham Municipality the authority to make byelaws for the good government of the city, it intended also to give the municipality the authority to segregate West Indians from Europeans in the use of public conveniences, provided that the facilities afforded West Indians were equivalent to those afforded to Europeans.[61]

Similarly *dicta* of Tredgold C. J. in *Estate of Mehta v. The Master*[62] point in the same direction. The court had to construe a taxing statute that contained the words "surviving spouse." The court held that this expression included the survivor of a polygamous marriage that was valid by the law of the place of its celebration. Thus for a limited purpose at any rate, recognition was given to a polygamous union, whereas this had been denied in the leading South African case.[63]

---

60. *Id.* at 686-87 quoting from DONGES AND VAN WINSEN'S MUNICIPAL LAW 717 (Juta), which was cited with approval in R. v. Carelse, [1943] C.P.D. 242, 253.

61. *Supra* note 59, at 687.

62. [1958] R & N 570 (F.C.).

63. Seedat's Executor v. The Master, [1917] A.D. 302. Simi-

There is in addition South African authority for the proposition that a Privy Council decision on a question involving public policy is binding. In *Patz v. Salzburg* [64] the Transvaal High Court held itself bound by a decision on appeal from India on what constituted champerty. Innes C. J. said:

> The rule was clearly laid down in the case referred to during the argument—*Ram Coomar Coondoo v. Chunder Canto Mookerjee.*[65] It is a general rule, not founded upon the law of India, but upon public policy, and therefore binding on this court.[66]

(iii) Conclusions

The following conclusions are tentatively submitted as to the effect of Privy Council decisions from other jurisdictions.

Such decisions are binding upon the courts of Lesotho in the following circumstances:

a. Where the decision is on a broad constitutional question, *e.g.*, dealing with English constitutional law (though there are only a few spheres in which such a decision could be relevant in Lesotho today).

b. Where the decision interprets a provision in a constitution identical to one in the Lesotho constitution, *e.g.*, on a question relating to a British Constitutional Convention [67] that had been written into both constitutions. This is subject to the proviso that there

---

lar decisions to this effect include the following: Mokwena v. Laub, [1943] W.L.D. 63; followed in Zulu v. Minister of Justice, [1956] 2 S.A. 128 (N.); Ngqobela v. Sihele, [1893] 10 S.C. 346; Meesedoosa v. Links, [1915] T.P.D. 357; R. v. Nalana, [1907] T.P.D. 407; S.A.N.T.A.M. v. Fondo, [1960] 2 S.A. 467 (A.D.).

64. [1907] T.S. 526.

65. 2 App. Cas. 186.

66. *Supra* note 64, at 527.

67. *See supra*, pp. 305-306.

is no significant difference in the surrounding circumstances between the two countries.

c. Where the decision is one interpreting a statutory provision *in pari materia* with one contained in a Lesotho statute, *e.g.*, a section of the English-model Companies Act [68] or Bills of Exchange Proclamation.[69] This is subject not only to the proviso about different surrounding circumstances, but also to a condition that Lesotho's common law does not require a different interpretation, *e.g.*, as to the meaning of the word "consideration" in the Lesotho Bills of Exchange Proclamation.[70]

This seems certain to be the case where the relevant Lesotho authorities are before the Privy Council as happened in the Swaziland case of *Gideon Nkambule v. R.*,[71] but it will probably be so even in the absence of consideration of Lesotho decisions.

In the *Nkambule* case the Judicial Committee had to decide whether to apply the English or the South African rule about accomplice evidence in a ritual murder case. The English rule is broadly to the effect that the evidence of one accomplice cannot be corroborated by that of another. The South African law considers the evidence of two accomplices to be sufficient even though there is no other evidence of the crime, and it is based upon judicial interpretation of provisions in a statute in the same terms as the Swaziland statute.[72] The particular provision the Committee was called upon to interpret was section 231 of

68. Companies Act, No. 25 of 1967.

69. Proc. 13 of 1912 as amended.

70. There is no requirement of consideration for the validity of a contract not under seal in the common law of Lesotho.

71. [1926-53] H.C.T.L.R. 181 (P.C.) (Swaziland).

72. The statute is the Criminal Procedure and Evidence Act No. 31 of 1917 which has been interpreted in R. v. Thielke, [1918] A.D. 373 and R. v. Ncanana, [1948] 4 S.A. 399.

the Swaziland Criminal Procedure and Evidence Proclamation 1938 [73] as amended, which provides:

> Any court which is trying a person on a charge of any offence may convict him of any offence alleged against him on the single evidence of any accomplice: Provided that the offence has, by competent evidence, other than the single and unconfirmed evidence of the accomplice, been proved to the satisfaction of such court to have been actually committed.

In *Tumahole Bereng v. R.*,[74] which was an earlier decision on appeal from Basutoland, the Committee had interpreted the statute to mean that a conviction could not be sustained on the evidence of two accomplices, other independent evidence being necessary. Apart from the conclusion reached on the construction of the proclamation, the Committee considered it was bound to follow the English cautionary rule which is set out in *R. v. Baskerville*,[75] and therefore decided it was unsafe to convict in *Tumahole Bereng v. R.* The proclamations of Basutoland and Swaziland were in identical terms on this point. Following certain of its *dicta* in the Basutoland case of *Lerotholi v. R.*,[76] which was decided after *Tumahole Bereng v. R.*, the Committee in the *Nkambule* case departed from its earlier ruling in *Tumahole Bereng v. R.* and held that

---

73. I LAWS OF SWAZILAND Ch. 35 at 526 (1959).

74. *Supra* note 26.

75. [1916] 2 K.B. 658; [1916-17] All E.R. 38. The cautionary rule is not absolute, but merely states that it is unsafe to convict on the testimony of an accomplice or accomplices, that one accomplice cannot corroborate another, and that a jury must have careful warning of these dangers, but that if such warning is given, a jury is entitled to convict on the evidence of a single accomplice alone. (It should be borne in mind that there are no juries in Lesotho, but that the courts often sit with assessors.)

76. *Supra* note 26.

the evidence of two accomplices, though unsupported by any other testimony, was sufficient.

It is clear that, since the relevant Lesotho decisions were before the Committee and detailed consideration given to them before that in *Tumahole v. R.* was departed from, the Swaziland decision is now binding on the courts in Lesotho, and it was so held by the High Court in 1954 in the case of *R. v. Kabi.*[77]

d. Where the decision was purely on a question of Roman-Dutch or South African common law and the relevant Lesotho authorities were before the Committee.

e. Probably, where the decision was purely on a question of Roman-Dutch or South African common law and although the Lesotho authorities were not cited, the circumstances in Lesotho do not require a different rule.

f. Where the decision was on the English common law and that law has been incorporated into the law of Lesotho by statute, for instance in various areas of the law of evidence.[78]

g. Possibly, where the decision was on a question of English common law and the position is the same under the common law in force in Lesotho and the circumstances in Lesotho permit. An example might be a case on a question of public policy, but public policy is an inconstant thing and subject to great changes due to time and place.

---

77. [1954] H.C.T.L.R. 27.

78. *See* Evidence in Civil Proceedings Ordinance of 1830, §§ 12, 15, 18, 21, 22, 23, 25, and 26; Criminal Procedure and Evidence Proclamation, 1938 (as amended), §§ 220, 221, 226, 230, 237, 249, 250, 251, and 272. The Mercantile Law Amendment Act of 1879 also introduces English law in various fields. *See supra* pp. 88-90.

h. Where the decision was concerned with questions of African customary law and the rule propounded was intended to be of general application. Thus in *Angu v. Attah,*[79] a case on appeal from the Gold Coast (as it then was) the Privy Council judgment contained the following statement:

> As is the case with all customary law it has to be proved in the first instance by calling witnesses acquainted with the native customs until the particular customs have, by frequent proof in the courts, become so notorious that the courts will take judicial notice of them.

While this was an *obiter dictum* in that case, it has been incorporated in later Privy Council decisions [80] and is thought to be binding in Lesotho in respect of proof of customary law in the higher courts.

(d) The Judicial Committee Is Not Bound by Its Own Previous Decisions

The decision in *Gideon Nkambule v. R.* (*supra*) illustrates the established practice of the Privy Council that it does not hold itself bound to follow its own previous decisions,[81] though it will naturally prefer not to dissent from any of them unless it appears very necessary to do so. The Committee stated the position in the *Nkambule* case in the following terms:

> Undoubtedly their Lordships must give a construction to the language used [in Section 231 *supra*] which differs from that adopted in *Tumahole's* case if they are to uphold the conviction now under appeal. In ordinary circumstances they

79. [1916] P.C. (1874-1928) 43, 44.

80. *E.g.*, Amissah v. Krabah, [1936] 2 W.A.C.A. 30, and Golightly v. Ashrifi (P.C. appeal No. 31 of 1958 from Ghana, reported 1961 J.A.L. 52). *See supra* pp. 122-123.

81. *See* Attorney-General for Ontario v. Canada Temperance Federation, [1946] 62 T.L.R. 199.

> would be very slow to take this course. It is true that the Board does not act, as the House of Lords acts,[82] on the strict rule that they are bound by a previous decision based on the same considerations. Nevertheless as was said in *Read v. Bishop of Lincoln*,[83] a decision on a given state of facts ought not to be reopened without the greatest hesitation, though the right to reopen it is not confined to cases where some fresh fact was adduced which had not been under consideration on the previous occasion. Still, the right to reopen remains, and from these observations it is apparent that the existence of some fresh material not communicated or, at any rate, not fully presented to the tribunal which heard and decided the earlier case is an element to be borne in mind when deciding whether that case should be followed or not. . . . The present case, therefore is one in which fresh facts have been adduced which were not under consideration when *Tumahole's* case was decided, and accordingly it is one in which, in their Lordships' view, they are justified in reconsidering the foundations on which that case was determined.[84]

The fresh facts unearthed in the *Nkambule* case were the existence of South African decisions interpreting identical wording to that in section 231, and the revelation that the law in force in Lesotho was not English law but Roman-Dutch law.[85]

(2) THE COURT OF APPEAL

Prior to independence Basutoland shared a Court

---

82. The House of Lords no longer adopts this rigid position —*see* pp. 78-79 *supra* for discussion of the change that took place in 1966.

83. [1892] A.C. 644; [1891-94] All E.R. 227 (P.C.). The case was concerned with whether or not the mixing of communion wine with water, and various other practices were contrary to the law of the church.

84. *Supra* note 71, at 186-87.

85. *Supra* note 26.

of Appeal with the Bechuanaland Protectorate and Swaziland. This court had been created in 1954; [86] before that date appeals went direct to the Privy Council from the High Court or its predecessor, the Resident Commissioner's Court. Since Independence, Lesotho has had its own Court of Appeal and the 1966 Constitution [87] governs its original and appellate jurisdiction. However, the personnel of the court is still broadly shared with the Courts of Appeal of Botswana and Swaziland.

(a) Appellate Jurisdiction

(i) Under the Constitution

Appeals lie as of right to the Court of Appeal from the High Court in respect of:

a. final decisions in any civil or criminal proceedings on questions as to the interpretation of the Constitution;

b. final decisions given in exercise of the jurisdiction conferred on the High Court by section 20 of the Constitution (which relates to the enforcement of fundamental human rights and freedoms);

c. final decisions of the High Court in the determination of any of the questions for the determination of which a right of access to the High Court is guaranteed by section 16 of the Constitution (which relates to the right of persons whose property is compulsorily acquired); [88]

d. final decisions in any civil proceedings where the matter in dispute on the appeal is of the value of R1,000 or upwards, or where the appeal involves di-

86. By the Basutoland, Bechuanaland Protectorate, and Swaziland Court of Appeal Order in Council, S. I. 1954 No. 1369.

87. 1966 CONSTITUTION, § 115.

88. *Id.* § 121(1).

rectly or indirectly a claim to or question respecting property or a right to the value of R1,000 or upwards;

e. final decisions in proceedings for dissolution or nullity of marriage;

f. such other decisions in civil proceedings as may be prescribed by Parliament.[89]

As we have seen, in all these cases an appeal also lies as of right from a decision of the Court of Appeal to the Judicial Committee of the Privy Council.[90]

Appeals also lie from the High Court to the Court of Appeal with the leave of the High Court in two further sets of circumstances:

a. from decisions in any civil proceedings where, in the opinion of the High Court, the question involved in the appeal is one that, by reason of its great general or public importance or otherwise, ought to be submitted to the Court of Appeal; and

b. from such other decisions in civil proceedings as may be prescribed by Parliament.[91]

As pointed out earlier, such appeals may go on to the Privy Council with the leave of the Court of Appeal. The Constitution expressly provides that certain decisions of the High Court are not subject to an appeal at all. These relate to decisions in respect of membership of Parliament.[92]

Appeals also lie direct to the Court of Appeal from decisions of a subordinate court or a court-martial in such cases as may be prescribed by any law.[93]

(ii) Under the Court of Appeal Proclamation, 1954 [94]

---

89. *Id.* § 122(2).
90. *Id.* §§ 121(1) and 122.
91. *Id.* § 122(3).
92. *Id.* § 54(6).
93. *Id.* § 123(3) and (4).
94. Proc. 72 of 1954 as amended by G.N. 102 of 1967.

Although the old Court of Appeal Order in Council [95] was repealed by the Independence Order, its counterpart Proclamation is still in force. Grave difficulties arise in attempting to work out whether all its provisions can operate consistently with the Constitution, as will be seen below.

a. Civil Appeals

The Proclamation provides that appeals shall lie as of right to the Court of Appeal from all final judgments of the High Court, and also, by leave of the Court of Appeal, from an interlocutory order, an order made *ex parte*, or an order as to costs only, where such judgments or orders are given in the exercise of the High Court's original jurisdiction.[96]

So far as decisions in its appellate jurisdiction are concerned any person aggrieved may appeal with the leave of the Court of Appeal or upon the certificate of the judge who heard the appeal on any ground that involves a question of law but not on a question of fact.[97]

It will be recalled that the Constitution provides for appeals as of right in nonconstitutional cases in two specified spheres, and then permits such appeals from "such other decisions in civil proceedings as may be prescribed by Parliament."

At first sight it might appear that in providing for prescription by Parliament the Constitution was referring to future legislation on the subject, of which there is none. However section 4 of the Independence Order declares that where something falls for prescription by Parliament and is presently provided for under an existing law, that provision shall have effect after Independence, with the necessary modifications,

95. S. I. 1954, No. 1369.
96. Proc. 72 of 1954, § 11.
97. *Id.* § 12.

as if it had been made under the Constitution by Parliament. This means that the words "as may be prescribed by Parliament" refer, for present purposes, to the Court of Appeal Proclamation.

Since the Constitution keeps the provisions of the Proclamation in being in this way the next question is the extent to which they need modification to bring them into line with the Constitutional provisions. The Constitution says that appeals lie as of right, for instance, where the subject matter in dispute is of the value of R1,000 or upwards,[98] whereas the Proclamation permits appeals from *all* final judgments of the High Court. On the one hand it may be argued that the Proclamation must be modified to limit appeals to where the value of the subject matter is R1,000 or upwards. On the other hand the Constitution expressly provides for "such *other* appeals" and therefore clearly contemplates appeals on grounds wider than those specified. On this line of argument the list of grounds for appeal enumerated in the Constitution is merely illustrative and not an exhaustive one. Perhaps the explanation is that the intention of the Constitution was to single out important areas where there was to be a right of appeal and entrench these, leaving less significant areas to be prescribed by Parliament and thus be amendable by a simple majority. If this is the correct inference, the exclusion of criminal appeals from those entrenched is a singular anomaly.

What has been stated above applies, *mutatis mutandis,* to appeals with leave when there is a similar inconsistency between the Constitution and the Court of Appeal Proclamation.[99]

---

98. In § 122(2)(a).

99. *I.e.*, between § 122(3)(a) of the Constitution and § 12 of the Court of Appeal Proclamation, linked with § 122(3)(b) of the Constitution.

b. Criminal Appeals

Whereas in the case of civil appeals the Constitution has created confusion by the grant of the right of appeal in specific instances, in the sphere of criminal appeals it is curiously silent (except in relation to questions involving an interpretation of the Constitution itself).

The Court of Appeal Proclamation makes provision for any person who is convicted by the High Court to appeal against conviction or against sentence [100] unless the sentence is one fixed by law.[101] In addition any person aggrieved by a judgment of the High Court given in its criminal appellate jurisdiction may appeal to the Court of Appeal with the leave of the Court of Appeal or upon the certificate of the judge who heard the appeal on any ground of appeal that involves a question of law, but not on a question of fact nor against severity of sentence.[102]

It would seem that these provisions have been continued in force by the Independence Order and do not require any modification in the light of the Constitutional provisions.

---

100. In Motsekae Motjolobela v. R., [1955] H.C.T.L.R. 19, the Court of Appeal laid down the following principles as a guide in considering an appeal against severity of sentence:

(i) Would a reasonable man have awarded such a sentence?

(ii) Are there any circumstances bearing upon the matter that the trial court has failed to consider?

(iii) Did the trial court follow a wrong principle in imposing the sentence?

(iv) Did the trial court exceed its powers?

The sentence was reduced in that case because the trial judge did not sufficiently take into consideration the extenuating circumstances.

101. Court of Appeal Proc., § 3(1).

102. *Id.* § 3(2).

(b) Original Jurisdiction

The Court of Appeal also has a limited original jurisdiction under the Constitution in relation to the succession to the throne and the regency. It is for the College of Chiefs to designate in accordance with customary law the person who is entitled to succeed to the office of King upon the death or abdication of the holder of that office. However, any person who claims that under customary law he should have been so designated, instead of the person who has been, may apply to the Court of Appeal within six months of the publication of the designation for the substitution of his own name.[103] It is also the duty of the College of Chiefs to designate a regent where necessary and if it has failed to do so within a reasonable time the Court of Appeal may, on the application of any person, itself designate a person to be regent in accordance with customary law.[104]

In the exercise of its original jurisdiction the Court of Appeal's decisions are not subject to appeal.[105]

The Court of Appeal must, whenever it determines any matter other than an interlocutory matter, be composed of an uneven number of judges, not being less than three.[106]

(3) THE HIGH COURT

Provision for the High Court to operate in Basutoland was first made in 1938.[107] Prior to this, a court exercising similar functions and jurisdiction was operating under the style of the court of the Resident Commissioner. The judicial powers of the Resident

103. § 33(5) of the Constitution.
104. *Id.* § 34.
105. *Id.* § 35.
106. *Id.* § 119(2).
107. Proc. 57 of 1938.

Commissioner dated back to the time when Basutoland became a British colony in 1884.[108] His court was vested with unlimited jurisdiction in civil and criminal matters.[109] As from 1889 a combined court could be formed of the Resident Commissioner and one or more European Officers.[110] Provision was also made in 1916 for the Deputy Resident Commissioner to hold court for the Resident Commissioner in certain cases.[111] In 1928 these judicial functions of the Deputy Resident fell away and instead the post of Judicial Commissioner was created.[112] He was to act as a substitute President of the Resident Commissioner's Court. In 1930 the system of appeals from the customary courts was modified [113] and this resulted in the Judicial Commissioner spending most of his time as a circuit appeal judge.[114]

The 1938 High Court Proclamation conferred the same jurisdiction upon the High Court as that possessed by the Supreme Court of South Africa,[115] and in a few specified areas it also had jurisdiction to hear civil cases in which the parties were Africans.[116] The judge of the High Court was also the judge of the High

---

108. Proc. 2B of 1884, § 1.

109. *Id.*

110. Proc. 1B of 1889, § 1.

111. Proc. 24 of 1916, repealed by Proc. 10 of 1928.

112. Proc. 10 of 1928.

113. Procs. 20 & 25 of 1930.

114. *See* HAILEY, NATIVE ADMINISTRATION IN THE BRITISH AFRICAN TERRITORIES Pt. V 90 (H.M.S.O. 1953). The role of the Judicial Commissioner under Proc. 10 of 1928 should not be confused with that of a later official with the same title whose jurisdiction is regulated by Proc. 25 of 1950, for which *see infra* pp. 487-488.

115. *Supra* note 107, § 2.

116. *Id.* at § 4 *and see* § 28 of the Subordinate Courts Proc. (No. 58 of 1938).

Courts of the Bechuanaland Protectorate and Swaziland, which were also established in 1938.

By 1954 the volume of criminal cases heard by the High Court had greatly increased and with the creation of a common Court of Appeal for Basutoland, the Bechuanaland Protectorate, and Swaziland, the time had come to consolidate and amend the law. The 1938 Proclamation was superseded [117] and provision made for the appointment of a Chief Justice and a puisne judge and also temporary appointments as an acting judge.[118] The original jurisdiction of the court was still broadly based on the race of the parties so far as civil proceedings were concerned.[119]

Up until 1965 the same person held the offices of Chief Justice for Basutoland, the Bechuanaland Protectorate, and Swaziland, but since that time there have been separate appointments.

The 1959 Constitution transferred the provisions establishing the High Court and prescribing its jurisdiction to itself [120] and this was followed through into the 1966 Constitution.[121] The High Court constituted in 1966 succeeded to the jurisdiction and powers of its predecessor [122] and therefore stepped into its shoes and is bound by the same decisions as its predecessors were. It is a superior court of record [123] and thus has inherent authority to fine and imprison for contempt of its authority; it cannot be directed by orders of mandamus and prohibition, nor can it be called for review.

---

117. By the High Court Proclamation (No. 18 of 1954).

118. *Id.* § 3.

119. *Id.* § 4.

120. Basutoland (Constitution) Order in Council 1959, § 65.

121. § 110 of the Constitution.

122. § 7(1) of the Independence Order in Council.

123. § 110(3) of the Constitution. As is the Court of Appeal —*see Id.* § 115(4).

The High Court sits in Maseru, but it may sit elsewhere if the Chief Justice so decides.[124]

Its present jurisdiction is set out below. There is, of course, no longer any distinction based upon the race of the parties to the proceedings.

(a) Original Jurisdiction

The Court has unlimited original jurisdiction to hear and determine any civil or criminal proceedings.[125] It also has powers, granted by the Constitution, to determine the following matters at first instance:

a. Claims by any persons (or in the case of a person detained, someone acting on his behalf) who allege that any of the provisions of sections 4 to 19 of the Constitution is being or is likely to be contravened in relation to them.[126] These sections relate to the protection of fundamental human rights and freedoms. The matter may come directly before the High Court or may be referred to it by a subordinate court.[127]

b. Questions as to the interpretation of the Constitution that arise in a subordinate court, and in that court's opinion involve a substantial question of law.[128] The subordinate court must refer such questions to the High Court if a party to the proceedings so requests, and may do so even if no such request is made.

c. Applications under section 16 of the Constitution. This section entitles any person having an interest in or right over property that has been compulsorily taken possession of, or whose interest in or right over any property has been compulsorily acquired, to

124. § 110(4) of the Constitution.
125. *Id.* § 110.
126. *Id.* § 20.
127. *Id.* § 20(3). *See supra* pp. 349-358.
128. *Id.* § 114(1). *See supra* pp. 356-358.

direct access to the High Court for the determination of: his interest or right, the legality of the taking of possession or acquisition of the property, interest or right and the amount of any compensation to which he is entitled, and for the purpose of obtaining prompt payment of that compensation; [129]

d. Questions as to membership of Parliament, namely:

(i) whether any person is validly nominated or designated as a senator; or

(ii) whether any person has been validly elected as a Member of the National Assembly; or

(iii) whether the seat in the National Assembly of any member thereof has become vacant.[130]

Decisions of the High Court on these matters are not subject to appeal.[131]

e. Applications for an order to quash a decision in respect of the allocation of land or the grant of any interest or right in or over land under sections 95 to 99 of the Constitution.[132]

(b) Appellate Jurisdiction

(i) Under the Constitution

Appeals lie as of right to the High Court from final decisions given by any subordinate court or a court-martial in any civil or criminal proceedings on questions as to the interpretation of the Constitution or as to the contravention of any of the sections of the Constitution protecting fundamental human rights and freedoms, save in the following circumstances:

a. if under any law an appeal lies as of right from that decision to another subordinate court or court-martial; or

---

129. *Id.* § 16(2).
130. *Id.* § 54(1).
131. *Id.* § 54(6).
132. *Id.* § 101(2).

b. if under any law an appeal lies from that decision to another subordinate court or court-martial with the leave of the court that gave the decision or of some other court and that leave has not been withheld.[133]

Subject to certain exceptions [134] appeals also lie as of right to the High Court from final decisions given by any subordinate court in any case in which, if the decision of the subordinate court were a decision of the High Court an appeal would lie as of right to the Court of Appeal.

In addition, appeals lie from a subordinate court or court-martial to the High Court in such cases as may be prescribed by any law.[135] Examples of such laws are the Subordinate Courts Proclamation [136] and the Central and Local Courts Proclamation.[137]

(ii) Under the Subordinate Courts Proclamation

a. Civil Appeals

The Subordinate Courts Proclamation provides for an appeal to the High Court against judgments in favour of plaintiff or defendant, absolution from the instance, judgments for costs, any rule or order having the effect of a final and definite sentence, and any decision overruling or upholding an exception.[138] Such appeals may be barred by an agreement of the parties in writing, lodged with the court before the hearing is

---

133. *Id.* § 123(1) and (2). *See supra* pp. 357-358.

134. The exceptions are where there is an appeal as of right to the Court of Appeal, or with leave and such leave has not been withheld; and where the same position applies in respect of appeals to another subordinate court—§ 123(3).

135. § 123(4) of the Constitution.

136. Proc. 58 of 1938 as amended—*see infra*, p. 483 *et seq.*

137. Proc. 62 of 1938 as amended—*see infra*, p. 489 *et seq.*

138. *Supra* note 136, § 54.

commenced, to the effect that the decision of the subordinate court shall be final.[139]

b. Criminal Appeals

A person convicted of any offence by the judgment of any subordinate court, including a person discharged after conviction, may appeal against conviction or sentence or against any consequent order to the High Court.[140] The Director of Public Prosecutions may also appeal where a criminal summons or charge is dismissed by the court.[141] Provision is also made for the Director of Public Prosecutions or the prosecutor to require the judicial officer to state a case for the consideration of the High Court where the subordinate court has given a decision in favour of the accused on any matter of law.[142]

(iii) Under the Central and Local Courts Proclamation [143]

Provision is made for appeals from local courts and central courts to the Court of the Judicial Commissioner and from there to the High Court in the following cases:

a. upon any question of law or of Sesotho law and custom reserved by the Judicial Commissioner at the instance of either party or of his own motion; or

b. upon the certificate of the Judicial Commissioner that it is a fit case for appeal on any other ground that appears to him to be a sufficient ground of appeal.[144]

---

139. *Id.* § 53.
140. *Id.* § 73(1).
141. *Id.* § 73(2).
142. *Id.* § 73(7) and (8).
143. Proc. 62 of 1938 as amended.
144. *Id.* § 28(3).

(c) Review Jurisdiction

Under the High Court Act of 1967 the Court has full powers, jurisdiction, and authority to review [145] the proceedings of all subordinate courts and if necessary to set aside or correct them.[146]

All sentences in criminal cases in which the punishment awarded is imprisonment for any period exceeding eighteen months or a fine exceeding R500 (in the case of a Resident Magistrate's Court), or imprisonment for more than six months or a fine of more than R100 (in the case of courts of the First Class), or imprisonment for more than three months or a fine of more than R50, or any whipping [147] (in the case of courts of the Second and Third Classes) are subject in the ordinary course to automatic review by the High Court. This is without prejudice to the right of appeal against such sentence whether before or after confirmation of the sentence by the High Court.[148] The system of automatic review provides a valuable safeguard against injustice, especially in keeping sentences uniform, since persons sentenced in the subordinate courts are often unrepresented and may be unaware of their right of appeal.

---

145. The difference between review proceedings and appeals was explained by the High Court in Kheoli v. Mapeshoane, [1963-66] H.C.T.L.R. 127, 128:

> In an appeal it may be said that there is a retrial, but in a review this is not the case; this Court is really only concerned to see whether the proceedings appear to be in accordance with real and substantial justice, and has not to go into the facts of the case. . . .

146. High Court Act (No. 4 of 1967), § 7.

147. Save in any case in which a male child under the age of eighteen has been sentenced under the Criminal Procedure and Evidence Proclamation.

148. Subordinate Court Proc., § 67 as amended by Proc. 5 of 1964, § 18.

(4) SUBORDINATE COURTS

The subordinate courts were established by the Subordinate Courts Proclamation of 1938.[149] The magisterial system was based on a few legally qualified magistrates supplemented to a large extent by administrative officers who were entitled to hold courts according to their rank. Subordinate courts were divided into three classes, and Senior District Officers and District Commissioners could hold Courts of the First Class. whereas District Officers could hold Courts of the Second Class, and cadets those of the Third Class.

The Subordinate Courts Proclamation was amended on many occasions prior to Independence,[150] and in 1964 the basis for the constitution of these courts was altered.[151] The Independence Order of 1966 left that arrangement unchanged [152] and the position at present is that there is provision for five classes of courts: [153]

(i) Resident Magistrate
(ii) First Class
(iii) Second Class
(iv) Third Class
(v) Special Class

However in 1967 there were no courts of third class or special jurisdiction actually operating.[154]

The judicial powers that administrative officers

---

149. Proc. 58 of 1938.

150. By Procs. 12 of 1943, 52 of 1947, 12 of 1948, 64 of 1951, 70 of 1952, 77 of 1954, 96 of 1955, 48 of 1959, 13 of 1960, and 5 of 1964.

151. By Proc. 5 of 1964.

152. § 120(1) of the Constitution read with § 4(2) of the Independence Order.

153. Proc. 5 of 1964, § 5(3).

154. There were five resident magistrates, four first class, and two second class.

used to possess have now been taken away from them so that there are currently only full-time magistrates. Resident Magistrates may exercise any powers and jurisdiction conferred on any magistrate of another class,[155] and their jurisdiction and powers extend the length and breadth of the country.[156] Other magistrates who are appointed are entitled to exercise powers and jurisdiction of such class as may be specified in their respective appointments.[157]

The powers and jurisdiction of a magistrate appointed to the special class are such as may from time to time be prescribed by the Chief Justice.[158]

(a) Original Jurisdiction

(i) Criminal

All subordinate courts have summary jurisdiction over all offences except treason, murder, and sedition, though this category of exceptions may be enlarged in relation to courts of the special class.[159] However there are various limitations on the punishments the different subordinate courts may impose: [160]

a. *Resident Magistrates:* imprisonment for a period not exceeding four years; fine not exceeding R1,000 or in default of payment, imprisonment not exceeding four years; whipping not exceeding fifteen strokes with a cane.[161]

b. *First Class:* imprisonment for a period not exceeding two years; fine not exceeding R200 or in de-

---

155. *Supra* note 153, § 4(4).

156. *Id.* § 5(3).

157. *Id.* § 4(2).

158. *Id.* § 5(6).

159. *Id.* § 14.

160. Subordinate Courts Proc. § 62 as amended by Proc. 5 of 1964, § 16.

161. This is subject to alteration under § 82 of the Subordinate Courts Proclamation by the Chief Justice.

fault of payment, imprisonment not exceeding two years; whipping not exceeding fifteen strokes with a cane.

c. *Second Class:* imprisonment for a period not exceeding one year; fine not exceeding R100 or in default of payment, imprisonment not exceeding one year; whipping not exceeding eight strokes with a cane.

d. *Third Class:* imprisonment for a period not exceeding six months; fine not exceeding R50 or in default of payment, imprisonment not exceeding six months. No punishment of whipping may be imposed.

A person convicted of any offence may be punished by both fine and imprisonment, or by both imprisonment and whipping, but not by both fine and whipping.[162]

Apart from their summary jurisdiction, subordinate courts may have cases remitted to them for trial or sentence. The remittal may be under the ordinary jurisdiction of the court or under an increased jurisdiction.[163]

In addition, subordinate courts hold preparatory examinations to determine whether or not an accused should be committed for trial.

(ii) Civil

Broadly it may be said that Resident Magistrates' Courts and Courts of the First and Second Class have civil jurisdiction over actions founded upon liquid documents, actions relating to the delivery of property, and other actions (with the exception of those mentioned below) within certain financial limits. A Resident Magistrate's Court has jurisdiction provided the amount of the claim or the value of the subject mat-

---

162. Subordinate Courts Proclamation, § 62(2).

163. *Id.* § 64.

ter does not exceed R2,000; for a Court of the First Class the figure is R1,000, and for a Court of the Second Class, R500. Courts of the Third Class have no civil jurisdiction, and courts of the Special Class are specifically allotted actions in which the dispute relates to *bohali* without any limit as to value.[164]

Subject to the exceptions below, subordinate courts have jurisdiction to determine any action or proceeding that would otherwise be beyond their jurisdiction if the parties consent thereto in writing.[165]

Matters in which subordinate courts have no jurisdiction whatever under the Subordinate Courts Proclamation are the following:

a. Dissolution of a marriage, or separation from bed or board or of goods of married persons;

b. The validity or interpretation of a will or other testamentary document;

c. The status of a person in respect of mental capacity (except as provided by any law relating to Mental Health);

d. Where a decree of specific performance of an act is sought without an alternative of payment of damages (except the rendering of an account or the delivery or transfer of property);

e. Where a decree of perpetual silence is sought;

f. Where provisional sentence is sought.[166]

The advantages of bringing an action in the subordinate courts are: there is less delay before trial than in the High Court and the scale of costs is lower. In addition, there are subordinate courts throughout Lesotho while the High Court invariably sits in the capital.

---

164. Proc. 5 of 1964, § 16(1).

165. *Supra* note 162, § 28.

166. *Id.* § 29 as amended by Proc. 5 of 1964, § 12.

(b) Review Jurisdiction

All sentences in criminal cases imposed by a subordinate court of the third class are subject to review as of course by a resident magistrate or a magistrate entitled to exercise first class powers and jurisdiction.[167]

In addition, every magistrate has access to all central and local courts in his district and to their records which he should check daily. He has wide powers to revise any proceedings of such courts, either of his own motion or on the application of the accused in a criminal case, or on the application of either of the parties in a civil case.[168]

(c) Transfer of Proceedings

Provision is made for the transfer of proceedings commenced in a subordinate court to a local or central court if the subordinate court considers the action would be more conveniently dealt with in that court.[169]

(5) JUDICIAL COMMISSIONER'S COURTS

These courts were established for the first time in 1944.[170] They have the same original jurisdiction as subordinate courts of the first class except that no civil suit or action or other civil proceedings can be commenced there.[171]

The bulk of their work, however, consists of hearing civil appeals from the Basotho central courts.[172]

---

167. *Id.* § 17.

168. Central and Local Courts Proc., § 26.

169. Proc. 5 of 1964, § 8(2) replacing § 16 of the Subordinate Courts Proclamation.

170. By Proc. 16 of 1944. They are presently governed by Proc. 25 of 1950 which replaced the earlier proclamation.

171. *Id.* § 4(1).

172. In 1967, 242 civil appeals and petitions were heard and only seventeen criminal.

The post of Judicial Commissioner is usually held by someone who has both an interest in and some experience of the customary law.[173] He does, however, have the aid of an assessor who can be of invaluable assistance to him. The penchant for litigation of the Basotho people is amply evidenced by the number of cases that go on appeal to the Judicial Commissioner's Court.[174] Usually they have already come through one appeal from a local court to a central court.

The court appears to rely mainly on its assessor and its own experience in the ascertainment of rules of customary law. Although previous decisions of the court are rarely cited, which is inevitable since they are not published or indexed, the rules propounded in previous cases are often recalled.

Appeals do not take the form of a complete rehearing, but are rather decided upon the basis of the record made by the lower court. Lawyers may appear before the court in both civil and criminal cases.

The courts are empowered to state a case for consideration by the High Court on a point of law, and an interesting example of this is found in the case of *Thipanyane v. R.*[175] The Judicial Commissioner requested guidance on whether or not he was bound by the Criminal Procedure and Evidence Proclamation in hearing criminal appeals from courts administering customary law. There was a conflict between this Proclamation and the 1938 Native Courts Proclamation which the High Court resolved.

---

173. The author of SOTHO LAWS AND CUSTOMS (O.U.P. 1960), PATRICK DUNCAN, was Judicial Commissioner from 1950 to 1952.

174. *See supra* note 172.

175. [1926-53] H.C.T.L.R. 203.

(6) CENTRAL AND LOCAL COURTS

This is the style and title recently conferred [176] on the Basotho courts, which were formerly known as native courts.[177] It is proposed to make a brief examination of their history and development before looking at their jurisdiction at the present time.

(a) History up to 1938 [178]

Following Basutoland's disannexation from the Cape in 1883, provision was made for customary law to continue to be administered in cases between Africans by the chief's courts.[179] This was in line with the policy of indirect rule. However by 1922 there was growing dissatisfaction with the delays that were a prominent feature of procedure in these courts. Proposals for the reform of the courts were placed before the Basutoland Council in 1928, but after lengthy debates no agreement was reached. During this time chiefs were adjudicating on disputes of virtually every conceivable nature between Basotho and were exercising their executive functions concurrently. The *Laws of Lerotholi* [180] provided that chiefs were bound to preside over cases of disputants unless they were prevented by illness from doing so. Some minor authorities did in fact preside personally over their courts, but often the more important chiefs left the hearing of cases to one of their deputies. The chiefs often set up an informal panel of assistants, usually

---

176. By the Native Courts Proclamation and Rules (Amendment) Regulations 1965 (Regulation No. 10 of 1965), § 22.

177. As constituted by the Native Courts Proclamation (N.C.P.), Proc. No. 62 of 1938.

178. *See generally* ASHTON, THE BASUTO Ch. XIV (2d ed. O.U.P. 1967) and HAILEY, *supra* note 114, §§ XI-XV.

179. *See* the General Law Proclamation (Proc. 2B of 1884).

180. In § 19 of the version of 1922.

drawn from their relations, from among whom the Court President would be chosen. The assistants could step in when the President was unable to hear a case. It appears that not infrequently there was a lack of communication between the various persons who heard cases and there were innumerable delays, both in securing the attendance of witnesses and parties, and in enforcing judgments. Thus a litigant might ask the President what had been done about his case and get an evasive reply to the effect that the President knew nothing about it as one of his assistants had dealt with it on the previous occasion. Litigants eventually got tired of the courts shirking their responsibilities and this fact, coupled with the charge that the chiefs were conniving in stocktheft, brought matters to a head and, together with Sir Alan Pim's Economic Report of 1935, finally culminated in the reforms of 1938.

In addition the chiefs were beginning to lose touch with the people. They were feathering their own nests and giving privileged positions to their sons by "placing" them. In this way the number of authorities increased and the number of people entitled to hold courts became greater each year.

(b) The Native Courts Proclamation of 1938

This proclamation gave the Resident Commissioner the power, with the approval of the High Commissioner, to issue warrants recognising or establishing such courts as he thought fit. Thus he exercised control over the number of courts as well as their personnel. The members of a court could be suspended and even dismissed with the approval of the High Commissioner. The extent of the courts' civil and criminal jurisdiction was set out in their respective warrants, with certain fields removed from their powers.

The Native Courts Proclamation has been

amended on several occasions since 1938,[181] but it is still substantially in force under its new title of the Central and Local Courts Proclamation.

One of the important changes made by the 1938 Proclamation was that, in theory at any rate, only courts with warrants could exercise jurisdiction under the law. Other courts continued to operate in practice in the traditional manner. Simultaneously under the 1938 Native Administration Proclamation,[182] 1,340 chiefs, sub-chiefs and headmen were recognised by identification in the Gazette and all these were issued with court warrants at the outset, until it was decided how many courts were in fact needed.

In 1946 a National Treasury was set up and this necessitated a careful scrutiny of the number of customary courts the country could afford. The Drafting Committee recommended a reduction of the courts to 117, including five Central Courts of Appeal. The Committee did not lay down any clear principle for the separation of executive and judicial functions; however it was assumed that the chiefs would not ordinarily sit in their courts but would rather appoint others to act as Presidents, perhaps from among responsible sub-chiefs. Eventually warrants were issued in 1946 to 121 Chiefs' Courts and this number was reduced to 106 in 1949. The other courts out of the original 1,340 could still function as courts of arbitrament but their decisions could not be enforced.

The difference between the relationship of a chief

181. By Procs. 23 of 1939, 16 of 1944, 9 of 1946, 25 of 1950, 39 of 1952, 46 of 1953, 58 of 1953, 1 of 1961, the Adaptation of Existing Laws (No. 1) Order 1964, and Regulation No. 10 of 1965.

182. Proc. 61 of 1938.

to his court before and after 1938 is well illustrated by the High Court decision in *R. v. Leteketa Rantletse.*[183] Chief Matlere of Mokhotlong District ordered the accused to remove his hut and reside in another village. The accused refused to obey the order and so Chief Matlere sent a headman and 30 messengers to demolish the hut. The accused, in resisting this attack killed one of the messengers. The question arose whether he was justified in using force to repel the invaders. The court held that he was, because the messengers were trespassers and he was entitled to defend his property against them. Section 8 of Part I of the *Laws of Lerotholi* states:

> No person shall be deprived of his hut or huts except under the authority of an order of a competent Court.

The crucial determination by the High Court was, therefore, that no court had in fact given its authority. Only Chief Matlere had authorised the "eating-up," as it is called, of the accused's hut, and thus it was an unlawful act. Harragin C. J. elaborated on the consequences of the 1938 changes:

> I do sympathise to some extent with the Chief in this case, because there is not the slightest doubt that before 1938, the Chief was the Court, but since then he has only become the senior member of it and he omitted what no doubt was to him an entirely unnecessary step in putting the matter before the Court. . . . I also think that Chief Matlere, wrong though he may be in law, was only carrying out what no doubt for a number of years every Chief has done, and I can only say that I hope this case will bring home to the Chiefs of this Territory that their authority to take drastic action does not lie in themselves, but in the Courts of the Territory, and that care should be taken

183. [1926-53] H.C.T.L.R. 226.

in future to see that the letter of the law is carried out.[184]

(c) Present Constitution of Central and Local Courts

The recognition, constitution, powers, and jurisdiction of these courts is now regulated by the Central and Local Courts Proclamation.[185] They are established or recognised by warrants under the hand of the responsible minister, acting with the concurrence of the Chief Justice.[186] At present there are thirteen central and fifty-eight local courts. The central courts hear appeals from the local courts, in addition to their jurisdiction in cases of first instance.[187]

(i) The Law To Be Administered [188]

This consists of:

a. The customary law prevailing in the country, so far as it is not repugnant to justice or morality or inconsistent with the provisions of any law in force in Lesotho. This "repugnancy clause" is discussed in Part I. [189]

b. The provisions of all rules or orders made by the King or a chief, sub-chief or headman under the Chieftainship (Powers) Proclamation,[190] which are in force within the area of jurisdiction of the Court. The Chieftainship (Powers) Proclamation, which was the

---

184. *Id.* at 228.

185. Reprinted, as amended, in X LAWS OF BASUTOLAND 186 (1965).

186. *See* § 2(1) of Central and Local Courts Proclamation.

187. In 1967 the central courts heard 928 civil cases and 736 criminal cases. The local courts during the same year heard 9,245 civil cases and 10,619 criminal cases. (LESOTHO—REPORT FOR YEAR 117) (Dept. of Information, Maseru 1967).

188. Central and Local Courts Proclamation, § 9.

189. *See supra* pp. 154-169.

190. Proc. 61 of 1938 as amended.

1938 Native Administration Proclamation embellished with a new title, has been repealed by the Chieftainship Act of 1968.[191] It used to list the various types of orders that the King might issue, *e.g.*, prohibiting or regulating the brewing and sale of intoxicating liquors, gambling, the possession of arms, the pollution of water, the cutting of trees, and the spread of disease.[192]

Parts II and III of the *Laws of Lerotholi* consist of rules and orders made under the Proclamation, and these remain in force despite the enactment of the Chieftainship Act except in one particular.[193]

c. The provisions of any law that itself authorises Basotho Courts to administer it. Examples of laws that fall into this category are the Partnerships Proclamation [194] and the Basic and Graded Tax (Consolidation) Act.[195]

d. The provisions of any law the court may be authorised to administer by an order made by the responsible minister with the concurrence of the Chief Justice.

(ii) Original Jurisdiction.

Subject to any express provision granting such jurisdiction, no central or local court has jurisdiction to try cases in which a person is charged with an offence in consequence of which death is alleged to have occurred or which is punishable with death or imprisonment for life. Nor can these courts try cases in connection with marriage other than a marriage con-

---

191. Act 22 of 1968.

192. § 9(1).

193. The Act in § 40 expressly repeals Order No. 10 of Part III of the LAWS OF LEROTHOLI which deals with chiefs and headmen absenting themselves.

194. Proc. 78 of 1957.

195. Act No. 24 of 1968.

tracted under or in accordance with the customary law, except where and insofar as the case concerns the payment or return or disposal of *bohali*.[196]

The courts have the civil and criminal jurisdiction set out in their respective warrants, and broadly speaking this jurisdiction is based on the cause of action having arisen in, or the defendant being ordinarily resident within the court's area in civil actions, and the offence having been committed therein in criminal proceedings.[197] The warrants specify certain financial limits for jurisdiction in civil proceedings and also lay down the maximum punishments that may be imposed in sentencing offenders.

(iii) Appellate Jurisdiction

Any person aggrieved by any order or decision of a local court may within 30 days from the date of such order or decision appeal to a central court.[198] From there appeals lie to the Court of the Judicial Commissioner.

(iv) Practice and Procedure in the Central and Local Courts.

Local courts theoretically sit five days a week, whereas central courts, being largely appellate, only sit at intervals.

Each court has a President and also a clerk who acts as prosecutor in criminal cases. The clerk does not however advise the President either on the law or on points of procedure. The President reaches his decision on the basis of his own knowledge and experience of the law and without the assistance of assessors or other advisers. He may on occasion recall one of his earlier decisions and follow it but extensive use can-

---

196. Central and Local Courts Proclamation, § 8(1).

197. *Id.* §§ 6 & 7.

198. *Id.* § 28(1).

not be made of precedent in the absence of indexed records of decisions in the Basotho courts and in the Judicial Commissioner's Court.[199]

The traditional procedure that used to obtain in the Basotho courts has been modernised and is now much closer to the procedure in the other courts.

The Basuto Courts (Practice and Procedure) Rules, 1961 [200] provide that practice and procedure shall be regulated in accordance with Sesotho custom and law and also in accordance with the provisions of the Rules. Certain specific directions of principle are laid down as follows: [201]

a. No court shall act in bad faith or from improper motives.

b. The President and every assessor shall apply his mind to the question under consideration and every President shall come in good faith to a genuine decision thereon.

c. No court President shall deliver judgment in a case in which he personally did not hear the evidence.

d. No Basotho Court shall act unlawfully in contravention of Sesotho law or any other law.

e. The proceedings of every court shall be conducted in such a way as to give fair hearing to all litigants including the accused person and the prosecutor in criminal cases; and all such litigants shall have the right to call, examine, and cross-examine witnesses, and to address the court on the merits or demerits of the matter before the Court.

It is clear that in the event of an inconsistency between Sesotho custom and the Rules, the latter must

---

199. The Judicial Commissioner occasionally circulates important decisions to the customary courts.

200. G.N. No. 21 of 1961.

201. *Id.* rule 8.

prevail [202] and it is proposed to examine a few of the respects in which Sesotho custom has been affected by the Rules.

Traditionally anyone present at a case was entitled to examine or cross-examine the witnesses, but now this may only be done by or on behalf of the parties or by the Court.[203]

Ashton reports that whereas in the Paramount Chief's Courts the wealthier people might employ special pleaders *(akhente)* this is contrary to traditional practice and theory, which place the burden on the judge to discover the truth and not merely to referee a struggle between the parties.[204] For this reason the employment of lawyers in the courts was forbidden by the old Native Courts Proclamation.[205] This is now permitted by the Central and Local Courts Proclamation [206] as well as guaranteed by the Constitution [207] in criminal cases. In civil proceedings no party can be represented by a legal practitioner, though the court may permit a husband or wife or guardian or other nonlegal representative who has that party's authority, to appear instead.[208]

A somewhat anomalous position has resulted in civil cases because whereas there has been a shift from the "inquisitorial" to the "accusatorial" system, legal representation has not been introduced and thus the onus lies on the parties to carry on any cross-examination. Formerly they could look to the judge to ask the necessary penetrating questions to ascertain the truth

---

202. See Central and Local Courts Proclamation § 9(a).
203. Basuto Courts Rules, rule 22.
204. *Supra* note 178, at 234.
205. § 20.
206. By Regulation 10 of 1965, § 14.
207. § 12(2)(d).
208. Central and Local Courts Proc., § 20.

or falsehood of testimony, and many litigants still lose cases today through a failure to appreciate the fundamental change that has occurred.[209]

The more important customary courts have been keeping records for many years, though somewhat erratically and with varying fullness. The Rules now provide that records of all proceedings must be kept [210] and in various prescribed books, records, and forms. All evidence given must be taken down in narrative form, read back to the witness or party and signed by him.[211]

Under the Rules, where judgment is given for the payment of money or stock, such payment must be made forthwith unless the court allows it to be made in instalments.[212] Traditionally fines went to the chief and he might slaughter a beast for the judges, but now fines go to the Government.

Formerly the ultimate sanction for a recalcitrant judgment debtor was for him to be "eaten up," *i.e.*, have his stock seized and his hut burnt. This practice was prohibited and has now died out.[213] The Rules provide for execution to be levied on a debtor's property and exempt certain items such as necessary bedding and wearing apparel, furniture, and household utensils up to R30, food and drink sufficient to tide him over until the next harvest, tools and implements of trade up to R40, professional books, documents, or instruments up to R40, and immovable property and growing crops.[214] Debts and emoluments may also be

---

209. *See, e.g.*, Mapane v. Motheolane, J.C. 112/1965; Ranthithi v. Khojane, J.C. 142/1967.

210. *Supra* note 203, rule 3.

211. *Id.* rule 19.

212. *Id.* rules 49 and 50.

213. On "eating-up," *see* DUNCAN, *supra* note 173, at 70.

214. *Supra* note 203, rule 47.

attached.[215] If a person willfully disobeys or neglects to comply with an order or judgment of the court, or fails to point out property to satisfy a judgment debt, or obstructs a messenger in the execution of his duty, he is guilty of contempt of court and on conviction he can be fined up to R50 and in default of payment sentenced to up to three months' imprisonment with or without hard labour.[216]

On the criminal side the procedure is similar to that followed in the subordinate courts.[217] Whereas previously the courts' powers were basically limited to fines, public ridicule, and occasional banishment (and in the time of Moshoeshoe even the death penalty for sorcery, inveterate thieving, and conspiring against the chief, until he abolished it) they can now imprison offenders. Fines used to be of animals but now all fines must be paid in cash.[218] Apart from fines and imprisonment, the court may inflict any punishment authorised by customary law, provided such punishment is not repugnant to natural justice and humanity. The fine or other punishment must in no case be excessive but always proportional to the nature and circumstances of the offence and the circumstances of the offender.[219] If a central or local court considers that a greater punishment should be inflicted on an offender than it has power to inflict, it may commit him in custody for sentence by a higher court.[220] Thus a local court may commit for sentence to a central court and a central court may commit to a subordinate court.

---

215. *Id.* rule 51.

216. Central and Local Courts Proclamation, § 15.

217. *See supra* note 203, rule 89.

218. *Id.* rule 97(2).

219. Central and Local Courts Proclamation, § 11(1).

220. Central and Local Courts (Amendment) Act (No. 35 of 1967), § 2.

In line with the traditional overlap of civil and criminal sanctions, the Rules permit a court to direct that any fine or part thereof shall be paid to the person injured or aggrieved by the act or omission in respect of which the fine has been imposed, on condition that if such person accepts the payment he shall not thereafter bring any civil proceedings to recover damages in respect of the same loss or injury.[221]

There are provisions in the Central and Local Courts Proclamation to counter delay, which was the bane of the litigant in former times. Aggrieved parties may apply in cases of unreasonable delay to a higher court which may then give such directions as it sees fit for the speedy hearing of the case.[222]

One of the fundamental features of customary law is its emphasis upon reconciliation, often through the good offices of a mediator (commonly a chief or headman). However there may be a risk that this will, on occasion, spread itself so widely as to constitute adjudication by unauthorised persons. For this reason it has been made an offence to exercise or attempt to exercise judicial powers within the area of a duly constituted central or local court without the proper authority to do so.[223] However it is still legitimate, and indeed common, for the traditional authorities to conduct proceedings in the nature of arbitrament with a view to settling disputes out of court, especially in

221. Central and Local Courts Proc., § 14. However we are informed that very little use is in fact made of this practice. In the non-Basotho courts, compensation may be awarded in criminal proceedings to any person who has suffered injury or loss through the offence of the convicted party—*see* Criminal Procedure and Evidence Proclamation (No. 59 of 1938), § 315. *See also* Brown, *The Award of Compensation in Criminal Cases in East Africa*, 1966 J.A.L. 33.

222. Central and Local Courts Proclamation, § 31.

223. *Id.* § 21.

matters relating to land. What is not so apparent is whether the regular courts still try to achieve the traditional result of a solution acceptable to the parties or whether they stick closely to the letter of the law. A court may sometimes enquire, to family disputes, whether or not any real attempt has been made to settle the matter within the family, and if no attempt has been made the court may on occasion refer the matter to the family first, if the parties are agreeable.

B. The Judiciary and the Magistracy

The rules governing the appointment of the judges of the superior courts are laid down in the Constitution.†† The ideal of judicial independence was clearly spelt out at the International Conference of Jurists at New Delhi in 1959 in the following terms:

Clause 1: [224]

> An independent Judiciary is an indispensable requisite of a free society under the Rule of Law. Such independence implies freedom from interference by the Executive or Legislative with the exercise of the Judicial function, but does not mean that the judge is entitled to act in an arbitrary manner. His duty is to interpret the law and the fundamental principles and assumptions that underlie it. It is implicit in the concept of independence set out in the present paragraph that provision should be made for the adequate remuneration of the Judiciary and that a judge's

---

†† Many of these rules have been re-enacted in the Court of Appeal and High Court Order, 1970 following upon the suspension of the 1966 Constitution. However, there are certain variations, in the main caused by the demise of the Judicial Service Commission which was a creature of the Constitution and has not been re-established. Moreover, the judges' security of tenure is not so carefully safeguarded as it was.

224. The Report of Committee IV.

right to the remuneration settled for his office should not during his term of office be altered to his disadvantage.

Clause 3:

The principle of irremovability of the Judiciary and their security of tenure until death or until a retiring age fixed by statute is reached, is an important safeguard of the Rule of Law. Although it is not impossible for a judge appointed for a fixed term to assert his independence, particularly if he is seeking reappointment, he is subject to greater difficulties and pressure than a judge who enjoys security of tenure for his working life.

Clause 4:

The reconciliation of the principle of irremovability of the Judiciary with the possibility of removal in exceptional circumstances necessitates that the grounds for removal should be before a body of judicial character assuring at least the same safeguards to the judge as would be accorded to an accused person in a criminal trial.[225]

This ideal of judicial independencc is safeguarded to a large extent in Lesotho both by the manner in which judges are appointed and by giving judges security of tenure.

(1) THE COURT OF APPEAL

The judges of the Court of Appeal are the President, together with such number (if any) of Justices of Appeal as may be prescribed by Parliament and the Chief Justice and the puisne judges (if any) of the High Court *ex officio*.[226] Parliament may provide for the office of President to be held by the Chief Justice *ex officio*, but otherwise the President is appointed by

225. REPORT OF THE INTERNATIONAL COMMISSION OF JURISTS 157 (1959).

226. § 115 of the Constitution.

the King acting in accordance with the advice of the Prime Minister. The Justices of Appeal are also appointed by the King but here he acts in accordance with the advice of the Judicial Service Commission.[227]

The qualifications for the President and Justices of Appeal are that they must hold or have held office as judges of a court of unlimited jurisdiction in civil and criminal matters in some part of the Commonwealth or in any country outside the Commonwealth that Parliament may prescribe, or a court having jurisdiction in appeals from such a court. Alternatively they must hold one or other of the qualifications necessary for admission as a legal practitioner in Lesotho and have held such professional qualification for a total period of not less than seven years.[228] Generally, judges of the Court of Appeal must retire on reaching the age of 62, but fixed appointments for three years may be made of those who have attained that age.[229]

A judge appointed to the Court of Appeal may only be removed from office for inability to perform the functions of his office or for misbehaviour, and even then only after advice has been so given to the King by a tribunal consisting of three persons who hold or have held high judicial office.[230] The salary of a judge of the Court of Appeal is a charge upon the Consolidated Fund and such salary and other terms of service cannot be altered to his disadvantage during his term of office.[231] The same applies for judges of the High Court (see below).

---

227. *Id.* §§ 115(2) and 116 (1) and (2).
228. *Id.* § 116(3).
229. *Id.* § 117(1) and (8).
230. *Id.* § 117(4), (5), and (6).
231. *Id.* § 107.

(2) THE HIGH COURT

The High Court is composed of the Chief Justice and one puisne judge.[232] At any session of the High Court, the Court consists of a single judge unless the Chief Justice directs otherwise.[233] The Chief Justice is appointed by the King acting in accordance with the advice of the Prime Minister. Puisne judges are appointed by the King, acting in accordance with the advice of the Judicial Service Commission[234]

The qualifications of judges of the High Court are the same as for judges of the Court of Appeal, save in one minor particular.[235]

The retirement age is 70 at present [236] with the same proviso about a possible further fixed term of three years as for judges of the Court of Appeal. A judge of the High Court may only be removed from office for inability to perform the functions of his office or for misbehaviour, and a tribunal must be set up first, as for the removal of a judge of the Court of Appeal.[237] In addition, the Judicial Committee of the Privy Council has to advise the King that the judge ought to be removed from office.

(3) THE SUBORDINATE COURTS

The staffing of the subordinate courts is regulated by the Judicial Service Commission. The Judicial Service Commission was established by the Constitution [238] and is made up of three members. These are the Chief Justice, the Chairman of the Public Service

232. *Id.* § 110(2) and High Court Act, 1967, § 3(1).
233. High Court Act, § 3(2).
234. Constitution, §§ 111(1) and (2).
235. *Id.* § 111(3).
236. High Court Act, § 4.
237. Constitution, § 112(3) *and see* § 112(4).
238. *Id.* § 125.

Commission (or a member of that Commission delegated by the Chairman), and a member appointed by the King acting in accordance with the advice of the Prime Minister, from among those who hold or have held high judical office.

Power is conferred upon the Judicial Service Commission to make various judicial appointments, confirmations in office, and dismissals as well as to exercise disciplinary control over the holders of various offices. The offices to which these powers relate are those of Registrar or Assistant Registrar of the High Court and Court of Appeal and the magistrates.[239] Assessors are not subject to the Commission.[240]

(4) THE JUDICIAL COMMISSIONERS' COURTS

At present there is only one Judicial Commissioner although there is provision for the appointment of more than one.[241] He is an itinerant magistrate travelling from district to district, although he also has a court in Maseru. He, like most other members of subordinate courts, is appointed by the Judicial Service Commission which also exercises disciplinary control over him.

(5) CENTRAL AND LOCAL COURTS

The central and local courts are staffed by court presidents, who are appointed by the Judicial Service Commission.[242] They generally have limited educational qualifications. They need only be literate in Sesotho,

---

239. *Id.* § 126.
240. *Id.* § 126(4).
241. Proc. 25 of 1950, § 3.
242. In 1967 there were eight Central Courts' Presidents, six Local Courts' Presidents Class I, and 54 Local Courts' Presidents Class II. (LESOTHO—REPORT FOR THE YEAR 117 (1967)).

for they must be able to keep proper records of the cases they hear. Only a small proportion of those appointed are chiefs. Presidents may on occasion be comparatively young men with little experience. The retiring age is 55, but this may be extended by short contracts for two years at a time.

C. The Legal Profession

The legal profession is divided into two branches, advocates and attorneys. This does not correspond, however, with the English division into barristers and solicitors, since there are equal rights of audience in the Court of Appeal, the High Court, Judicial Commissioner's courts, and the subordinate courts.[243] There is also a right of audience in the central and local courts, but this is limited to criminal proceedings.[244] An important respect in which the branches of the profession diverge is in the keeping of accounts. Attorneys are required to keep separate trust accounts of clients' moneys together with proper books of accounts [245] and must furnish the Law Society with an accountant's certificate at least once in each calendar year.[246] Advocates are not subject to these regulations.

Members of both professions must be duly admitted to practice under the provisions of the Legal Practitioners Act 1967 [247] or its predecessors. In this respect the branches of the profession also diverge.

---

243. Legal Practitioners Proclamation, § 33.

244. Central and Local Courts Proclamation, § 20, *and see* § 12(2)(d) of the Constitution.

245. *Id.* § 24.

246. *Id.* § 25.

247. Act 11 of 1967, repealing the Legal Practitioners Proclamation (No. 93 of 1935), the Legal Practitioners (Temporary Provision) Law 1962, and the Legal Practitioners (Temporary Provision) Law (Amendment) 1966.

Petitions for admission and enrolment as a legal practitioner are made to the High Court, a copy being served on the Law Society.[248] A proper Law Society has not yet been created by Parliament and until this has been done its functions are performed by the Principal Legal Adviser. Every person who wishes to be admitted and enrolled as an *advocate* must prove to the satisfaction of the High Court that he is over 21 years of age and that he is a fit and proper person to be admitted. In addition he must satisfy one of the professional qualifications laid down.

The newest of these qualifications and the one that is most likely to be used for the future is possession of the degree of Bachelor of Laws from the University of Botswana, Lesotho and Swaziland. The LL.B. degree course is made up of three parts, with the first two years in Lesotho followed by two years at Edinburgh University and a final six months in Lesotho. The first LL.B. students graduated in 1969 after four and a half years. Other qualifications for enrolment are:

(i) Admission and present enrolment as a barrister in England or Ireland, or as an advocate in Scotland.

(ii) Admission and present enrolment as an advocate in the Republic of South Africa, South West Africa, or Rhodesia.

(iii) Possesson of qualifications entitling the applicant to be admitted to any of the above.

(iv) Having been or being entitled to be admitted to practise as an attorney of the courts of Lesotho under the Act.[249]

(v) Admission and enrolment as a barrister, advocate, solicitor, or attorney of the courts of any coun-

---

248. *Supra* note 244, § 29.
249. Legal Practitioners Act, § 6.

try (other than those mentioned in (i) and (ii) above) approved by regulations made by the Chief Justice.[250] Such regulations have not yet been made.

Similar application must be made for admission as an *attorney.* A person possessing the degree of Bachelor of Laws from the University of Botswana, Lesotho and Swaziland will, however, have to pass a practical examination covering the practice and procedure of the different courts of Lesotho, such practical bookkeeping as may be necessary for the keeping of books of account, and the conduct and duties of the profession.

Another method of becoming an attorney is to serve a period of articles of clerkship with a practising attorney. The period is three years for a person holding an approved degree (which includes a degree of Bachelor of Laws at the University of Botswana, Lesotho and Swaziland).[251] In addition, two examinations must be passed, including the practical examination referred to above. In view of the long period of articles required, it seems unlikely that this method will be used except by persons who do not hold approved degrees.[252] In certain circumstances articled

---

250. *Id.* § 21.

251. *Id.* § 7 and the Schedule. Provision is also made for admission as attorneys of British solicitors and attorneys enrolled in S. Africa, S. W. Africa, and Rhodesia. *Also* any person entitled to be admitted as an advocate of the Courts of Lesotho can be admitted as an attorney provided he has passed the practical examination—§ 7(c)(iii).

252. In the absence of an approved degree, a person intending to serve articles must have passed the Cambridge Overseas School Certificate, or the matriculation examination conducted and controlled by the Joint Matriculation Board of the University of South Africa, or an examination certified by the Permanent Secretary for Education to be equivalent or superior thereto: *Id.* § 9(b)(i).

clerks are entitled to appear in subordinate courts and before any board, tribunal, or similar body on behalf of their principals.[253]

Attorneys may apply to be admitted as notaries public and conveyancers.[254]

Disciplinary control over legal practitioners is exercised by the High Court and the Law Society. The registrar refers to the Law Society any complaint of professional misconduct and the Law Society may take appropriate action. However the Law Society has no power to strike practitioners off the roll or suspend them. It must apply to the High Court for such an order.[255]

D. Law Reporting

Most of the important cases decided in the Basutoland High Court, as well as those that went up to the Court of Appeal for Basutoland, the Bechuanaland Protectorate, and Swaziland, and the Privy Council are to be found in the several volumes of the High Commission Territories Law Reports (H.C.T.L.R.).

This series was started in 1955 with the publication of a volume spanning the years 1926 to 1953, edited by the then Chief Justice of the three High Commission Territories. It included decisions of the three High Courts and appeals to the Privy Council.

Annual volumes appeared from 1954 until 1960, and from 1955 onwards these contained, in addition, decisions of the new joint Court of Appeal.

Since 1960 only two volumes have been published, one for the years 1961-62 and the other for the period 1963 to 1966. An index was also compiled down to 1962.

---

253. *Id.* § 20(3).
254. *Id.* §§ 22 and 23.
255. *Id.* § 28.

No cases decided since 1966 have yet been reported and it remains to be seen whether Lesotho will continue the practice of joint reports with Botswana and Swaziland.

Decisions of the Judicial Commissioner's Court are not reported at all. This is a lamentable state of affairs since most of the important decisions on the customary law are given here and not in the superior courts. The availability of these decisions would seem to be a prerequisite for any research leading to the writing down of the customary law, *e.g.*, for purposes of a restatement, and also for the enactment of comprehensive legislation in some fields. Moreover it is thought that the central and local courts would be greatly assisted by knowledge of the decisions of the Judicial Commissioner's Court.

APPENDIX A

EXCERPTS FROM THE LESOTHO INDEPENDENCE ORDER 1966

Constitution of Lesotho

CHAPTER II

PROTECTION OF FUNDAMENTAL HUMAN RIGHTS AND FREEDOMS

4.—(1) Whereas every person in Lesotho is entitled, whatever his race, tribe, place of origin or residence, political opinions, colour, creed or sex, to fundamental human rights and freedoms, that is to say, to each and all of the following—

(a) the right to life;
(b) the right to personal liberty;
(c) freedom of movement and residence;
(d) freedom from inhuman treatment;
(e) freedom from slavery and forced labour;
(f) freedom from arbitrary search or entry;
(g) the right to respect for private and family life;
(h) the right to a fair trial of criminal charges against him and to a fair determination of his civil rights and obligations;
(i) freedom of conscience;
(j) freedom of expression;
(k) freedom of assembly and association;
(l) freedom from arbitrary seizure of property;
(m) freedom from discrimination; and
(n) the right to equality before the law and the equal protection of the law,

the provisions of this Chapter shall have effect for the purpose of affording protection to those rights and freedoms, subject to such limitations of that protection as are contained in those provisions, being limitations designed to ensure that the enjoyment of the said rights and freedoms by any person does not prejudice the rights and freedoms of others or the public interest.

(2) For the avoidance of doubt and without preju-

dice to any other provision of this Constitution it is hereby declared that the provisions of this Chapter shall, except where the context otherwise requires, apply as well in relation to things done or omitted to be done by persons acting in a private capacity (whether by virtue of any written law or otherwise) as in relation to things done or omitted to be done by or on behalf of the Government of Lesotho or by any person acting in the performance of the functions of any public office or any public authority.

5.—(1) No person shall be deprived of his life intentionally save in execution of the sentence of a court in respect of a criminal offence under the law of Lesotho of which he has been convicted.

(2) Without prejudice to any liability for a contravention of any other law with respect to the use of force in such cases as are hereinafter mentioned, a person shall not be regarded as having been deprived of his life in contravention of this section if he dies as the result of the use of force to such extent as is necessary in the circumstances of the case—

(a) for the defence of any person from violence or for the defence of property;

(b) in order to effect a lawful arrest or to prevent the escape of a person lawfully detained;

(c) for the purpose of suppressing a riot, insurrection or mutiny; or

(d) in order to prevent the commission by that person of a criminal offence,

or if he dies as the result of a lawful act of war.

6.—(1) Every person shall be entitled to personal liberty, that is to say, he shall not be arrested or detained save as may be authorised by law in any of the following cases, that is to say—

(a) in execution of the sentence or order of a court, whether established for Lesotho or for some other country, in respect of a criminal offence of which he has been convicted;

(b) in execution of the order of the High Court or the Court of Appeal punishing him for contempt of that court or of another court or tribunal;

(c) in execution of the order of a court made to se-

cure the fulfilment of any obligation imposed on him by law;

(d) for the purpose of bringing him before a court in execution of the order of a court;

(e) upon reasonable suspicion of his having committed, or being about to commit, a criminal offence under the law of Lesotho;

(f) in the case of a person who has not attained the age of eighteen years, for the purpose of his education or welfare;

(g) for the purpose of preventing the spread of an infectious or contagious disease;

(h) in the case of a person who is, or is reasonably suspected to be, of unsound mind, addicted to drugs or alcohol, or a vagrant, for the purpose of his care and treatment or the protection of the community;

(i) for the purpose of preventing the unlawful entry of that person into Lesotho, or for the purpose of effecting the expulsion, extradition or other lawful removal of that person from Lesotho or for the purpose of restricting that person while he is being conveyed through Lesotho in the course of his extradition or removal as a convicted prisoner from one country to another; or

(j) to such extent as may be necessary in the execution of a lawful order requiring that person to remain within a specified area within Lesotho or prohibiting him from being within such an area, or to such extent as may be reasonably justifiable for the taking of proceedings against that person with a view to the making of any such order or relating to such an order after it has been made, or to such extent as may be reasonably justifiable for restraining that person during any visit that he is permitted to make to any part of Lesotho in which, in consequence of any such order, his presence would otherwise be unlawful.

(2) Any person who is arrested or detained shall be informed as soon as is reasonably practicable, in a language that he understands, of the reasons for his arrest or detention.

(3) Any person who is arrested or detained—

(*a*) for the purpose of bringing him before a court in execution of the order of a court; or
(*b*) upon reasonable suspicion of his having committed, or being about to commit, a criminal offence,

and who is not released, shall be brought before a court as soon as is reasonably practicable, and where he is not brought before a court within twenty-four hours of his arrest or from the commencement of his detention, the burden of proving that he has been brought before a court as soon as is reasonably practicable shall rest upon any person alleging that the provisions of this subsection have been complied with.

(4) Where any person is brought before a court in execution of the order of a court in any proceedings or upon suspicion of his having committed or being about to commit an offence, he shall not be thereafter further held in custody in connection with those proceedings or that offence save upon the order of a court.

(5) If any person arrested or detained upon suspicion of his having committed, or being about to commit, a criminal offence is not tried within a reasonable time, then, without prejudice to any further proceedings that may be brought against him, he shall be released either unconditionally or upon reasonable conditions, including in particular such conditions as are reasonably necessary to ensure that he appears at a later date for trial or for proceedings preliminary to trial.

(6) Without prejudice to the generality of any other provision of this Constitution or any other law by virtue of which a person is entitled to redress for a contravention of this section, any person who is unlawfully arrested or detained by any other person shall be entitled to compensation therefor from that other person or from any other person or authority on whose behalf that other person was acting.

7.—(1) Every person shall be entitled to freedom of movement, that is to say, the right to move freely throughout Lesotho, the right to reside in any part of Lesotho, the right to enter Lesotho, the right to leave Lesotho and immunity from expulsion from Lesotho.

(2) Any restriction on a person's freedom of move-

ment that is involved in his lawful detention shall not be held to be inconsistent with or in contravention of this section.

(3) Nothing contained in or done under the authority of any law shall be held to be inconsistent with or in contravention of this section to the extent that the law in question makes provision—

(a) for the imposition of restrictions in the interests of defence, public safety, public order, public morality or public health on the movement or residence within Lesotho of any person or any person's right to leave Lesotho:

Provided that a person shall not be permitted to rely in any judicial proceedings upon such a provision of law as is referred to in this paragraph except to the extent to which he satisfies the court that the provision or, as the case may be, the thing done under the authority thereof does not restrict the movement or residence within Lesotho or the right to leave Lesotho of the person concerned to a greater extent than is necessary in a practical sense in a democratic society in the interests of any of the matters specified in this paragraph; or

(b) for the imposition of restrictions, by order of a court, on the movement or residence within Lesotho of any person or on any person's right to leave Lesotho either in consequence of his having been convicted of a criminal offence under the law of Lesotho or for the purpose of ensuring that he appears before a court at a later date for trial in respect of such a criminal offence or for proceedings preliminary to trial or for proceedings relating to his extradition or lawful removal from Lesotho;

(c) for the imposition of restrictions on the freedom of movement of any person who is not a citizen of Lesotho;

(d) for the imposition of restrictions on the acquisition or use by any person of land or other property in Lesotho;

(e) for the imposition of restrictions upon the movement or residence within Lesotho or on the right to leave Lesotho of any public officer;

(f) for the removal of a person from Lesotho to be

tried or punished in some other country for a criminal offence under the law of that other country or to undergo imprisonment in some other country in execution of the sentence of a court in respect of a criminal offence of which he has been convicted under the law of Lesotho; or

(g) for the imposition of restrictions on the right of any person to leave Lesotho that are necessary in a practical sense in a democratic society in order to secure the fulfilment of any obligations imposed on that person by law.

(4) If any person whose freedom of movement has been restricted by virtue of such a provision as is referred to in subsection (3) *(a)* of this section so requests at any time during the period of that restriction not earlier than three months after the order was made or three months after he last made such a request, as the case may be, his case shall be investigated by an independent and impartial tribunal presided over by a person appointed by the Chief Justice:

Provided that a person whose freedom of movement has been restricted by virtue of a restriction that is applicable to persons generally or to general classes of persons shall not make a request under this subsection unless he has first obtained the consent of the High Court.

(5) On any investigation by a tribunal in pursuance of subsection (4) of this section of the case of any person whose freedom of movement has been restricted, the tribunal may make recommendations concerning the necessity or expediency of continuing that restriction to the authority by whom it was ordered and, unless it is otherwise provided by law, that authority shall be obliged to act in accordance with any such recommendations.

(6) Nothing contained in or done under the authority of any provision of the customary law of Lesotho shall be held to be inconsistent with or in contravention of this section to the extent that that provision authorises the imposition of restrictions upon any person's freedom to reside in any part of Lesotho.

8.—(1) No person shall be subjected to torture or to inhuman or degrading punishment or other treatment.

(2) Nothing contained in or done under the authority of any law shall be held to be inconsistent with or in contravention of this section to the extent that the law in question authorises the infliction of any description of punishment that was lawful in Lesotho immediately before the coming into operation of this Constitution.

9.—(1) No person shall be held in slavery or servitude.

(2) No person shall be required to perform forced labour.

(3) For the purposes of this section, the expression "forced labour" does not include—

(a) any labour required in consequence of the sentence or order of a court;

(b) any labour required of any person while he is lawfully detained that, though not required in consequence of the sentence or order of a court, is reasonably required in the interests of hygiene or for the maintenance of the place at which he is detained;

(c) any labour required of a member of a disciplined force in pursuance of his duties as such or, in the case of a person who has conscientious objections to service as a member of a naval, military or air force, any labour that that person is required by law to perform in place of such service;

(d) any labour required during any period when Lesotho is at war or a declaration of emergency under section 21 of this Constitution is in force or in the event of any other emergency or calamity that threatens the life or well-being of the community, to the extent that the requiring of such labour is reasonably justifiable, in the circumstances of any situation arising or existing during that period or as a result of that other emergency or calamity, for the purpose of dealing with that situation; or

(e) any labour reasonably required by law as part of reasonable and normal communal or other civic obligations.

10.—(1) Every person shall be entitled to freedom from arbitrary search or entry, that is to say, he shall not (except with his own consent) be subjected to the search of his person or his property or the entry by others on his premises.

(2) Nothing contained in or done under the authority of any law shall be held to be inconsistent with or in contravention of this section to the extent that the law in question makes provision—

(a) in the interests of defence, public safety, public order, public morality, public health, town and country planning, the development or utilisation of mineral resources or the development or utilisation of any other property in such a manner as to promote the public benefit;

(b) for the purpose of protecting the rights or freedoms of other persons;

(c) that authorises an officer or agent of the Government of Lesotho or of a local government authority or of a body corporate established by law for public purposes to enter on the premises of any person for the purpose of inspecting those premises or anything thereon in connection with any tax, rate or due or for the purpose of carrying out work connected with any property that is lawfully on those premises and that belongs to that Government, authority or body corporate, as the case may be; or

(d) that authorises, for the purpose of enforcing the judgment or order of a court in any civil proceedings, the entry upon any premises by order of a court.

(3) A person shall not be permitted to rely in any judicial proceedings upon such a provision of law as is referred to in subsection (2) of this section except to the extent to which he satisfies the court that that provision or, as the case may be, the thing done under the authority thereof does not abridge the freedom guaranteed by subsection (1) of this section to a greater extent than is necessary in a practical sense in a democratic society in the interests of any of the matters specified in paragraph *(a)* of subsection (2) of this section or for any of the purposes specified in paragraph *(b)*, paragraph *(c)* or paragraph *(d)* of that subsection.

11.—(1) Every person shall be entitled to respect for his private and family life and his home.

(2) Nothing contained in or done under the authority of any law shall be held to be inconsistent with or in contravention of this section to the extent that the law in question makes provision—

(a) in the interests of defence, public safety, public order, public morality or public health;
(b) for the purpose of protecting the rights and freedoms of other persons.

(3) a person shall not be permitted to rely in any judicial proceedings upon such a provision of law as is referred to in subsection (2) of this section except to the extent to which he satisfies the court that that provision or, as the case may be, the thing done under the authority thereof does not abridge the right guaranteed by subsection (1) of this section to a greater extent than is necessary in a practical sense in a democratic society in the interests of any of the matters specified in paragraph *(a)* of subsection (2) of this section or for the purpose specified in paragraph *(b)* of that subsection.

12.—(1) If any person is charged with a criminal offence, then, unless the charge is withdrawn, the case shall be afforded a fair hearing within a reasonable time by an independent and impartial court established by law.

(2) Every person who is charged with a criminal offence—

(a) shall be presumed to be innocent until he is proved or has pleaded guilty;
(b) shall be informed as soon as reasonably practicable, in a language that he understands and in adequate detail, of the nature of the offence charged;
(c) shall be given adequate time and facilities for the preparation of his defence;
(d) shall be permitted to defend himself before the court in person or by a legal representative of his own choice;
(e) shall be afforded facilities to examine in person or by his legal representative the witnesses called

by the prosecution before the court and to obtain the attendance and carry out the examination of witnesses to testify on his behalf before the court on the same conditions as those applying to witnesses called by the prosecution; and

(f) shall be permitted to have without payment the assistance of an interpreter if he cannot understand the language used at the trial of the charge.

and except with his own consent the trial shall not take place in his absence unless he so conducts himself as to render the continuance of the proceedings in his presence inpracticable and the court has ordered him to be removed and the trial to proceed in his absence.

(3) When a person is tried for any criminal offence, the accused person or any person authorised by him in that behalf, shall, if he so requires and subject to payment of such reasonable fee as may be prescribed by law, be given within a reasonable time after judgment a copy for the use of the accused person of any record of the proceedings made by or on behalf of the court.

(4) No person shall be held to be guilty of a criminal offence on account of any act or omission that did not, at the time it took place, constitute such an offence, and no penalty shall be imposed for a criminal offence that is severer in degree or description than the maximum penalty that might have been imposed for that offence at the time when it was committed.

(5) No person who shows that he has been tried by a competent court for a criminal offence and either convicted or acquitted shall be tried for that offence or for any other criminal offence of which he could have been convicted at the trial for that offence, save upon the order of a superior court in the course of appeal or review proceedings relating to the conviction or acquittal.

(6) No person shall be tried for a criminal offence if he shows that he has been pardoned for that offence.

(7) No person who is tried for a criminal offence shall be compelled to give evidence at the trial.

(8) Any court or other adjudicating authority prescribed by law for the determination of the existence or extent of any civil right or obligation shall be established by law and shall be independent and impartial;

and where proceedings for such a determination are instituted by any person before such a court or other adjudicating authority, the case shall be given a fair hearing within reasonable time.

(9) Except with the agreement of all parties thereto, all proceedings of every court and proceedings for the determination of the existence or extent of any civil right or obligation before any other adjudicating authority, including the announcement of the decision of the court or other authority, shall be held in public.

(10) Nothing in subsection (9) of this section shall prevent the court or other adjudicating authority from excluding from the proceedings persons other than the parties thereto and their legal representatives to such extent as the court or other authority—

(a) may by law be empowered to do and may consider necessary or expedient in circumstances where publicity would prejudice the interests of justice or in interlocutory proceedings or in the interests of public morality, the welfare of persons under the age of eighteen years or the protection of the private lives of persons concerned in the proceedings; or
(b) may by law be empowered or required to do in the interests of defence, public safety or public order.

(11) Nothing contained in or done under the authority of any law shall be held to be inconsistent with or in contravention of—

(a) subsection (2) *(a)* of this section to the extent that the law in question imposes upon any person charged with a criminal offence the burden of proving particular facts;
(b) subsection (2) *(e)* of this section to the extent that the law in question imposes conditions that must be satisfied if witnesses called to testify on behalf of accused persons are to be paid their expenses out of public funds; or
(c) subsection (5) of this section to the extent that the law in question authorises a court to try a member of a disciplined force for a criminal offence notwithstanding any trial and conviction or acquittal of that member under the disciplinary

law of that force, so, however, that any court so trying such a member and convicting him shall in sentencing him to any punishment take into account any punishment awarded him under that disciplinary law.

(12) In the case of any person who is held in lawful detention the provisions of subsection (1) paragraphs *(d)* and *(e)* of subsection (2) and subsection (3) of this section shall not apply in relation to his trial for a criminal offence under the law regulating the discipline of persons held in such detention.

(13) Nothing contained in subsection (2) *(d)* of this section shall be construed as entitling a person to legal representation at public expense.

(14) In this section "criminal offence" means a criminal offence under the law of Lesotho.

13.—(1) Every person shall be entitled to, and (except with his own consent) shall not be hindered in his enjoyment of, freedom of conscience, including freedom of thought and of religion, freedom to change his religion or belief and freedom, either alone or in community with others, and both in public and in private, to manifest and propagate his religion or belief in worship, teaching, practice and observance.

(2) Every religious community shall be entitled, at its own expense, to establish and maintain places of education and to manage any place of education which it wholly maintains; and no such community shall be prevented from providing religious instruction for persons of that community in the course of any education provided at any places of education which it wholly maintains or in the course of any education which it otherwise provides.

(3) Except with his own consent (or, if he is a minor, the consent of his guardian), no person attending any place of education shall be required to receive religious instruction or to take part in or attend any religious ceremony or observance if that instruction, ceremony or observance relates to a religion other than his own.

(4) No person shall be compelled to take any oath which is contrary to his religion or belief or to take

any oath in a manner which is contrary to his religion or belief.

(5) Nothing contained in or done under the authority of any law shall be held to be inconsistent with or in contravention of this section to the extent that the law in question makes provision—

(a) in the interests of defence, public safety, public order, public morality or public health; or

(b) for the purpose of protecting the rights and freedoms of other persons, including the right to observe and practice any religion without the unsolicited intervention of members of any other religion.

(6) A person shall not be permitted to rely in any judicial proceedings upon such a provision of law as is referred to in subsection (5) of this section except to the extent to which he satisfies the court that that provision or, as the case may be, the thing done under the authority thereof does not abridge the rights and freedoms guaranteed by this section to a greater extent than is necessary in a practical sense in a democratic society in the interests of any of the matters specified in paragraph *(a)* of subsection (5) of this section or for the purpose specified in paragraph *(b)* of that subsection.

(7) References in this section to a religion shall be construed as including references to a religious denomination, and cognate expressions shall be construed accordingly.

14.—(1) Every person shall be entitled to, and (except with his own consent) shall not be hindered in his enjoyment of, freedom of expression, including freedom to hold opinions without interference, freedom to receive ideas and information without interference, freedom to communicate ideas and information without interference (whether the communication be to the public generally or to any person or class of persons) and freedom from interference with his correspondence.

(2) Nothing contained in or done under the authority of any law shall be held to be inconsistent with or in contravention of this section to the extent that the law in question makes provision—

(a) in the interests of defence, public safety, public order, public morality or public health; or

(b) for the purpose of protecting the reputations, rights and freedoms of other persons or the private lives of persons concerned in legal proceedings, preventing the disclosure of information received in confidence, maintaining the authority and independence of the courts or regulating the technical administration or the technical operation of telephony, telegraphy, posts, wireless broadcasting or television; or

(c) for the purpose of imposing restrictions upon public officers.

(3) A person shall not be permitted to rely in any judicial proceedings upon such a provision of law as is referred to in subsection (2) of this section except to the extent to which he satisfies the court that that provision or, as the case may be, the thing done under the authority thereof does not abridge the freedom guaranteed by subsection (1) of this section to a greater extent than is necessary in a practical sense in a democratic society in the interests of any of the matters specified in paragraph *(a)* of subsection (2) of this section or for any of the purposes specified in paragraph *(b)* or paragraph *(c)* of that subsection.

15.—(1) Every person shall be entitled to, and (except with his own consent) shall not be hindered in his enjoyment of, freedom of assembly and association, that is to say, freedom to assemble and associate with other persons and in particular to form or belong to trade unions and other associations for the protection of his interests.

(2) Nothing contained in or done under the authority of any law shall be held to be inconsistent with or in contravention of this section to the extent that the law in question makes provision—

(a) in the interests of defence, public safety, public order, public morality or public health; or

(b) for the purpose of protecting the rights and freedoms of other persons; or

(c) for the purpose of imposing restrictions upon public officers.

(3) A person shall not be permitted to rely in any judicial proceedings upon such a provision of law as is referred to in subsection (2) of this section except to the extent to which he satisfies the court that that provision or, as the case may be, the thing done under the authority thereof does not abridge the rights and freedoms guaranteed by subsection (1) of this section to a greater extent than is necessary in a practical sense in a democratic society in the interests of any of the matters specified in paragraph *(a)* of subsection (2) of this section or for any of the purposes specified in paragraph *(b)* or paragraph *(c)* of that subsection.

16.—(1) No property, movable or immovable, shall be taken possession of compulsorily, and no interest in or right over any such property shall be compulsorily acquired, except where the following conditions are satisfied, that is to say—

(a) the taking of possession or acquisition is necessary in the interests of defence, public safety, public order, public morality, public health, town and country planning or the development or utilisation of any property in such manner as to promote the public benefit; and

(b) the necessity therefor is such as to afford reasonable justification for the causing of any hardship that may result to any person having an interest in or right over the property; and

(c) provision is made by a law applicable to that taking of possession or acquisition for the prompt payment of full compensation.

(2) Every person having an interest in or right over property which is compulsorily taken possession of or whose interest in or right over any property is compulsorily acquired shall have a right of direct access to the High Court for—

(a) the determination of his interest or right, the legality of the taking of possession or acquisition of the property, interest or right and the amount of any compensation to which he is entitled; and

(b) the purpose of obtaining prompt payment of that compensation:

Provided that if Parliament so provides in relation

to any matter referred to in paragraph *(a)* of this subsection the right of access shall be by way of appeal (exercisable as of right at the instance of the person having the interest in or right over the property) from a tribunal or authority, other than the High Court, having jurisdiction under any law to determine that matter.

(3) The Chief Justice may make rules with respect to the practice and procedure of the High Court or any other tribunal or authority in relation to the jurisdiction conferred on the High Court by subsection (2) of this section or exercisable by the other tribunal or authority for the purposes of that subsection (including rules with respect to the time within which applications or appeals to the High Court or applications to the other tribunal or authority may be brought).

(4) Nothing contained in or done under the authority of any law shall be held to be inconsistent with or in contravention of subsection (1) or subsection (2) of this section—

(a) to the extent that the law in question makes provision that is necessary in a practical sense in a democratic society for the taking of possession or acquisition of any property, interest or right—

(i) in satisfaction of any tax, duty, rate, or other impost;

(ii) by way of penalty for breach of the law, whether under civil process or after conviction of a criminal offence under the law of Lesotho;

(iii) as an incident of a valid contract or of the terms and conditions of service of a public officer;

(iv) in the execution of judgments or orders of a court in proceedings for the determination of civil rights or obligations;

(v) in circumstances where it is reasonably necessary so to do because the property is in a dangerous state or injurious to the health of human beings, animals or plants;

(vi) in consequence of any law with respect to prescription or limitation of actions; or

(vii) for so long only as may be necessary for

the purposes of any examination, investigation, trial or inquiry or, in the case of land, for the purpose of carrying out thereon of work of soil conservation or the conservation of other natural resources or work relating to agricultural development or improvement (being work relating to such development or improvement that the occupier of the land has been required, and has without reasonable excuse refused or failed, to carry out); or

(*b*) to the extent that the law in question makes provision for the taking of possession or acquisition of the following property (including an interest in or right over property), that is to say—

(i) enemy property;

(ii) property of a deceased person, a person of unsound mind or a person who has not attained the age of 21 years, for the purpose of its administration for the benefit of the persons entitled to the beneficial interest therein;

(iii) property of a person adjudged insolvent or a body corporate in liquidation, for the purpose of its administration for the benefit of the creditors of the insolvent or body corporate and, subject thereto, for the benefit of other persons entitled to the beneficial interest in the property; or

(iv) property subject to a trust, for the purpose of vesting the property in persons appointed as trustees under the instrument creating the trust or by a court or, by order of a court, for the purpose of giving effect to the trust.

(5) Nothing contained in or done under the authority of any Act of Parliament shall be held to be inconsistent with or in contravention of this section to the extent that the Act in question makes provision for the compulsory taking possession of any property or the compulsory acquisition of any interest in or right over property where that property, interest or right is vested in a body corporate established by law for public purposes in which no moneys have been invested other than moneys provided by Parliament.

17.—(1) Subject to the provisions of subsections (4), (5) and (8) of this section, no law shall make any provision that is discriminatory either of itself or in its effect.

(2) Subject to the provisions of subsections (6), (8) and (9) of this section, no person shall be treated in a discriminatory manner by any person acting by virtue of any written law or in the performance of the functions of any public office or any public authority.

(3) In this section, the expression "discriminatory" means affording different treatment to different persons attributable wholly or mainly to their respective descriptions by race, tribe, place of origin or residence, sex, political opinions, colour or creed, whereby persons of one such description are subjected to disabilities or restrictions to which persons of another such description are not made subject or are accorded privileges or advantages which are not accorded to persons of another such description.

(4) Subsection (1) of this section shall not apply to any law to the extent that that law makes provision—

(a) with respect to persons who are not citizens of Lesotho; or

(b) for the application, in the case of persons of any such description as is mentioned in subsection (3) of this section (or of persons connected with such persons), of the law with respect to adoption, marriage, divorce, burial, devolution of property on death or other like matters which is the personal law of persons of that description; or

(c) for the application of the customary law of Lesotho with respect to any matter in the case of persons who, under that law, are subject to that law; or

(d) for the appropriation of public revenues or other public funds; or

(e) whereby persons of any such description as is mentioned in subsection (3) of this section may be made subject to any disability or restriction or may be accorded any privilege or advantage which, having regard to its nature and to special circumstances pertaining to those persons or to persons

of any other such description, is reasonably justifiable in a democratic society.

(5) Nothing contained in any law shall be held to be inconsistent with or in contravention of subsection (1) of this section to the extent that it makes provision with respect to standards or qualifications (not being standards or qualifications specifically relating to race, tribe, place of origin or residence, sex, political opinions, colour or creed) to be required of any person who is appointed to any office in the public service, any office in a disciplined force, any office in the service of a local government authority or any office in a body corporate established by law for public purposes.

(6) Subsection (2) of this section shall not apply to anything which is expressly or by necessary implication authorised to be done by any such provision of law as is referred to in subsection (4) or subsection (5) of this section.

(7) No person shall be treated in a discriminatory manner in respect of access to shops, hotels, lodging houses, public restaurants, eating houses, beer halls or places of public entertainment or in respect of access to places of public resort maintained wholly or partly out of public funds or dedicated to the use of the general public.

(8) Nothing contained in or done under the authority of any law shall be held to be inconsistent with or in contravention of this section to the extent that the law in question makes provision whereby persons of any such description as is mentioned in subsection (3) of this section may be subjected to any restriction on the rights and freedoms guaranteed by sections 7, 10, 11, 13, 14 and 15 of this Constitution, being such a restriction as is authorised by paragraph *(a)* or paragraph *(c)* of section 7(3), section 10(2), section 11(2), section 13(5), section 14(2) or section 15(2), as the case may be.

(9) Nothing in subsection (2) of this section shall affect any discretion relating to the institution, conduct or discontinuance of civil or criminal proceedings in any court that is vested in any person by or under this Constitution or any other law.

(10) The provisions of this section shall be without

prejudice to the generality of section 18 of this Constitution.

18. Every person shall be entitled to equality before the law and to the equal protection of the law.

19.—(1) Nothing contained in or done under the authority of an Act of Parliament shall be held to be inconsistent with or in contravention of section 6, section 17 or section 18 of this Constitution to the extent that the Act authorises the taking during any period when Lesotho is at war or when a declaration of emergency under section 21 of this Constitution is in force of measures that are necessary in a practical sense in a democratic society for dealing with the situation that exists in Lesotho during that period.

(2) When a person is detained by virtue of any such law as is referred to in subsection (1) of this section the following provisions shall apply, that is to say—

(a) he shall, as soon as reasonably practicable after the commencement of his detention, be furnished with a statement in writing in a language that he understands specifying in detail the grounds upon which he is detained;

(b) not more than fourteen days after the commencement of his detention, a notification shall be published in the Gazette stating that he has been detained and giving particulars of the provision of law under which his detention is authorised;

(c) not more than one month after the commencement of his detention and thereafter during his detention at intervals of not more than six months, his case shall be investigated by an independent and impartial tribunal established by law and presided over by a person appointed by the Chief Justice;

(d) he shall be afforded reasonable facilities to consult a legal representative of his own choice who shall be permitted to make representations to the tribunal appointed for the investigation of the case of the detained person; and

(e) at the hearing of his case by the tribunal appointed for the investigation of his case he shall be permitted to appear in person or by a legal representative of his own choice.

(3) On any investigation by a tribunal in pursuance of this section of the case of a detained person, the tribunal may make recommendations concerning the necessity or expediency of continuing his detention to the authority by which it was ordered but, unless it is otherwise provided by law, that authority shall not be obliged to act in accordance with any such recommendations.

(4) Nothing contained in subsection (2) *(d)* or subsection (2) *(e)* of this section shall be construed as entitling a person to legal representation at public expense.

20.—(1) If any person alleges that any of the provisions of sections 4 to 19 (inclusive) of this Constitution has been, is being or is likely to be contravened in relation to him (or, in the case of a person who is detained, if any other person alleges such a contravention in relation to the detained person), then, without prejudice to any other action with respect to the same matter which is lawfully available, that person (or that other person) may apply to the High Court for redress.

(2) The High Court shall have original jurisdiction—

(a) to hear and determine any application made by any person in pursuance of subsection (1) of this section; and

(b) to determine any question arising in the case of any person which is referred to it in pursuance of subsection (3) of this section

and may make such orders, issue such process and give such directions as it may consider appropriate for the purpose of enforcing or securing the enforcement of any of the provisions of sections 4 to 19 (inclusive) of this Constitution:

Provided that the High Court may decline to exercise its powers under this subsection if it is satisfied that adequate means of redress for the contravention alleged are or have been available to the person concerned under any other law.

(3) If in any proceedings in any subordinate court any question arises as to the contravention of any of the provisions of sections 4 to 19 (inclusive) of this

Constitution, the person presiding in that court may, and shall if any party to the proceedings so requests, refer the question to the High Court unless, in his opinion, the raising of the question is merely frivolous or vexatious.

(4) Where any question is referred to the High Court in pursuance of subsection (3) of this section, the High Court shall give its decision upon the question and the court in which the question arose shall dispose of the case in accordance with that decision or, if that decision is the subject of an appeal under section 121 of this Constitution to the Court of Appeal or to the Judicial Committee, in accordance with the decision of the Court of Appeal or, as the case may be, of the Judicial Committee.

(5) Parliament may confer upon the High Court such powers in addition to those conferred by this section as may appear to be necessary or desirable for the purpose of enabling that court more effectively to exercise the jurisdiction conferred upon it by this section.

(6) The Chief Justice may make rules with respect to the practice and procedure of the High Court in relation to the jurisdiction and powers conferred on it by or under this section (including rules with respect to the time within which applications may be brought and references shall be made to the High Court).

21.—(1) The Prime Minister may, by proclamation which shall be published in the Gazette, declare that a state of emergency exists for the purposes of this Chapter.

(2) Every declaration of emergency shall lapse at the expiration of fourteen days, commencing with the day on which it was made, unless it has in the meantime been approved by a resolution of each House of Parliament.

(3) A declaration of emergency may at any time be revoked by the Prime Minister by proclamation which shall be published in the Gazette.

(4) A declaration of emergency that has been approved by a resolution of each House of Parliament in pursuance of subsection (2) of this section shall, subject to the provisions of subsection (3) of this section,

remain in force so long as those resolutions remain in force and no longer.

(5) A resolution of either House of Parliament passed for the purposes of this section shall remain in force for six months or such shorter period as may be specified therein:

Provided that any such resolution may be extended from time to time by a further such resolution, each extension not exceedng six months from the date of the resolution effecting the extension.

(6) Any provison of this section that a declaration of emergency shall lapse or cease to be in force at any particular time is without prejudice to the making of a further such declaration whether before or after that time.

(7) Before exercising his powers under this section, the Prime Minister shall whenever practicable consult with the King's Privy Council.

(8) The King may summon the two Houses of Parliament to meet for the purposes of this section notwithstanding that Parliament then stands dissolved, and the persons who were members of either House immediately before the dissolution shall be deemed, for those purposes, still to be members of that House, but, subject to the provisions of sections 47(4) and 49(4) of this Constitution, neither House shall, when summoned by virtue of this subsection, transact any business other than debating and voting upon resolutions for the purposes of this section.

22.—(1) In this Chapter, unless the context otherwise requires—

"contravention", in relation to any requirement, includes a failure to comply with that requirement, and cognate expressions shall be construed accordingly;

"court" means a court of law having jurisdiction in Lesotho other than a court established by a disciplinary law, and includes the Judicial Committee and, in sections 5 and 9 of this Constitution, a court established by a disciplinary law;

"disciplinary law" means a law regulating the discipline of any disciplined force;

"disciplined force" means—

(a) a naval, military or air force;

(*b*) the Police Force; or
(*c*) a prison service;

"legal representative" means a person entitled to practise as a legal practitioner in Lesotho; and

"member", in relation to a disciplined force, includes any person who, under the law regulating the discipline of that force, is subject to that discipline.

(2) Nothing contained in any of the provisions of section 7, section 16 or section 17 of this Constitution shall be construed as affecting any law for the time being in force relating to the allocation of land or the grant of any interest or right in or over land or as entitling any person to any greater such interest or right than he would otherwise have and, without prejudice to the generality of the foregoing, nothing done under the authority of Chapter VIII of this Constitution shall be held to be inconsistent with or in contravention of any of the provisions of any of those sections.

(3) In relation to any person who is a member of a disciplined force raised under a law made by any legislature in Lesotho, nothing contained in or done under the authority of the disciplinary law of that force shall be held to be inconsistent with or in contravention of any of the provisions of this Chapter other than sections 5, 8 and 9.

(4) In relation to any person who is a member of a disciplined force raised otherwise than as aforesaid and lawfully present in Lesotho, nothing contained in or done under the authority of the disciplinary law of that force shall be held to be inconsistent with or in contravention of any of the provisions of this Chapter.

APPENDIX B

STANDARDS

The different standards have been analysed in the following way. Our thanks are owed to Mr. J. E. Beardsley for permission to include the following chart.

In dealing with burdens of proof and persuasion below the term "government" is used to indicate the party defending the constitutionality of the act or law in question (it need not in fact be the government in every case). The word "petitioner" denotes the party challenging constitutionality.

"Standards" are those formulae which are employed to direct the judge in assessing the validity of an action or law restrictive of a protected right or rights.

Section	*Standard Applies to:*	*Standard:*
7 (3)(a)—(Movement)	Such restrictions in interest of defence, public safety, public order, public morality, or public health as are not otherwise specifically provided for in 7(3)(b)-(g)	"Necessary in a practical sense in a democratic society"
10—(Arbitrary search and entry)	Any restriction of protected right	-do-
11—(Respect for private and family life)	-do-	-do-
13—(Conscience)	-do-	-do-
14—(Expression)	-do-	-do-
15—(Assembly and association)	-do-	-do-
7(3)(g)—(Movement)	Restrictions of departure from Lesotho to secure fulfilment of legal obligations	-do-
16(4)(a)—(Arbitrary seizure of property)	Taking of property for any of a number of specified reasons mainly dealing with the fulfilment of legal obligations	-do-
19(1)—(Declaration of emergency)	Measures which may be taken when a declaration of emergency is in force	-do-
17(4)(e)—(Discrimination)	Discriminatory legislation in favour of or imposing restrictions upon specified classes of persons	"Reasonably justifiable in democratic society"
6(1)(i)—(Personal liberty)	Making of orders implementing restrictions on right to be within specified areas of Lesotho (See s. 7)	"Reasonably justifiable"
9(3)(d)—(Slavery and forced labour)	Labour required in emergency, war, or calamity	-do-
16(1)(b)—(Arbitrary seizure of property)	One of conditions for taking of property	-do-
9(3)(b)—(Slavery and forced labour)	Labour in interests of hygiene or maintenance by one lawfully detained	"Reasonably required"
9(3)(e)—(Slavery and forced labour)	Labour in interests of civil obligations	-do-
6(2)—(Personal liberty)	Period of detention before being brought before judge	"Reasonably practicable"

APPENDIX C

DIAGRAM SHOWING THE STRUCTURE OF COURTS IN LESOTHO

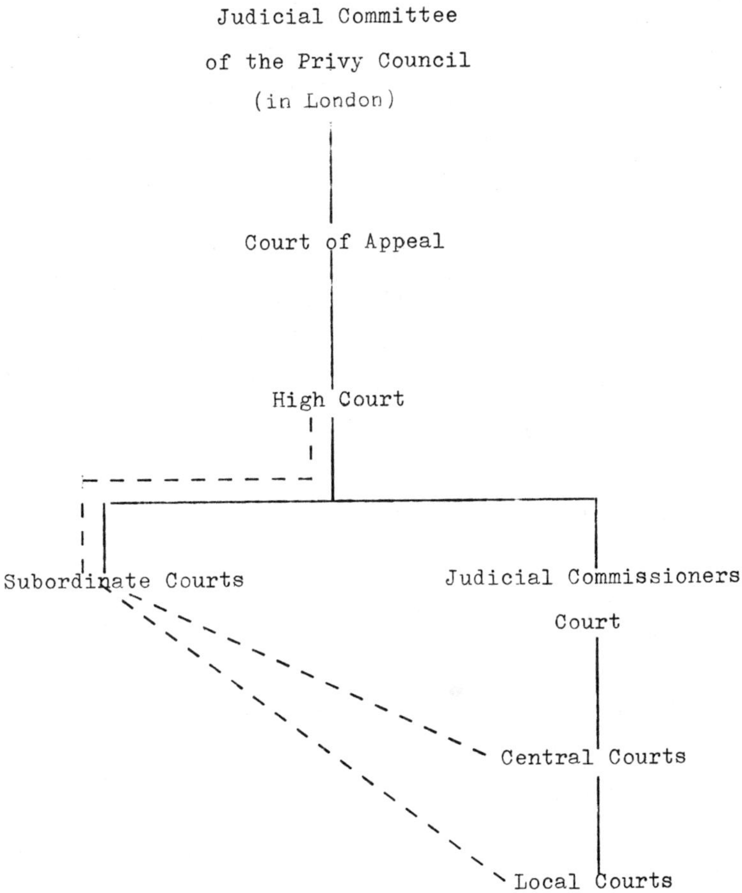

________ indicates channel of appeal

_ _ _ _ _ indicates channel of revisory jurisdiction.

Table of Cases

Farrelly's Trustee, Smith v.
Fatuma binti Mohamed bin Salim Backhshuwen v. Mohamid bin Salim Backhshuwen, [1952] A.C. 1—IIIA(1)(c)(i), n. 41.
Fellner v. Minister of the Interior, [1954] 4 S.A. 523 (A.D.)—I, n. 44, n. 128.
Ferguson, Plessy v.
Ferguson v. Skrupa, 372 U.S. 726 (1963)—II, n. 378.
Fijabi v. Odumola, [1955-56] W.R.N.L.R. 133—I, n. 238.
Fitzgerald, Green v.
Flast v. Cohen, 392 U.S. 83 (1968)—II5A(6)(b)(iv)a, n. 350.
Fondo, S.A.N.T.A.M. v.
Fortuin, R. v.
Fraenkel N.O. v. Sechele, [1964-65] Bech. L.R. 5 (C.A.)—I3C(5), n. 316.
Friesland Hotel, Catering Equipment Centre v.
Frothingham v. Mellon, 262 U.S. 447 (1923) — II, n. 334; II5A(6)(b)(iv)a, n. 346.
Gagnon, Prince v.
Gamioba v. Esezi II, [1961] All N.L.R. 584—II5A(5)(d)(i), n. 326.
Gayle v. Browder, 352 U.S. 903—II, n. 492.
Geldenhuys and Neethling v. Beuthin, [1918] A.D. 426—II, n. 344.
Georgia, Manley v.
Ghamboye, Buraimo v.
Gibson v. van der Walt, [1952] 1 S.A. 262 (A.D.—I, n. 158.
Gideon Nkambule v. R., [1926-53] H.C.T.L.R. 181 (P.C.) (Swaziland)—IIIA(1)(c)(iii), n. 71.
Gikanga, Kimani v.
Giwa v. Erinmilokun, [1961] 1 All N.L.R. 294—I, n. 204.
Golightly v. Ashrii, P.C. appeal No. 31 of 1958 (Ghana) reported 1961 J.A.L. 52—I, n. 203; III, n. 80.
Goodinson v. Goodinson, [1954] 2 Q.B. 118; [1954] 2 All E.R. 255—I, n. 352.
Gopalan v. State of Madras, [1950] S.C.R. 88 — II, n. 172; II5A(1)(b), n. 273.
Goseb, R. v.
Government of East Pakistan, Hossain v.
Government of Nigeria, Eleko v.
Governments Stock and Other Securities Investment Company v. Manila Railway Company, [1897] A.C. 81—I2B(1), n. 24.
Green v. Fitzgerald, [1914] A.D. 88—I, n. 489.
Guri v. Hadejia Native Authority, [1959] 4 F.S.C. 44 (Nigeria) —I, n. 331.